THE LEARNING COMPASS

MASTER THE SKILLS TO GET WHAT YOU WANT IN LIFE

CHRISTOPHER S. MUKIIBI

JORDAN IVY PUBLISHING

CONTENTS

chrismukiibi.com

ISBN: 979-8-9921390-0-6 (ebook)

ISBN: 979-8-9921390-1-3 (print)

ISBN: 979-8-9921390-3-7 (audio)

Dedications & Acknowledgements

Kyra, *your love and passion for writing is so potent that it has overwhelmed me and birthed this book. Your love and encouragement kept me going and helped me conquer my fears. Without your seemingly endless support, devotion, and sacrifice, this book would never have been considered or written.*

Mom, *for loving me unconditionally so I may have the confidence to march to my own drum and for showing me that not only can we live out our dreams, but we must through focus and commitment.*

Dad, *for loving me unconditionally and instilling the values of prioritizing education, nurturing intelligence, eradicating ignorance, embodying excellence, and cherishing creativity.*

Madelynne, *for showing me responsibility, giving me an opportunity to care about more than just myself, and always supporting me no matter what.*

Students & Families, *for trusting me with your education and the education of your children. Your incredible support and feedback that has allowed me to see myself as an effective educator and refine these ideas.*

Friends, for loving me despite my differences and helping me see that I have something unique to give to the world. Your friendship is a beacon of light in the abyss.

Myla & Kalia, for making all things new and an undeniable reason to be the best I can be. Many of the lessons I wrote in here are for you both to read when the time is right. I hope this book may deepen your knowledge of learning and give you a skill that you can trade for anything you want.

HOW TO USE THIS BOOK
A PERSONALIZED GUIDE

This book has three key goals.

First, it offers practical systems to help learners navigate the world with greater ease, making school and life feel less overwhelming.

Second, it challenges us to rethink education—not just as a means to success, but as a way to reduce unnecessary suffering and create lives filled with beauty, meaning, and fulfillment.

Finally, it shows that anyone can thrive as a student. By embracing the science and art of learning and following evidence-based strategies, we can accomplish more than we ever thought possible.

"Absorb what is useful, discard what is useless, and add what is uniquely your own. " - Bruce Lee

Rules on How to Use this Book

1. *Treat the book as a buffet* - do not feel like you need to go through the whole thing. Find your main goals and

check out the relevant sections. Start wherever you like and read in any order you please.

  ○ There are 6 sections:
1. Discovering Potential
2. Skills & Habits
3. Mindful Learning
4. Elevating Our Study Game
5. Navigating Academic Success
6. Integrative Growth

2. *My goal is for each of my readers to like 50%, love 25%, and never forget 10% of this book.* The best part is the 50/25/10 split will be different for everyone. Write down what sticks out to you the most.

3. *Skip, but skip intentionally and intelligently* - Occasionally, I may dive too deeply into a subject. If I get too into detail for you, look for the main message. I will do my best to make them as clear as possible. On the other hand, I may not dive deep enough— if something interests you please find other resources to go further. At the end of each section, I have included the books I referenced and recommend reading for further learning.

4. *Please be skeptical* - From what I have found, the how-to is correct but the why could be wrong as we learn more. Feel free to contact me with any inaccuracies you find - chris@chrismukiibi.com

5. *Don't use skepticism as an excuse for inaction* - be proactively skeptical, but not defensively skeptical. If you disagree with anything I say in this book, I challenge you to come up with a different solution. *Progress only occurs when the critics offer solutions.* Doing this helps prevent inaction.

6. *Enjoy it* - I poured my heart and soul into this book. I took years of learning and condensed them down here so you don't have to go through the same struggles I went through. This book contains over 12 years of

experience in education, written over the course of 7 years, with 7 extensive rewrites. It was brutal and challenging, but a labor of love.

~

Come back to this as a reference guide if you need it.

Thanks to Tim Ferriss for inspiring the format of this book. (Rules are taken from Tim Ferriss' *4-Hour Body*.)

"This book is not simply a prescription for success; it's a call to arms. But this call to arms is not a call to do battle. It's a call to learning." - Michael E. Gerber (*The E-Myth Revisited*)

Disclaimer: Some parts are going to be more valuable than others. Everyone is in different places, and what may apply to you may not necessarily apply to someone else. This book is my attempt to capture everything I know about learning and being a successful student. Some of it may be revolutionary, some of it may be useless, but I believe all of it is good.

1

DISCOVERING POTENTIAL
THE PERSONAL JOURNEY OF EDUCATION

ON EDUCATION
WHY IT MATTERS

"A single day among the learned lasts longer than the longest life of the ignorant." - Posidonius

When I was a boy, my parents taught me to value education—not just because it could bring power, wealth, and a good life, but because education was something no one could ever take away from me. It was a lifelong investment, one I could carry anywhere I went. No matter the path I chose, education had to be part of it.

Every person's education is different. For a musician, it's the stage. For an athlete, it's the court. For a teacher, the classroom. However, as I grew older, I realized education is much more than equations or dates in history. True education is training ourselves for a mission worthy of our talents and potential. It's learning how to face challenges, even the ones we don't want to tackle. It is, as far as I know, the key to freedom.

I worked hard in school, took challenging classes, went to college, chose a practical major, and followed the path my teachers and parents endorsed. I was after a "great education," and all it promised. But after the graduation celebration ended, I was met with a subtle disappointment every time I looked at my degree. I felt school had let me down—let all of us down.

Getting the degree, "getting educated," didn't prepare me for the reality I was facing. I was confronted by practical problems I had no clue how to solve. School taught me nothing about:

- Applying for a mortgage
- Building wealth
- Buying a car
- Understanding credit
- Planning meals and grocery shopping
- Finding good books
- Raising happy children
- Knowing and understanding myself
- Coping with family struggles or dealing with addictions
- Living with purpose
- Starting a business
- Having honest conversations
- Maintaining healthy relationships
- Navigating the digital world
- Managing my emotions
- And so much more...

I could go on forever. It was frustrating to realize I'd spent almost two decades in school, and yet maybe only a fraction of that time had yielded valuable, practical knowledge. College did help me grow in unexpected ways, throwing me into challenging situations that broadened my view. But I still felt let down—not just by my teachers but by the momentum of our culture.

The world is changing faster than any generation before us could have anticipated, and those responsible for teaching us had no guide to follow either. They were trying to prepare us for a world they themselves were struggling to understand. In their time, a formal education was the path to success. While that path still holds value, it needs adaptation.

Consider school schedules, they mimic a typical 9-to-5 job:

- Start in the morning
- Take a short break after a few hours
- Wait for time to pass
- Lunch around noon
- Continue waiting
- Go home
- Repeat

Why? This structure was designed during the Industrial Revolution to prepare future factory workers. Schools trained kids to follow instructions and stay put when the bell rang. They were not built for complex problem-solving, critical thinking, or creativity. Yet, thanks to this system, we made incredible advancements and launched our civilizations into the modern age.

But times have changed, and so must we. Today, not knowing something, ignorance, is a choice. With modern access to information, we can learn almost anything at anytime. We can connect, create, and become anything faster than ever. Yet, most schools remain structured as they were over a century ago. Minor adjustments have been made, but they're often just variations of the same outdated approach. We need tools and structures that align with today's world, which demands knowledge and the ability to build meaningful lives.

Responsibility first belonged to schools, but since they dropped the ball, it falls on us. It is up to us as individuals to seek out the education we need and deserve.

"The way you teach your kids to solve interesting problems is to give them interesting problems to solve. And then, don't criticize them when they fail... What we can say to that 11-year-old is: 'I really don't care how you did on your vocabulary test. I care about whether you have something to say.'" - Seth Godin (*Linchpin*)

Using today's resources, I've taken it upon myself to fill the gaps in my education—not just to survive but to thrive. Our current institutions aren't fit to fully prepare the next generation.

"Sooner or later, parents have to take responsibility for putting their kids into a system that is indebting them and teaching them to be cogs in an economy that doesn't want cogs anymore." - Seth Godin (*Stop Stealing Dreams*)

Changing schools overnight isn't feasible, and I'm not suggesting we abandon them. Instead, we can use school as an opportunity to practice facing what we don't want to do, building resilience for life's inevitable challenges. Life is filled with things we don't want to do; ask anyone. Knowing ourselves as people who can tackle challenging tasks is invaluable.

But that's only one lesson. Education should also teach us to:

- Read well, expanding our understanding
- Write well, so we can think and communicate effectively
- Think critically, seeing beyond the obvious
- Develop character, which determines our opportunities
- Build the best version of ourselves, making life worth the effort

Beyond school, we each need to seek our own education—the one perfect for who we are. The right education minimizes needless suffering. Life without it can feel like a struggle.

I remember when my wife and I first became parents and struggled with breastfeeding. It was painful and challenging, but as we learned more, the suffering decreased.

"Oh, how beautiful life could be..." - Viktor Frankl (*Man's Search for Meaning*)

Life holds more beauty than we know, and education helps us see it. Without it, we risk losing access to that beauty.

To start, we can approach life with discipline and curiosity. Keep searching for answers until we find those that satisfies our hunger. If we don't know where to begin, we can start with the great works of culture. These resources, often free, provide a fantastic foundation. Seth Godin offers two suggestions for young people:

1. Learn to lead.
2. Learn to solve interesting problems.

If that doesn't resonate, consider this: education helps us understand ourselves. Ignorance leads to suffering, while knowledge alleviates it. The more we educate ourselves, the more tools we gain to handle life's challenges.

Connecting to collective wisdom deepens our vision. We become more thoughtful, communicate more clearly, and better navigate relationships. Education helps us become permanently stronger and healthier.

The right education makes us not only better people but happier, wealthier, and more capable.

THE ROLES OF EDUCATION
ACCESSING POTENTIAL

W hat is the role of education?
Education has many different roles. What constitutes a good education for an individual varies, but I want to touch upon a few that are worth considering.

I mentioned a few of them earlier:

- To prevent and minimize needless suffering

Needless suffering comes from not knowing or understanding something. Note: suffering is distinct from pain. Education cannot help alleviate pain, but it can help ease the suffering associated with it.

- To give access to a beautiful life

Life is always full of more beauty if only we knew it was there. Part of my education is to challenge myself to see the beauty in life, especially when I believe there's none to be found. I often find more beauty than I would have initially noticed. Additionally, aiming to notice beauty is free, contingent on no one except myself, dramatically improving my overall life experience. Through education, we can turn ourselves into who we want to be, and we don't have to be stuck with who we are.

- To train us in the face of adversity

School is good for training us to do what is necessary and prioritize what we may not want to do in the face of adversity. While school can be optimized to set students up to live meaningful, fulfilling, and productive lives, we are closer to the beginning of that optimization rather than the end.

That being said, for students stuck in an antiquated system, we can pursue an education that is meaningful to us while using traditional education systems to train us to do things we may not want to. After all, life is full of things we do not want to do, no matter which path we take.

There are more roles that Education can fill:

- To create the future we want

To manipulate the world around us, we must first understand how it works and how we can act. Education should make people prosperous and happy, not stressed and exhausted.

- To develop the feeling of community and social interest

This belief was the foundation of Alfred Adler's work. The world-renowned Austrian medical doctor, psychotherapist, and the founder of the school of individual psychology. He believed that the goal is education is to connect people by helping them understand one another. He mentioned it in his book Understanding Human Nature.

- To develop our ability to meet life's situations

This idea was popularized by the former president of Princeton University, Dr. John G. Hibben. Life is full of difficulty and complexity. Education allows us to navigate those situations with grace or even survive them.

- To inspire action

Education is not merely the accumulation of knowledge. Without consequent action, knowledge is wasted, and education is incomplete. Many people accumulate knowledge but never act upon it, bringing out more tragedy than necessary. They know things could be better, but they are not. Knowledge can exacerbate suffering, but education alleviates it.

- To educe latent potential

The word "educate" comes from educe, which means to bring out or develop (something latent or potential). It also means to infer something from data. Both of these definitions lie at the heart of education. Educating ourselves is making inferences from various data to bring out our latent potential. A child learning mathematics, physical sciences, and coding takes in new information to bring out their potential as an engineer. We all bring out our potential when we infer something from data. Putting ourselves before relevant data and making sense of it will bring out the most in us.

- To have our knowledge and the knowledge of the world be indistinguishable.

Plato put forth an idea known as Reciprocal Revealing, which is rooted in Plato's Theory of Forms, which asserts that our worldly experiences are mere shadows of ideals, absolute forms, or truths that exist in a higher realm of reality. Plato believed that as we learn more about the world, our knowledge becomes similar to our understanding of the world until we reach the perfect form. Information gets us in formation. Getting informed gets us in form. That etymology is not an accident.

In other words, when we study and learn in school, we're not just remembering things our teachers tell us. We're also exploring, like in a game. Each time we learn something new, we get better at the game. That's because we're learning about the subject and how we think and learn.

- To love life and serve ourselves

Education is rooted in human relationships. If we look at what makes relationships successful, it could be described as us knowing them like they know us, we know ourselves, and they know themselves. Education is the path of knowing, and knowing ourselves and our loved ones is our primary orientation as human beings. Education gives us access to more intimacy.

"Education is not the answer to the question. Education is the means to the answer to all questions. - Bill Allin (Sociologist and Education Activist)

THE ROOTS OF LEARNING
THE ORIGINS & INFLUENCES OF WESTERN EDUCATION

"The roots of education are bitter, but the fruit is sweet." - Aristotle

People who want to do well in school usually feel that way because they've been told that it's the primary route to doing well in life.

Performance in school is usually measured by grades, and those who get A's are considered the cream of the crop. It's no surprise that students tend to fall in love with A's.

I know plenty of students who will do anything for the A. It's so prevalent in society I was able to start a profitable tutoring business based on this need with no business experience and little marketing.

Some students genuinely needed help, but most just wanted the A.

Those who are interested in a fancy career, a nice house, and respect from others are the most likely to fall in love with the A's. They believe that having the A's will give them a fancy career, a nice house, and the respect they desire.

However, sometimes it doesn't work out like that.

Sometimes people who *succeed in school, fail in life.*

At other times the people who *fail in school, succeed in life.*

The Issue with Curricula

There are many reasons for this, but I will start with the school curricula.

Most curricula were created for students to succeed in The World of Academics, not reverse-engineered to help students succeed in The World Beyond.

The typical school curriculum is not tailored to *The World Beyond* and the skills needed to succeed within those curriculums are not necessarily the skills we need in everyday life.

Many students pick up on this well before they enter the job market, and educators have to dedicate a lot of energy just to prove they're teaching relevant information.

Students ask me at increasingly younger ages why they have to learn what they're being taught in school, and they have every right to wonder.

The worst part (in my opinion) is that as time goes on, more of the curricula become harder to justify.

Origins and Influences of Western Education

To understand why this is the case, we'll have to examine what influences these curricula and why they are even being taught. After all, these institutions were brought about through tremendous effort and intentionality, and to carelessly denigrate an institution without understanding its purpose or origins increases our chances of undoing valuable work. Like Chesterton's Fence, it's not wise to destroy something without understanding its origins.

Our current education system has roots in the Industrial Revolution back in 1760. The West had a massive transformation turning their textiles, agriculture, and handcrafts into large-scale factories with machines run by factory workers. Since there was a high demand for factory workers, *the school systems were designed to educate as many people as possible so that they could be employed at the factories.*

Undoubtedly, at the time, this was a wonderful thing.

Factory jobs provided people with a higher quality of life (believe it or not) and were highly sought after. Nowadays, most people see education as a way to avoid those kinds of jobs specifically.

However, we can still see echoes of this influence just by looking at a typical school schedule:

- Start in the morning
- Take your 10-minute break roughly 2-3 hours in
- Back to work
- Lunch around the 5th hour
- Work again
- Go home.
- Repeat.

It's just like working at a 9-5. Just like working in the factories. (Except breaks and lunches were monitored in the factories.)

It's not like this system wasn't good. It was wonderful at the time. It was effective and helped launch the Western world into the marvel it is today. We would not be here without industrialization.

Without industrialization, we wouldn't be in the Information Age, where not knowing something is a matter of choice.

Today, we can learn anything at any moment and talk to anyone in the world at any time. We can know almost everything that everyone else knows in mere moments.

But the education system hasn't been updated for this. There have been small improvements here and there, but not enough to address the issues many students are dealing with today.

The same teaching methods are practiced year in and year out and are becoming exponentially irrelevant, especially with the growth of accessible technology, information, and artificial intelligence.

There are almost no efforts to teach students more effectively and efficiently in a way that matches up with the speed of today.

There have been some curriculums that are updated and more tailored to today's dynamic and complex world, but traditions from the Industrial Revolution still carry the most weight.

The Industrial Revolution wasn't the only influence on our education system. The content that is taught has a long line of historical influence that is worth paying attention to.

Much of today's school curriculums are based on the curriculums of medieval monasteries, the ideas of 19th-century German educationalists, and the concerns of aristocratic court societies.

Those 19th-century educationalists designed their curriculums with a few key assumptions that underly most school curriculums today:

1. The most important things are already known.
2. What currently is, is all that could ever be.
3. Being original is dangerous.

These are all incorrect assumptions.

Part of the solution, in my opinion, will be to move larger parts of the curriculums towards concepts and ideas that teach students useful skills.

School is for learning, not job training.

Most places train on the job anyway. Realistically, there are only a few professions where the training is happening in the classroom.

Here's something fun to think about. Below is a mini timeline of the goals of education throughout history:

- 753 BC - The cultivation of virtue
- 33 AD - The cultivation of virtue
- 313 AD - The cultivation of virtue
- 800 AD - The cultivation of virtue
- 1517 - The cultivation of virtue
- 1865 - The cultivation of virtue

- 1965 - College and career readiness

Perhaps returning to the deeper roots of education - cultivating virtue could be a more meaningful and relevant goal of education than solely "college and career readiness." It is through the cultivation of virtue that we become ready to create our careers, but ultimately our lives.

Wrong Messages

Students are implicitly being taught that the only way to go about life is to ask permission and beg for acceptance.

Ask permission to use the restroom.

Ask permission to answer questions.

Ask permission to work at a job.

Ask permission to make money.

Ask permission to buy something.

Ask permission to make something.

Ask permission to live.

Too many people believe that they aren't successful until someone else has permitted them to do something.

In traditional classrooms, a large part of why students have to ask for so many things is to maintain order, but I believe the implicit lesson being taught is horrible. Therefore, it would be helpful for teachers (and other educators) to intentionally include times for students to not ask for permission. That could look many different ways, but we cannot have another generation of students who believe it is more important to ask permission than to act on their ideas. If given a compelling purpose, people will act constructively more often than not.

So many people believe that they're limited by the income approved by their "boss." Many people believe their boss intrinsically knows their value and compensates them accordingly.

Too many people believe that we cannot create opportunities for ourselves.

We're taught to deliver on expectations, not change them.

We're taught to regurgitate ideas instead of originating them.

We're taught to respect people in authority, rather than honestly contemplate the possibility that no one else really knows what's going on.

Change expectations! Originate ideas! Internalize that no one knows what is going on!

There are liberating perspectives that can enrich the experience of our lives. If we search further than what our current systems are spoon-feeding us, we will find a new and beautiful world where we can exercise our will to our fullest expression.

> "Teachers should prepare the student for the student's future, not for the teacher's past." - Richard Manning (Engineer)

Evolving Education & Critical Targets

> "One of my deepest concerns is that while education systems around the world are being reformed, many of these reforms are being driven by political and commercial interests that misunderstand how real people learn and how great schools actually work. As a result, they are damaging the prospects of countless young people. Sooner or later, for better or for worse, they will affect you or someone you know." - Sir Ken Robinson (Creative Schools)

There were many key players in the evolution of education since the early days of the industrial revolution, and even earlier days of Ancient Greece.

One of the first was the teacher Noah Webster, who contributed several ideas to education like incorporating patriotism, establishing a national language and curriculum in the classroom, and lastly, that education should be free.

Horace Mann is described as the "Father of American Education". His accomplishments included increasing public support for education that was for all children and supported by the state government, as well as bringing attention to the actual teacher profession and creating normal schools which were teacher training institutes. Mann believed in a child-centered approach to learning.

John Dewey was a person who brought about progressive education change in the classroom by making curriculum and pedagogy more student-centered, with problem-solving and learning through experience becoming more popular.

United States of America Founding Father, Benjamin Rush, laid out similar plans that would unify higher education as well. He sought colleges should teach higher branches of science, laws, physics, divinity, the law of nature, and economics.

In 1779, Thomas Jefferson, a huge proponent of accessible education, signed the *Bill for the More General Diffusion of Knowledge*. This bill provided for the establishment of a system of public schools that would educate the masses with the basic education necessary to ensure good government, public safety, and happiness, Jefferson proposed school would be free for white children, male and female, for three years as they study reading, writing, arithmetic, and history.

Now, I'm not just bashing the education system without respect for its miraculous achievements. Those key players along with countless others have helped make the unbelievable and unlikely progress that we have made. Incredibly, we have an institution that educates its young so they can go out and be enriched and powerful. We just need to modernize and improve effectiveness.

In any system, there are cracks and imperfections, and given the nature of a youth's education, the consequences are not trivial. School teaches us so much, except for two critical subjects:

• *How to Work* – choose the right job for us and work in a way that doesn't take away from our lives. The right work will allow us to connect and contribute to our fellow humans and justify our existence.

• *How to Love* – how to form satisfactory relationships with others and ourselves. It is no secret that our quality of life is highly correlated with the quality of our relationships.

If I had to write what education should be on a sticky note, it would be those two topics. A proper education, rich in meaning and purpose, will teach people how to work and love.

There is a huge need for a reverse-engineered curriculum that allows students to develop skills needed for *The World Beyond*. Something that shows students how to be outwardly obedient, but inwardly independent.

ON GOING TO GOOD SCHOOLS
WHY YOU (PROBABLY) DON'T NEED TO GO

I used to think that to be successful, I had to go to a top-notch university. I've noticed that many of my students feel the same way. They put all their energy into getting into big-name schools instead of figuring out what they truly want in life.

Yes, attending a fancy university means meeting brilliant people and reading the best books ever written. But students often end up in super intense jobs that, while great for some, are not what most people want or need.

It's better to figure out what we want our lives to look like and find places that can help us realize those dreams. Going to a pricey Ivy League school doesn't replace knowing what you want and being genuinely excited to learn.

That's not to say that going to one of those places isn't valuable. They offer a lot.

For example, professional programs like MBAs or doctorates have a dramatically lower value if you do not attend a top 10 or top 15 school.

However, top universities are not for everyone, and that's fine.

There are a few ideas that helped me realize that I didn't need to attend a fancy institution to get a good education, and I didn't even need to go to one to be "successful".

In my case, I just needed to find the institution that helped me achieve my desired lifestyle.

Asking for Permission

"The education-industrial complex has grown up around the idea that no one has the ability to create useful work without a certificate" - Seth Godin (*The Practice*)

People can create and act without a certificate; they just need to learn. We do not need a degree to start a business or to succeed.

We need to focus on doing useful work.

Don't wait for permission to do the thing. Start.

Seeking to Be An Authority

"Famous colleges need to enforce the regime of compliance and scarcity, so they seek our cooperation and belief to build their reputation. They're only famous because we want them to be famous. That desire is about credentialing. The magic power a famous institution has to bless us with status and authority." - Seth Godin (*The Practice*)

Seeking to join a good college often equates to seeking authority.

Authority, at least the kind that is worthwhile, is earned, not artificially given.

This is not to say that aiming to go to a "*good*" college is not worthwhile.

"There's no such thing as a best school or a best job. There's only the best fit for your values and goals." - Adam Grant

Going to a "good" college is a byproduct of having worthwhile goals, not the goal itself.

People are not successful because they went to a top university, but you do have to be successful to go to a top university.

Internalizing this idea helped me free myself from the notion that faceless administrators determine the trajectory of my life at a random university. My life is determined by my choices and perceptions, and if our values match, a *"good"* university is just another tool I could use.

I learned to move the trust I put in institutions and give it to myself instead. I stopped shaping my life according to a university's expectations and started working towards internal *rather than external approval.*

Credentials, Not an Education

"Credentialing lulls us into false confidence about who is actually an expert" - Seth Godin (*The Practice*)

Many of these institutions are in the business of providing credentials. Credentials have their place and are necessary for functioning institutions, but it is critical not to conflate credentials with an education.

Institutions are designed to give us credentials, not an education.

Credentials do not make us experts, but they do give us some authority in society. People who have both credentials and true expertise are rare.

I believe that those with credentials have a responsibility to society to have a robust education.

And *education is something that we must take into our own hands.* Only we can make ourselves true experts in our endeavors.

Many people, including myself, are upset with the rising cost of higher education. Still, the truth is that many of *those institutions sell credentials instead of education, and they come at a high cost.*

These institutions allow people to buy society's trust rather than earn it. Societal trust is earned through true competence and demonstrations with repeated results.

~

LET'S talk about successful college dropouts.

College is *not* a must for everyone.

However, most people will probably benefit from a college degree. Aside from access to better-paying jobs that require less physical work, there are many other reasons to pursue a college education. However, given the rising costs of higher education each person needs to assess if the cost is worth the value for them.

Everyone hears the stories about Zuckerberg or Bill Gates dropping out of college, but there are two small caveats to this:

• *These people are outliers.*

They are the exception to the rule. If we plan to be the exception, we set ourselves up for failure.

Hope to be the exception. Plan to be the exception. Do not expect to be the exception.

• *These people didn't actually "drop out."*

Universities typically offer these high achievers a leave of absence where they can leave and finish their degree later.

Many of these people were also qualified to gain admission to top-performing universities. Being a college dropout is not an excuse for being incompetent or uneducated.

Initially, taking generalized coursework seems like a waste of time, but it broadens our thinking. If we attend university, we will probably encounter classes we expected to like but don't. The opposite is also true; we may discover that we enjoy a class we initially expected to dislike.

Most college students do not know what they want and do not accurately assess their strengths and weaknesses. Studying generalized coursework can help highlight our likes, dislikes, strengths, and weaknesses.

BUILDING STRONG FOUNDATIONS FOR LEARNING

CHARACTERISTICS OF HIGH ACHIEVING HOMES & FOUNDATIONS FOR SELF-EDUCATION

"Don't let school interfere with your education." - Mark Twain

L earning isn't just about school. Real education happens everywhere, especially at home. However, even if we don't have a strong foundation at home, we can still build one. No matter where we go, we will need an education.
Sometimes it's in the classroom, and other times it isn't.

It's up to us to figure out what we need to know, and self-education is key.

My Personal Experience with Self-Directed Learning

A few months into my self-directed learning, something amazing happened. I could focus better and understand new ideas faster. I wasn't as easily distracted, and I could remember things I had learned weeks earlier. This focus gave me energy and curiosity I never had before. Suddenly, I could read and understand things in a fraction of the time they previously took. This was when I really started to believe that anything is possible.

Characteristics of Homes with High-Achieving Children

"If knowledge is power, then learning is our superpower." - Jim Kwik (*Limitless*)

A strong foundation for learning begins at home. Here are some characteristics of homes with high-achieving children. Every characteristic has to do with parents because they are the most influential factor when it comes to a child's educational outcomes. The best part is that these are simple things that anyone can do.

- *The parents believe in a better world*

Parents who believe the world can improve pass on that hope to their kids. Optimism is critical to learning, and children who believe in a better future are more motivated to learn.

- *The parents offer consistency*

Clear rules and routines give kids stability, helping them focus on self-improvement over time. Consistency is vital for growth.

- *The parents give praise*

Positive reinforcement encourages children to repeat good behaviors. Everyone wants to do the right thing and know when they are on the right track.

- *The parents are the primary educators*

Parents who see themselves as their children's primary educators tend to have better-performing children. Schools are important, but children learn even more at home.

. . .

I HAVE NOTICED these characteristics in the homes of high-performing students, and I've also had conversations with other educators who have noticed something similar. These characteristics are low-cost and can be done by anyone everywhere.

Maybe our parents did these things, perhaps they didn't. Regardless, achievement is still possible even without these things. It's more challenging, but humans are built to do hard things.

Building a Strong Foundation for Self-Education

A good foundation is essential because we will judge what we learn later by what we learned earlier. We can't discern what is true or false if we have a bad foundation. We can create a good foundation by studying foundational topics and practicing efficient learning methods.

Key Foundational Topics for a Strong Foundation

- Hard Sciences (like biology, physics, chemistry, and derivative fields)
- Psychology
- Philosophy
- Game Theory
- Logic & Mathematics
- Computers

A strong understanding of these subjects makes learning nearly anything else much easier.

Efficient Learning Methods for Self-Education

There are two powerful ways to learn efficiently:

- Teaching: we become experts by teaching others.

We immediately discover our knowledge gaps and are incentivized to fill them quickly.

I teach because it helps me learn. We can pick a topic we want to master and teach it to others. I want to become a learning expert, so I teach others how to learn. I also do this with other subjects like psychology, philosophy, finance, and entrepreneurship.

- Reading: learning is faster when we love reading.

Read what you love until you love to read.
Learn what you love until you love to learn.

Learning Pokémon gave me the confidence to study chemistry. Learning chemistry gave me the confidence to study chemical engineering. Learning chemical engineering gave me the confidence to study philosophy. If anyone had told me as a kid that I would love reading philosophy, I wouldn't have believed them. Leveraging my love for Pokémon led me to learn more complex topics.

We will know when we have built a good foundation when we are comfortable picking up any book in any library and feel confident that we can:

- Read it.
- Understand it.
- Determine if it is true or false.

Analyzing Dominant Questions

Thinking is all about asking and answering questions. Every day, we ask ourselves thousands of questions, but a select few dominate our thoughts. The most common questions shape how we see the world and behave. For example, someone constantly asking, "How do I get people to like me?" may become a people pleaser, hiding their thoughts and feelings.

Pay attention to dominant questions. Jim Kwik recommends these questions to guide our learning:

- How can I use this?
- Why must I use this?
- When will I use this?

These questions help us take action and turn knowledge into power. Every time we answer a question or try something new, we rewire our brains.

Purpose and Passion

Knowing our purpose and passion drives us to succeed. I see passion as experimenting and finding what gives us joy, while purpose is sharing that joy with others. A worthwhile goal is to help others through our passions.

Passions change over time. We will likely have many different passions throughout life, and embracing those changes is essential. I know my passions have changed throughout my life. Creativity is expressed by making unique connections. With each passion I explore, I can make more and more unique connections.

Who Do We Think We Are?

"The two most powerful words in the English language are the shortest: 'I am.' Whatever you put after those two words determines your destiny." - Jim Kwik (*Limitless*)

What we believe about ourselves shapes our lives. I often experience the effects of what I tell myself. For example, when I say "I am tired" I will typically take actions of a tired person. However, when I say "I am someone who takes advantage of the day," I tend to take actions that make the most of my time.

Whether we're building strong foundations at home or guiding our self-education, it all starts with our mindset.

Let's work together to give the next generation—and ourselves—the best chance at success. Whether they're ours or someone else's, the future depends on the foundations we lay today.

DEVELOPING INDEPENDENT THOUGHT

THE POWER OF SELF-LEARNING & SELF-RELIANCE

Self-Education Starts with Independent Thought Habits

In my experience, the people most capable of self-education have the following characteristics:

- High-performing
- Want to reach their highest potential
- Insatiably curious
- Committed to consistent improvement
- Want to see their actions make a difference
- Want to be leaders

If these characteristics aren't applicable to you, don't worry. We can still access a prolific education. What matters most is training ourselves to think independently.

In my opinion, the most important qualities to access high-quality self-education are to be insatiably curious and an independent thinker. Most people are insatiably curious when they are children or connected to their inner child. Independent thought is a skill that can be developed.

The lack of the other characteristics are not main barriers to learning something new. The main barrier to learning anything is not physical, it's emotional. However, emotions can be changed with new perspectives or insights.

> "To educate educators! But the first ones must educate themselves! And for these I write." - Friedrich Nietzsche (*Twilight of the Idols*)

Self-Reliance

Education is a fundamental layer of who we are, so we cannot entrust the process entirely to others.

Learning how to educate ourselves starts with learning how to rely on ourselves and think independently. There are many beautiful books on this topic, but one that I want to touch upon is *Self-Reliance* by Ralph Waldo Emerson.

Self-Reliance is a short series of essays that explain the significance and benefits of relying on ourselves and how that plays a critical role in our education.

> "My life is for itself and not for a spectacle." - Ralph Waldo Emerson (*Self-Reliance*)

Life is for ourselves, not for other people to watch. We must live for our own experience.

Thinking independently begins with living for ourselves and disregarding how it appears to others.

> "There is a time in every man's education when he arrives at the conviction that envy is ignorance; that imitation is suicide; that he must take himself for better for worse as his portion; that though the wide universe is full of good, no kernel of nourishing corn can come to him but through his toil bestowed on that plot of ground which is given to him to till." - Ralph Waldo Emerson (*Self-Reliance*)

Emerson is saying that through education we discover three things:

- Everyone has their problems and no one is worth envying.
- Being ourselves is the only way to live.
- Good comes to us through working for it.

How each of us gets to these conclusions is unique and incomparable. Our education is each our own. There are opportunities to learn all around us, but we cannot know anything until we take the time to plant the seeds and tend to the garden. A worthwhile education is an internal achievement brought about through work and sacrifice.

"Trust thyself: every heart vibrates to that iron string. Accept the place the divine providence has found for you, the society of your contemporaries, the connection of events. Great men have always done so, and confided themselves childlike to the genius of their age, betraying their perception that the absolutely trustworthy was seated at their heart, working through their hands, predominating in all their being. And we are now men, and must accept in the highest mind the same transcendent destiny; and not minors and invalids in a protected corner, not cowards fleeing before a revolution, but guides, redeemers and benefactors, obeying the Almighty effort and advancing on Chaos and the Dark." - Ralph Waldo Emerson (*Self-Reliance*)

The only way to access the unique education we need for our lives is to trust ourselves.

We need to accept that there is a divine power in us, our society, and everything that connects them.

All great people trust themselves and commit to the genius within them.

The ancient Romans called the guardian spirit of a person or place a "genius". The word "genius" comes from the Latin word "gignere", which means "to give birth". The Romans believed that the genius was present at the moment of a person's birth and would stay with them throughout their life. The genius was responsible for a person's unique personality and disposition, as well as their talents and abilities.

That commitment to honor the genius advances humanity and makes life worthwhile.

"He cumbers himself never about consequences, about interests; he gives an independent, genuine verdict. You must court him; he does not court you." - Ralph Waldo Emerson (*Self-Reliance*)

If a man can be over-cumbered with consequences and biases but still can provide an independent and genuine opinion, then he will never have to fight for other people's attention or approval because everyone else will be fighting for his.

Learning to provide an independent and honest opinion is a key goal of self-learning. If we are constantly fighting for other people's approval, we end up just thinking what everyone else thinks.

"What I must do is all that concerns me, not what the people think. This rule, equally arduous in actual and in intellectual life, may serve for the whole distinction between greatness and meanness. It is the harder because you will always find those who think they know what is your duty better than you know it. It is easy in the world to live after the world's opinion; it is easy in solitude to live after our own; but the great man is he who in the midst of the crowd keeps with perfect sweetness the independence of solitude." - Ralph Waldo Emerson (*Self-Reliance*)

What we do is our business and not everyone else's, even though it's easy to fall into believing that our business is other people's.

People will always think they know what we "should" do better than us, but this isn't the case.

Only we know our lives and ourselves better than anyone else. It's easy to live in a world based on everyone else's thoughts and opinions, it's much harder to live for ourselves. Some people even lose this connection and don't know what their own thoughts and ideas are.

However, we can find it easy to listen to ourselves by living in solitude. If we've lost access to our independent thoughts and opinions, we can spend some time alone and reconnect with this part of ourselves because greatness is given to those who keep their independence of solitude when they are around others.

"Well, most men have bound their eyes with one or another handkerchief, and attached themselves to some one of these communities of opinion. This conformity makes them not false in a few particulars, authors of a few lies, but false in all particulars. Their every truth is not quite true. Their two is not the real two, their four not the real four" - Ralph Waldo Emerson (*Self-Reliance*)

People tend to practice willful ignorance and intentionally blind themselves to independent thought by mindlessly adopting the opinions of others around them.

Quite often, the opinions of a community are an ideology. These ideologies make our entire reality a lie.

By maintaining and pursuing an independent thought connection to ourselves, we bolster ourselves against the dangers of miseducation and ideology.

"The other terror that scares us from self-trust is our consistency; a reverence for our past act or word because the eyes of others have no other data for computing our orbit than our past acts, and we are loath to disappoint them." - Ralph Waldo Emerson (*Self-Reliance*)

We are hesitant to trust ourselves because we only have our past experiences as a guide. People trap themselves into thinking "what we thought and did in the past is what we'll think and do in the future." We hold the past in such high regard because we have no other concrete evidence to base our decisions on. If we can see that this is simply a mind game, an illusion, then we can set ourselves free of the unconscious patterns of the past and create a new future. A future completely independent of thoughts and habits dictated by the community, a future of our design.

This is the first step of tapping into our divine powers as conscious beings.

> "Ah, so you shall be sure to be misunderstood.'—Is it so bad then to be misunderstood? Pythagoras was misunderstood, and Socrates, and Jesus, and Luther, and Copernicus, and Galileo, and Newton, and every pure and wise spirit that ever took flesh. To be great is to be misunderstood." - Ralph Waldo Emerson (*Self-Reliance*)

Thinking independently is hard, especially because it makes us different from others. But is it so bad to be different? Greatness is only achieved by being different than others. Greatness is so separate from the crowd, that it's almost a different being entirely.

When we harness independent thought, we will often be misunderstood. We will not think like other people and when we share our thoughts, we will be met with confusion, misunderstanding, and judgment.

If being misunderstood was so bad, why were the best minds in history misunderstood?

Being misunderstood is not a sign that we are thinking wrong, it is a sign that we are thinking differently.

Taking the extra step of recognizing when people misunderstand us and being articulate enough to explain why we think the way we do can deepen our own understanding of our independent thoughts.

"Many who are self-taught far excel the doctors, masters, and bachelors of the most renowned universities. - Ludwig Von Mises (Austrian Economist and Author of *Human Action*)

When we are self-taught and driven by our internal desires, we tend to dive deeper and retain more information than in traditional settings. It's easy to fall into thinking that someone is incompetent because they are self-taught. While being self-taught cannot guarantee a competency, neither can be taught from a traditional institution.

In my experience, self-taught students are masters in their own right. For me personally, I believe I have deeper competence in my self-taught endeavors compared to my formal training.

It is possible to have world-class skill and be self-taught.

"He cumbers himself never about consequences, about interests; he gives an independent, genuine verdict. You must court him; he does not court you." - Ralph Waldo Emerson (*Self-Reliance*)

When someone thinks independently, they have more control over what they are convinced by. When dealing with an independent thinker, we must be the one who convinces them. They are not concerned with trying to convince anyone else that they are correct.

Being an independent thinker means that we will be free of trying to convince others of our positions, instead, they will be the ones convincing us.

Additionally, we will build a different relationship with ourselves. We learn that we become the one who is capable of building an accurate understanding when we are presented with new information without needing validation from authority. In a sense, harnessing independent thought can make us an authority. If not for others, at least to ourselves.

"What I must do is all that concerns me, not what the people think. This rule, equally arduous in actual and in intellectual life, may

serve for the whole distinction between greatness and meanness. It is the harder because you will always find those who think they know what is your duty better than you know it. It is easy in the world to live after the world's opinion; it is easy in solitude to live after our own; but the great man is he who in the midst of the crowd keeps with perfect sweetness the independence of solitude."
- Ralph Waldo Emerson (*Self-Reliance*)

It is better to focus on what we need to do rather than the opinions of others. Many times people will tell us that they know what is good for us or what we should be doing, but those are just opinions of others.

Being able to keep our vision for ourselves and maintain our independence is what will make us great.

Not being swayed by the opinions of the world is a challenge worth taking on.

"Well, most men have bound their eyes with one or another hand-kerchief, and attached themselves to some one of these communities of opinion. This conformity makes them not false in a few particulars, authors of a few lies, but false in all particulars. Their every truth is not quite true. Their two is not the real two, their four not the real four." - Ralph Waldo Emerson (*Self-Reliance*)

People will frequently practice willful blindness and attach themselves to other's opinions. They will intentionally ignore the flawed details of these opinions for the sake of "belonging" to or "being accepted" by the community.

This comes at a huge risk. This prevents us from seeing reality as it is, which prevents us from knowing what is true.

If we want to take independent thought seriously, we have to be able to see the flaws in collective opinions as well as the truth of reality. If we can't do this, self-education will collapse upon itself.

Being possessed by a community of opinion, also known as ideology, makes our reality a lie. All of the details become lies. This is why rigid adherence to ideology can lead to miseducation and struggle.

"The other terror that scares us from self-trust is our consistency; a reverence for our past act or word because the eyes of others have no other data for computing our orbit than our past acts, and we are loath to disappoint them." - Ralph Waldo Emerson (*Self-Reliance*)

Self-trust is critical for harnessing independent thought. That being said, we have to act in a way that preserves self-trust and avoid actions that corrode it.

Consistently maintaining our word, and keeping promises to ourselves and others is critical for trusting ourselves.

Keeping our word to ourselves is the most important commitment we have. We are the only person who knows all of our experiences, what we have done, and what we have failed to do.

When we keep our promises to ourselves, our self-trust stays whole, and we can properly harness independent thought.

If we break our self-commitments, we give ourselves evidence to not trust our perceptions, intentions, or instincts.

More On Independent Thought

Here are some more thoughts from other thinkers that I believe relate to this topic:

"Selection pressure is the mechanism through which animals evolve." - Temple Grandin (*Animals Make Us Human*)

Homo Sapiens have survived because we are wise. Our ability to know, to determine what is important, and to seek out and disseminate wisdom has been foundational to our survival.

Evolution is selecting more knowledgeable and wise humans.

"Man is tradition or imitation. He is not born, but rather mould-
ed." - Arthur Schopenhauer (*The World as Will and Representation*)

It is in our nature to not think for ourselves, so it is critical to
pay attention to what we accept to be true.

If the only mechanisms for change are tradition or imitation,
then it is imperative that we identify why we are doing things.

Do we do things simply because that's the way they've always
been done?

Do we do things simply because others around us are doing the
same thing?

How much do we agree with these actions? Do they lead us
where we want to go?

On the flip side, we can enhance our influence on others by
providing them with something worthwhile to imitate. Over time,
this can become a tradition.

"Many who are self-taught far excel the doctors, masters, and
bachelors of the most renowned universities." - Ludwig Von Mises
(Austrian Economist and Author of *Human Action*)

The most comprehensive education is through self-education.
When we are pursuing self-education, we are driven to learn more
and learn deeply. It is guided with the help of others, but the
responsibility of the learning is taken on by the individual.

ACADEMIC SUCCESS VS. REAL-WORLD SUCCESS
BEYOND THE CLASSROOM

School prepares us for challenges in the world beyond. I like to ask my students some questions throughout the school year to show them how some of their thought patterns may not be well received in the workplace.

Some of these questions include:

- Do you think your boss will care if you don't feel like coming to work today?
- Do you think your boss will give you a retake?
- Do you think your boss will excuse you if you are absent without proper communication?

If there is one thing to get from school, it is to learn how to do tasks even when you don't want to.

School is an opportunity to train ourselves in the face of what we don't like. Some people will argue that is precisely the reason to not go to school, but I believe there is a lot to gain from learning how to do things despite our moods.

The Destructive Force of Competition

As someone who deeply appreciates competition, it is not always a valuable aspect of an institution. A portion of Peter Thiel's book *Zero to One* outlines how the academic system incentivizes thought patterns that are maladaptive to the world beyond the classroom.

"Competition is an ideology—the ideology—that pervades our society and distorts our thinking. We preach competition, internalize its necessity, and enact its commandments; and as a result, we trap ourselves within it—even though the more we compete, the less we gain." - Peter Thiel (*Zero to One*)

Thiel argues that our educational system both motivates and is a reflection of our cultural obsession with competition.

"Grades themselves allow precise measurement of each student's competitiveness; pupils with the highest marks receive status and credentials." - Peter Thiel (*Zero to One*)

This happens as young as 4 or 5 years old. Kids are learning to build their identity based on how competitive they are with their peers. I cannot tell you how many times I've heard students say they don't care about learning, they just want an A.

Unfortunately, much of standard public education teaches every young person the same subjects in the same ways, regardless of individual talents or preferences.

"Students who don't learn best by sitting still at a desk are made to feel somehow inferior, while children who excel on conventional measures like tests and assignments end up defining their identities in terms of this weirdly contrived academic parallel reality." - Peter Thiel (*Zero to One*)

Learning is a more dynamic process than the rigid norms of

classroom behavior allow. Education is similar to the electromagnetic spectrum - we only see a small portion of it, but there is so much more that is there.

Learning can be more than what we normalize in classrooms.

"Elite students climb confidently until they reach a level of competition sufficiently intense to beat their dreams out of them." - Peter Thiel (*Zero to One*)

Higher education is where those with big plans will pay hundreds of thousands of dollars to conform in these intense competitions with equally intelligent peers over careers they aren't passionate about like management consulting or investment banking. Unfortunately, the price of tuition is still growing and outpacing inflation.

Academic success incentivizes blindly following the competition, which can be dangerous.

Thiel also provides a short story about big tech that illustrates the danger of focusing on competition.

"Let's test the Shakespearean model in the real world. Imagine a production called Gates and Schmidt, based on Romeo and Juliet. Montague is Microsoft. Capulet is Google. Two great families, run by alpha nerds, sure to clash on account of their sameness.

As with all good tragedy, the conflict seems inevitable only in retrospect. In fact it was entirely avoidable. These families came from very different places. The House of Montague built operating systems and office applications. The House of Capulet wrote a search engine. What was there to fight about?

Lots, apparently. As a startup, each clan had been content to leave the other alone and prosper independently. But as they grew, they began to focus on each other. Montagues obsessed about Capulets obsessed about Montagues. The result? Windows vs. Chrome OS, Bing vs. Google Search, Explorer vs. Chrome, Office vs. Docs, and Surface vs. Nexus.

Just as war cost the Montagues and Capulets their children, it cost Microsoft and Google their dominance: Apple came along and overtook them all. In January 2013, Apple's market capitalization was $500 billion, while Google and Microsoft combined were worth $467 billion. Just three years before, Microsoft and Google were each more valuable than Apple." - Peter Theil (*Zero to One*)

Competition and rivalry causes us to overemphasize old opportunities and mindlessly copy what has worked in the past. Our focus on competition blinds us to new methods and can make us believe there are opportunities where none exist.

"Competition is a destructive force instead of a sign of value" - Peter Theil (*Zero to One*)

Competition in the world of academics is a sign of value and it is useful to be competitive with your classmates. However, this competitive bias is dangerous in the world beyond.

Just in Case Information vs. Just in Time Information

Most of the concepts in school don't help students build a coherent picture of the world.

The students learn how to graph conic sections without getting a chance to build anything with that information.

Everything we teach is out of context.

Children are *confused* about how things fit together. They are being overloaded with information just in case they need it instead of learning information just in time.

Just in case information is useful for success in the academic world.

Just in time information is useful for success in the world beyond.

Everyone Has a Proper Place in the Pyramid

Schools teach students that they must stay in the class where they belong.

They learn how to stay put, mature at the same rate as everyone else, and fit the mold of the "perfect" student. Schools have an orderly category for everyone, which teaches the students to seek status, compete, and please adults.

Instead, they need to learn how to learn and collaborate. Learning and collaboration are much more useful in the world beyond. Especially when compared to status-seeking, competing, and people-pleasing.

Don't Care Too Much

Students are forced to turn their interests on and off as soon as the bell rings or as soon as a unit is over. No matter how much they enjoy studying a topic, they must move on because the system dictates it.

It becomes increasingly difficult for a student to follow their obsessions or dive deep into topics they genuinely love.

The ones who end up diving deeper or following their obsessions end up "falling behind" because they are not keeping up with the pace of the curriculum.

Some of the most rewarding and useful work in the "real world" comes from deep focus and obsession.

Schools need to incentivize diving deep and obsession, but they probably won't. So we need to cultivate and nourish these impulses within ourselves. We need to recognize when we want to dive deep and when we are obsessed because that is what leads to success in the world beyond.

Emotional Reliance

Students learn how they should feel based on the feedback their teacher gives them.

As much as we should encourage students to develop their own emotional connections, they learn emotional dependence through grades, prizes, and punishments.

I see this all the time as a teacher. My body language is one of my strongest tools in the classroom...and it really shouldn't be.

Students are conditioned to feel what their teachers want them to feel and have few opportunities for emotional independence.

The world beyond demands emotional independence and students can only solve meaningful problems if they are connected to their emotions informed by their unique experiences.

Intellectual Reliance

Students rarely have a chance to think for themselves in the world of academics. The best students wait for the teacher to tell them what to do, tell them what to learn, and tell them what to think.

Students learn to let other people determine the meaning of their lives. If they do things their own way or ask hard questions, they are quickly labeled as "a problem child."

There is almost no opportunity to develop their own ideas. Students are rewarded for championing the ideas of the teachers.

The world beyond demands that people develop their own ideas and determine their own meaning.

Provisional Self-Esteem

The world of academics creates situations where students learn that their worth comes from what a professional thinks of them.

Students learn that they should not trust themselves, but instead rely on the evaluations of their report cards, grades, or trained professionals.

To succeed in the world of academics, we have to suspend our trust in ourselves to make room for professionals to evaluate us.

The world beyond demands that we trust ourselves. This is a critical first step in any worthwhile endeavor.

No Privacy or Personal Space. Little to No Rights.

In traditional schools, students are always watched and under consistent surveillance.

This prevents students from developing true autonomy and can lead to issues such as excessive screen time. (Screens are typically a method for escape.)

In the world beyond the classroom, people discover creative solutions when they have the freedom to experiment, fail, and experiment again.

Constant evaluation kills this dynamic and prevents creative problem-solving.

~

Where does this leave us?

Real-World Success is determined by different metrics and values than Academic Success.

However, the academic world is not inherently bad. There are just unintended effects of the dated and centralized system.

Independent thinkers and innovators are the antidote to many of these issues. This is largely why independent thought is so critical, especially in alternative education. There are many people frustrated with the current state of the traditional education system and are taking it into their own hands. There are many people calling for system reform, combining existing systems, or even starting their own schools.

In a 2015 interview, Elon Musk shared two core principles that would guide the school he wants to start:

- Ditch the assembly line model—no grade levels.

Allow the students to operate at the level that they are, not the level the system thinks they are in. He believes that age segregation doesn't work because kids have different aptitudes and interests that vary across time.

- Problem-focused, not tool-focused.

This prioritizes the idea of "just in time" information over "just in case" information. The students have a problem and will learn along the way. This allows them to actually build with the information they are learning, which provides more neural connections. This improves retention and relevance for more efficient and effective learning.

Learning to use tools is pointless and boring unless those tools help us solve a real problem.

PERSONALITY DIMENSIONS
DEFINING OUR OWN SUCCESS

**Success Redefined: Risk, Admiration, and Personality
Preferences**

Most parents push their children toward mediocrity because they prioritize safety over excellence. Safe choices have become synonymous with success, even if we don't find happiness or fulfillment in them.

This book, in part, is focused on obtaining excellence. This means we'll be thinking of things differently & independently. Excellence requires unconventional choices and risk.

If we have a few critical stable pillars in life, then we can afford to take bigger risks.

These pillars are:

- gainful employment
- stable relationships
- a good home

"I think people who do what they have an aptitude to do are much happier than unfortunately a very large amount of people who are stuck in occupations they don't like." - Conrad M. Black

There is a deeper satisfaction and happiness found in careers that match our natural talents. Unfortunately, most people experience discontent in jobs they don't enjoy.

Success comes from defining it on our own terms, rather than adhering to societal expectations. By understanding and embracing individual strengths and passions, people can forge a path to a fulfilling and authentically successful life.

I believe we can discover what success means to us by paying attention to who and what we admire. Admiration is instinctive, but it manifests differently for each person. So, the best way to define success is to pay attention to what we admire — that gives us a hint. However, that is not the only thing we can pay attention to. We can also start uncovering what success means to each of us by learning about personality.

Personality and Trajectory

"The privilege of a lifetime is to become who you truly are." - Carl Jung

I've always found personality to be a fascinating subject. I've always been interested in what makes people tick and what separates an individual from the rest of the crowd.

Personality is one of the many factors which determine individuality.

Personality can be thought of as a collection of qualities that make up our overall character.

Over the years, there has been much debate over what those qualities are and how they are present in human behavior. Today, multiple theories have been widely accepted by the public and are used in business practices.

Studying personality is a fantastic way to connect with and understand more people than we otherwise might, but I don't just stop there, I like to use it to help determine a complimentary life trajectory.

Learning about our own personality gives us an insight into what kind of life we would actually enjoy.

It's too easy to get caught up in building our lives for other people or chasing romanticized ideals. This is how people get stuck with jobs and relationships that they hate. People think they want certain things because someone else told them it was worth having or because they saw it in the media. I see this with my students all the time, they stress out over which career pays the most, is the most "secure," or looks the most glamorous.

I frequently see many people intentionally repress themselves in order to fit into a mold that they will never truly accept. The trick to avoiding this pitfall is learning about what makes up our personalities and tailoring our trajectories to fulfill ourselves.

If we know what we would like to do, then we can pick a role within society that is complementary to that.

Sounds simple enough, but people don't really act this way. We live in a complex society and there are roles that need to be filled by people of a certain temperament. It's better to fill these roles with people who naturally fit into them, rather than waste resources trying to fit a square peg in a round hole.

Our personality is something to take into account when we are designing the trajectory of our lives. It's something we need to grapple with. It's much easier to put ourselves in an environment that compliments our strengths and preferences, rather than reject or ignore parts of ourselves that cannot be easily changed.

Myers-Briggs Personality Types

This is a popular theory of personality. It's slightly outdated and not entirely scientifically inaccurate, but it is widely accepted and used in many institutions so it's useful to "be in the know" with this information. Plus it's fun party talk.

The *Myers-Briggs Personality Type Indicator* (MBTI) categorizes people based on how they perceive the world and make decisions. It was created by American mother-daughter duo, Katharine Cook Briggs and Isabel Briggs Myers.

MBTI is widely accepted throughout the business world as well as socially, especially in the United States.

Contrary to popular belief, the MBTI has significant scientific limitations, including poor reliability and an incomplete depiction of human personality.

However, MBTI is useful to know because it gives us a common language with people who accept it.

MBTI is popular in the corporate world because it does an excellent job of categorizing people without hurting anyone's feelings. This theory of personality has a way of making everyone seem like they have no downfalls and can always contribute, which is powerful in business environments. Businesses tend to do better when the people in it feel better. In the business world, empirical personality data isn't as relevant to performance as we would expect.

MBTI is fantastic at providing a basic structure for understanding personality, but it's crucial to know that it does not supply us with the whole picture. It assumes that people have distinct preferences for interpreting experiences and making decisions.

It draws from Carl Jung's typology theories which suggest people have four modes of cognitive functions (*Thinking, Feeling, Sensation, and Intuition*) as well as one of two polar orientations (*Extraversion or Introversion*).

Even though Jung's theory of psychological types was not based on empirical scientific studies, they were based on clinical observation, introspection, and anecdotes. Since the conclusions did not originate from controlled scientific studies, they are not accepted by the scientific community. However, Carl Jung was an profound thinker and I do believe he was one of the few operating with precision at the edge of our collective understanding. His conclusions, from his observations or otherwise, were always made with the intention of bringing man closer to a truth that we all can accept.

MBTI sorts what personality is in 4 major continuums.

Each person leans more towards one pole of each pair similar to right-handedness or left-handedness. When a person determines which side of each continuum they express, they are assigned a type.

There are a total of 16 different types, 1 for each combination of the letters.

Let me give an example using my own letters:

I'm more *introverted* than extroverted.

I'm more *intuitive* than sensory.

I'm more of a *thinker* than a feeler.

Usually, I'm more perceiver than judger, but recently I have been more *judger* than perceiver.

This gives me the letters INTJ. (Some days I'm an INTP) The letters come from the capitalized letter in each word: Introverted, iNtuitive, Thinking, and Judger.

Extroversion vs. Introversion

MBTI and Jung use introversion and extroversion in similar ways. Introversion means *inward-turning* and extroversion means *outward-turning*. These both are often referred to as attitudes that one uses to function in the external world.

Simply put, extroverts are recharged by people while introverts are recharged by alone time.

Each type is usually drained by the opposite activity, extroverts are drained by alone time and introverts are drained by social interaction. However, there are other notable differences between them.

Extroverts direct their energy towards people and objects while introverts direct theirs towards concepts and ideas.

We can find out which attitude people take by paying attention to the topics of their conversation or asking them what their ideal weekend would look like. If someone is frequently talking about people and things they're most likely extroverted. If someone is frequently talking about concepts and ideas they're most likely introverted. An extrovert's ideal weekend is probably spent going out and seeing a bunch of people, celebrating at the club, or another type of high-energy ordeal. An introvert's ideal weekend would probably be spent inside with a good book or TV show along with ample time for reflection.

This is not to say that extroverts can never be alone, or that introverts hate being with people. Everyone needs some amount of social interaction and alone time.

Our attitudes merely reflect our preferences and how we choose to interact with the world around us. There are not concretely who we are and are likely to change as we go through life.

Neither attitude is more advantageous or otherwise, they are simply two sides of the same coin.

The following statements may apply if you are more *extroverted*:

- I am seen as "outgoing" or as a "people person."
- I feel comfortable in groups and like working in them.
- I have a wide range of friends and know lots of people.
- I sometimes jump too quickly into an activity and don't allow enough time to think it over.
- Before I start a project, I sometimes forget to stop and get clear on what I want to do and why.

The following statements may apply to you if you are more *introverted*:

- I am seen as "reflective" or "reserved."
- I feel comfortable being alone and like things, I can do on my own.

- I prefer to know just a few people well.
- I sometimes spend too much time reflecting and don't move into action quickly enough.
- I sometimes forget to check with the outside world to see if my ideas really fit the experience.

Sensing vs. Intuition

This dichotomy is based on how we psychologically perceive the external world. These are both functions of gathering information.

Sensing individuals tend to trust information that is tangible, concrete, and understood by the five senses.

They're less likely to trust "gut feelings" or other "hunches" that come out of nowhere. For them, meaning lies in the data, what is in front of them.

Individuals driven by intuition tend to trust information that is remembered or discovered through analyzing patterns.

Since they trust information that doesn't have to fit within the five senses, they tend to be more excited by what the future has in store. For them, meaning is not in the data but in the principles and theories which underlie the data.

The following statements may apply if you perceive through *sensing*:

- I remember events as snapshots of what actually happened.
- I solve problems by working through facts until I understand the problem.
- I am pragmatic and look to the "bottom line."
- I start with facts and then form a big picture.
- I trust experience first and trust words and symbols less.
- Sometimes I pay so much attention to facts, either present or past, that I miss new possibilities.

The following statements may apply if you perceive through *intuition*:

- I remember events by what I read "between the lines" about their meaning.
- I solve problems by leaping between different ideas and possibilities.
- I am interested in doing things that are new and different.
- I like to see the big picture, and then find out the facts.
- I trust impressions, symbols, and metaphors more than what I actually experienced.
- Sometimes I think so much about new possibilities that I never look at how to make them a reality.

Thinking vs. Feeling

Thinking and feeling are based on how we prefer to make choices in the external world. Both thinkers and feelers make rational choices based on certain kinds of information that were gathered from their senses or intuition.

Thinkers tend to make their decisions based on objective measures while aiming to be reasonable, logical, or causal.

They are usually personally detached from their decisions and try to match their choices to a given set of rules. Thinkers also tend to have a low tolerance for those who are inconsistent or illogical. Thinkers give direct (and sometimes harsh) feedback and view the truth as more important than feelings.

This is not to say that thinkers never make emotional decisions, MBTI simply lets us know one's preference in decision-making and is *not* a predictor of behavior. They also don't "think better" than their feeling counterparts. MBTI doesn't measure cognitive ability, just preferences.

Feelings types tend to make their choices based on empathy, balance, harmony, and consideration for others' needs. They will try to see what works best for everyone involved and are willing to sacrifice logic and truth for the good of the majority.

Thinking types will have a hard time leading a healthy and productive life if they make their choices based on their feelings while feeling types will have a harder time leading a healthy and productive life if they make their choices based on their logical reasoning.

Both types tend to lack the opposite senses necessary to make well-informed choices.

Similar to our attitudes toward the external world (extraversion vs. introversion), one isn't better than the other, they are both different sides of the same coin.

The following statements may apply if you decide through *thinking*:

- I enjoy technical and scientific fields where logic is important.
- I notice inconsistencies.
- I look for logical explanations or solutions to almost everything.
- I make decisions with my head and want to be fair.
- I believe telling the truth is more important than being tactful.
- Sometimes I miss or don't value the "people" part of a situation.
- I can be seen as too task-oriented, uncaring, or indifferent.

The following statements may apply if you decide through *feeling*:

- I have a people or communications orientation.
- I am concerned with harmony and nervous when it is missing.

- I look for what is important to others and express concern for others.
- I make decisions with my heart and want to be compassionate.
- I believe being tactful is more important than telling the "cold" truth.
- Sometimes I miss seeing or communicating the "hard truth" of situations.
- I am sometimes experienced by others as too idealistic, mushy, or indirect.

Judging vs. Perceiving

This dichotomy is based on how we relate to our perceptions of the external world. This continuum is heavily influenced by our sensing and/or intuitive natures because we are either judging or perceiving the information obtained through those perceptions.

Judging types take in information with the intention of using it later and, in the words of Myers, like to "have matters settled." They usually have a plan in mind and are only interested in information if it's related to their goal in some way. They tend to be more comfortable once decisions have been made and the environment around them is under control.

Perceiving types take in information for the sake of learning. They love knowing things just to know them. Perceiving types learn about and adapt to the world around them rather than structure it themselves.

The following statements may apply if you perceive your information through *judging*:

- I like to have things decided.
- I appear to be task-oriented.
- I like to make lists of things to do.
- I like to get my work done before playing.
- I plan to work to avoid rushing just before a deadline.

- Sometimes I focus so much on the goal that I miss new information.

The following statements may apply if you perceive your information through *perceiving*:

- I like to stay open to respond to whatever happens.
- I appear to be loose and casual. I like to keep plans to a minimum.
- I like to approach work as play or mix work and play.
- I work in bursts of energy.
- I am stimulated by an approaching deadline.
- Sometimes I stay open to new information so long I miss making decisions when they are needed.

For more information on each of the MBTI traits, I suggest going to myersbriggs.org. It's the place to go for more thorough explanations of everything MBTI and where I got most of this information, like the relevant statements for each type.

LIKE I SAID EARLIER, personality changes throughout our lives, and these letters are just letting us know our proclivities, not defining who we are as people. However, knowing my MBTI can give me an insight into what kind of life trajectory I would be the most satisfied with with the least friction.

According to my MBTI, I would most enjoy a trajectory that:

- provides me with ample alone time (I)
- opportunities to discover new information (N)
- puts me in environments where the culture values reason, logic, and causality (T)
- gives me the opportunity to make decisions on my own time at my own pace (J)

By understanding our personality, we can create paths for ourselves which complement our proclivities. For example, if I were extroverted, I would probably best enjoy myself in an environment surrounded by others.

MBTI Critiques & Justifications

While MBTI provides valuable insight into complementary life trajectories would best complement our nature, there are some criticisms that are important to consider:

- These types are generalizations that do not accurately describe an individual.
- There are people who do not fit nicely into these 16 groups.
- MBTI suggests that there are no negative personality traits.
- MBTI is widely accepted in the workplace, even though there is no evidence that supports MBTI is predictive of performance.
- There are others, but these are the ones I've encountered to be the most substantial.

All these criticisms bring up the question:
Why should we still use MBTI?

It can give us a rough idea of what kind of life trajectory we would fit well with and as I've talked about in my other posts, we do things badly before we can do them well. If we want to design a beautiful life trajectory, we need a rough starting point. MBTI is great for that. Plus it's a fun party conversation if you ever run into an MBTI nerd. Additionally, since MBTI is commonly accepted in the workplace, it's useful to be in the know when people try to use its coded language.

Find our letters and start discovering which paths most align with us.

In the modern world, we have choices, why not choose what fits us?

~

The Big 5

"No matter who you are, The Man does occasionally bend his ear to you even if his eyes are looking elsewhere, he does now and then condescend to listen to your demands and let you appear at his side. But you never think to listen to yourself, to bend your own ear to what you yourself have to say."- Seneca (*On the Shortness of Life*)

The Big 5 Model, also known as the five-factor model (FFM) or the OCEAN model, provides descriptions of each dimension of personality according to the FFM, as well as what success would look like for people who score high or low in each particular dimension. I will also discuss how we can use The Big 5 Model to add on to and polish our pre-existing trajectory framework based on MBTI.

This model proposes five main dimensions of personality.

Each dimension is identified through factor analysis of personality surveys. The factor analysis was applied to the surveys to discern commonalities between descriptive words that people would use to describe themselves. This means that these experiments were based on semantic associations and not quantitative empirical data. However, no personality model is perfect and knowledge of The Big 5 can be extremely valuable for developing an even deeper understanding of our personalities.

Critics argue that the Big 5 dimensions are too simplistic to fully capture human complexity. While it is true that The Big 5 Model probably does not accurately capture a human being in its entirety, I do believe five dimensions do carry sufficient complexity to describe human behavior. Newtonian physics occurs in three dimensions (four at max) and that's enough to invite serious complexity. Five dimensions provide ample complexity, especially when examining how individual personalities align with these traits.

Another thing to keep in mind is, similarly to MBTI, these personality traits can fluctuate over our lifetime and that is okay. Humans are constantly growing and changing and personality goes along for the ride.

Our personality must be one of the biggest factors when we are considering which choices to make when building our lives. If we're high in extraversion, then we probably won't want a job that sits us in front of computer screens all day with little social interaction. If we're lower in conscientiousness, we wouldn't want to be in a position of high power and authority because people are going to need things from us all the time and that would drive us crazy.

The 5 dimensions of personality are:

- Openness
- Conscientiousness
- Extraversion
- Agreeableness
- Neuroticism

Percentage vs. Percentile

The FFM is measured by percentiles. This is not to be confused with the percentage.

Let me give an example to make this clear:

If someone were to score 90th percentile in extraversion, this would mean out of 100 people they are more extraverted than 90 of them while being less extraverted than 9 of them.

This does not mean that they are 90% extravert and 10% introverted, although that is a common interpretation.

All the traits are normally distributed, meaning most people are in the 50th percentile range while there are fewer people who score high or low.

Openness

Or to be more specific, *openness to experience*. This dimension explores how open to new experiences someone is. Openness can be broken up into six subcategories which are:

- Active Imagination
- Aesthetic Sensitivity or Artistic Interests
- Awareness of Inner Feelings or Emotionality
- Preference for Variety or Adventurousness
- Intellectual Curiosity
- Liberalism
- Artistic Interests

Openness can be expressed through any of these six categories but does not have to be in all of them. For example, someone who is high in openness may express it through their heightened preference for variety, but may not have a particular aesthetic sensitivity. However, that same person will most likely have a higher aesthetic sensitivity than one who is less open.

People who are high in openness tend to be more liberal, have more imaginative sexual fantasies, and experiment with drugs or participate in other risky activities. Novelty excites the open person. Open people also need to be creative, if they aren't they lose their vitality quickly.

Openness has also been found to be positively correlated with intelligence. Right now, it's unclear whether intelligence may predispose the individual to openness or if openness predisposes to intelligence but nonetheless, they are correlated.

People who are low in openness (closed) tend to be more conservative, don't like trying new things, and enjoy routines.

Closed individuals are less flexible than their open counterparts and tend to be more analytical.

Individuals who score low in openness may do well at jobs that don't require creativity and involve routines.

High-openness individuals excel in roles requiring creativity and adaptability.

Success to the open person can look like large blocks of time for creative work and exploration while success to the closed person can be predictable and orderly environments.

Conscientiousness

This is one of the biggest predictors of long-term life success.

People who score high in conscientiousness tend to be responsible, organized, hard-working, intentional, goal-oriented, self-disciplined, and serious. These are the types of people who would spend all day chopping down trees to build a cabin if we left them alone in a forest with an axe. Conscientious people tend to be in leadership positions along with earning more and better work relationships. These folks also love to plan things.

Similar to openness, conscientiousness can be broken up into the following six subcategories:

- Self-Efficacy
- Orderliness
- Dutifulness
- Achievement-striving
- Self-discipline
- Cautiousness

Conscientiousness can be expressed through any of these categories, but not all.

Highly conscientious people are often responsible, organized, goal-oriented, and disciplined. When taken to the extreme, conscientiousness is responsible for the "workaholics" and "perfectionists". These types rarely miss bill payments, take notes, keep promises, and are punctual. They are less likely to engage in risky behavior. High-scoring conscientious types also tend to keep to-do lists and attend to tasks with little delay.

People who are low in conscientiousness tend to be laid-back, less achievement-driven and are more likely to commit anti-social or criminal behavior. Especially if they are paired with low agreeableness. Non-conscientious types are also more likely to oversleep, be late, or avoid tasks that demand action.

Success for conscientious people looks like the most conventional sense of the term. They would excel in high-powered positions with clearly defined rules. Their life would be full of routines and order. Clean environments where everything is in its place.

Success for non-conscientious types may look like surrounding themselves with automated actions and little external responsibility. They would probably excel in positions requiring creative work with a fair amount of flexibility, not the types of jobs that require someone to show up and act on a regular basis. They would prefer a little more chaos in their environments and would probably be bothered by too much order. Non-conscientious types would probably love having pets (as long as they are conscientious enough to take adequate care of them).

Extraversion

This trait is the dimension of positive emotion and an indicator of how outgoing or social someone is. Highly extroverted types love to be around people, go to social gatherings, and work well in groups. They also tend to seek out the company of others, are enthusiastic, energetic, and action-oriented. These people are the life of the party and love being the center of attention.

The six subcategories in which extraversion is expressed are as follows:

- Friendliness

- Gregariousness
- Assertiveness
- Activity level
- Excitement-seeking
- Cheerfulness

Unlike MBTI, there is no introversion dimension. In The Big 5 Model, introversion is just the absence of extraversion. Kind of like cold from the scientific perspective. There is no cold, just the absence of heat.

People who score low in the extraversion dimension are commonly referred to as introverts. Introverts have less enthusiasm and energy than extroverts, are less involved in social activities, and tend to be quiet and keep to themselves.

Matching a job to our level of extraversion is crucial in building a satisfying life trajectory for ourselves. Higher-scoring extroverts may want to go into jobs that need a high level of interaction like teaching, sales, nursing, PR, or other service jobs.

Introverts may want to find jobs that allow them to work independently or don't require much social interaction. Excellent jobs for that could be authors, librarians, engineers, music or video editors, or computer scientists.

Success to an extrovert would require them to nurture their relationships carefully so they can have people there to celebrate their big wins with them. Success for an introvert would require them to create plenty of opportunities for space for recharging in between their other activities.

We can't talk about this dimension without talking about *ambiverts*. These types are equal parts of extroverted and introverted. They don't have preferences for working in groups or alone. They are not uncomfortable in social settings, but being around people can tire them out. They love being the center of attention, but only for a short time. Some people think they're quiet, while others think they are social. They lose themselves in conversation just as easily as they can lose themselves in their own thoughts. Ambiverts tend to do extremely well in both personal and professional settings.

Agreeableness

This is the social harmony and cooperation dimension.

High scorers of agreeableness tend to be friendly, self-sacrificing, warm, polite, helpful, considerate, and generous. They usually take the John Locke approach to human nature and believe that people are fundamentally good. Agreeable people see others as decent, honest, and trustworthy much like themselves. Agreeable people are more than willing to put aside their own interests for the good of other people or social harmony. In unhealthy doses, agreeable people could end up as pushovers.

Agreeableness can be expressed in these six subcategories:

- Trust
- Morality
- Altruism
- Cooperation
- Modesty
- Sympathy

People who are low in agreeableness are known as disagreeable and tend to put their own needs above those of others. They are also more distant, less friendly, and less cooperative than their agreeable counterparts. Highly disagreeable people tend to gravitate towards anti-social or criminal behavior.

Success to an agreeable person will have a lot of social cohesion. They would love to be surrounded by people who like them and are great at building teams and maintaining relationships. Some great careers for agreeable types include nurses, counselors, teachers, or HR specialists.

Success to a disagreeable person will have a lot to do with how they feel about their own desires. Since social harmony is not a big goal of disagreeable folks, their own interests will take that place. So a successful disagreeable person would be more satisfied with getting what they want at the cost of social cooperation than being tactful and considerate of others' needs. Some great careers for disagreeable people include scientists, critics, or soldiers.

Neuroticism

This dimension determines our susceptibility to negative emotions. Negative emotions are anxiety, fear, anger, frustration, envy, jealousy, depression, worry, or loneliness, not negativity.

Highly neurotic individuals tend to respond worse to stressors and interpret them as more severe than they are. People who score highly in neuroticism have a harder time remaining emotionally stable and balanced. People who are high in neuroticism feel negative emotions faster and more intensely than less neurotic types. They are emotionally reactive and tend to give emotional responses to situations that normally wouldn't affect many people. Highly neurotic types tend to be self-conscious, shy and have trouble controlling urges or delaying gratification.

The six sub-traits of neuroticism are as follows:

- Anxiety
- Anger
- Depression
- Self-consciousness
- Immoderation
- Vulnerability

Individuals who score low in neuroticism are known as emotionally stable. People with lower levels of neuroticism are desired in most professions because they tend to get less distracted by work, their personal lives, or other stressors.

High levels of neuroticism are associated with a higher risk of mental illness and less favorable results on measures of health and relationships.

However, neuroticism provides a higher sensitivity to potential threats which is a useful survival mechanism. People with high levels of neuroticism also learn faster than their emotionally stable counterparts. There is a strong utility in experiencing negative emotion, which I will talk about in future lessons. We learn faster when we experience negative emotions and since neurotic types are more sensitive to negative emotions, they experience this sooner.

The knowledge of our own sensitivity to negative emotion is critical when examining the potential realities in front of us.

Fairly neurotic types may want to consider that they don't work well under pressure and plan ahead so their work can be done at a leisurely pace.

Emotionally stable types may not have to exercise that type of consideration and would be a fantastic fit for high-pressure careers like firefighting or surgery.

Methods of Identifying Personality

All of this knowledge is great, but how do we determine exactly where we land on each dimension?

There are multiple methods with some being more accurate and precise.

The easiest is taking a test while in a neutral psychophysiological state. There are tons of resources online. I recommend understandmyself.com.

Take the test while feeling as neutral as possible. Don't take the test upset, tired, or hungry. On the flip side, don't take the test happy, excited, or anxious.

This knowledge is crucial to take into account when we plan our futures including study schedules, career goals, relationship choices, and other life plans.

Keep in mind that personality, especially since there are no flawless models, is *just a starting point* when it comes to designing a life trajectory.

Paying attention to our inclinations is a promising way to know what kind of life fits us best.

Knowing ourselves takes time because we have multiple levels all working together like an orchestral symphony.

Personality is a great starting point for building a foundation for the knowledge and cultivation of our inclinations. People like Steve Jobs or Robert Greene achieved the levels of success they had because they took the time to get to know themselves and cultivated their personal interests.

Knowing ourselves intimately gives us access to deep satisfaction that we couldn't get anywhere else.

I was lucky enough to have parents support my inclination to music at a young age. I got to explore my love for music and the deeper I got, the more I fell in love with it.

Fast forward to post-college where I am forced to deal with the realities of life and decide what my life will mean, I learn that I'm high in trait openness. From my own analysis and reflection, I discovered that long periods of time where I can be creative will satisfy my openness appetite. Combining the knowledge of these two ideas, I spent years slowly molding my schedule into one that provides me ample time to be creative. Today, I can say with 100% certainty that it gives me inner peace and a pure sense of satisfaction to have connected with something deep within me. Getting to know ourselves is truly the best way to spend our time. It enriches every aspect of our existence.

Another method of identifying personality is writing an autobiography. Now, this doesn't have to be some thick book. It could be short with just a few paragraphs. There are no rules for writing an autobiography other than we have to write it ourselves.

The real meaning lies in what we write and not how much we write.

This method is less quantitative than the online exams but could offer deeper insights.

Articulating the past is helpful because we can clearly see how we understand the past. We can stand back, look at the picture as an outsider, and make sound judgments about what we think, feel, or know.

Writing an entire biography is difficult, so to make it a little more manageable, just start by breaking our life story up into 5 episodes. The way in which we divide up our lives gives us a hint into what we value.

For example, when I last did this exercise I noticed that my epochs were based on what my main occupation was at the time. This particular division suggests my proclivity towards high conscientiousness. The time before last, I split my life up by which people I spent the most time around, which can suggest my agreeable tendencies.

When we write our story, we see how we know ourselves. It can be quite interesting to examine our lives through our own eyes.

Correlations

The world of personality research has given us a wealth of knowledge that we can use to better understand ourselves and others. Relationships regarding personality are not blanket statements about any specific group of people. There will be exceptions in every case. For example, women tend to be more agreeable than men but that does not mean there are no agreeable men or disagreeable women.

One personality relationship worth paying attention to is between gender differences.

Across cultures, women tend to report higher levels of neuroticism, conscientiousness, agreeableness, friendliness (extraversion subset), and emotionality (openness subset).

Men, on the other hand, typically report higher levels of assertiveness (extraversion subset), and adventurousness (openness subset).

There is much overlap between men and women except for the

difference in neuroticism, which is the biggest and most prominent difference in these self-reported studies.

Each of these traits has been believed to have evolved out of survival.

However, success in the modern world and survival in the wild require different abilities and skills.

Agreeableness, for example, is great for caring for infants. That's why we choose to take care of them if they're crying at 3 AM rather than throw them out the window. On the other hand, agreeableness isn't great for moving up the corporate ladder. We do need some agreeableness to cooperate with everyone, but we need to be disagreeable enough to fight for opportunities and look out for our own interests. All of these traits are useful for survival, but not in the modern world.

There are also trends with personality and birth order. Frank Sulloway, an American psychologist best known for his work on birth order personality research, argues that firstborns are higher in conscientiousness and lower in openness than their later-born siblings. He also argues that firstborns are more socially dominant. There have been other studies conducted that have fallen in line with Sulloway's claims but with a small correlation.

There are some correlations between personality and substance abuse as well. The personality profile of a typical heroin user would be low in neuroticism, high in openness, low in agreeableness, and low in conscientiousness. The personality profile of a typical ecstasy user would be high in extraversion, high in openness, low in agreeableness, and low in conscientiousness.

There are also connections between personality and health. Being high in conscientiousness can add five years to our life and being high in neuroticism is related to less favorable health outcomes. People who report high levels of conscientiousness, extraversion, and openness tend to have lower risks of mortality as well. It seems like it pays off to try to be conscientious, extroverted, and open.

There are some connections between academic achievement and personality: conscientiousness is predictive of GPA and exam performance. Students who report higher levels of conscientiousness and agreeableness tend to have higher GPAs and exam scores. Those who report higher levels of neuroticism tend to have less desirable academic outcomes.

Personality can also be a predictor of job performance. This is partly why I suggest using personality to help shape our life trajectory. We are more likely to enjoy jobs that we would excel in. People who excel in leadership positions are perceived to have low levels of neuroticism and high levels of openness while maintaining balanced levels of conscientiousness and extraversion. Studies have found that employees are less likely to view their supervisor's actions as abusive if they consider their supervisor to be high in conscientiousness. Professional burnout is highly correlated with high levels of neuroticism. People who report higher levels of agreeableness tend to make less money than their disagreeable counterparts.

Conscientiousness is the biggest predictor of overall job performance, the higher the conscientiousness the better the performance. Extraversion is the 2nd biggest predictor of overall job performance, the higher the extraversion the better their performance. Agreeableness and Neuroticism are tied for 3rd, with lower levels of each being tied to higher performance.

Research on how individual traits affect individuals and organizations at work found that individuals (or organizations of individuals) who are higher in openness are more proactive with tasks but less organized and proficient. Both of these effects are mutually exclusive. Those who are more agreeable tend to be less proactive with tasks. Those who are higher in extraversion are, on average, less proficient at tasks. Those who are high in conscientiousness tend to relate positively to all forms of work performance. Highly neurotic individuals often struggle with various aspects of work performance.

In romantic relationships, personality could predict satisfaction and relationship quality during the various stages of a romantic relationship.

Dating couples' studies suggest that people will have higher relationship satisfaction and quality if they see their partner with lower levels of neuroticism and higher levels of conscientiousness as well as see themselves with higher levels of conscientiousness.

Engaged couples' studies suggest that relationship satisfaction and quality are higher among those who report their partner as high in openness, agreeableness, and conscientiousness and lower in neuroticism. Satisfaction and quality are also higher for those who report themselves as higher in extraversion and agreeableness. Neuroticism predicts worse relationship satisfaction and quality for both self-reported and partner-reported studies.

Married couples, on the other hand, demonstrate higher levels of relationship satisfaction and quality when self-reporting higher levels of neuroticism, extraversion, and agreeableness as well as partner-reported agreeableness.

Personality can also show up with people's political identification, but not with all 5 traits. People who are higher in conscientiousness tend to be more conservative, while people who are higher in openness tend to be more liberal. The other three traits have not been found to be linked to preferred political preferences.

Personalities are subject to change as our lives move and one of the traits that changes the most with age is neuroticism. Research has found that neuroticism tends to decrease with age and after major life events.

Big 5 Critiques

Similar to MBTI, The Big 5 has a few critiques as well. While The Big 5 is more based on empirical evidence, it is still limited in its predictive power and does not accurately encompass all of the human personality. However, it's one of the best models we have and that doesn't mean that we can't use it to our advantage.

Since there is more research related to the Big 5, we can use what rings true from The Big 5, MBTI, our personal experiences, and other sources to clearly articulate our preferences. We can use everything we know about personality to create a more refined way of determining our life trajectory. Keep in mind which traits we have and how they will change and use that knowledge to inform our choices when we choose what we do for work, who we marry, where we live, and why we do what we do.

Aiming with Precision

While it's great to tailor our life trajectory to our personalities, that does not mean we should avoid exposing ourselves to the opposites of our preferences.

Wisdom is found on the other side of what we are.

"Become who you are. Become all that you are. There is still more of you – more to be discovered, forgiven, and loved." - Carl Jung

Personality is just one way of defining success. It can be a powerful starting point, but life is about refining that definition and going after it relentlessly. It is critical that we set realistic, but optimistic, expectations of our lives so we bolster ourselves up against depression and suicide. Many of our life expectations are developed in adolescence and are used as benchmarks for success in adult life. Getting clear on those expectations is the foundation for understanding our definition for success.

Keeping the Big 5 traits in mind, we can get an idea of what success would look like.

- Extraversion - success in social domains
- Agreeableness - success in intimate relationships
- Disagreeableness - success in competitions

- Openness - success in creative pursuits
- Neuroticism - success is predictable and stability

In order to know where we are and where we are going, we use a map.

If we don't know where we want to go, we can run through a mental exercise.

Here are a few guidelines we can use to discover our preferred pathway:

- We have to treat ourselves like we're someone we have to take care of.
- If we can have the family we want, what would that look like?
- If we could have the career we want, what would that look like?
- How will we take care of ourselves mentally and physically?
- How are we going to educate ourselves?
- How are we going to resist the temptation of drugs and alcohol?
- How will we use our time meaningfully and productive outside of work?
- Do we want a long-term stable relationship? How will it lay itself out?
- What are our weaknesses? What would happen if we let them run wild?

This will help us see what we want. When we establish aims we see pathways and obstacles. A bad plan is better than no plan. We can always recalculate.

- Use this knowledge to make 8 goals.
- Rank the goals

Now we can articulate why these goals are good for us.

- Why do we want to accomplish the goal?
- Why it is good for our family?
- Why it is good for our community?

These reasons will arm us against haters, but also ourselves when we're feeling down. Success is best when it is our own definition. We just need to take the time to understand ourselves and what we want for our lives.

EDUCATION AS TRANSFORMATION
HOW LEARNING INFORMS, FORMS, & TRANSFORMS US

The word *education* originates from the Latin *educere*, meaning "to bring out" or "develop." At its essence, education is a process that brings out more of who we are and shapes us into what we can become.

> "The intellect, through a species of being informed in the act of intelligence, forms itself some intention of the understood thing." - Rollo May (*Love and Will*)

The key concept here is being "in-formed." To inform someone is to shape that person. Education is not merely about filling us with facts; it is about shaping us, defining who we are, and what we can become.

This raises essential questions:

- What are we being formed into?
- Who is forming us?
- How are we allowing this information to shape us?

In essence, our intellect uses the knowledge we acquire to

shape intentions, choices, and our very identity. When we know and understand less, we remain smaller, less capable. But when we learn, we *become* more capable, evolved, and prepared for life's challenges.

Education shapes us. It gives substance to our souls, allows us to transcend our limitations, and propels us into greater possibilities. Yuval Noah Harari, in *Sapiens*, argues that Homo Sapiens thrived not because we were stronger than other species, but because we were *wiser*. We survived through our understanding of knowledge, and our ability to learn and adapt.

"Selection pressure is the mechanism through which animals evolve." - Temple Grandin (*Animals Make Us Human*)

Humans evolved, in part, because they prioritized wisdom and education. Through this process of being informed, we change our form—transcending our previous selves, becoming something new.

However, this transformation is double-edged. Education allows us to create the future we want, but it can also lead us into futures we don't want. If we aren't mindful, we may be shaped in ways that don't align with our goals or values. This is why it's crucial to discern what information we allow to shape us.

"Education is not the answer to the question. Education is the means to the answer to all questions." - Bill Allin (Sociologist)

Education offers us the tools we need to avoid being stuck in our current forms. It enables us to become the versions of ourselves that we aspire to be, instead of being bound by what we already are.

"Education is the ability to meet life's situations." Dr. John G. Hibben (former president of Princeton University)

Education is not just knowledge—it's a skill, one that can be sharpened through effort and practice, empowering us to navigate life's complexities.

"The great aim of education is not knowledge but action." - Herbert Spencer

The true value of education lies not in accumulating facts, but in applying them to improve ourselves and our world. Without action, knowledge is inert and wasted.

Plato's Reciprocal Revealing

One of the greatest insights into education comes from Plato, who presents the concept of *Reciprocal Revealing*. This principle argues that true understanding comes from a mutual exchange between the student and the subject. In Plato's theory of Forms, he suggests that what we encounter in the world are mere shadows of deeper truths, and that our learning journey is one of actively uncovering these truths.

In education, Reciprocal Revealing emphasizes an interactive process of discovery. We don't merely absorb knowledge; we actively engage with it, revealing new insights about both the subject and ourselves. It's a dynamic, two-way street of learning.

This form of education is not passive. It requires critical thinking, curiosity, and a deep engagement with the material. As we grapple with new ideas, we uncover truths not just about the world but about ourselves. Education becomes an active, self-transformative journey.

The goal of education should be to integrate our knowledge with the world's, making them indistinguishable—where our understanding becomes so intertwined with reality that it feels like second nature. Education allows us to transcend who we are, meet life's challenges head-on, and discover our full potential.

Education is far more than the acquisition of information. It is a transformative force that shapes us into something new. Through education, we gain not only the knowledge to understand the world but also the wisdom and power to change it. It is a process of mutual discovery between ourselves and the universe, a journey where learning transforms us into more capable, adaptable, and enlightened beings.

THE LIMITS OF LEARNING
WHY WISDOM REQUIRES MORE THAN JUST KNOWLEDGE

There's an arrogance in learning. I've long believed that education is a solution to many of life's problems, but it's not the answer to everything. For an insightful critique on the limits of intelligence and learning, I turn to Michel de Montaigne's *Essays*.

"Even on the highest thrones in the world, we're still seated upon our asses." - Michel de Montaigne

No matter how much we learn or how high we rise, we remain human—flawed and limited. Education can help us understand and control the world, but it can also inflate our confidence in ways that blind us to our own limitations.

When we learn something new, it's hard to remember what it felt like to *not* know it. Once knowledge becomes part of us, it's impossible to un-know. This creates a danger: we start believing we know more than we truly do. Intellectual pride creeps in, making us forget that knowledge is imperfect and that we are inherently fallible.

True wisdom, as Montaigne would argue, doesn't come from

knowing everything—it comes from recognizing what we *don't* know. It comes from keeping our minds open to other perspectives and being willing to learn from those around us.

Everything I've learned has come from two places: either through personal struggle or from reading about the experiences of others. For every ounce of wisdom I've gained, I've lived through equal, if not greater, moments of foolishness.

> "Our life consists partly in madness, partly in wisdom. Whoever writes about it merely respectfully and by rule leaves more than half of it behind." - Michel de Montaigne

It's through embracing both the wisdom and the madness that we truly grow.

So, if education doesn't provide all the answers, what *should* we value? Montaigne suggests that the worth of anything comes from its usefulness and relevance to our lives.

> "If man were wise, he would gauge the true worth of anything by its usefulness and appropriateness to his life." - Michel de Montaigne

Critiques are only helpful if they offer solutions. If we measure the value of knowledge by how useful it is, then education needs to follow the same principle. For example, take Montaigne's disdain for overly complex books. If a book is too difficult to read, its wisdom can't be absorbed. Despite its knowledge, the book becomes worthless because it fails in its primary purpose: to communicate. Unfortunately, many textbooks in traditional education fall into this trap, making learning harder than it needs to be.

> "Difficulty is the coin which the learned conjure with so as not to reveal the vanity of their studies, which human stupidity is keen to accept as payment." - Michel de Montaigne

Complexity often serves as a disguise for the emptiness behind it, and we must guard against being impressed by difficulty for its own sake.

The path to building a strong education is both deep and accessible. As we become more competent, what is easy to understand expands. When starting out, we can focus on what we can grasp and build our abilities gradually to match the complexity of the world.

Montaigne argues that academic culture often teaches us to study the works of others before studying ourselves. Perhaps the better path is to reverse this: we should first study our minds before turning to the thoughts of others.

"For education is to natural faculty what a wax nose is to a real one... In virtue of his education, a man says, not what he thinks himself, but what others have thought and he has learned as a matter of training." - Arthur Schopenhauer

Formal education can train people to mimic the ideas of others instead of thinking for themselves. Formal education often shapes us more to fit society's expectations rather than to explore our true potential.

This is why it's crucial to approach education with intention and openness. Without careful reflection, we risk filling our minds with useless knowledge, dictated by the flawed and often arbitrary forces of society. By studying ourselves first, we can break free from these constraints and focus on what is truly important.

Study yourself. Study your mind. Don't be swayed by the arrogance or cleverness of others. Even the most intelligent minds, like Montaigne's, say that they shouldn't always be taken so seriously.

THE COST OF IGNORANCE
HOW BAD CHOICES & MISINFORMATION SHAPE OUR LIVES

Bad Choices Made Worse

I t's easy to make terrible choices. It's even easier when we are ignorant. Without education, we are ruled by madness.

"Well, most men have bound their eyes with one or another handkerchief, and attached themselves to some one of these communities of opinion. This conformity makes them not false in a few particulars, authors of a few lies, but false in all particulars. Their every truth is not quite true. Their two is not the real two, their four not the real four" - Ralph Waldo Emerson (*Self-Reliance*)

When we are ignorant, we adopt the opinions of our communities, not our own. Being possessed by a community of opinion—also known as ideology—makes our reality a lie and leaves us vulnerable to false or harmful information.

Here is a real headline from the COVID-19 pandemic in 2020:

"At least 800 people died around the world because of coronavirus-related misinformation in the first three months of this year, researchers say."

Historical Examples of Miseducation

In many ways, miseducation causes more harm than anything else.

- The "Lost Cause" Narrative in American History

After the Civil War, many Southern schools romanticized the Confederacy and downplayed the horrors of slavery. This led to generations of Americans misunderstanding the causes and effects of the Civil War, which contributed to racial biases and the perpetuation of systemic racism.

- Eugenics Education in the Early 1900s

In the early 20th century, various educational institutions in the United States and Europe taught a theory advocating for controlled breeding to increase the frequency of "desirable" heritable characteristics. These theories were the basis of racist and ableist policies, including forced sterilizations, and influenced Nazi ideology.

- Racial Segregation and Education in Apartheid South Africa

Under Apartheid, a racial-based policy of segregation, Black South Africans received an intentionally inferior education designed to limit their opportunities and maintain racial segregation. This created a long-lasting impact on economic disparities, social inequalities, and limited career opportunities for multiple generations of Black South Africans.

- Propaganda in Totalitarian Regimes

In Nazi Germany, Stalinist USSR, and Maoist China, education systems were used to indoctrinate youth with propaganda, rewriting history, and promoting the regime's ideology. This resulted in the widespread acceptance of oppressive policies, human rights violations, and in some cases, the facilitation of genocides.

- Religious Fundamentalism in Education

In various historical and contemporary contexts, education systems have been used to promote religious fundamentalism, often at the expense of scientific understanding and pluralistic values. Which has led to societal divisions, conflict, and the suppression of scientific and cultural advancements.

- Colonial Education Systems

All over the world and throughout history, colonial powers often established education systems in their colonies that devalued indigenous cultures and languages, promoting the superiority of the colonizer's language and culture. Which caused long-term impacts including cultural erosion, identity crises, and ongoing struggles for indigenous rights and recognition.

No education is the breeding ground for miseducation, which propagates misinformation. This dangerous road has devastating effects that could last generations. At its worst, it reinforces harmful stereotypes, perpetuates social injustices, and can kill millions of people.

Practical Impacts In The Absence of Education

On a more practical level, without education, we can never realize our full potential. There are many impacts we can experience when we don't have an education.

- Limited Career Opportunities

Without adequate education, we often have limited access to high-quality job opportunities. This can lead to a cycle of low-income jobs and diminished career progression.

This idea is preached by educators all over the world and is frequently rejected by the youth. Many times I see my students say that they don't need to go to college to be successful. While that is true, they will still need an education.

Without education, we are not useful to others or to ourselves.

- Reduced Critical Thinking Skills

Education fosters critical thinking and problem-solving skills. A lack of education can hinder an someone's ability to analyze, evaluate, and create solutions effectively.

Many of life's challenges come from problems and cCritical thinking is essential for solving those problems..

While I believe critical thinking is a separate skill all on its own. Education is what gives us a foundation to think critically. Without it, the solutions are weak or don't exist.

- Lower Self-Esteem and Confidence

Education often boosts self-esteem and confidence. Without it, individuals may struggle with self-doubt and a sense of inadequacy, affecting their personal and professional lives.

With education comes the ability to know ourselves and pursue what is meaningful to us. When we pursue meaning, we are more competent and have better follow-through. This naturally creates higher self-esteem and confidence.

- Diminished Awareness of Rights and Responsibilities

An educational background contributes to our understanding of civic duties, rights, and social responsibilities. Lack of education can lead to less engagement in societal issues and lower awareness of our rights and responsibilities, which can impact both our lives and the community.

People who are not educated tend to take more from society than they contribute.

- Stunted Personal Development

Education is not just about academic learning; it also includes personal growth and development. Without education, individuals may miss out on opportunities to explore and develop their interests, talents, and personal values.

Every aspect of my life that makes it worth living has come from educating myself in subjects that I am genuinely interested in. When I take the path of self-education, I learn more, faster, and deeper with higher levels of retention. Additionally, my passion for these subjects was able to inspire others to learn about those topics as well.

- Limited Access to Information and Resources

Education often provides skills in seeking, evaluating, and using information effectively. Without these skills, individuals might struggle to access or leverage information and resources beneficial for their growth and success.

- Economic Disadvantages

On a broader scale, a lack of education can lead to economic disadvantages. This not only affects individual earning potential but can also impact the economic development of communities and nations.

- Health Risks and Lack of Awareness

Education plays a crucial role in health awareness and practices. A lack of education can lead to a lack of understanding about health risks, poor health choices, and reduced access to healthcare services.

- Social Exclusion and Marginalization

Education is a key factor in social integration. Those lacking education may find themselves excluded or marginalized in society, leading to social isolation and a lack of social mobility.

- Hindered Innovation and Creativity

Education often stimulates creativity and innovation. A lack of educational opportunities can stifle the development of new ideas and solutions, impacting both individual expression and broader societal progress.

Self-Education Despite Ignorance and Adverse Conditions

We don't have to suffer the consequences of the absence of education, we can still educate ourselves to empower us to take on the forms we desire. Frederick Douglass serves as an excellent example of this.

He was born into slavery and faced immense challenges in his quest for education. His initial exposure to literacy came unexpectedly when his slaveholder's wife, Sophia Auld, began teaching him the alphabet. However, once her husband forbade these lessons, citing the belief that literacy would make slaves unmanageable, Douglass's formal education ended abruptly. This obstacle, however, only fueled his determination to learn. Douglass ingeniously traded bread for reading lessons with poor white children in his neighborhood, capitalizing on the little he had to further his education. He also made use of his limited resources, often reading newspapers and books he could find, which were scarce in his condition as a slave. Additionally, Douglass observed the writings of the people around him, slowly teaching himself to write. Through these methods, Douglass overcame his oppressive environment, demonstrating that determination and ingenuity can triumph even in the most challenging circumstances.

Douglass's story is proof that the human spirit is resilient and of the transformative power of education, even when acquired under dire conditions. His journey from a slave with limited access to education to a renowned abolitionist, writer, and speaker is an inspiring example of self-education and the pursuit of knowledge against all odds.

Let's break down what he did to elevate himself from ignorance to being highly educated:

- He Traded for Lessons:
  - He exchanged bread for reading lessons with poor white children.
  - He traded what he could for what he wanted (even if it wasn't much).
- He Used Observation and Imitation:
  - Imitated the writing he saw to teach himself how to write.
- Using What Was Available To Him:
  - He would read newspapers and books he could find, despite their scarcity.
  - Used any accessible written material for learning.
- He Leveraged Work Assignments:
  - He used his work tasks, which sometimes involved errands in the city, to find opportunities to learn.
- He Engaging in Intellectual Conversations:

- Participated in discussions with other slaves and free blacks to refine his understanding and opinions.
- He Practiced Critical Thinking and Reflection:
  - He engaged in self-reflection and critical thinking about what he read and experienced.
  - He formed his interpretations of religious and political texts, challenging conventional views.
- Developed Practicing Writing Skills:
  - Practiced writing in secret whenever he had the chance.
- Eavesdropping and Absorbing Information:
  - Practiced writing in secret whenever he had the chance.

Douglass found opportunities wherever he could. We can protect ourselves from the consequences of a lack of education by staying open to opportunities and learning whenever possible. Sometimes this starts with being able to identify the opportunities that exist.

The risk is too high to let ignorance or circumstance get in the way of our quest for education.

BOOK REFERENCES & RECOMMENDATIONS
FOR DISCOVERING POTENTIAL

"It's not about the book, it's about the book the book leads you to."
- Austin Kleon (*Steal Like an Artist*)

Book References & Recommendations

<u>On Education: Why It Matters</u>

- **"Man's Search for Meaning"** by Viktor E. Frankl
- **"Limitless"** by Jim Kwik
- **"The Hero with a Thousand Faces"** by Joseph Campbell
- **"Games People Play"** by Eric Berne
- **"12 Rules for Life"** by Jordan B. Peterson
- **"The 48 Laws of Power"** by Robert Greene
- **"The Obstacle Is the Way"** by Ryan Holiday
- **"The Courage to Be Disliked"** by Ichiro Kishimi and Fumitake Koga
- **"The 7 Habits of Highly Effective People"** by Stephen Covey
- **"Stop Stealing Dreams"** By Seth Godin

- "The Power of Now" by Eckhart Tolle
- "The Four Agreements" by Don Miguel Ruiz
- "Atomic Habits" by James Clear
- "Outliers" by Malcolm Gladwell
- "Grit" by Angela Duckworth
- "Flow" by Mihaly Csikszentmihalyi
- "The War of Art" by Steven Pressfield
- "Mindset" by Carol S. Dweck
- "Deep Work" by Cal Newport
- "Linchpin"By Seth Godin

The Roles of Education: Accessing Potential

- "Pedagogy of the Oppressed" by Paulo Freire
- "The Republic" by Plato
- "Understanding Human Nature" by Alfred Adler
- "How Children Succeed" by Paul Tough
- "The Art of Learning" by Josh Waitzkin
- "The Courage to Teach" by Parker J. Palmer
- "The School and Society" by John Dewey
- "The Ignorant Schoolmaster" by Jacques Rancière
- "Drive" by Daniel H. Pink
- "Sapiens" by Yuval Noah Harari
- "The Talent Code" by Daniel Coyle
- "The Innovator's Dilemma" by Clayton M. Christensen
- "A Mind for Numbers" by Barbara Oakley
- "Emotional Intelligence" by Daniel Goleman
- "An Astronaut's Guide to Life on Earth" by Chris Hadfield
- "Teaching Community" by Bell Hooks
- "The Structure of Scientific Revolutions" by Thomas S. Kuhn
- "The Tao of Physics" by Fritjof Capra
- "The Wisdom of Crowds" by James Surowiecki

- **"The Art of Possibility"** by Rosamund Stone Zander and Benjamin Zander
- **"Make It Stick"** by Peter C. Brown, Henry L. Roediger III, and Mark A. McDaniel

The Roots of Learning: Western Education's Origins & Influences

- **"Creative Schools"** by Sir Ken Robinson
- **Deschooling Society"** by Ivan Illich
- **"The End of Education"** by Neil Postman
- **"Dumbing Us Down"** by John Taylor Gatto
- **"The Underground History of American Education"** by John Taylor Gatto
- **"Why Don't Students Like School?"** by Daniel T. Willingham
- **"Schooling in Capitalist America"** by Samuel Bowles and Herbert Gintis
- **"Teach Like a Champion"** by Doug Lemov
- **"The Smartest Kids in the World"** by Amanda Ripley
- **"Experience and Education"** by John Dewey
- **"Mindstorms"** by Seymour Papert
- **"The Schools Our Children Deserve"** by Alfie Kohn
- **"The Learning Gap"** by Harold W. Stevenson and James W. Stigler
- **"The One World Schoolhouse"** by Salman Khan
- **"The Element"** by Sir Ken Robinson
- **"The Global Achievement Gap"** by Tony Wagner
- **"Teaching as a Subversive Activity"** by Neil Postman and Charles Weingartner
- **"A Mathematician's Lament"** by Paul Lockhart
- **"The Death and Life of the Great American School System"** by Diane Ravitch
- **"The Learning Game"** by Ana Lorena Fabrega

On Going To Good Schools: Why You (Probably) Don't Need To Go

- "The Practice" by Seth Godin
- "Originals" by Adam Grant
- "The Dip" by Seth Godin
- "So Good They Can't Ignore You" by Cal Newport
- "Excellent Sheep" by William Deresiewicz
- "The Education of Millionaires" by Michael Ellsberg
- "The Icarus Deception" by Seth Godin
- "Range" by David Epstein
- "The End of Jobs" by Taylor Pearson
- "Rework" by Jason Fried and David Heinemeier Hansson
- "The Millionaire Fastlane" by MJ DeMarco
- "Choose Yourself" by James Altucher
- "Deep Work" by Cal Newport
- "Linchpin" by Seth Godin
- "The Personal MBA" by Josh Kaufman
- "The Startup of You" by Reid Hoffman and Ben Casnocha
- "The Defining Decade" by Meg Jay
- "The 4-Hour Workweek" by Timothy Ferriss
- "How Will You Measure Your Life?" by Clayton M. Christensen
- "The Education of a Value Investor" by Guy Spier

Building Strong Foundations for Learning: Characteristics of High Achieving Homes & Foundations for Self-Education

- "Limitless" - Jim Kwik
- "Games People Play" - Eric Berne
- "The Almanack of Naval Ravikant" - Eric Jorgenson

Developing Independent Thought: The Power of Self-Learning & Self-Reliance

- "Self-Reliance" by Ralph Waldo Emerson

- "Twilight of the Idols" by Friedrich Nietzsche
- "Human Action" by Ludwig von Mises
- "On Liberty" by John Stuart Mill
- "The World as Will and Representation" by Arthur Schopenhauer
- "Walden" by Henry David Thoreau
- "The Wisdom of Insecurity" by Alan Watts
- "Flow" by Mihaly Csikszentmihalyi
- "Antifragile" by Nassim Nicholas Taleb
- "The War of Art" by Steven Pressfield
- "Mindset" by Carol S. Dweck
- "The Power of Myth" by Joseph Campbell
- "Zen and the Art of Motorcycle Maintenance" by Robert M. Pirsig
- "The Art of Learning" by Josh Waitzkin
- "Animal Farm" by George Orwell
- "The Myth of Sisyphus" by Albert Camus
- "Thinking, Fast and Slow" by Daniel Kahneman
- "The Courage to Be Disliked" by Ichiro Kishimi and Fumitake Koga
- "Animal Make Us Human" by Temple Grandin
- "Quiet" by Susan Cain

Academic Success vs. Real-World Success: Beyond the Classroom

- "Zero to One" by Peter Thiel
- "The End of Education" by Neil Postman
- "The Innovator's Dilemma" by Clayton M. Christensen
- "The Learning Revolution" by Gordon Dryden and Jeannette Vos
- "Dumbing Us Down" by John Taylor Gatto
- "Excellent Sheep" by William Deresiewicz
- "The Case Against Education" by Bryan Caplan
- "Creative Schools" by Sir Ken Robinson
- "Mindstorms" by Seymour Papert

- "The Talent Code" by Daniel Coyle
- "Outliers" by Malcolm Gladwell
- "Drive"by Daniel H. Pink
- "Range" by David Epstein
- "Linchpin" by Seth Godin
- "The Power of Unlearning" by Scott H. Young
- "Educated" by Tara Westover
- "The Power of Now" by Eckhart Tolle
- "Radical Candor" by Kim Scott
- "Grit" by Angela Duckworth
- "Thinking, Fast and Slow" by Daniel Kahneman
- "The Learning Game" by Ana Lorena Fabrega

Personality Dimensions: Defining Our Own Success

- "The Practicing Mind" by Thomas M. Sterner
- "Grit" by Angela Duckworth
- "The Four Tendencies" by Gretchen Rubin
- "Atomic Habits" by James Clear
- "Drive" by Daniel H. Pink
- "Quiet" by Susan Cain
- "The Slight Edge" by Jeff Olson
- "The Power of Habit" by Charles Duhigg
- "Self-Reliance" by Ralph Waldo Emerson
- "The Path to Purpose" by William Damon
- "Mindset" by Carol S. Dweck
- "How to Win Friends and Influence People" by Dale Carnegie
- "Mastery" by Robert Greene
- "The Talent Code" by Daniel Coyle
- "The Road Less Traveled" by M. Scott Peck
- "Flow"by Mihaly Csikszentmihalyi
- "Daring Greatly" by Brené Brown
- "The War of Art" by Steven Pressfield
- "Deep Work" by Cal Newport

- **"The Compound Effect"** by Darren Hardy

Education as Transformation: How Learning Informs, Forms, & Transforms Us

- **"Man's Search for Meaning"** by Viktor Frankl
- **"Sapiens"** by Yuval Noah Harari
- **"The Courage to Teach"** by Parker J. Palmer
- **"The Power of Now"** by Eckhart Tolle
- **"Zen and the Art of Motorcycle Maintenance"** by Robert M. Pirsig
- **"Thinking, Fast and Slow"** by Daniel Kahneman
- **"A Theory of Justice"** by John Rawls
- **"The Republic"** by Plato
- **"The Art of Learning"** by Josh Waitzkin
- **"Love and Will"** by Rollo May

The Limits of Learning: Why Wisdom Requires More Than Just Knowledge

- **"Essais (The Essays)"** by Michel de Montaigne
- **"The Art of Controversy"** by Arthur Schopenhauer

The Cost of Ignorance: How Bad Choices & Misinformation Shape Our Lives

- **"Self-Reliance"** by Ralph Waldo Emerson
- **"Sapiens"** by Yuval Noah Harari
- **"Narrative of the Life of Frederick Douglass, an American Slave"** by Frederick Douglass

2

SKILLS & HABITS

MASTERING OURSELVES FOR LIFELONG SUCCESS

WHAT ARE SKILLS?

THE BASIS OF KNOWLEDGE

S kills are the building blocks of success, both personally and professionally. Whether we're students seeking to expand our knowledge, professionals looking to advance in our careers, or individuals striving for self-improvement, understanding the importance of skills is key to mastering the art of learning and thriving in life. Many things we find challenging or don't yet understand are often skills we haven't developed—skills that can be learned, refined, and improved over time.

What Are Skills, Exactly?

At their core, skills are learned abilities that enable us to perform specific tasks. They are like tools in our personal toolkit, each designed for a particular purpose. Whether we're writing an email, resolving a conflict, or baking a cake, we're using different skills to interact with the world and handle everyday challenges. The more skills we develop, the better equipped we become to face diverse situations with confidence and effectiveness.

It's important to recognize that many of the things we struggle with aren't fixed traits or personal deficiencies—they're simply *skill deficits.* Instead of thinking, "I'm just not good at this," realize that it's a skill we haven't yet acquired or refined. Understanding that most things can be learned and improved makes it easier to overcome challenges and grow.

The Two Sides of the Skill Coin: Hard and Soft Skills

Skills generally fall into two main categories: hard skills and soft skills, each playing a vital role in personal and professional development.

- *Hard skills* are technical or administrative abilities we acquire through education, training, or experience. These are tangible, measurable, and often specific to particular tasks or industries. Examples include coding, proficiency in a foreign language, or graphic design. These skills can be easily quantified and are usually showcased on a résumé to demonstrate expertise.
- *Soft skills*, on the other hand, are more nuanced and harder to measure. These interpersonal abilities help us navigate social and professional relationships. Skills like communication, teamwork, leadership, and problem-solving are crucial for working effectively with others and managing the complexities of human interactions. While they may not be as easily quantifiable, they are essential for long-term success in both the workplace and life.

For instance, knowing how to code (a hard skill) is crucial for a software developer, but being able to communicate effectively with team members and collaborate on projects (soft skills) is just as essential. If we are deficient in any area, it's likely just a skill we haven't honed yet—not something innately lacking within us.

Acquiring Skills: A Lifelong Journey

One of the most empowering aspects of skills is their potential for growth. Skills aren't fixed—they can be developed, refined, and expanded over time. With practice, training, and real-world experience, we can continuously add new abilities to our toolkit while sharpening the ones we already have.

Think of how a professional musician evolves over time. They begin with basic lessons but, through years of focused practice, feedback, and dedication, their talent grows into mastery. The same concept applies to any skill. Whether we're learning to cook, lead a team, or manage our time, skill-building is a lifelong journey filled with challenges and rewards. The key is to understand that anything we don't yet know can be learned.

Why are Skills so Important?

In the professional world, skills are the currency of the workforce. They determine our career trajectory and open doors to new opportunities. Employers value candidates who possess not only the hard skills necessary to perform a job but also the soft skills required to thrive in a collaborative environment. The more developed our skillset, the more marketable we become, allowing us to advance and succeed in our careers.

In our personal lives, skills are equally important. They allow us to handle daily tasks more efficiently, solve problems with creativity, and foster meaningful relationships. Trying to manage our time effectively without strong organizational skills or resolving a disagreement without solid communication abilities would be nearly impossible. Whether it's mastering budgeting, improving emotional intelligence, or learning to cook, the skills we cultivate directly impact the quality of our lives.

Reframing Challenges as Skills Deficits

One powerful mindset shift is realizing that most of the challenges we face come from skills we haven't yet developed, not from inherent personal flaws.

When we struggle with something, whether it's public speaking, leadership, or time management, it's not because we "just don't have it"—it's because those are skills we haven't learned yet. By seeing challenges through this lens, we can approach them with curiosity and openness, ready to learn rather than feeling inadequate.

This realization makes it easier to identify what's missing. Once we know which specific skills we need to develop, we can take actionable steps to grow. Instead of thinking, "I'm bad at communicating," try reframing it as, "I need to work on my communication skills." This perspective shift empowers us to take control of our learning and growth.

The Pathway to Success

Recognizing and developing our skills is not just about career advancement; it's about enhancing our ability to navigate life's countless challenges and seize its many opportunities. Every new skill we acquire adds value to our personal and professional journey, making us more capable, confident, and adaptable.

Skill development is an ongoing process, and the beauty of it lies in its infinite potential. The more we learn, the more we can learn. Each skill we acquire opens up new doors to other skills, creating a compounding effect on our growth and success.

Skill-building is a lifelong journey. Every challenge we encounter is an opportunity to add a new skill to our toolkit. The more we acquire, the more we can acquire.

Stay curious, continue growing, and never stop learning.

LEARNING AS A SKILL
MASTERING KNOWLEDGE

Why Understanding and Developing Skills is Crucial to Learning

Many of us focus solely on study strategies, but there's much more to the learning process. Learning isn't just about memorizing information: it's about developing the skills that enable us to absorb, retain, and apply knowledge effectively.

Why Skills Matter in Learning

Education is essentially the process of acquiring skills. But which skills we acquire, and how we choose to use them, is up to us.

Skills aren't static; they're developed through consistent practice, feedback, and refinement. This is what makes them so powerful. We don't need to be born with a talent for learning, problem-solving, or creativity—these are all skills we can build over time.

Learning itself is a skill—one that can be cultivated and mastered. In fact, being a student is a skill. Some people may struggle in the beginning, but with the right tools and mindset, they can become excellent learners. This is what I call a *meta-skill*— a skill that enhances our ability to develop other skills.

Learning is so powerful because it is a skill that can be traded for any other skill.

Learning and Intelligence: The Dynamic Duo

Consider this: *learning involves adapting behaviors to the same environment, while intelligence refers to the speed at which we learn.* If learning is a skill, that means we can get better at it, just like improving at sports or music with practice.

But it's not just about getting better quickly—it's about *how* we learn. The more intentional and reflective we are about the process, the more we can grow.

The Gap in Traditional Education Systems

Unfortunately, traditional education systems often fall short of teaching us *how* to learn. We're taught subjects like math, science, and history, but rarely are we given tools for becoming better learners. In most schools, there's little focus on teaching students how to study effectively, manage their time, or retain knowledge over the long term.

Imagine if schools offered a semester-long course on the skill of learning itself. Students would have a toolkit they could apply to every class and project. We need to understand how to build the skill of learning if we want to become exceptional learners.

The Power of Learning to Learn

Once we grasp how to develop skills, we can apply this knowledge to virtually anything. For example, when I first started cooking, I didn't know how to balance flavors or time my ingredients properly. But by applying the meta-skill of learning—seeking feedback from experienced cooks, experimenting in the kitchen, and analyzing my mistakes—I gradually became more confident and skilled. The same happened when I tackled other challenges, like web design or emergency medicine.

Learning is our superpower, and when applied with intention, it can unlock any skill we desire.

Schools and Meta-skills

A great education begins with teaching meta-skills.

I believe some of the foundational meta-skills include *learning, reading, focus,* and *writing.*

Each of these meta-skills makes acquiring other skills easier, more efficient, and more effective.

First Principles of Effective Learning

To master the art of learning, consider these principles:

1. *Repeat Successful Actions:* Identify what works well and repeat it. For instance, if using flashcards or scheduling focused study sessions helps, reinforce that habit.
2. *Seek Feedback:* Feedback from those who are ahead of us is crucial for growth. It gives us insights into what we're doing well and where we need to improve.
3. *Expand Our Timelines for Results:* Learning is a long game. We can measure our progress over months or years rather than only focusing on immediate results.
4. *Narrow Our Timeline for Inputs:* On the other hand, we need to be deliberate about what we're working on now. Focus on immediate actions and improvements.
5. *Prioritize progress over outcomes:* The goal isn't just to achieve a specific result but to continually refine our skills.

Bridging the Effort and Knowledge Gap

Between where we are now and where we want to be, there are two gaps we need to bridge:

- *The knowledge gap:* What we don't know yet.
- *The effort gap:* The discipline and commitment required to put in the work.

Learning helps us fill the knowledge gap, but it takes effort to close the distance between our current abilities and our goals. Many give up too soon, not because they lack intelligence, but because they haven't learned the discipline of sticking with the process.

The Transformative Power of Skills

Understanding and developing skills, especially the skill of learning, is transformative. It gives us the ability to be anything and learn whatever we want.

By seeing learning as a skill that can be developed, we can achieve anything we desire.

Learning is not just a process but a journey—one that, when navigated with the right skills, can lead to unimaginable growth and achievements.

THE SCIENCE BEHIND GAINING SKILLS
HOW OUR BRAINS SHAPE AND RETAIN SKILLS

Our ability to learn and develop skills goes far beyond academics; it has profound implications for how we grow, adapt, and thrive throughout life. The process of skill development is intricately tied to how our brain functions, and understanding this connection empowers us to become more effective learners.

Understanding the Brain's Role in Skill Development

Our brain is an intricate organ that manages everything from voluntary to involuntary functions. It's intriguing to think about how the brain (which named itself) can contemplate its existence yet still hold mysteries about its function.

Here's some of what we do know:

- The brain is a network of neurons that communicate through electrochemical signals.
- These neurons connect at synapses and use electrochemical neurotransmitters to communicate.

- Specific synaptic connections are formed for each
  activity we engage in.

Let's explore how our brain shapes and retains skills. This goes deeper than academics; it has profound implications for how we learn and maintain our abilities throughout life.

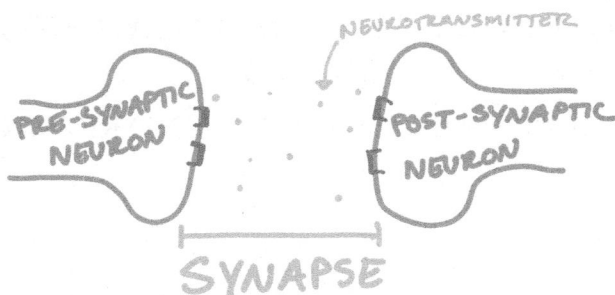

Synaptic Connection

The Dynamic Nature of Synaptic Connections

The brain is adaptable, constantly reorganizing itself based on our experiences. This process is known as *neuroplasticity*—our brain's ability to reorganize its structure by forming new connections and refining existing ones.

It strengthens connections we frequently use and prunes those that are less active. This ongoing process optimizes our brain's efficiency, allowing us to focus more energy on what's most relevant.

Neural Pruning vs. Long-Term Potentiation

Our brain functions like a highly efficient system, managing resources through two key processes:

- *Neural Pruning:* Think of this as the brain's way of decluttering. When we don't practice a particular skill or retain specific information, the brain prunes those synaptic connections to make room for new, more relevant ones. This is why skills we neglect tend to deteriorate time.

- *Long-Term Potentiation (LTP):* On the flip side, the brain strengthens the synaptic connections we frequently use, making these actions easier to perform. For example, daily tasks like putting on pants or brushing our teeth become second nature due to these strong, efficient connections.

The more we repeat an action or engage in learning, the less effort it requires over time. This is why repetition is crucial in mastering complex subjects like math or science.

Practical Implications for Learners

So, what does this mean for students and lifelong learners?

When we first encounter new information or try to learn a new skill, it often feels challenging. This difficulty is a natural part of the process as our brain forms new synaptic connections. However, with consistent practice, these actions become effortless. Neglecting practice, on the other hand, leads to neural pruning, where the brain reallocates resources to focus on new information.

Here's what to keep in mind:

- *For the Younger Generation:* Invest time in honing skills that will serve you in the long term. Every repetition strengthens your brain's ability to retain and execute these skills.
- *For Older Learners:* Embrace learning new skills. It not only enhances cognitive flexibility but can bring excitement and new possibilities into our lives.

Learning Beyond The Classroom

The beauty of learning is that it's not confined to a classroom. The world is rich with opportunities to develop new skills—whether it's mastering a language, learning how to cook, or picking up a musical instrument. Any challenge can be overcome by acquiring the right skills, but the key lies in mastering the process of learning itself.

Unfortunately, many educational systems don't teach us *how* to learn effectively. We often go through school memorizing facts and passing tests, without ever being taught to think independently, solve problems creatively, or absorb information efficiently. This gap leaves many students unprepared for the challenges of lifelong learning.

The Power of Learning to Learn

By understanding how our brain adapts and retains skills, we can become more effective learners at any stage of life. Learning itself is a skill—one that can be honed through the right strategies, consistent practice, and patience. Whether we're young or old, remember that the ability to learn and adapt is one of our greatest strengths.

THE BRAIN & LEARNING
ANATOMICAL PERSPECTIVES

"Biology gives you a brain. Life turns it into a mind." - Jeffrey Eugenides

Our brains are incredible organs that define how we interact with the world. While we often think of it as just a thinking machine, it's so much more. Its a control center that shapes our learning, creativity, and ability to adapt to new challenges.

The Earth's Most Powerful Machine

Have you ever wondered why some things stick with us forever while other information fades as soon as we learn it? The answer lies in our brain's structure and how it functions. Our brains generate up to 70,000 thoughts per day and have virtually infinite storage capacity. Humans have become Earth's most dominant species largely due to the advanced capabilities of our brains.

But how does the brain do this? The answer is in the basic anatomy of the brain and how its different parts contribute to learning.

The Brain's Building Blocks: Neurons and Synapses

Our brains are made up of 100 billion neurons—nerve cells that send electrochemical signals to each other. Imagine neurons as the messengers, constantly passing notes through a network of connections called *synapses*. Neurons fire electrical signals through synapses, where *neurotransmitters* carry messages to neighboring neurons. It's like a well-oiled communication system, where each neuron knows exactly when to pass on information.

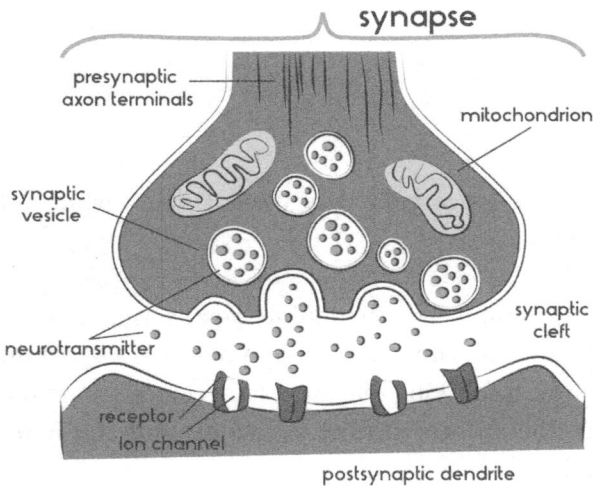

Synapse from simplypsychology.org

These connections between neurons form *neurological pathways*. Every single thing we think and do has its own unique pathway in the brain. The more we repeat a behavior or thought, the stronger that pathway becomes. This process, known as *neuroplasticity*, is the brain's ability to rewire itself, creating new pathways and strengthening old ones. It's like carving a path through a forest —the more we walk it, the clearer it becomes.

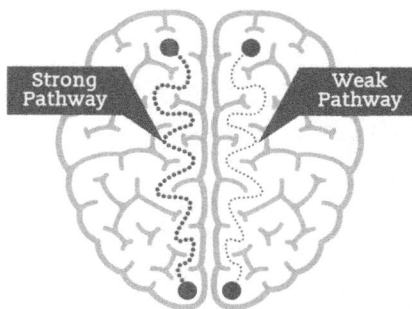

Neural Pathways from altamirarecovery.com

How Neuroplasticity Fuels Learning

Neuroplasticity is our brain's superpower. It allows us to learn new skills, change old habits, and adapt to new challenges. The best part? It never stops. Our brains are constantly changing, no matter our age. Learning doesn't stop as we age; it stops only when we decide to stop learning. So, how can we make the most of this ability?

Repetition.

The more we practice a skill, the more your brain prioritizes that pathway, making it easier to access in the future. This is why *practice makes perfect*—not because we're simply getting better, but because our brain is reorganizing itself to make the skill feel natural.

Anatomy of the Brain: The Big 3

Understanding the brain's structure can help us take better care of it and use it more effectively for learning. While the brain is a complex organ, knowing the three major parts can make a big difference.

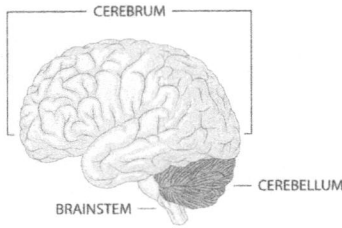

Brain Anatomy from physio-pedia.com

1. *Cerebrum:* This part handles higher-order thinking, like reasoning, emotions, and learning new information.
2. *Cerebellum:* It coordinates muscle movements and helps with balance. It's key when we're mastering physical skills like riding a bike or playing an instrument.
3. *Brainstem:* It controls automatic functions like breathing, heart rate, and sleep. It's the oldest part of the brain, ensuring we survive without thinking about it.

Left Brain vs. Right Brain: A Unified Approach to Learning

There is a stereotype that some people are "left-brained" analytical thinkers while others are "right-brained" creatives. This is an over-simplification. We use both sides of the brain for different tasks. The *left hemisphere* helps us navigate familiar situations, while the *right hemisphere* kicks in when we're facing new, unfamiliar challenges.

In learning, different brain regions work together, with the left hemisphere often associated with processing familiar information and the right hemisphere aiding in creative problem-solving. Knowing this balance can help us push past frustration when learning new skills—it's just our brain adjusting.

The Lobes of the Cerebrum

Each lobe of our brain plays a role in how we process information. They all work together to help us interpret and interact with the world. When we're learning something new, different parts of our brain work in harmony to process the new information and store it for later use.

Frontal Lobe

The frontal lobe plays a crucial role in shaping our personalities, behaviors, and emotions. It is responsible for planning, problem-solving, and judgment, and is where most of our executive and higher-level functions occur. This includes cognitive abilities like concentration and self-awareness, which help us think critically and pursue our goals. The Broca's area, responsible for speaking and writing, also resides in the frontal lobe, along with the motor strip that controls voluntary body movements.

Additionally, the frontal lobe houses the prefrontal cortex, a region involved in complex cognitive tasks, personality expression, and decision-making. It also helps moderate social behavior. This part of the brain is key to our willpower, enabling us to regulate impulsive or instinctual urges. A well-developed prefrontal cortex allows individuals to better follow through on what they set out to do.

Parietal Lobe

The parietal lobe, located at the top of the brain, acts as the brain's sensory processing center. It is responsible for interpreting language and processing tactile, thermal, visual, auditory, and other sensory stimuli. Additionally, the parietal lobe plays a key role in managing both spatial and visual perception, helping us understand and navigate the world around us.

Occipital Lobe

The occipital lobe, located at the back of the head, serves as the brain's primary visual processing center. It interprets visual information in three key ways: color, light intensity, and movement. While our eyes capture the light from what we see, it's the occipital lobe that processes this data and helps us make sense of the visual world around us.

Temporal Lobe

The temporal lobe is located on the sides of the head, just beneath the temples, where the skull fuses. This area excels at processing auditory stimuli, as well as handling sequencing, organization, and memory. Think of it as the brain's mission control center for understanding sounds, recalling memories, and deciphering languages. The Wernicke's area, located in the temporal lobe, plays a crucial role in language comprehension. We can picture the temporal lobe as the brain's music and memory box, keeping track of all the sounds, stories, and languages we've encountered.

The Brain's Internal Structures for Memory and Learning

Beyond the lobes, there are deeper structures in our brains that play crucial roles in learning:

Hippocampus

The hippocampus is the part of the brain responsible for information consolidation and spatial memory, which helps with navigation. Its primary role is to move memories from short-term (working memory) to long-term memory. This process is crucial for learning because it transforms temporary information into lasting knowledge. Damage to the hippocampus can lead to anterograde amnesia, which is the inability to form new memories. In essence, learning is what the hippocampus does—it ensures that the information we're engaging with right now becomes something we can access and use indefinitely.

Amygdala

The amygdala, an almond-shaped cluster of neurons, is responsible for processing our emotions. It is closely linked to our fear response and pleasure. Understanding how the amygdala works is essential for grasping how emotions influence learning.

For instance, fear enhances memory retention—when we encounter something that triggers fear, our brain is more likely to remember it. This is because, from an evolutionary standpoint, remembering dangers is crucial for survival. At the same time, our pursuit of pleasure serves as a powerful motivator, driving us to seek experiences and learn skills that bring us joy or satisfaction. These emotional drivers play a key role in shaping how and what we learn.

Basal Ganglia

The basal ganglia, also known as the basal nuclei, work in tandem with the cerebellum to coordinate voluntary motor movements. This region of the brain plays a crucial role in procedural learning, habit formation, eye movements, cognition, and emotions. It's the part of the brain that we rely on when we learn how to perform skills like typing, tying our shoes, riding a bike, or playing a musical instrument.

The basal ganglia receive input from the cerebellum to encode these skills, which is why people often refer to it as the source of muscle memory. However, it's not the muscles that remember; it's the basal ganglia's strong neural pathways that deeply encode these actions. When we first attempt a new action, the cerebellum helps initiate it. But after deliberate practice, the basal ganglia's pathways become so strong that the action feels automatic, like second nature.

Optimizing Our Brain for Learning

Our brain has evolved for survival, but that doesn't mean we can't train it to excel in today's world. To improve learning, it's essential to:

- *Practice regularly:* The more we repeat something, the stronger our brain's neural pathways become.
- *Engage in active recall:* Test ourselves on what we've learned. This forces our brain to retrieve information, strengthening those neural connections.
- *Get enough sleep:* Sleep is essential for consolidating memories. During deep sleep, our hippocampus works to move new information from short-term to long-term memory.

OUR BRAINS ARE incredible organs designed to help us thrive in any situation. By understanding how it works, we can take control of our learning and unlock our true potential. The next chapter will dive into the metaphysical aspect of learning—the mind—and how we can use it to further maximize our learning abilities.

Our brains are always ready to learn. It's never too late to start developing new skills, mastering new concepts, and embracing the power of our brain's plasticity.

THE MIND & LEARNING
METAPHYSICAL LEVERAGE

"The mind is its own place, and in itself can make a heaven of hell, a hell of heaven." - John Milton (*Paradise Lost*)

I magine if we could access the full potential of our minds. Whether we're tackling complex problems, mastering new skills, or generating creative ideas, understanding how the brain and mind function together can transform our approach to life. The brain and mind work hand-in-hand, and we can harness this relationship to learn faster, think better, and create more.

The Brain and the Mind: Our Hardware and Software

The brain is the physical organ that processes information, while the mind is the metaphysical realm where our thoughts, creativity, and imagination reside. Together, they form the control center that guides our actions, perceptions, and interactions with the world. While we often associate the mind with the brain, the mind transcends physical boundaries, influencing everything from how we solve problems to how we dream. Understanding both can help us optimize our thinking and learning processes.

Modes of Thinking

Thinking is a core cognitive function essential for problem-solving, decision-making, and responding to the world. Theories like *diffuse vs. focused thinking* offer insight into how we approach different tasks. Mastering both styles can unlock more powerful cognitive abilities.

Focused thinking is deliberate and concentrated, relying on the prefrontal cortex. We use it when we're consciously trying to solve a problem or learn something specific. It's the kind of thinking we engage in when solving a math problem or focusing on a project with clear steps. Focused thinking is most effective when we have high energy, and the solution is just outside our current level of understanding.

Diffuse thinking, on the other hand, occurs in the background. It's the brain's creative, exploratory mode, making connections across different areas of the brain. Diffuse thinking is the kind of thinking that happens when we're walking, daydreaming, or taking a shower—moments when our brain can wander freely. Diffuse thinking helps when we're faced with a complex problem that requires out-of-the-box solutions. For example, Benjamin Franklin used a special napping technique to induce this creative state whenever he encountered a problem he couldn't immediately solve. He would sit in a chair holding a metal object, like a spoon, in his hand and rest it over a plate on the floor. As he started to fall asleep and enter a relaxed, diffuse thinking state, the spoon would drop, hitting the plate and waking him up. This brief moment of rest allowed his mind to wander, make creative connections, and often helped him find solutions to the problems he couldn't solve while fully awake.

By switching between focused and diffuse thinking, we can maximize both our problem-solving and creative abilities.

Daniel Kahneman, in his bestselling book *Thinking, Fast and Slow*, introduces a similar concept to focused and diffuse thinking, called *System 1* and *System 2*. These systems represent the two ways our brain operates:

- *System 1* is fast, automatic, and intuitive. It handles routine tasks and quick decisions effortlessly. It's perfect for situations that don't require deep thought, like recognizing familiar faces or making simple choices.
- *System 2*, on the other hand, is slow, deliberate, and analytical. This system kicks in when we need to solve complex problems or make important decisions. It requires more mental energy and focus.

Kahneman emphasizes that while System 1 is efficient for everyday tasks, people often rely on it too much, even when they should engage System 2. This can lead to hasty decisions and unnecessary mistakes. By understanding when to slow down and switch to System 2, we can make better, more thoughtful choices.

Top-Down & Bottom-Up Processing: Two Paths to Understanding

Learning involves two types of cognitive processing:

- *Top-down processing*: when we use what we already know to make sense of something. For example, if we see the word "rcoking," we might recognize it as "rocking" because our brains expect that word in the context.
- *Bottom-up processing*: when we start with small details and put them together to figure out the bigger picture. In this case, we'd look at each letter of "rcoking" carefully before realizing it should spell "rocking."

When learning, bottom-up processing is ideal for understanding new material, while top-down processing helps apply what we already know to new situations. Balancing both is essential for deep learning.

Different Types of Memory

Memory is crucial to how we interact with the world and retain information. There are different types of memory, each playing a distinct role in how we learn and behave.

- *Declarative (Explicit) Memory* is the conscious storage of facts, events, and concepts. It can be divided into two types:
  - *Episodic memory:* our autobiographical memory of specific life events.
  - *Semantic memory:* our memory of words, concepts, and general knowledge.
- *Implicit Memory* operates unconsciously and influences our behaviors and thoughts without our direct awareness. An example is *procedural memory*, which is responsible for skills like riding a bike or typing without consciously thinking about each movement.

Understanding how different types of memory work can help us tailor our study and practice methods. For example, practicing a skill repeatedly reinforces procedural memory, while active recall strengthens declarative memory.

Imagination and Problem Solving

"Scientists must have a vivid intuitive imagination, for new ideas are not generated by deduction, but by an artistically creative imagination." - Max Planck

Imagination is the engine of creativity, allowing us to envision new possibilities, empathize with others, and solve problems. It's not limited to artists and scientists—imagination is a skill everyone uses in everyday life, whether we're daydreaming, picturing a future scenario, or solving a challenge at work.

Imagination fuels creativity, and creativity leads to innovation. From technological breakthroughs to social change, the world's most complex problems will be solved through imaginative thinking. Cultivating imagination isn't just about fostering creativity—it's about solving real-world problems by thinking beyond the obvious.

Assimilation and Accommodation

Learning involves two key processes: *assimilation* and *accommodation*.

- *Assimilation* is when we apply existing knowledge to new situations. For example, when teaching algebraic inequalities, I show my students how they are similar to solving regular equations. This helps them relate the new concept to something familiar.
- *Accommodation* happens when new information doesn't fit into our existing knowledge. When this happens, we modify or create new frameworks to make sense of the novel information. This is the process that allows us to truly learn new things and expand our understanding.

By mastering both processes, we continuously build on what we know, allowing us to adapt and grow.

Identity, Self, & Personal Growth

Our identity shapes how we see ourselves and drives much of our behavior. *Our actual self,* the person we are in reality, is influenced by both our *ideal self* (who we aspire to be) and our *ought self* (who others expect us to be).

Understanding these different facets of identity can motivate us to grow. For example, the closer our actual self aligns with our ideal self, the higher our self-esteem. Similarly, improving our *self-efficacy* (belief in our own abilities) makes us more likely to embrace challenges and learn new things. I'll talk about identity more in a later chapter.

Cognitive Load: Our Brain's Processing Power

Cognitive load refers to the brain's processing capacity. Think of it as our brain's "RAM." Every task, decision, or piece of information uses up some of this mental energy, so managing cognitive load is key to effective learning and problem-solving. I'll talk more about Cognitive Load later in the next chapter.

Here are some ways to reduce cognitive load:

- Simplify tasks whenever possible.
- Prioritize important decisions early in the day when your cognitive load is high.
- Use cognitive aids like checklists, calendars, and reminders to offload unnecessary mental effort.

By managing cognitive load, we free up more brainpower for the tasks that matter most.

The Mind as Our Most Powerful Ally

The brain and mind work together to shape our thoughts, creativity, and actions. Understanding the difference between focused and diffuse thinking, mastering both System 1 and System 2, and recognizing the role of top-down and bottom-up processing can transform the way we approach problem-solving and decision-making. These mental processes not only help us learn more effectively but also tap into our creative potential.

Our mind is a powerful ally. When we harness its abilities—

whether by managing cognitive load, improving memory, or fostering imagination—we are able to thrive in every aspect of life. From the practical use of memory to the abstract power of creativity, our mental faculties give us the tools to adapt, grow, and innovate.

When we master the balance between these modes of thinking, we can learn more efficiently, solve problems more creatively, and make better decisions. The mind, as John Milton suggests, can turn any situation into a heaven or a hell—it's up to us to choose how we use it. With this knowledge, we can start discovering our mind's full potential, shaping our reality in powerful, positive ways.

LEARN FASTER, ACHIEVE MORE
THE 20 HOUR RULE & META-SKILLS

"The future belongs to those who learn more skills and combine them in creative ways." - Robert Greene (*Mastery*)

The 20-Hour Rule: A Game-Changer in Learning

Many of us have heard of the 10,000-hour rule, which suggests it takes around 10,000 hours of deliberate practice to become a master in any field. But here's the exciting part: we don't need 10,000 hours to be proficient in a new skill.

Research suggests it takes just 20 hours of focused, deliberate practice to become reasonably competent at a new skill. In other words, only 20 hours to make significant progress in something we've never done before.

This is revolutionary because it means that success in any field can be broken down into learning a specific combination of skills, one 20-hour chunk at a time. We don't need to wait for mastery to see progress—we just need to start.

The Beginner's Advantage

The first 20 hours of learning a new skill provide the most significant gains. It's like charging a phone battery from 20% to 80%—we see rapid and meaningful improvement. For example, a beginner hurdler might improve their time dramatically in the first few sessions, whereas an Olympic hurdler might train for years just to shave off milliseconds.

In the beginning, progress feels fast and rewarding. That's the beginner's advantage.

Different types of skills—whether physical (like playing tennis), cognitive (like solving math problems), or social (like public speaking)—follow this same pattern. Initially, everything feels new, but with practice, our brains form neural pathways that make the task easier and more automatic.

Meta-skills: The Key to Versatile Success

The real magic happens when we develop *meta-skills*—skills that help us acquire other skills. Meta-skills are like universal tools, making it easier to learn and succeed in a wide range of domains.

Take me, for example: developing as a musician taught me self-control, focus, and problem-solving—skills that I later found invaluable as a student, tutor, and EMT. Learning one skill made learning others easier. That's the power of meta-skills.

Meta-skills are like multipliers—they amplify our ability to succeed in any field by making the learning process more efficient.

A Growing Arsenal of Skills

Each skill we learn adds to our personal toolkit, giving us the resources to handle life's challenges. Skills aren't confined to specific domains like academics or sports. They are transferable. For example, being a successful student involves multiple skills:

time management, study strategies, critical thinking, and independent learning.

Once we've mastered these, they can be applied to new challenges at work or in personal growth.

My Top Recommendations for Meta-skills

Here are the top meta-skills I recommend for building a versatile skill set.

- *Cognitive Skills*
    - *Writing:* Effective communication is essential in every field.
    - *Quantitative Reasoning:* Understanding numbers helps with decision-making and problem-solving.
    - *Critical Thinking:* Analyze and evaluate ideas objectively.
- *Emotional and Social Skills*
    - *Self-awareness:* Understand our strengths, weaknesses, and triggers.
    - *Resilience:* Bounce back from failure and learn from it.
    - *Leadership:* Guide others while staying open to feedback.
- *Practical Skills*
    - *Time Management & Scheduling:* Prioritize tasks and make the most of our time.
    - *Focus:* Eliminate distractions and concentrate on the task at hand.
    - *Public Speaking:* Articulate our thoughts confidently in front of others.

Dedicating just five minutes a day to any of these can lead to significant growth over time. Conquering our goals is about mastering one skill at a time, building upon each success.

Learning Beyond the Classroom

Contrary to popular belief, learning doesn't stop with school—and it doesn't have to get harder as we age. By focusing on meta-skills, we can continue learning effectively throughout our lives. The 10,000-hour rule is about mastery, but the *20-hour rule* tells us that starting something new is within everyone's reach.

THE VALLEY OF DISAPPOINTMENT & THE TRANSITION CURVE
EMBRACING THE LEARNING JOURNEY

L et's dive into two powerful concepts that every learner needs to understand: *The Valley of Disappointment* and *The Transition Curve*. These ideas reshape how we view progress and dramatically improve how we approach challenges in skill development.

The Valley of Disappointment: Navigating the Dip in Progress

In his book *Atomic Habits*, James Clear introduces the concept of *The Valley of Disappointment*. This phase occurs when we expect immediate, linear improvement in our skills but instead experience slow or even invisible progress. The Valley of Disappointment is where many learners give up because, despite their hard work, they don't see quick results.

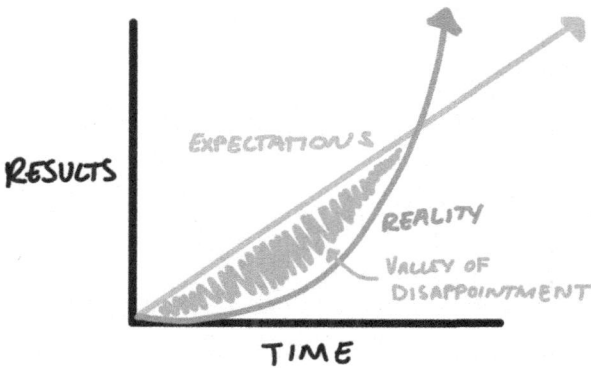

James Clear's The Valley of Disappointment

Imagine trying to learn a new language. In the first few lessons, we might feel like we're making great progress, but as we advance, the grammar becomes more complex, and our confidence falters. This is the Valley of Disappointment—a point where the effort we're putting in hasn't yet turned into tangible results.

The key is to recognize that progress is compounding. Even when it seems like nothing is happening, our brain is absorbing, adjusting, and storing information. Just as compound interest in finance takes time to grow, so does our skill development. Keep going, and soon we'll see a surge in improvement. Mastery requires patience and trust in the process.

The Transition Curve: Moving from Novice to Master

While the Valley of Disappointment focuses on the perceived lack of progress, the *Transition Curve* shows the different stages we go through as we develop competence in a new skill. Developed from research at Cranfield University, this curve outlines the emotional and cognitive stages of skill acquisition—from initial excitement to deep frustration, and eventually, to mastery. It illustrates the relationship between our competence and confidence over the time we spend developing a skill.

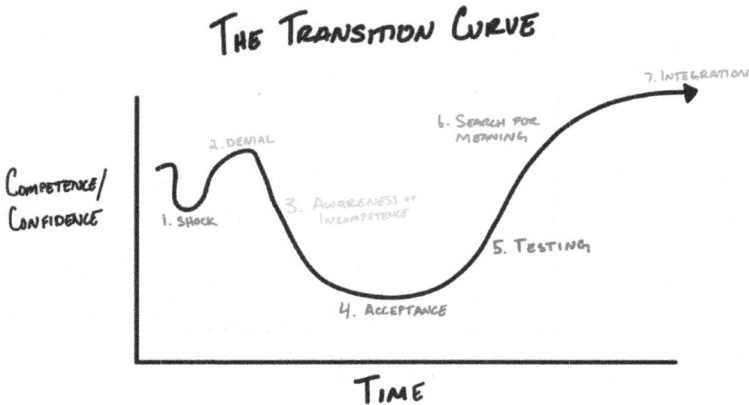

Kübler-Ross Change Curve

The Transition Curve has several phases:

1. *Shock and Denial:* When starting something new, we often feel excited, but the complexity of the task can quickly catch us off guard. We might think, "This is harder than I expected."
2. *Awareness of Incompetence:* This is the most challenging phase for many. When we realize how little we know, our confidence dips. This is the critical point where most people quit, believing they're not cut out for the task.
3. *Testing and Acceptance:* If we push through the discomfort, we'll start experimenting with new approaches, learning from mistakes, and refining our technique.
4. *Integration and Mastery:* Finally, after consistent practice, the skill becomes second nature, and we reach a level of unconscious competence where things flow smoothly.

The Transition Curve reminds us that struggle is a natural part of learning. Instead of feeling discouraged by mistakes or setbacks, celebrate them as signs of growth. When we recognize that we don't know something, that's the moment when true learning begins. Embrace the awareness of incompetence as a sign we're on the right path.

Navigating These Concepts in Real Life

Let's apply these principles to a common example: learning how to drive. In the beginning, it feels overwhelming—balancing the pedals, watching the mirrors, and staying aware of the road. At first, progress is quick: we figure out the basics, like turning the car on and driving in a straight line. But soon, we enter the Valley of Disappointment when it feels like every new lesson reveals how much more there is to learn. We might struggle with parallel parking or highway merging, thinking we'll never get it.

However, by sticking with it and deliberately practicing those challenging areas, you progress through the Transition Curve. Soon, those actions become automatic, and driving becomes second nature. The struggle we faced earlier fades, and the skill is now integrated into our routine.

How to Stay Consistent and Overcome the Valleys and Curves

So, how do we navigate these challenging phases?

- *Break it Down:* Set small, achievable milestones. If we're learning to code, don't aim to build a complex app on day one. Start by understanding basic syntax and solving simple problems. Celebrate each step forward.
- *Track Our Progress:* Keep a journal or log of our practice sessions. By documenting what we've learned, we'll see improvement over time, even if it's not immediately visible.
- *Seek Feedback:* Don't go through the Valley of Disappointment alone. Find a mentor, coach, or peer to

provide guidance and encouragement. Outside feedback can offer new perspectives and keep us motivated.

- *Create a Consistent Schedule:* Mastery comes from consistency. Dedicate time each day to deliberate practice, even if it's just 15 minutes. Consistency builds momentum and helps us push through plateaus.
- *Reflect and Adjust:* Regularly assess what's working and what's not. If a particular approach isn't yielding results, don't be afraid to pivot and try something new.

Why These Concepts Matter

Both the Valley of Disappointment and the Transition Curve remind us that learning is not a linear process. Understanding these concepts helps us prepare for the inevitable ups and downs, and embrace the struggles as necessary parts of growth.

Progress often comes after a period of stagnation. By keeping these concepts in mind, we can tackle new challenges with greater resilience and optimism. In the end, the struggle makes the reward that much sweeter.

The Journey to Mastery

The Valley of Disappointment and the Transition Curve teach us one critical lesson: the journey is just as important as the destination. Every challenge, mistake, and frustrating plateau is a stepping stone toward greater skill and understanding. If we can endure the valleys and stay the course through the transitions, we'll emerge more skilled and confident than we ever imagined.

THE MYTH OF MOTIVATION
THE POWER OF DISCIPLINE

"We are always complaining that our days are few, and acting as though there would be no end of them." - Seneca (*On The Shortness of Life*)

Missing Pieces

Motivational books, speakers, quotes, videos, blog posts, et cetera, are fantastic for getting us pumped up enough to dominate any obstacle in our way. When we're motivated, we can do anything, but motivation doesn't stick around for very long and is difficult to recover once lost.

Action beyond motivation is necessary for achieving many of the goals we set for ourselves. Acting only when we feel motivated, while expecting to accomplish all our dreams, sets us up for massive disappointment and wasted energy. Substantial achievement requires acting even when we don't feel like it.

If I only studied when I felt like studying, I would never have even finished high school let alone a chemical engineering or master's degree. If I only wrote when I felt like it, then I wouldn't have a blog or a book. If I was only a good husband or father when

I felt like it, then I wouldn't have a happy family. I can literally go on forever about this. Over and over again I have discovered that all of my goals cannot be accomplished only when I feel motivated.

On the flip side, I only make music when I feel like it, and I have almost nothing to show for it.

Motivation is a fantastic tool, but it isn't reliable enough to take us to the promised land—so to speak. So that poses the question:

What is motivation missing?

Without discipline and purpose, motivation is only a short-term solution. Motivation fueled by purpose and discipline is enough to get us anywhere we need to go. Discipline gets us through when we don't want to and purpose gets us through when things are hard. They are like two engines to a plane, and both give us access to action beyond motivation.

Purpose has many parts which I will discuss in other chapters, but this chapter is going to mainly focus on discipline. What it is, why it's necessary, how to develop it within ourselves, and specific methods to create action beyond motivation.

Discipline and Its Components

"Discipline equals freedom." - Jocko Willink (*Discipline Equals Freedom: Field Manual*)

When most people think of discipline, they think of punishment. That is *not* what I am talking about here.

What I mean by discipline is taking on the challenge of creating a relationship with ourselves, knowing ourselves as people who do the right things. We continuously have an opportunity to change our relationship with ourselves and know ourselves as the kind of people who can focus on the task in front of us and do it as well as we possibly can.

I like to think of discipline as a way to learn how to deliberately narrow our focus to the one thing that our highest selves want to be doing.

Without discipline, we are victims of our circumstances, environments, and unconscious desires.

I spent a few weeks trying to wrap my head around discipline and in doing so, I had a fantastic conversation with my wife.

She was telling me about how her relationship with discipline can be broken up into two subcategories: taking responsibility and making decisions.

She told me that when she started taking responsibility for everything in her life, endless opportunities for decisions emerged. When we take responsibility, we empower ourselves, which gives us vitalizing freedom and insight into what we can and cannot change. Once we see our options, it is up to us to do something about it (or not).

Taking responsibility gives us options.

Let me root this in a simple example:

Let's say we're trying to study for a test but can't get ourselves to crack open the book and start. What we lack is discipline. A disciplined person would just sit down and start working without wasted energy dedicated to convincing themselves that studying is a good idea.

In order to navigate our way from not being able to open the book to sitting and starting flawlessly, we first need to take responsibility for our learning.

We can take on a perspective:

How much we understand and how much we are able to demonstrate is solely a function of our own effort and dedication.

Once we genuinely take that on, we can see the decisions to be made in front of us.

We can either study or not.

The choice is ours—not up to our professors, parents, or the economy (common scapegoats people often use).

Now we can make the decision to study or not. That is where we want to be mentally. We can choose to not study, but if we run through this thought process and still decide not to, the pain is so much worse.

Nothing sucks more than suffering and knowing that it's all because of us and our stupid choices.

More often than not, we will end up doing what we "should" be because of loss aversion. People will go to greater lengths to not lose $5 than gain $20.

If we take responsibility for our lives, we can see how much power we truly have. Usually, it's much more than we like to think. Opportunities for decisions appear to us and all we have to do is make a choice.

Taking responsibility and making decisions is what we need to create a foundation for developing discipline.

Access to a New Life

Most of what we want to accomplish requires tremendous amounts of effort, time, energy, and attention. Our resources are best spent moving closer to those goals, not convincing ourselves we need to.

Here's a fun little exercise to show us how we have access to a new life. I found this from one of Jordan Peterson's lectures:

- Ask yourself – *How many hours a day do I waste?*
- Write that number down.....really write it down.
- Now, let's say you value your time at $50/hour, which is probably on the low end.
- *How much money do you waste per day?*
- Most people write anywhere from 4-6 hours. Let's say we waste 4 hours a day valued at $50/hr. That's a loss of $200/day or $1000/work week.
- That's $52,000/year wasted, *at least.*

This is just one of the costs of a lack of discipline.

If we value ourselves more, then the cost is even more expensive.

I like to do this exercise with my students at the start of the semester and it's always so funny to see the look on their faces when they're present to how much time they really have access to.

The best part of this exercise is that I *don't* define waste.

The students waste 1/6 of their day by their own standards!

Discipline is more than just preventing waste, it helps develop a powerful relationship with ourselves.

Preventing wasted time and developing a powerful relationship with ourselves provide incredible benefits, but the real sweetness of discipline comes from accomplishing what we set out to accomplish.

This is how we live a life by design.

Since external discipline can be hard to find in some occupations, cultivating self-discipline is key to making all of this possible. We need to learn how much self-discipline we have and how we need to adjust. Some people are too lax with themselves while others are too stern.

How to Develop Discipline within Ourselves

"A paradox of life: The problem with patience and discipline is that developing each of them requires both of them." - Thomas M. Sterner (*The Practicing Mind*)

We can increase our discipline by changing our self-image.

If we think of ourselves as lazy, then we will be lazy. If we think of ourselves as focused, then we will be focused. The trick is actually believing it.

Our identity is one of the strongest motivational forces if we learn how to use it correctly. We hate being wrong and being wrong about our identity is something we will go to the ends of the earth to prevent, this is known as *identity defense*.

We just need to work on changing our identity to someone who is disciplined and the discipline will follow.

We can also do short-term challenges that train the "discipline muscle." These challenges will give us opportunities to be disciplined if we don't have something else requiring that of us. For example: taking cold showers for 30 days. It's tempting to want to take a hot shower (especially for me), but with the challenge in place, we can decide to stick to our word or give in to our animalistic needs. Doing something like cold showers is great because it's excuse-proof. We're already taking showers daily (I hope) so it's already integrated into our routines, we just need to make a simple and small adjustment. Remember: anyone can do anything for a month.

Another method for increasing discipline is setting up a system that requires you to show up every day. Yes, I do mean every damn day. This is powerful because it forces us to act even if "we don't feel like it." At first, it will be painful, but after each day the part of us that perseveres will become stronger and stronger until we have the self-discipline to get through it. Create a nice reward for afterward, but also create a punishment so there is even more of a reason to do it. Make it short and manageable so it will will actually get done every day.

An example of this in my life is my exercise habits. I used to hate working out and I never had the discipline to do it, until I told myself I wasn't going to eat in the morning until I did a few kettlebell swings. The reward is eating and the punishment is going hungry. Pretty simple if you ask me.

Now we could say, "Chris why don't you just eat anyway if you don't feel like working out?" and my reply to that would be because it destroys the relationship I have with myself. Letting ourselves slide with things has a detrimental effect on how we relate to ourselves and I've worked too hard to develop a positive and strong relationship with myself where I know myself to be a person who follows through on his commitments.

Getting Started Anyway

Acting when we aren't motivated is difficult. It's expensive in terms of cognitive load, not because the tasks are hard, but because we have to overcome so much within ourselves to get going.

Since I'm a physics nerd, I'm going to put it like this: Action beyond motivation is similar to overcoming friction. Friction is a force that works against another force, usually slowing or preventing the displacement of an object.

There are two types of friction – static friction and kinetic friction.

Static friction is tougher to overcome than kinetic friction.

We can try this with a box sitting on the ground. If we apply pressure on the box, we will notice that it takes more pressure to get the box moving than to keep the moving moving. The same principles apply in other places. It's harder to get things starter than to keep things going.

If we overcome the static friction, then we won't have to push as hard to keep going.

Procrastination is a huge ally to static friction. Usually, we procrastinate because we feel like overcoming that static friction is too expensive. Finding ways to get started is the secret to action beyond motivation.

Methods to Fight Procrastination

There are a ton of methods to get started, but I'm just going to share two of them right now.

One of my favorite methods I use to fight procrastination and overcome static friction is *The 5-Second Rule*. I first heard of this idea from the renowned and respected author and motivational speaker, Mel Robbins. It's pretty simple, right before you get yourself to do something just count down from 5 then begin.

5...4...3...2...1... Go!

There is something about counting down that primes our

minds to overcome static friction. I do this all the time when I'm working out. Right before I do a set (that I really don't want to do) I count down from 5 and begin. Once I start, I just focus on getting through it. The push I give myself (the willpower I exert) to start is more than enough to keep the workout going as long as I keep pushing.

This idea set me free from believing that "things are hard to start and keep getting harder."

The opposite is actually true, *getting started is the hardest part and it gets easier over time.*

Something I do want to mention about this technique is how it is easier to get derailed if we are interrupted.

Let me use the example of my workouts again. I can use the 5-second rule to get started and push through to the finish line, but if I'm interrupted while I'm doing my workout the process has to start over again. I will have to overcome the static friction over again. The force I was applying while I had momentum will not be enough to start again.

Beware of interruptions when doing demanding activities.

Another fantastic method of fighting procrastination and over-coming static friction is implementing starting rituals. Starting rituals are fantastic for tricking our brain into doing things we don't want to do. (The 5-Second Rule is really just a simplified starting ritual).

In later chapters, I will talk about the *habit cycle* and how we can design the lives we want if we work on designing our habits. It's difficult to do what we tell ourselves, but with knowledge of the habit cycle, we can see our patterns and manipulate them to our own advantage.

The first stage of the habit cycle is *Cue*. This means our cravings and responses which come afterward are influenced by cues.

We are extremely susceptible to subconsciously perceiving cues and we can use this potential vulnerability to create powerful starting rituals.

Doing the same thing over and over right before we do an activity primes our brains to do that activity.

Let me solidify this with an example. I remember to brush my teeth when I walk into my bathroom and see my toothbrush. As much as I'd like to say I remember to brush my teeth every morning, the truth is that I'm reminded by the cue. Walking into the bathroom is my starting ritual to brushing my teeth.

Another example is when I'm writing. I always grab a drink, place it on my right side, turn on classical music, set my Pomodoro timer, and start typing away. All the things I do before I actually start writing I consider my starting ritual. Doing these things helps me get ready to work and it really helps with overcoming the huge amounts of static friction that come with writing.

I've tried to write without the ritual and it usually ends in disaster. I would try to tell myself all those little routines are a waste of time and I should just start writing, but I end up writing for a short amount of time while easily distracted. This results in worse writing and wasted energy. Starting rituals help us get in the mode.

We can create our own starting rituals, which I think can be a lot of fun.

Like with any habit, it takes a while before our brain starts to understand these cues and cravings so stick with it for at least 5 sessions.

Aim for the Success Spiral

The Matthew Effect (also known as the Matthew Effect of Accumulated Advantage or the Matthew principle) was popularized by American sociologist, Robert K. Merton, and is named after *The Parable of Talents* from the biblical Gospel of Matthew.

"For to every one who has will more be given, and he will have abundance; but from him who has not, even what he has will be taken away." - Gospel of Matthew (25:29 Revised Standard Version)

Regardless of religious affiliation, The Matthew Effect is a phenomenon we can observe time and time again even in the modern world.

I recently started seriously investing in the stock market and I see exactly how people who already have money can make more money.

People who invest more money have the potential to make more money, people who invest little money have the potential to make little money.

This is also visible in something like a small bank account, the more money we have in the account, the more money can we get back in interest. People who don't have a lot of money in their bank account are subject to low-interest yields and overdraft fees, which prevent them from effortless wealth building.

On an academic level, students who get A's on the first few exams are going to have an easier time getting an A on future assessments or the final exam. The students who failed the first few exams are more likely to fail the final unless they put in even more effort than the A students.

When it comes to exercise, it's actually easier to work out once we're in shape and healthy. If we aren't, exercise can seem like an impossible mountain to climb, and we are more likely to become even unhealthier.

In Jeff Olsen's book, *The Slight Edge*, he brings up the idea of the *Two Life Path*. This concept clearly illustrates The Matthew Effect.

Our choices compound on each other, and while it doesn't seem like it at the moment, the good choices can easily become great and the bad choices can easily become terrible.

We just need to add time.

This knowledge is powerful because we can use it to our advantage. All we have to do is aim for the success spiral. Once we reach a critical point of good decisions, the benefits compound on each other and create even more benefits as long as we don't destroy the structure.

Focus on making the small wins and watch them evolve into big ones.

It's much easier to win once we've been winning. On the flip side, the small losses can spiral out of control. At that point, it becomes too easy to lose and seemingly impossible to win. Don't let it get to that point, take the wins wherever possible.

There's no win that is too small.

Half a push-up? Fantastic, next time we can do 1. The time after that we can do 2. Keep that up for a year and we'll be surprised how far that can take us.

A big part of aiming for the success spiral is tracking our habits. Tracking is important because we can see how we've been performing over time and determine if we are on a success spiral or if we need to make changes.

For the past few months I've been using the Streaks app on iOS and I highly recommend it. Best $5.99 I've spent this year for sure. Creating streaks builds momentum and that momentum gives us an extra push.

Remember: kinetic friction is easier to overcome than static friction.

It's easier to maintain a streak than to start one.

I also reward myself whenever I finish my streaks, so I have an incentive to start again the next day.

Good Feelings Come After Action

"Chase after money and security, And your heart will never unclench. Care about people's approval, And you will be their prisoner. Do your work, then step back. The only path to serenity." - Lao Tzu (*Tao Te Ching*)

Waiting until we feel good about doing something is similar to waiting until we feel motivated. It's futile and we will never get enough done to obtain significant achievement. Action beyond motivation is the muscle we need to develop within ourselves and the same principles can apply to action beyond feeling good.

What makes people happy is not obtaining goals, but observing themselves move towards a goal.

Knowing that our actions are "correct" gives us bursts of dopamine, which make us feel good. The truth is that the good feelings come after the actions.

We will feel like doing it, once we are doing it.

I encounter this every time I start reading or writing a blog post. Every time it's a struggle to start, but once I'm started I tend to lose myself in my work and I feel genuine pleasure while I'm doing it. The feelings I wanted to have before I started came to me while I was doing the work.

Good feelings come *after* accomplishment, not before

Do good, feel good.

THE MAMBA MENTALITY
CULTIVATING CONSISTENCY

"To sum up what Mamba Mentality is, it means to be able to constantly try to be the best version of yourself. That is what the Mentality is—it's a constant quest to try to be better today than you were yesterday." — Kobe Bryant

Unlocking the Mamba Mentality

What does it take to achieve greatness? For Kobe Bryant, the answer was simple: relentless dedication to improving every single day. This drive, famously termed the *Mamba Mentality*, became his guiding philosophy—one that transcended the basketball court. It's a mindset that applies to anyone seeking to reach their full potential, regardless of their field.

But what exactly is the Mamba Mentality, and how can we apply it in our own lives?

Kobe's Inspiring Journey

Before Kobe became one of the most iconic athletes of all time, he faced failure head-on. At 10 or 11 years old, Kobe played in a summer basketball league and scored zero points for the entire season. For a child with big dreams, this was devastating.

His father, Joe Bryant, gave him the confidence he needed with one simple message: *"It doesn't matter if you score 0 or 60 points, I'm going to love you either way."* This reassurance allowed Kobe to confront failure without fear, but it didn't mean he accepted being average. He didn't want to score 0 points again.

After that season, Kobe focused intensely on the fundamentals, while his teammates relied on raw athleticism. As the years passed, his dedication to mastering the basics began to pay off. By age 14, Kobe had surpassed his peers, becoming the best basketball player in his state. For Kobe, it was a matter of simple math: *If you practice 2–3 hours every day, while others practice 1–2 hours twice a week, who will improve more?*

His story highlights a key aspect of the Mamba Mentality: Skill development isn't just a function of talent; it's a result of consistent, focused effort over time.

Understanding the Mamba Mentality

At its core, the Mamba Mentality is the relentless pursuit of becoming the best version of oneself. It's not about instant success or overnight achievements. Rather, it's a daily commitment to progress—improving a little bit every day until those small gains add up to something extraordinary.

This mindset isn't exclusive to athletes; it's universal. Whether we're an artist, entrepreneur, teacher, or scientist, the Mamba Mentality can serve as a roadmap for achieving excellence in any domain.

The Pillars of the Mamba Mentality

Kobe Bryant's philosophy can be broken down into three key principles—pillars that anyone can adopt to level up in their craft.

1. *Show Up and Work Every Day:* The first pillar is about unwavering commitment. It means showing up, putting in the work, and giving your 100%, no matter the circumstances. Consistent effort over time creates a significant edge over the competition. The people who show up, even on their worst days, are the ones who stand out.

2. *Rest at the End, Not in the Middle:* Endurance is key to achieving long-term success. This pillar emphasizes the importance of pushing through discomfort and delaying gratification. Resting only after the task is complete ensures that we've truly earned it. Resting prematurely can lead to stagnation.

3. *Obsess Over the Fundamentals:* Mastering the basics is crucial. Kobe spent hours honing his footwork, shooting form, and defensive skills, never getting bored of the essentials. When we build a strong foundation, everything else becomes easier.

Applying the Mamba Mentality to Life

The Mamba Mentality isn't just a mindset for the basketball court —it's a philosophy for life. I've applied it to various aspects of my own life, whether it's learning something new, working out, or creative endeavors like writing and music production. The principles of daily dedication, patience, and perseverance through discomfort have transformed my approach to challenges.

For example, in writing, the Mamba Mentality encourages me to push through writer's block or the days when creativity feels absent. It's about showing up at the desk, even when it's hard, and trusting that the consistency will lead to breakthroughs.

Incremental, Consistent Progress

One of the most powerful lessons from the Mamba Mentality is the importance of incremental progress. Improving by just 1% each day may seem insignificant, but over time, those small gains compound into massive growth. If we improve by 1% every day, we'll be 37 times better by the next year.

The key is patience. It's okay to be terrible when we start something new, but what matters is our dedication to getting better every single day.

Dedication + Time = Success

The combination of dedication and time is what drives skill development. Kobe's story teaches us that putting in the hours, day after day, will eventually lead to mastery. It's not glamorous, and it often feels slow, but success is the result of these two simple ingredients: effort and time.

In my own life, I apply this principle by dedicating specific time slots to skill-building. Whether it's dedicating two hours a day to my craft or practicing something new for 30 minutes on weekdays, consistency is the key that unlocks progress.

A Blueprint for Greatness

The Mamba Mentality is more than just a mindset—it's a blueprint for achieving excellence in anything we pursue. By showing up every day, focusing on the fundamentals, and committing to incremental progress, we can transform not only our skills but our entire approach to challenges and opportunities.

If we're willing to embrace the grind, push through discomfort, and commit to becoming just a little better every day, success is inevitable. The journey may be long, but if we follow the Mamba Mentality, greatness is within reach.

FAIL FORWARD

WHY MISTAKES ARE THE KEY TO MASTERY AND SUCCESS

"There are two kinds of failure. The first comes from never trying out your ideas because you are afraid, or because you are waiting for the perfect time. This kind of failure you can never learn from, and such timidity will destroy you. The second kind comes from a bold and venturesome spirit. If you fail in this way, the hit that you take to your reputation is greatly outweighed by what you learn. Repeated failure will toughen your spirit and show you with absolute clarity how things must be done." - Robert Greene (*Mastery*)

The Power of Failure

What if the key to success wasn't avoiding failure but actively seeking it out? It might sound counterintuitive, but failure is one of the most powerful tools for growth and learning. In fact, failing is not just okay, it's necessary for any kind of meaningful progress.

Why I Love Failing

It might sound strange, but failure has become one of my favorite things in life. Why? Because failure is an honest teacher. It strips away illusions and excuses, showing us exactly where we need to improve.

Despite societal beliefs painting failure as something negative to be avoided at all costs, the reality is quite the opposite. Failure is a powerful tool that teaches us lessons we remember forever. It guides us toward success more effectively than success itself.

Active Recall and the Power of Getting It Wrong

One of the most fascinating aspects of failure is its role in memory and learning. When students engage in active recall—attempting to remember information without looking at notes—they tend to retain what they got wrong more effectively than what they got right. This phenomenon also applied to my experience studying for the MCAT. The parts I initially got wrong were the ones I remembered most clearly.

It's as if failure engraves knowledge into our brains in a way that success cannot. The act of making mistakes and correcting them is essential to truly mastering any subject.

Sensitivity to Failure: An Evolutionary Perspective

Why do failures seem to hit us harder than successes? From an evolutionary perspective, humans are wired to be more sensitive to negative stimuli. In our ancestors' time, mistakes often carried higher stakes—sometimes even life or death. Our brains evolved to prioritize learning from failures quickly, allowing us to adapt and survive.

This heightened sensitivity means that failure feels like a threat, and our brains treat it as such. But the silver lining is that this sensitivity to failure makes us learn and adapt rapidly, helping us grow faster in the long run.

Failure is Inevitable

"Failure had better be an option because, whether or not you consider it an option, it's going to happen! If you go through life with the philosophy that 'failure is not an option,' then you'll never have any good opportunities to learn." - Jeff Olson (*The Slight Edge*)

Failure isn't just an option; it's inevitable. No matter how skilled, prepared, or cautious we are, mistakes are part of the process. The key to thriving in the face of failure is to see it as a learning opportunity rather than a setback.

Every time we fail, we learn what *not* to do, and that is incredibly valuable. Failure is not the opposite of success—it's part of the journey toward it.

Failure Reveals What Needs Improvement

One of the most valuable aspects of failure is that it reveals our inadequacies. It shows us exactly where we are lacking and where our ideas or methods are flawed. This kind of clarity is a gift because it points us directly to the areas that need improvement.

Failure is half the battle in the learning process. Once we know where we need to grow, we can take deliberate steps toward mastery.

The Unexpected Formula for Success

"Would you like me to give you the formula for success? It's quite simple, really. Double your rate of failure. ... You're thinking of failure as the enemy of success. But it isn't at all. You can be discouraged by failure—or you can learn from it. So go ahead and make mistakes. Make all you can. Because, remember, that's where you'll find success. On the other side of failure." - Thomas Watson (Founder of IMB)

The idea of doubling our rate of failure may seem shocking, but Watson's point is clear: the more we fail, the more we learn, and the closer we get to success. Failure should not discourage us; it should propel us forward by teaching us the lessons we need to succeed.

Detaching Identity from Failure

One of the biggest challenges we face when dealing with failure is that we often tie our self-worth to our successes or failures. In reality, neither failure nor success defines who we are. They are simply results—indicators of what worked and what didn't.

By detaching our identity from the outcomes, we free ourselves to embrace failure as a learning tool, not as a judgment of our worth.

The Seed of Equal or Greater Benefit

"Every adversity, every failure, every heartache carries with it the seed of an equal or greater benefit."- Napoleon Hill (*Think and Grow Rich*)

Every failure carries with it the potential for growth. It's not a permanent defeat, but a stepping stone on the path to mastery and success. Failure forces us to reassess, re-strategize, and ultimately come out stronger on the other side.

FAILURE IS NOT THE ENEMY—IT'S a teacher, a guide, and a necessary step on the path to mastery. True defeat only happens when we choose to stop trying. Embrace failure, learn from it, and let it fuel our journey to success.

THE PATH TO GROWTH

THE POWER OF DEVELOPMENT AND MENTORSHIP

"The principal goal of education in the schools should be creating men and women who are capable of doing new things, not simply repeating what other generations have done; men and women who are creative, inventive, and discoverers, who can be critical and verify, and not accept everything they are offered." - Jean Piaget

Education is more than the mere transferring knowledge from one generation to the next. True education fosters creativity, discovery, and the development of critical thinking skills. To understand how we can foster this kind of growth, we can look to the transformative ideas of Jean Piaget and Lev Vygotsky. Their theories about how we learn, combined with the right mentorship, can dramatically enhance both personal and professional growth.

Building Knowledge with Piaget's Constructivism

Jean Piaget, a Swiss developmental psychologist, pioneered the theory of *constructivism*. According to Piaget, learning isn't about passively absorbing information; it's an active process of building new knowledge on top of what we already know.

Imagine we're building a wall. Every experience, every new piece of knowledge, is like adding a brick to that wall. But these new bricks don't just sit on top of old ones—they reshape and integrate with the foundation below. This is how Piaget saw learning: each new idea or skill is layered on top of the previous one, continually evolving and becoming more complex over time. Piaget believed that people build new representations of the world on top of their preexisting knowledge, with the new interpretation incorporating the old.

We can see this in action when learning to play the piano. Initially, we might only know how to play individual notes. But as we practice, we start building on that knowledge, learning chords and eventually entire songs. Each new skill depends on the foundation we've built, allowing we to grow in complexity.

In Piaget's view, we continually adjust our understanding of the world as we encounter new experiences. Education should encourage this growth, helping learners to actively construct their own knowledge rather than simply repeat what others have done.

Vygotsky's Zone of Proximal Development & The Power of Mentorship

While Piaget focused on how we construct knowledge, Lev Vygotsky emphasized the role of social interaction in learning. His concept of the *Zone of Proximal Development (ZPD)* explains the gap between what a person can do on their own and what they can achieve with help.

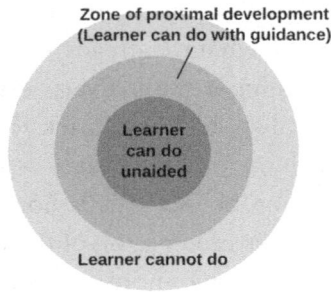

Zone of proximal development
(Learner can do with guidance)

Learner
can do
unaided

Learner cannot do

Image from wikipedia.org

The Zone of Proximal Development (ZPD) is where true learning happens. When a task is just beyond our current abilities, we need a mentor to help us bridge that gap. Over time, with the right guidance, we can master the skill and eventually perform it on our own. This concept highlights the importance of mentorship in helping us grow beyond our current capabilities.

Think about a student struggling with math. They can solve simple problems on their own, but when it comes to more complex equations, they need guidance from a teacher. The teacher provides the right level of support—just enough to challenge the student without causing them to feel hopeless. Over time, the student is able to solve the complex equations on their own, thanks to the teacher's mentorship within the ZPD.

How Piaget and Vygotsky's Theories Work Together

Piaget and Vygotsky's theories are complementary. Piaget's constructivism focuses on how we build knowledge over time, while Vygotsky's ZPD shows us how mentorship accelerates that process. Together, these ideas emphasize the importance of both self-directed learning and mentorship in developing new skills.

For instance, in the example of learning to play the piano, Piaget's theory would suggest that we gradually build new skills as we practice. Vygotsky's theory, on the other hand, reminds us that we need a teacher or mentor to guide us through the more challenging aspects, such as learning complex pieces or techniques that we can't yet grasp on our own.

This synergy of personal growth and mentorship is the key to transformative learning. By understanding how we learn independently and how others can guide us, we can develop a more holistic and effective approach to education.

Building Own Personal Panel of Mentors

To accelerate our learning and personal growth, we need more than just theories—we need mentors. But what if we don't have immediate access to someone who can guide us? That's where the idea of creating a personal panel of mentors comes in.

We can build our own council of mentors. These mentors can include real-life guides or figures whose work inspires and informs us. This council is most effective when it's diverse, balancing strengths and weaknesses across various domains. The idea is to stand on the shoulders of giants, creating a mastermind group that can guide us through different aspects of life and learning.

How to Build A Panel

1. *Identify Areas of Growth:* What skills or knowledge do we want to develop? Do we want to improve in leadership, creativity, or perhaps technical skills?
2. *Find Mentors in Different Disciplines:* These mentors don't have to be people we know personally. They can be authors, public figures, or experts whose work resonates with us. For example, if we're learning about education, we might include Jean Piaget and Lev Vygotsky as theoretical guides, alongside modern educators or leaders whose work we admire.
3. *Balance Strengths and Weaknesses:* Each mentor should bring something unique to the table. Where one mentor

lacks timeless wisdom, another may provide cutting-edge insights. For instance, pairing a figure like the philosopher Seneca with someone like Tim Ferriss gives us a mix of ancient wisdom and modern productivity strategies.

Even without direct access to these mentors, their books, talks, and videos can offer valuable guidance, aiding us in navigating our personal and professional journeys.

Key Skills to Develop in Our Zone of Proximal Development

Now that we understand the importance of mentorship and self-directed learning, let's focus on some of the key skills that can yield lifelong benefits. These are skills that can be nurtured within our Zone of Proximal Development and continuously refined as we grow.

Here are some crucial skills to consider developing:

- Lifelong learning and skill acquisition
- Grit and resilience
- Adaptability
- Critical and creative thinking
- Emotional intelligence
- Leadership and decision-making
- Personal effectiveness and time management
- Reflection and meditation
- Self-control and discipline

Each of these skills can help us grow, both personally and professionally. By identifying which areas are most relevant to our goals and finding mentors to guide us, we can make consistent progress and continue evolving throughout our lives.

Stepping Into Our Zone of Proximal Development

Understanding and applying the concepts of the *Zone of Proximal Development* and *constructivism*—combined with the strategic use of mentorship—can profoundly enhance our personal development. By building on the knowledge we already have and seeking guidance from mentors, we can step into our ZPD and achieve growth that goes beyond what we thought possible.

Becoming better individuals is a continuous journey, and with the right mentors by our side, we can keep evolving. Whether we're learning a new skill, navigating a career change, or pursuing personal growth, stepping into our Zone of Proximal Development —and being guided by those who've walked the path before us— will ensure that we keep moving forward.

Every significant leap in development begins with the courage to step beyond what we know and the wisdom to seek guidance along the way.

THE POWER OF STRUGGLE
OPPONENT PROCESS & SKILL REFINEMENT

Understanding the Opponent Process Theory

Acquiring and refining skills is difficult, but these struggles are essential to achieving mastery. This concept is powerfully illustrated by the *Opponent Process Theory*, which posits that contrasting experiences—such as hardship followed by relief—create balance.When we apply this to learning, we see that challenges aren't obstacles to skill acquisition; they are the fuel that drives progress. The struggles we face during the process of skill development are not only inevitable but beneficial, which leads to greater mastery.

Struggle as a Catalyst for Skill Improvement

When it comes to skill acquisition, struggle and success are two sides of the same coin. Every time we wrestle with a difficult concept, we are laying the groundwork for getting better in the future. The initial frustration and difficulty learners face are crucial. As we persist through challenges, we develop more effective strategies, deeper understanding, and enhanced skills.

I found this to be true when I would learn difficult pieces of music as a musician. At first, the complexity of the notes and rhythms seems overwhelming, and frustration sets in. But with each practice session, I saw the small improvements accumulate. My struggle to master the intricate passages sharpened my technique, deepened my understanding of the music, and strengthened my confidence. What was once overwhelming became second nature, and the struggle itself was a key part of that growth.

I see this happen with my chemistry students as well. When they first encounter a difficult concept, I observe them struggle with it until it clicks.

Improving Skills Through Struggle

Skill acquisition is often marked by plateaus and frustrations. The Opponent Process Theory suggests that overcoming these challenges is the key to advancing to higher levels of skill. When learners face difficulties, those moments of discomfort trigger adaptation, allowing them to break through learning plateaus. The intensity of the struggle directly correlates with the depth of the learning that follows.

Athletes, for example, often talk about "hitting the wall" during training—where it seems like no amount of effort will make them better. But pushing through this phase leads to breakthroughs in performance.

The harder the struggle, the greater the potential reward that awaits on the other side.

Across fields—from academics to sports to the arts—people will face the initial challenges of learning new skills. A student wrestling with advanced mathematics may feel overwhelmed by the complexity of new concepts, but through persistence and practice, they become better at problem-solving. A dancer learning a new routine stumbles through the first few rehearsals; yet, those early missteps become the foundation for eventual precision and grace.

Implications for Learners and Educators

For both learners and educators, the Opponent Process Theory holds significant implications. Educators can create learning environments that embrace challenge, helping students see struggle as an essential part of the learning process. By designing tasks that stretch students just beyond their comfort zone, educators can foster resilience and deep learning.

A practical example is incorporating reflective practices after students face challenges. When students pause to reflect on their learning, they often realize that the struggle they faced was an essential part of their growth. This not only builds confidence but also encourages them to tackle future challenges with a stronger mindset.

Chase the Struggle

Chase the struggle. That's where the learning is. Every obstacle we face during skill acquisition refines not only our abilities but also our character. Struggle isn't just a byproduct of the learning process —it's a powerful driver of mastery. Challenges don't stop us from getting better, they elevate our skills to new heights.

The greater the intensity of the struggle, the more profound the learning. Embracing this dynamic allows us to transform difficulties into stepping stones toward mastery. Real growth occurs when we push through frustration, and on the other side, we discover a higher level of proficiency, resilience, and self-confidence.

SMALL WINS
THE 1% RULE

"We are what we repeatedly do. Excellence, then, is not an act, but a habit." - Will Durant (*The Story of Philosophy*)

Excellence isn't achieved in a single moment but through the accumulation of small, intentional actions. Every day, the decisions we make—no matter how small—contribute to shaping our lives and bringing us closer to the person we aspire to be. This brings us to the 1% Rule, a powerful principle that illustrates how we can create lasting change through consistent, small wins.

The Essence of Habit Formation

Life consists of small, seemingly insignificant moments. Our future is determined by the choices we make during these moments—whether we decide to take action or remain stagnant. The key to building the life we dream of lies in embracing these moments and making decisions that align with our highest ideals. By consistently embodying our ideal self, we gradually construct our dream life, one step at a time.

However, maintaining such a high standard of decision-making on a daily basis can be daunting. This is where habits come in, acting as the autopilot for our brains, allowing us to conserve energy while staying on course toward our goals.

Habits in Lifestyle Design

In his book *Atomic Habits*, James Clear emphasizes that our habits serve as the building blocks of success. Habits automate repetitive tasks, freeing up cognitive resources for learning and mastering new skills. When we design our habits intentionally, we lay the foundation for an ideal lifestyle.

The small actions we take today, when repeated over time, can produce massive results.

The 1% Rule and Continuous Improvement

"Small helpful or harmful behaviors and inputs tend to accumulate over time, producing huge results. According to *Lean Thinking* by James P. Womack and Daniel T. Jones, Toyota's approach is based on the Japanese concept of kaizen, which emphasizes the continual improvement of a system by eliminating muda (waste) via a lot of very small changes. Many small improvements, consistently implemented, inevitably produce huge results." - Josh Kaufman (*The Personal MBA*)

The 1% Rule, promoted by authors like James Clear, Josh Kaufman, and Jeff Olsen, focuses on the power of small, consistent improvements. Whether we're blogging, producing music, or learning a new skill, aiming for just a 1% improvement with each attempt can lead to massive growth over time. This principle is versatile and can be applied to virtually any aspect of life—physical fitness, career advancement, relationships, or personal development.

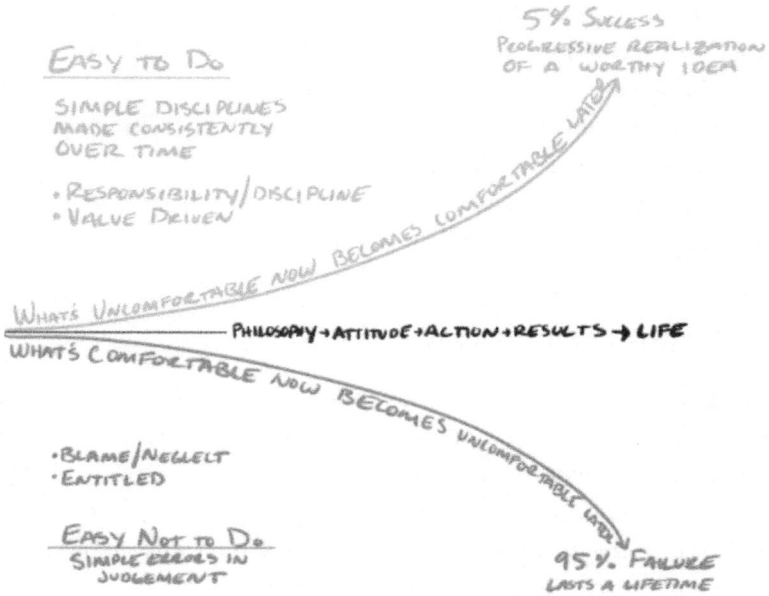

The hand-drawn figure shows:

EASY TO DO

SIMPLE DISCIPLINES MADE CONSISTENTLY OVER TIME

- RESPONSIBILITY/DISCIPLINE
- VALUE DRIVEN

5% SUCCESS
PROGRESSIVE REALIZATION OF A WORTHY IDEA

WHAT'S UNCOMFORTABLE NOW BECOMES COMFORTABLE LATER

PHILOSOPHY → ATTITUDE → ACTION → RESULTS → LIFE

WHAT'S COMFORTABLE NOW BECOMES UNCOMFORTABLE LATER

- BLAME/NEGLECT
- ENTITLED

EASY NOT TO DO
SIMPLE ERRORS IN JUDGEMENT

95% FAILURE
LASTS A LIFETIME

The Two Life Path from The Slight Edge

At first glance, a 1% improvement may seem insignificant. But over time, these small gains compound, transforming who we are day by day. Clear suggests that success isn't a one-time achievement but rather the cumulative result of our daily habits.

The Compounding Nature of Habits

The compounding effect of habits can work for or against us. Just as positive actions accumulate toward success, negative habits can drag us toward failure. This is why it's essential to recognize that every decision, no matter how small, contributes to the direction of our lives. We either climb toward our best selves, or we slide toward a life of regret.

"If you do not change direction, you may end up where you are headed" - Confucius

This principle extends beyond our actions, and also includes our thoughts. What we repeatedly tell ourselves shapes our identity. When we consistently affirm our strengths, we're more likely to believe in our power. Conversely, if we constantly reinforce feelings of inadequacy, those beliefs will take root and limit us. Our thought habits are just as malleable as our physical habits, and they too can be shaped by small, consistent changes.

The Math & Science Behind the 1% Rule

The 1% Rule is not just an abstract idea—it's rooted in scientific principles, like the second law of thermodynamics, which states that entropy (disorder) naturally increases over time. In life, if we are not actively improving, we are inevitably decaying. This is why continuous improvement is essential: it's not only a pathway to growth but also a means of preventing decline.

We need to put in effort simply to maintain where we are. Without deliberate action, entropy will lead us into stagnation. By applying the 1% Rule, we can combat this natural tendency toward disorder and create a life of continuous progress.

A 1% daily improvement results in a 37.8-fold gain over a year, while a 1% daily decline results in a 97% loss over the same period. These numbers illustrate the profound impact small, consistent actions can have over time.

$$1.01^{365} = 37.8$$
$$0.99^{365} = 0.03$$

Practical Steps for Implementing the 1% Rule

Implementing the 1% Rule in our lives begins with setting realistic, achievable goals that encourage incremental progress. Focus on improving just a little each day, and over time, we'll experience significant growth.

For example, if we're bloggers and we commit to improving our writing by 1% each week, we'll naturally build the habit of writing regularly. This small goal not only helps us improve our craft but also builds consistency—an essential factor for success in any endeavor.

Similarly, if we aim to improve our fitness by 1% each day, we might start with small changes like adding an extra five minutes to our workouts or swapping out one unhealthy snack. These seemingly minor actions accumulate, and before we know it, we've made substantial progress.

The Compounding Power of Small Wins

The 1% Rule provides a powerful framework for personal and professional development. By embracing the principle of compound improvements, we can counteract the natural tendency toward entropy and achieve significant growth. Every day presents a new opportunity to improve, and with each small win, we move one step closer to becoming the best version of ourselves.

Success, like failure, is the result of compounded habits. The difference between those who succeed and those who fail often lies in the small choices they make each day. Successful people choose the path of continuous improvement, even when it's difficult in the short term, knowing it will bring long-term rewards. Those who fail tend to choose what's easy in the moment, only to face discomfort later on.

In the end, the choice is simple: will we improve by 1% today, or will we let entropy take its course?

THE LONG GAME
PATIENCE, PERSISTENCE, AND SYSTEMS THINKING

"We often overestimate what we can do in a year, but underestimate what we can do in ten." - Bill Gates

What if we could have whatever we wanted in 20 years —our dreams realized, our goals achieved—but it would take two whole decades? Would it still be worth pursuing? Now, what if we couldn't get *any* of it until the full 20 years had passed—no shortcuts, no instant rewards? Would we still stay the course?

What if the challenge we face today took 9 months to solve? Would it still be worth our effort?

Take a moment to zoom in on where we are right now on this long, invisible timeline of our life. What actions should we take today, this week, this month, to move forward—one tiny step at a time?

The Valley of Disappointment

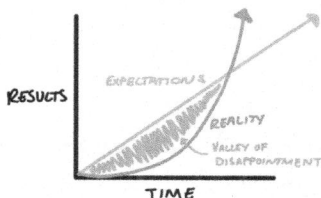

James Clear's The Valley of Disappointment

New habits rarely make a noticeable difference at first because real progress doesn't follow a linear path. As James Clear's *expectancy curve* suggests, progress often resembles a logarithmic curve: initial results are slow and almost invisible. It's not until reality meets our expectations, also known as the *critical point*, that the real transformations begin to show.

The Valley of Disappointment is a period during which effort seems to outweigh results, causing many people to give up too soon. But real progress often happens underground, much like the growth of a bamboo tree. During the first years, the bamboo appears to be doing nothing. But beneath the surface, roots are stretching deep and strong. And then, one day, it surges upward seemingly overnight.

It's the same with habit development. We won't always see instant gratification, but that doesn't mean progress isn't happening. To witness the transformative power of new habits, we must persist beyond *The Valley of Disappointment*: stay patient, stay focused, and, most importantly, create systems that support our growth.

Confronting Challenges with Constant Rigore

"How you do anything is how you do everything." - Dr. Andre Pinesett

This philosophy shapes my approach to life. Whether I'm writing a blog post or tackling mundane tasks, I strive for excellence in everything I do. It's not about being perfect—it's about showing up consistently and doing my best. This shapes my identity as someone who doesn't settle for half-measures, no matter the task at hand.

One of the greatest lessons I've learned, especially from teaching, is that how we confront challenges defines who we become. I've seen students approach the same problem in very different ways. Some get frustrated and try to bypass it, others double down and work through the frustration, and a few pretend they understand when they really don't. I don't judge their choices—each choice reveals a different relationship with challenges.

My role as a teacher is to help students enhance their problem-solving skills by meeting them where they are and guiding them through their struggles. Finding their zone of proximal development and guiding them forward. I believe life's challenges are similar—every obstacle is an opportunity to practice resilience and grow stronger.

If we were to take only one thing away from our education, it should be the ability to surmount challenges in a healthy way. The math problems my students face are low-risk training grounds for much bigger challenges in life. Learning to face challenges head-on is invaluable practice.

Leonardo da Vinci has a famous mantra, *Ostinato rigore*— constant rigor. Consistency in effort and persistence in the face of difficulty create the foundation for true mastery. Our performance in life reflects our training, not our goals. Rigorous, steady practice leads to a baseline of excellence, which is essential for changing habits and achieving success.

Set Up Systems, Not Goals

Goals define what we want to achieve; systems determine the processes that get us there. The truth is, people who achieve massive success don't win because they set big, ambitious goals. They win because they run better systems. Here's why:

- *Winners and losers often have the same goals.* It's not the goal that makes the difference, but the system behind achieving it. Winners focus on the process.
- *Achieving a goal is satisfying—but only for a moment.* If all you're chasing is the end result, you'll need a new goal as soon as the first is achieved. And if you fail to meet that goal, disappointment follows. But if you fall in love with the *process* of improvement, you allow yourself to be happy, no matter the outcome.
- *Solving problems at the goal level is momentary.* Solving them at the systems level, however, prevents similar problems from recurring. Systems are sustainable.

When I set up systems in my life, I look for patterns in my repeated decisions or actions. For example, if I notice that I'm always struggling to find time for exercise, I might create a system where I schedule a specific time every day for a 20-minute workout. I don't have to think about it, I just follow the system. Over time, these results compound.

Systems don't need to be complex at the start; in fact, they shouldn't be. Simple systems are easier to stick with, and over time, you can refine and expand them. The key is consistency.

Practical Tips for Building Systems

So how do we build systems in our lives?

1. *Identify one habit to develop.* Maybe it's getting fitter, learning a new skill, or reading more. Start small.
2. *Create a system around that habit.* If we want to exercise more, for example, schedule a specific time each day. Keep it simple, like 20 minutes of walking or 10 minutes of stretching.
3. *Track progress.* Even if it seems like nothing is changing, stick with it. Remember, the early results may be invisible, but we're building a foundation.
4. *Refine the system over time.* As we get more comfortable, we can adjust and improve. Add new elements or change the routine to keep it engaging.

The key to long-term success lies in focusing on systems, not just goals. Systems keep us on track during the hard, slow phases of growth. They provide the structure needed to push through *The Valley of Disappointment* and reach the *critical point* where results begin to compound.

SHAPING IDENTITY
THE KEY TO PERSONAL TRANSFORMATION

"Few are born bold. Even Napoleon had to cultivate the habit on the battlefield, where he knew it was a matter of life and death. In social settings, he was awkward and timid, but he overcame this and practiced boldness in every part of his life because he saw its tremendous power, how it could literally enlarge a man (even one who, like Napoleon, was in fact conspicuously small)." – Robert Greene (*The 48 Laws of Power*)

Identity isn't just how we see ourselves; it's a dynamic force that shapes our habits, actions, and life trajectory. Far from being fixed, our identity is something we can consciously craft, using it as the foundation for profound personal growth.

The Power of Habits in Identity Formation

Habits are the building blocks of our lives, yet they can be notoriously difficult to form or break. This struggle underscores the significance of motivation, discipline, and patience in habit formation. Yet, at the heart of this process is something even more fundamental—our identity.

The relationship between habits and identity is not one-way; they are deeply intertwined, continuously reinforcing one another in a feedback loop. When we act in ways that align with a particular identity, those actions solidify that identity, making it easier to repeat those behaviors.

Identity and Habit: A Feedback Loop

Identity is our most powerful motivational force. At its core, *Identity Defense* posits that our actions tend to align with how we perceive ourselves. If our sense of self doesn't match a task, we'll resist doing it. However, when a behavior aligns with our identity, we naturally lean into it.

For instance, when I first started writing my blog, it felt awkward and foreign, like I was playing a role I hadn't earned. I wasn't a writer—at least, not yet. But over time, as I continued to write, the act became easier, and soon enough, it felt like a natural part of who I was. Writing transformed from something I did into a part of who *I was*.

This same process unfolded when I took on other identities— whether as a musician, an EMT, or even as a teacher. At first, these roles felt uncomfortable, like putting on a jacket that didn't fit. But with consistent action, these identities became my own. Our actions provide evidence of who we are, and over time, that evidence reshapes our sense of self.

Identity Shape Our Habits Shape Our Identity

The Identity Feedback Loop

1. *Decide who we want to become*
2. *Take consistent actions that align with that identity*
3. *Watch as our actions reinforce our identity, making future behaviors easier*

This cycle works both ways. If we can consciously shape our identity, we can harness the immense power of our self-perception. The more deeply we anchor our habits to an identity, the greater our motivation to maintain those habits. The reverse is true as well: the more we engage in habits, the more our identity will shift to match.

Creating Evidence for Identity

"Every action you take is a vote for the type of person you wish to become. No single instance will transform your beliefs, but as the votes build up, so does the evidence of your new identity." – James Clear (*Atomic Habits*)

Every action, no matter how small, helps construct our identity. When we consistently engage in a behavior—whether it's writing, exercising, or studying—we accumulate evidence that reinforces a specific identity. Over time, this incremental process transforms our self-perception.

The key lies in shifting our focus from *doing* to *being*. Instead of merely reading, we can see ourselves as readers. Instead of simply writing a blog post, we can view ourselves as writers. This subtle shift in perspective profoundly impacts both motivation and behavior.

- Don't read—*be* a reader.
- Don't study—*be* a scholar.
- Don't write—*be* a writer.

By focusing on being rather than doing, we shift our actions to align with the identity we want to embody.

The Pitfalls of Over-Attachment to Identity

While identity can be a powerful motivator, it's important to remain flexible. Over-identifying with certain traits—such as being a 'winner' or 'intellectual'—can lead to cognitive dissonance and stifle growth. A rigid attachment to any one identity can make it difficult to adapt when things don't go as planned.

Common Problematic Identities

- *Success/Failure* – Defining ourselves strictly as a 'success' sets us up for disappointment when we inevitably encounter failure. Conversely, identifying too much with failure can lead to decision paralysis and a fear of taking risks. The truth is, success and failure are merely indicators of the effectiveness of past actions, not reflections of our worth.
- *Youth/Young* – Youth is fleeting, and over-identifying with being young or "cool" can create emotional distress when time passes and new generations take the stage. As Seneca once said, "What is more foolish than identifying with that which is fleeting?"
- *Intelligent* – While intelligence is a valuable trait, identifying too strongly with it can lead to intellectual arrogance. The moment we believe we are infallible, we stop growing. True wisdom comes from recognizing the limits of our knowledge.

Overcoming Imposter Syndrome

Imposter Syndrome often arises when we lack sufficient evidence to support our new identity. It's the voice that tells us we're not good enough, that we don't deserve our accomplishments. However, experiencing Imposter Syndrome doesn't mean we're incapable; it simply means we need more proof.

The way to overcome it is simple: *keep creating evidence.* Small, consistent wins eventually silence the voice of doubt. Even Leonardo Da Vinci struggled with self-doubt, as evidenced in his notebooks, but he pushed forward regardless.

> "Many will think they may reasonably blame me... not considering that my works are the issue of pure and simple experience, who is the one true mistress." – Leonardo Da Vinci (*The Notebooks of Leonardo Da Vinci*)

If Da Vinci could struggle with self-doubt and still achieve greatness, so can we. Imposter Syndrome is just another obstacle to overcome, a signal that we need to keep improving, not that we aren't good enough.

Crafting the Identity We Desire

Identity is not static; it is something we can shape and mold through our habits and actions. By consciously deciding who we want to become and taking consistent actions that align with that vision, we can create profound, lasting change in our lives. The power of identity lies not in who we are today, but in who we choose to become tomorrow.

BREAKING OLD HABITS, BUILDING NEW HABITS
THE HABIT CYCLE AND CHANGING OUR LIVES

E ver wondered why it's so hard to start a good habit and so easy to fall into a bad one? Whether it's scrolling social media or hitting the gym, habits shape almost half of our daily actions. 40-50% of what we do every day is governed by habits —automatic behaviors that save our brains from being over-whelmed by decision-making. Understanding how habits work helps us take control and intentionally shape the lives we want to lead.

We can learn a lot about the intricacies of habit formation, from James Clear's *Atomic Habits* and Josh Kaufman's *Personal MBA*.

The Power of Habit Loops

Without habits, our brains would shut down, overwhelmed by the minutiae of daily life.

> "Without habit loops, our brains would shut down, overwhelmed by the minutiae of daily life. People whose basal ganglia are damaged by injury or disease often become mentally paralyzed. They have

trouble performing basic activities, such as opening a door or deciding what to eat. They lose the ability to ignore insignificant details—one study, for example, found that patients with basal ganglia injuries couldn't recognize facial expressions, including fear and disgust, because they were perpetually uncertain about which part of the face to focus on." - Charles Duhigg (*The Power of Habit*)

In essence, habits free up our mental energy for bigger decisions, but they can also lock us into cycles we'd rather escape. The key is understanding how these cycles work.

Four Categories of Habits

Josh Kaufman, author of *Personal MBA*, breaks down habits into four categories:

- Things we want to start doing
- Things we want to stop doing
- Things we want to do more
- Things we want to do less

This simple framework helps us analyze our habits and make conscious changes.

I use this framework to categorize my habits. It helps me focus on which specific behaviors I want to change. I try to focus on one habit that I want to stop doing or do less and one habit that I want to start doing or do more. When I try to stop more than one habit, I tend to get off track. The same is true for when I try to start more than one habit. However, I have found success with stopping one habit and starting a new habit.

The Habit Cycle

James Clear outlines four stages of habit formation:

1. *Cue:* The trigger that initiates the behavior.
2. *Craving:* The desire or motivation that follows the cue.
3. *Response:* The action we take in response to the craving.
4. *Reward:* The satisfying feeling we get from completing the action.

By understanding this loop, we can either strengthen or weaken the habits that shape our lives.

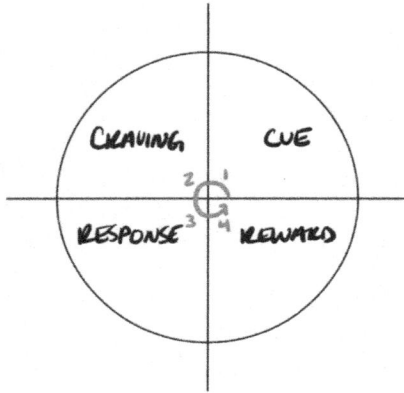

The Habit Cycle

The Habit of Escapism

Let's say I'm working on a blog post and hit a difficult section.

- *Cue:* I encounter a frustrating problem.
- *Craving:* I want relief from the frustration.
- *Response:* I turn off my computer and start playing video games.
- *Reward:* I feel relieved and entertained, temporarily forgetting about the problem.

Although this may bring temporary relief, recognizing the cycle enables me to decide whether to reinforce or break this habit. To break it, I could replace video games with a quick walk or some stretching—activities that relieve tension without pulling me away from my goal.

We can take intentional steps to create the life we desire by paying attention to what causes our cravings.

Breaking Old Habits: Replace, Resist, and Reinvent

Many believe the best way to break a bad habit is to replace it with a better one. Dr. Elliot Berkman from the University of Oregon supports this, noting that it's easier to start doing something new than to stop an old habit cold turkey.

When trying to break a habit, we can consider three factors:

- *Desire:* How badly do we want to break the habit?
- *Time:* How long have we had the habit? New habits are easier to stop than deeply ingrained ones.
- *Consequences:* What will happen if we don't break the habit?

Harnessing Friction

One of the most effective ways to break a bad habit is to add *friction*—obstacles that make it harder to perform the unwanted behavior. For example, placing your phone across the room at night reduces the temptation to scroll first thing in the morning.

Friction is a powerful tool. I use it constantly in my life. When I want to stop a habit, I increase the friction. When I want to build a new one, I reduce it. This method works about 90% of the time for me, and it can work for others too.

Inverting the Habit Loop

Another strategy to break habits is to invert each step of the habit cycle:

1. *Cue:* Remove or hide the trigger. Out of sight, out of mind.
2. *Craving:* Make the desire unattractive, such as by reminding ourselves of the long-term negative consequences of indulging in the craving.
3. *Response:* Increase the difficulty of performing the habit. Adding friction is key here.
4. *Reward:* Make the reward unsatisfying. If the reward isn't worth the effort, we're less likely to repeat the habit.

Emotional states like hunger, anger, loneliness, and tiredness (H.A.L.T) can weaken our willpower and make us more susceptible to falling into old habits. Recognize these states and prepare accordingly.

Building New Habits

When we try to create new habits, it's useful to keep in mind that we only want to do things when we believe it will pay off for us. If we believe it won't pay off or might harm us, we're unlikely to do it.

We have to believe it is worth it. We can get to this place through careful reflection.

Encouraging the Habit Cycle

To build new habits, make each stage of the habit loop work in our favor:

1. *Cue:* Make it obvious. Use visual reminders or tie the habit to an existing routine.
2. *Craving:* Make it attractive. Associate the habit with something you enjoy.
3. *Response:* Make it easy. Start with small, manageable tasks.

4. *Reward:* Make it satisfying. Celebrate small wins to reinforce the behavior.

Traits Are Habits in Disguise

Our habits don't just influence what we do—they shape who we are. Habits can build traits like honesty, courage, or reliability. By consciously choosing habits, we can develop traits we admire in others.

This means we can create habits that mirror the qualities we respect in our role models. We can look to people we admire to get an idea of which habits to build.

How Long Does It Take to Form a Habit?

Research from University College London found that, on average, it takes 66 days to form a new habit. Some people take as few as 18 days, while others need up to 254 days. The key is repetition in the same context—over time, the behavior becomes automatic.

Tim Ferriss, in *Tools of Titans*, emphasizes the importance of starting small. When building new habits, it's crucial to rig the game in our favor. It takes only five sessions to start forming a habit. These sessions don't have to be long—keep them short and simple. The goal is consistency, not perfection. Additionally, these sessions don't just need to be short—they can also be easy.

For example, when I first started exercising regularly, I kept my sessions short and easy for the first five times. Now, it feels strange if I don't get some form of exercise each day.

Conserve and Focus Willpower

Building new habits takes willpower, but it's not an infinite resource. To conserve it, optimize the environment. Arrange your environment to encourage good habits and discourage bad ones by introducing friction where necessary. This is known as building a guiding environment.

Additionally, focus on one habit at a time.

"For best results, focus on installing one Habit at a time. Remember, you only have so much Willpower to use each day, and overriding your default mode of action depletes it quickly. If you try to install too many Habits at the same time, you probably won't succeed at adopting any of them for long. Focus on installing one Habit until taking action feels automatic, then move on to the next." - Josh Kaufman (*The Personal MBA*)

By focusing our attention, we increase our chances of success.

Win the Moment in Front of Us

Creating and breaking habits is a gradual process that requires patience, practice, and discipline. If our efforts don't seem to be working, try again and give it more time. We are surprisingly adaptable creatures, even though we're hardwired for routine.

At first, it's uncomfortable. But over time, it becomes worth it.

Remember, it all starts with the present moment. Win that moment, and we're on our way to creating the life we want.

THE ESSENCE AND POWER OF PRACTICE
PROCESS OVER PRODUCT

"Everything in life worth achieving requires practice. In fact, life itself is nothing more than one long practice session, an endless effort of refining our motions. When the proper mechanics of practice are understood, the task of learning something new becomes a stress-free experience of joy and calmness, a process which settles all areas in your life and promotes proper perspective on all of life's difficulties." - Thomas M. Sterner (*The Practicing Mind*)

Practice is not merely a means to an end but also a way to alleviate stress, enhance learning, and lead a fulfilling life. It's more than repetition; it's a pathway to presence and peace.

The Essence of Practice

At its core, practice is the *continuous effort to refine our actions and thoughts toward mastery*. But many of us see it as a chore, something to get through rather than to enjoy. This perception changes when we view practice not as a burden but as a source of freedom and therapy—a perspective beautifully articulated by Thomas M. Sterner. With the right mindset, practice transforms from a duty into a journey—one that calms the mind and brings clarity to all areas of life.

To truly appreciate the value of practice, let's see what makes it effective and meaningful.

Foundations for Effective Practice

"Practice encompasses learning but not the other way around." - Thomas M. Sterner (*The Practicing Mind*)

Self-Control and Awareness

The foundation of practice lies in *self-control* and *self-awareness*, both of which are anchored in the power of *attention*. Our ability to regulate emotions and focus thoughts is essential for meaningful practice. Without these elements, we're riding a horse with no reins —drifting aimlessly without control over where we're headed.

Self-control gives us the internal power to guide our actions, while self-awareness ensures that we engage with purpose. This is why an *internal locus of control*—the belief that we control our lives, not outside circumstances—is critical for effective practice.

Life as Practice

When we view life as one long practice session, every action, from the mundane to the complex, becomes an opportunity for growth. This shift in perspective helps us to approach all aspects of life with a dedication to constant improvement.

Our "life's work" doesn't emerge from a single moment of brilliance but rather from countless hours of practice, honing our craft day by day. I experienced this firsthand when I started writing this book. Initially, I was impatient and hard on myself for not finishing faster. But I didn't yet have the skills or knowledge to write the book I had envisioned. The skills and understanding had to be developed through practice—step by step, chapter by chapter.

Even though I know this intellectually, I still struggle with the idea that "this project should have been done yesterday." Sterner addresses this frustration in *The Practicing Mind* and lets us know that learning along the way is not only acceptable but necessary. There is no way I could have written this book without the time it took to practice writing day after day.

Mechanisms of Practice

Focus on the Process, Not the Outcome

One of the most profound lessons Sterner offers is the idea that we must focus on the process rather than the outcome. This shift in mindset is crucial for maintaining motivation and avoiding burnout. When we value each step of the journey, progress unfolds naturally, and we find satisfaction in the effort itself.

Focusing on the process, not the product, is the key to making practice effective, consistent, and cathartic.

This is analogous advice to "Set up systems, not goals."

I used to think that if I wanted to perform better, I needed to apply more pressure. But humans aren't diamonds; we don't thrive under constant, crushing stress. In fact, focusing too much on the end result often leads to frustration, impatience, and burnout. By shifting our focus to the process, we free ourselves from this pressure and allow growth to happen naturally. Pressure naturally dissipates when we focus on the process.

This is something I apply with my students. When they struggle with complex problems, I remind them to focus on the next step rather than the entire solution. One small step at a time often leads to the solution faster—and with less stress.

"When you focus on the process, the desired product takes care of itself with fluid ease. When you focus on the product, you immediately begin to fight yourself and experience boredom, restlessness, frustration, and impatience with the process." - Thomas M. Sterner (*The Practicing Mind*)

The last point about focusing on the process is that it's crucial to recognize there are no mistakes or judgment when we are truly immersed in the process. We are simply executing actions, observing the results, and making adjustments accordingly. There is no bad or wrong when we are focused on the process.

Judgment is the death of deliberate practice.

Focusing on the process seems like a great idea, but how do we start doing that?

Detachment and Presence

Detaching from the outcome doesn't mean abandoning our goals; it means freeing ourselves from the anxiety tied to them. By letting go of the need for immediate results, we open ourselves to the joy of being fully present in the process. This presence allows for deeper engagement and ultimately leads to better outcomes.

Mindfulness meditation is a great tool for cultivating this presence. It helps us train our attention, recognize when our mind is wandering, and bring it back to the present moment. When we focus solely on the task at hand, we make more meaningful progress.

We are capable of letting go of any attachments we develop, nothing is too substantial that it ought to take us from the present moment.

Once we cultivate healthy detachment, we focus solely on what we're doing in the present moment. As long as we can keep this up, we are accomplishing our goal in every moment.

Staying Present

Sterner provides four key principles to help us maintain a practicing mind. He calls them the "4 S Words":

- *Simple:* Keep things simple to reduce friction. Break large tasks into smaller, manageable pieces. Simplicity fosters momentum and makes progress feel attainable.
- *Small:* Focus on small, incremental steps. Tackling smaller sections of a task builds a series of small victories that fuel further progress.
- *Short:* Keep practice sessions short, especially when building new habits. It's easier to commit to a few minutes of effort daily than to an overwhelming, multi-hour session.
- *Slow:* Slow down. Taking things slowly allows us to be more mindful of each action, reducing mistakes and making the task less daunting.

The D.O.C. Cycle

Sterner also introduces the *D.O.C. cycle—Do, Observe, Correct—*as a simple yet powerful framework for engaging in practice. The D.O.C. cycle is also known as the practice cycle. This cycle guides us to take action, observe the outcome, and adjust accordingly. It's a feedback loop that keeps us moving forward without judgment.

When we step out of this cycle and allow frustration, impatience, or judgement to take over, we lose our ability to practice effectively. The key is to recognize when we've strayed from the cycle and bring ourselves back into it.

For example, when I write, I often feel judgmental or insecure. This is the death of practice. I've learned to quiet those thoughts, focus on the writing itself, and trust the process. Observing my work objectively and making small corrections is far more productive than succumbing to self-criticism.

Simply do the action, observe how we are doing, and correct course. Repeat.

The Power of Perspective: Perfection & Patience

Finally, practice teaches us the power of perspective. When is the flower perfect? Is it at the seed, or when it sprouts, or only when it blooms? The truth is, the flower is perfect at every stage. It's doing exactly what it needs to do in every moment.

We are the same. By focusing on the process and growing every day, we, too, are always perfect. This perspective takes the pressure off and helps us enjoy the journey.

Patience is key here. Practice without patience is fruitless. Patience allows us to appreciate the gradual progress that comes with deliberate practice. The only way we can see the results of our practice is through patience.

So how can we cultivate patience?

Sterner suggests that we can develop patience by changing our perspective. Sterner likes to think of patience more as *quiet perseverance*. By changing the vocabulary, we change our perspective of ourselves. Rather than seeing ourselves as someone waiting patiently for things to finally work out, we can become someone who is quietly overcoming all the obstacles thrown in front of them time and time again. This may seem like a small change, but humans are creatures of conversation and our worlds are created by our speech.

Impatience usually comes from trying to live in the future and being unsatisfied with the present. In my experience, the best way to cultivate patience is to be present in the moment and focus on what I can do in that moment, nothing else. Impatience is an indicator that we are being product focused. Another indicator is when our internal chatter starts going haywire. We have to be able to recognize when our thoughts are going off on a tangent and return ourselves to the present. Controlling our minds like this is challenging at first, but as I mentioned earlier, mindfulness meditation is excellent for cultivating this skill — noticing when the mind runs wild and pulling it back in. Like a wild horse, it's going to fight us but if we can tire it out then it'll stop running away.

Patience naturally comes with a change in perspective, just trying to "be more patient" is a fool's errand and is incredibly expensive from a cognitive load perspective. If we correctly change our perspective, we can feel the impatience vanish.

> "The problem with patience and discipline is that developing each of them requires both of them." - Thomas M. Sterner (*The Practicing Mind*)

Practical Advice for Cultivating a Practicing Mind

- *Remain Process-Oriented:* Focus on the current action, not the distant goal.
- *Stay Present:* Engage fully with the task at hand.
- *Make the Process the Goal:* Let the larger goal guide, not dictate, your actions.
- *Be Deliberate:* Practice with intention and maintain awareness of that intention.

Practice, Practice, Practice

Thomas M. Sterner's *The Practicing Mind* reminds us that life is a long practice session. Through patience and persistence, the art of practice leads not only to the achievement of our goals but to a deeper understanding of life itself. Every moment spent in practice is a victory, and with the right mindset, we win each day—not just at the finish line.

By cultivating a practicing mind, we not only enhance our skills but also enrich our lives with joy, calmness, and a sense of accomplishment.

We are always perfect, but we are always practicing.

We are always growing; the only question is, in which direction?

BOOK REFERENCES & RECOMMENDATIONS

FOR SKILLS & HABITS

"It's not about the book, it's about the book the book leads you to."
- Austin Kleon

Book References & Recommendations

What are Skills?: The Basis of Knowledge

- **"Outliers"** by Malcolm Gladwell
- **"Mindset"** by Carol S. Dweck
- **"Atomic Habits"** by James Clear
- **"Grit"** by Angela Duckworth
- **"The Talent Code"** by Daniel Coyle

Learning as a Skill: Mastering Knowledge

- **"Mindset"** by Carol S. Dweck
- **"Atomic Habits"** by James Clear
- **"The Talent Code"** by Daniel Coyle
- **"Grit"** by Angela Duckworth

- **"Peak"** by Anders Ericsson and Robert Pool
- **"Deep Work"** by Cal Newport
- **"The Power of Now"** by Eckhart Tolle
- **"Outliers"** by Malcolm Gladwell
- **"The 7 Habits of Highly Effective People"** by Stephen Covey
- **"A Mind for Numbers"** by Barbara Oakley

The Science Behind Gaining Skills: How Our Brains Shape and Retain Skills

- **"The Talent Code"**by Daniel Coyle
- **"Peak"** by Anders Ericsson and Robert Pool
- **"Atomic Habits"** by James Clear
- **"Mindset"** by Carol S. Dweck
- **"Deep Work"** by Cal Newport

The Brain & Learning: Anatomical Perspectives

- **"The Practicing Mind"** by Thomas M. Sterner
- **"The Power of Habit"** by Charles Duhigg
- **"How the Mind Works"** by Steven Pinker
- **"Thinking, Fast and Slow"** by Daniel Kahneman
- **"Atomic Habits"** by James Clear
- **"Principles: Life and Work"** by Ray Dalio
- **"MCAT Complete 7-Book Subject Review"** by Kaplan Test Prep

The Mind & Learning: Metaphysical Leverage

- **"Paradise Lost"** by John Milton
- **"The Practicing Mind"** by Thomas M. Sterner
- **"Thinking, Fast and Slow"** by Daniel Kahneman
- **"Atomic Habits"** by James Clear
- **"The Power of Habit"** by Charles Duhigg

- "The Personal MBA" by Josh Kaufman
- "The Slight Edge" by Jeff Olson
- "Man and His Symbols" by Carl Jung
- "The Power of Now" by Eckhart Tolle
- "Memory: From Mind to Molecules" by Larry Squire and Eric Kandel
- "The Interpretation of Dreams" by Sigmund Freud
- "Cognitive Load Theory" by John Sweller

Learn Faster, Achieve More: The 20 Hour Rule & Meta-Skills

- "Mastery" by Robert Greene
- "The First 20 Hours" by Josh Kaufman
- "Atomic Habits" by James Clear
- "Peak"by Anders Ericsson and Robert Pool
- "Deep Work" by Cal Newport

The Valley of Disappointment & The Transition Curve: Embracing the Learning Journey

- "Atomic Habits" by James Clear
- "Mastery" by Robert Greene
- "Grit" by Angela Duckworth
- "The Talent Code" by Daniel Coyle
- "Deep Work" by Cal Newport

The Myth of Motivation: The Power of Discipline

- "On The Shortness of Life" by Seneca
- "Discipline Equals Freedom" by Jocko Willink
- "The Practicing Mind" by Thomas M. Sterner
- "The Slight Edge" by Jeff Olson
- "Atomic Habits" by James Clear
- "Extreme Ownership" by Jocko Willink and Leif Babin
- "The Power of Habit" by Charles Duhigg

- **"Mindset"** by Carol S. Dweck
- **"Can't Hurt Me"** by David Goggins
- **"Flow"** by Mihaly Csikszentmihalyi
- **"Deep Work"** by Cal Newport
- **"The War of Art"** by Steven Pressfield
- **"Ego Is the Enemy"** by Ryan Holiday
- **"The Power of Now"** by Eckhart Tolle
- **"The Tao of Physics"** by Fritjof Capra
- **"The Obstacle Is the Way"** by Ryan Holiday
- **"Grit"** by Angela Duckworth
- **"Limitless"** by Jim Kwik
- **"Make Your Bed"** by Admiral William H. McRaven
- **"The Compound Effect"** by Darren Hardy

The Mamba Mentality: Cultivating Consistency

- **"The Mamba Mentality"** by Kobe Bryant
- **"Relentless"** by Tim S. Grover
- **"Atomic Habits"** by James Clear
- **"Grit: The Power of Passion and Perseverance"** by Angela Duckworth
- **"Mindset"** by Carol S. Dweck

Fail Forward: Why Mistakes Are the Key to Mastery and Success

- **"Mastery"** by Robert Greene
- **"The Slight Edge"** by Jeff Olson
- **"Outwitting the Devil"** by Napoleon Hill
- **"Failing Forward"** by John C. Maxwell
- **"Atomic Habits"** by James Clear

The Path to Growth: The Power of Development and Mentorship

- **"Outwitting the Devil"** by Napoleon Hill
- **"The Personal MBA"** by Josh Kaufman

- "Constructivism in Education" by Jean Piaget
- "Mind in Society"by Lev Vygotsky
- "Letters from a Stoic" by Seneca
- "Tribe of Mentors" by Tim Ferriss

The Power of Struggle: Opponent Process & Skill Refinement

- "Mastery" by Robert Greene
- "The Talent Code" by Daniel Coyle
- "Grit" by Angela Duckworth
- "Peak"by Anders Ericsson and Robert Pool

Small Wins: The 1% Rule

- "Atomic Habits" by James Clear
- "Lean Thinking" by James P. Womack and Daniel T. Jones
- "The Personal MBA" by Josh Kaufman
- "The Slight Edge" by Jeff Olson
- "The Story of Philosophy" by Will Durant

The Long Game: Patience, Persistence, and Systems Thinking

- "Atomic Habits" by James Clear
- "The Slight Edge" by Jeff Olson
- "The Power of Habit" by Charles Duhigg
- "Lean Thinking" by James P. Womack and Daniel T. Jones

Shaping Identity: The Key to Personal Transformation

- "The 48 Laws of Power" by Robert Greene
- "Atomic Habits" by James Clear
- "The Notebooks of Leonardo Da Vinci" by Leonardo Da Vinci

- **"Letters from a Stoic"** by Seneca

Breaking Old, Building New: The Habit Cycle and Changing Our Lives

- **"Atomic Habits"** by James Clear
- **"The Power of Habit"** by Charles Duhigg
- **"The Personal MBA"** by Josh Kaufman
- **"Tools of Titans"** by Tim Ferriss

The Essence and Power of Practice: Process Over Product

- **"The Practicing Mind"** by Thomas M. Sterner
- **"Atomic Habits"** by James Clear
- **"Tools of Titans"** by Tim Ferriss

3

MINDFUL LEARNING

THE ART AND SCIENCE OF METACOGNITION

DISTINGUISHING KNOWLEDGE FROM WISDOM

THE FOUNDATIONS OF BEING A BETTER LEARNER

Knowledge and wisdom are often used interchangeably, but they fulfill distinct roles in how we navigate the world. Knowledge refers to the accumulation of facts, data, and information, while wisdom transcends this—applying knowledge thoughtfully by considering context, ethics, and long-term impact. Let's explore the key differences between knowledge and wisdom through philosophical, psychological, and cultural perspectives, while examining how metacognition transforms raw knowledge into actionable wisdom.

Philosophical Perspectives

In ancient philosophy, knowledge and wisdom were defined differently but recognized as interconnected. Plato described knowledge, or *episteme*, as justified true belief—a systematic understanding of why things are the way they are. In today's terms, we can compare this to our approach to scientific facts and objective truths, which are supported by reasoning and evidence.

Aristotle provided a more nuanced view, distinguishing between theoretical knowledge (*episteme*) and practical knowledge (*techne*). He introduced a third concept, *phronesis*, or practical wisdom. Unlike theoretical knowledge, *phronesis* represents the practical wisdom we employ to navigate daily complexities, particularly moral dilemmas. It's not just about knowing what is true but about understanding *how* to act ethically in specific situations.

This distinction between theoretical knowledge and practical wisdom reminds us that wisdom is not just about knowing facts but about making sound decisions in real-world contexts.

Psychological Perspectives

In the realm of psychology, the distinction between knowledge and wisdom takes on another dimension. Jean Piaget, a developmental psychologist, believed that knowledge is formed through a dynamic interaction between the individual and their environment. He described two processes that shape our understanding:

- *Assimilation:* Incorporating new information into existing frameworks without changing them.
- *Accommodation:* Adjusting cognitive frameworks to fit new information.

These processes explain why learning new ideas can be challenging—our minds must adapt to fit new information (accommodation) or conform new information to existing beliefs (assimilation).

However, wisdom goes beyond this. According to Robert J. Sternberg, wisdom is the application of intelligence and experience toward a common good. It requires balancing our interests with the interests of others, across both short and long-term perspectives. Wisdom, according to Sternberg, involves ethical action and demands a profound understanding of human behavior and values.

Where knowledge builds through direct experience and factual learning, wisdom involves the ability to make ethical judgments that benefit not just ourselves, but others around us. Sternberg's theory shows wisdom as contextual, relying on situational awareness and emotional intelligence.

Cultural Perspectives

Across different cultures, the distinction between knowledge and wisdom is shaped by values and traditions. In Eastern philosophies like Buddhism and Taoism, knowledge is often seen as external—gained through observation and study. Wisdom, by contrast, is an inner understanding that allows individuals to live in harmony with the Tao, or the natural way of things. Wisdom in these traditions emphasizes compassion, insight, and a deep awareness of the interconnectedness of all beings.

In Indigenous cultures, knowledge is often passed down through generations and is practical, focused on survival, understanding the land, and maintaining relationships with the natural world. Wisdom is the ethical and responsible use of this knowledge, guided by respect, spirituality, and the recognition of community. It teaches that knowing something is not enough—how we apply that knowledge determines its true value.

These cultural perspectives remind us that wisdom is not just about intellect or skill but about how knowledge is used in harmony with others and the world.

The Essence of Wisdom and Knowledge

"Wisdom is not accidental." - Friedrich Nietzsche

Nietzsche's insight that "wisdom is not accidental" points to an essential truth: wisdom must be pursued intentionally, with effort and self-awareness. It is not simply the byproduct of random experiences but is cultivated through reflection and deliberate practice.

In an age of information overload, intentional pursuit of wisdom is more critical than ever.

Nietzsche argued that knowledge should invigorate life rather than merely fill the mind with facts. It must be a catalyst for action and purpose. Similarly, Ryan Holiday reminds us that the pursuit of wisdom enables us to think independently, beyond what society or "the mob" expects. This independent critical thinking is crucial in an age where information is abundant, but wisdom is scarce.

While knowledge can be seen as the accumulation of facts, wisdom is about the thoughtful application of those facts. Wisdom demands that we consider the broader context, exercise judgment, and act with empathy and ethics.

The Role of Metacognition in Developing Wisdom

Metacognition—reflecting on how we think—is essential for transforming knowledge into wisdom. By reflecting on our own thought processes, we can become more aware of how we learn, solve problems, and make decisions.

Understanding our cognitive strengths and weaknesses allows us to optimize study strategies, tailor learning techniques to our personal needs, and make better, wiser decisions. This awareness not only improves how we acquire knowledge but also how we apply it to real-world situations.

Through metacognitive practices, learning becomes not just a matter of memorizing facts but of engaging deeply with the material, leading to greater retention and a stronger ability to apply that knowledge wisely.

The Universal Arts of Wisdom and Philosophy

Seneca, the Stoic philosopher, contended that wisdom and philosophy are universal arts, accessible to anyone willing to cultivate them. Although it was not called this at the time, he advocated for the cultivation of what John Keats called *Negative Capability*—the ability to entertain a thought without accepting it. This openness to diverse perspectives without immediate judgment is a hallmark of an educated, wise mind.

Anyone open to exploring diverse ideas can cultivate wisdom. It's a matter of patience, practice, and openness to learning from experience.

Bloom's Taxonomy: A Framework for Understanding

Bloom's Taxonomy is a useful framework for distinguishing different levels of thinking, from simple memorization to deep analysis and creation. It is a reminder that moving from knowledge to wisdom requires higher-order thinking, such as evaluation and creation.

Bloom's Taxonomy is organized into six major categories, each representing a distinct level of cognitive processing in learning. These categories, listed from the simplest form of thinking to the most complex, are:

1. *Remembering:* Recalling basic facts and concepts.
2. *Understanding:* Interpreting, summarizing, and paraphrasing information.
3. *Applying:* Using information in new situations.
4. *Analyzing:* Breaking information into parts to explore understandings and relationships.
5. *Evaluating:* Justifying a decision or course of action based on criteria and standards.
6. *Creating:* Combining elements to form a new coherent or functional whole.

When acquiring knowledge, the simpler forms of thinking—remembering and understanding—are most effective.

When we are transforming knowledge into wisdom, the more complex forms—analyzing, evaluating, and creating—become essential.

The more we engage in these higher-order processes, the deeper our understanding becomes, and the more likely we are to apply that knowledge wisely.

The Path to Wisdom

Knowledge and wisdom play distinct roles in our understanding of the world. Philosophical, psychological, and cultural perspectives show that knowledge is the foundation of facts and theories, while wisdom is the art of applying that knowledge with ethics, empathy, and judgment.

Through metacognition, we can enhance both our learning and decision-making, turning knowledge into wisdom. Ultimately, wisdom is a deliberate and lifelong pursuit, cultivated through self-awareness, ethical action, and a willingness to explore ideas deeply and critically.

As we strive to balance the accumulation of knowledge with the pursuit of wisdom, we come closer to living a more meaningful, purposeful life—one that benefits not only ourselves but also the world around us.

THE PARETO PRINCIPLE
THE 80/20 RULE IN LEARNING

"The 80/20 Principle tells us that a minority of causes, inputs, or effort usually lead to a majority of the results, outputs, or rewards."
- Richard Koch (*The 80/20 Principle*)

Ever feel like we're doing so much work, but only a little of it really pays off? Or maybe we've noticed that a few key habits bring us most of our success? That's the Pareto Principle in action—a simple idea that can change the way we learn, work, and live. Understanding the Pareto Principle, commonly referred to as the 80/20 rule, can make both our learning and life more efficient.

The Birth of the 80/20 Rule

The Pareto Principle is named after Vilfredo Pareto, an Italian economist from the 19th century. In 1896, Pareto observed that 80% of the land in Italy was owned by just 20% of the population. Curious, he started looking at other areas, like his garden. He noticed that 20% of his pea plants produced 80% of the peas.

Later, Dr. Joseph Juran, a management consultant, brought this idea into business and called it the "vital few and trivial many." Over time, this concept became known as the 80/20 rule: 80% of outcomes often result from 20% of inputs.

What Does This Have to Do with Learning?

> "Some material is more important than other material; focusing on what's essential helps to make your studying more productive."
> - Peter C. Brown (*Make It Stick*)

In learning, the Pareto Principle shows up everywhere. Here are a few examples:

- *Studying for Tests:* 20% of the material may account for 80% of the exam questions. If we can figure out which topics are most important, we can focus our time more wisely.
- *Skill Mastery:* When learning a new language, 20% of the vocabulary is used in 80% of conversations. Learning these key words first will get us speaking faster.
- *Improving Grades:* Small changes, such as reviewing notes for 15 minutes daily or asking one thoughtful question in class, can lead to significant improvements in understanding.

Other Everyday Examples

The Pareto Principle isn't just about learning. Once we see it, we'll notice it everywhere:

- *Business:* 80% of a company's profits often come from 20% of its products or customers.
- *Relationships:* 20% of your relationships bring 80% of your happiness.

- *Fitness:* 20% of exercises (like squats or push-ups) can give you 80% of the benefits.
- *Cleaning:* The initial 20% of effort (e.g., picking up clutter) often achieves 80% of the impact in how clean a room feels.

How to Use the Pareto Principle in Our Learning

Knowing about the Pareto Principle isn't enough. We need to use it! Here's how:

1. *Identify the Vital Few:* We can ask ourselves, "What's the 20% that will make the biggest difference?" Maybe it's reviewing core concepts, practicing key problems, or getting feedback from a teacher.
2. *Focus on Quality, Not Quantity:* Don't waste time on the "trivial many." Instead, spend energy on what matters most.
3. *Adjust as We Go:* Learning is not a one-size-fits-all process. Continuously assess whether you're focusing on the right things.

Why This Matters

"Doing less is not being lazy. Don't give in to a culture that values personal sacrifice over personal productivity." - Tim Ferriss (*The 4-Hour Workweek*)

Applying the Pareto Principle doesn't mean doing only 20% of the work. It means we work smarter. It helps us save time and energy while still achieving our goals.

When we apply this rule to learning, it's like finding a shortcut —but an honest one. It doesn't skip the hard work; it just focuses it where it counts most.

.   .   .

THE PARETO PRINCIPLE serves as a tool, not a law of nature. It won't always be exactly 80/20. Sometimes it's 70/30 or 90/10. The point is to notice patterns and direct our effort where it matters most.

Vilfredo Pareto probably never imagined his garden peas would inspire a way to rethink how we learn and live. But the next time we're overwhelmed with too much to do, we can remember: not everything is equally important. Prioritize the vital few, and allow the trivial many to take care of themselves.

And who knows? Maybe our 20% effort will lead to 80% of our success.

By learning smarter, not harder, we create more time for what truly matters—whether mastering a new subject, spending time with loved ones, or finally pursuing a long-delayed hobby.

EAT THE FROG
MASTERING COGNITIVE LOAD

"Eat a live frog first thing in the morning and nothing worse will happen to you the rest of the day." — Mark Twain

Every day, our brains juggle countless tasks, from remembering deadlines to tackling complex problems. But what happens when our mental to-do list becomes overwhelming? Enter *cognitive load*—the amount of mental effort required to complete a task. Managing this load is crucial for improving productivity, learning, and overall well-being.

Think of the brain like a computer. Just like a computer has limited RAM, our brain has limited mental capacity. When overloaded, it slows down, and our ability to process new information diminishes. To perform at our best, we need to manage that mental bandwidth.

Cognitive Load 101: What Is It?

Cognitive Load Theory, introduced by Australian psychologist John Sweller, helps us understand how much mental effort our working memory can handle at one time. Our working memory is where we process and store information in the short term. When it gets over-loaded, it's like trying to load too many programs on a computer—it crashes. Cognitive overload is like pulling an all-nighter and struggling to focus the next day.

Cognitive load comes in three types:

- *Extraneous Load*: This refers to the mental energy drained by distractions—such as noisy environments or unclear instructions. It's the 'mental static' that complicates learning and task completion.
- *Intrinsic Load*: This type of load is tied to the task's complexity. The more complicated the task, the more cognitive load it demands. Learning difficult subjects, like chemistry or calculus, naturally creates a heavier intrinsic load.
- *Germane Load*: This is the beneficial type of cognitive load—the mental effort dedicated to understanding and retaining new information.

The Consequences of Unfinished Tasks: The Zeigarnik Effect

Unfinished tasks seem to nag at us, even when we try to relax. This is called the *Zeigarnik Effect*, named after Russian psychologist Bluma Zeigarnik. She observed that waiters in a restaurant could easily remember customers' orders—until the food was served. Once the task was complete, the orders disappeared from memory.

In a study, Zeigarnik found that people remember incomplete tasks much better than finished ones. Unfinished tasks create mental tension, keeping them at the forefront of our minds until completed. This can make us feel overwhelmed, as we constantly replay what still needs to be completed.

When cognitive load is already high, unfinished tasks can push things beyond manageable levels. That's why we might find ourselves lying in bed at night, thinking about everything we didn't get done that day.

"Incomplete tasks and procrastination often lead to unhelpful thought patterns, impacting sleep, triggering anxiety, and draining mental resources." - *Hadassah Lipszyc*

Managing Cognitive Load

To be productive and mentally sharp, we need to know how to manage our *cognitive load threshold (CLT)*—the point when our brains say, "Enough!" Our CLT fluctuates throughout the day, with mornings typically being the time when we can handle the most mental effort.

This is why Mark Twain's advice about eating the frog—tackling the hardest task first thing in the morning—is so powerful. When we address challenging work early, we use our cognitive resources more effectively, leaving easier tasks for later in the day when our mental energy wanes.

Here's how we can optimize our cognitive load throughout the day:

- *Maximize the Signal-to-Noise Ratio:* Minimize distractions (the noise) and focus on what truly matters (the signal). This can mean turning off notifications, working in a quiet space, or using noise-canceling headphones. The less clutter in our environment, the more mental bandwidth we have for important tasks.
- *Minimize Daily Decisions:* Decision fatigue is real. The more decisions we make in a day, the more we drain our cognitive load. Streamline routines by creating a weekly meal plan, simplifying your wardrobe, and automating repetitive tasks to conserve mental energy for more significant decisions.
- *Tackle Tough Tasks First:* Our cognitive load threshold is highest in the morning. Use this time to dive into complex, demanding tasks. Once those are completed,

we'll feel more accomplished and can shift our focus to simpler, low-effort tasks later in the day.

- *Avoid Redundancy:* Engage the brain with novel challenges. Repetitive tasks can drain our cognitive load without adding value. Instead, focus on learning new skills or tackling fresh problems to keep sharp.
- *Collaborate:* Sharing the cognitive load with others— whether through teamwork or delegation—can prevent mental fatigue. Working together often leads to more creative solutions and allows us to divide and conquer.
- *Use Cognitive Aids:* Checklists, calendars, and reference guides are our brain's best friends. Offload mental effort onto these tools, freeing up cognitive capacity for more demanding tasks.
- *Minimize Context Switching:* Every time we switch tasks, our brain has to readjust, increasing our cognitive load. Concentrate on one task at a time to reduce the mental strain caused by task-switching.
- *Leverage the Modality Effect:* Combine visual and auditory learning to reduce cognitive load. For example, when learning a new concept, watch an explainer video while taking notes. This multimodal approach makes it easier to absorb and retain information.

The Yerkes-Dodson Curve

Our performance is directly tied to our cognitive load, but there's a sweet spot. Too little cognitive load leads to boredom, while too much causes anxiety and stress. This relationship is known as the *Yerkes-Dodson Curve*—a bell-shaped curve that shows how performance improves with moderate cognitive load and decreases with overload.

To perform at our best, we need to find that sweet spot—where we're challenged enough to stay engaged, but not so overwhelmed that we burn out.

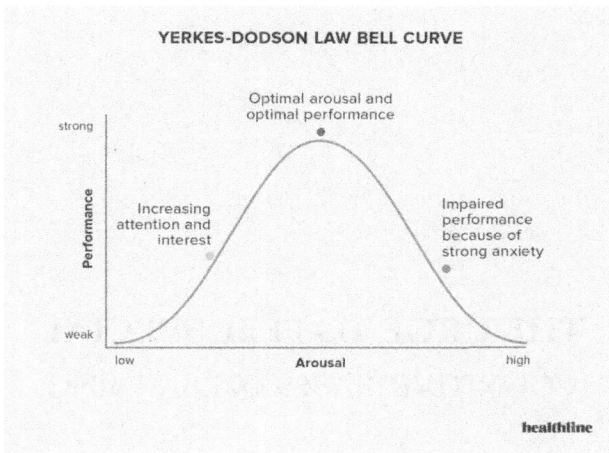

YERKES-DODSON LAW BELL CURVE

Image from healthline.com

Mastering Mental Bandwidth for Better Living

Managing cognitive load is not just about working smarter; it's about living better. By understanding the different types of cognitive load and implementing strategies to manage them, we can optimize our mental bandwidth and achieve more without feeling overwhelmed. Our brains are a powerful tool—when we give it the right conditions, it can handle anything we throw at it.

Begin each day by tackling your hardest task first, and observe how smoothly the rest of the day unfolds.

THE URGE TO FEEL SPECIAL
COGNITIVE BIASES IN LEARNING

I f we were to find a $5 bill on the ground, we would feel like luck was on our side. But we often overlook all the times we didn't find money on the ground. This simple moment reveals a profound truth: our interpretation of reality is shaped more by how we think than by what we know.

In learning and in life, we constantly face challenges. The key question is: when we encounter a problem, do we walk away, or do we try to solve it? Our cognitive biases—mental shortcuts that distort our perception—play a massive role in how we approach these challenges.

Why Cognitive Biases Matter in Learning

Cognitive biases influence how we process information, solve problems, and make decisions—often without our awareness. Neil deGrasse Tyson, in his MasterClass, emphasizes the importance of recognizing these biases to think more critically and effectively. This is especially crucial for students. Understanding cognitive biases isn't just about boosting academic performance; it's about seeing the world more clearly and solving problems more realistically.

Here are some of the most common cognitive biases, how they impact our learning journey—and more importantly, how to overcome them.

Key Cognitive Biases and Their Implications for Learners

Confirmation Bias: Seeing What We Want to See

Picture researching a paper and finding evidence that perfectly aligns with existing beliefs. We immediately latch onto that information, ignoring any data that contradicts your views. This is *confirmation bias* in action—our tendency to seek out and favor information that supports our preconceptions while dismissing or overlooking evidence that doesn't.

Horoscopes are a prime illustration of this. If our horoscope says we'll experience a positive change today, we're more likely to notice small positive events, reinforcing our belief in astrology—even though it's vague and unfounded. In learning, confirmation bias can hinder openness to new ideas or adjustment of beliefs based on new evidence.

How to Combat It: Practice open-mindedness. When researching or learning, actively seek out opposing viewpoints or contradictory evidence. Challenge your own assumptions and be willing to revise them.

Cultural Bias: The Lens Through Which We See the World

Cultural bias refers to the tendency to interpret other people's behavior, values, or beliefs through the lens of our own culture, often leading to misunderstandings. This bias can create barriers in diverse settings, including classrooms.

For example, if we're working in a multicultural group, we

might judge someone's communication style based on our cultural norms, without realizing that their approach is influenced by their background. This can lead to unfair assessments and missed opportunities for collaboration.

How to Combat It: Be culturally aware. Learn to recognize and respect different cultural values and approaches, particularly in group projects or discussions. Acknowledge that your cultural perspective is just one of many.

Availability Heuristic: The Danger of Anecdotal Evidence

Ever notice how vivid, memorable events seem more frequent than they actually are? That's the *availability heuristic* at work—a mental shortcut where we judge the likelihood of events based on how easily they come to mind.

For example, if we see news reports of airplane accidents, we might overestimate the dangers of air travel, even though it's statistically one of the safest modes of transportation. Similarly, students might overestimate the importance of anecdotal evidence over data, which can skew their understanding.

How to Combat It: Trust data, not just stories. Whether it's in our studies or daily life, rely on research and statistics rather than memorable anecdotes to form conclusions.

Dunning-Kruger Effect: Overestimating Our Abilities

The *Dunning-Kruger effect* occurs when people with limited knowledge or competence in a subject overestimate their abilities, while those with more expertise tend to underestimate theirs. This can be particularly deceptive for students, who might assume they've mastered a topic after covering the basics, not realizing how much more there is to learn.

For example, a novice chess player might challenge an expert with confidence, not understanding the depth of skill involved, while the expert may downplay their own abilities due to awareness of what they don't know.

How to Combat It: Maintain humility and curiosity. Acknowledge the limits of our knowledge and commit to continuous learning. Seek feedback and challenge ourselves to deepen our understanding.

Strategies for Overcoming Cognitive Biases

Now that we've explored a few key biases, how can students overcome them? Here are some practical strategies:

Critical Thinking and Skepticism

Neil deGrasse Tyson emphasizes the importance of healthy skepticism. This doesn't mean being cynical, but rather questioning the validity of information and seeking evidence before accepting claims. When faced with new information, ask yourself: *What's the evidence? How strong is it? Is it supported by research?*

Valuing Evidence Over Authority

Tyson encourages scientific thinking—not just acquiring knowledge, but also developing a mindset that values evidence over authority. In learning, this means questioning assumptions, seeking empirical evidence, and avoiding the trap of simply accepting information from "authoritative" sources without validation.

Self-Awareness and Reflection

Recognizing our biases is the first step toward overcoming them. We can take time to reflect on our thought processes and learning strategies. Are there biases influencing how we approach a problem or make decisions? Regular self-reflection can help us identify areas for growth.

Embrace Diverse Perspectives

Group work can be a powerful tool for challenging biases. By engaging with different viewpoints, learners can broaden their understanding and challenge their preconceptions. We can actively listen to others and be open to changing our minds.

Experimentation and Bias

Tyson uses a coin flip experiment to show how biases like confirmation bias can cloud our judgment. When participants predict a series of coin flips, those who guess correctly attribute their success to skill rather than recognizing it's just luck. This is a reminder of how easily we fall into cognitive traps. Be mindful of attributing success or failure to the wrong causes. Adopt a scientific mindset, particularly in experiments and decision-making.

Communication Tactics to Overcome Biases

Preparation and Communication

Preparation is key to clear communication. To deliver a message effectively, whether in a classroom presentation or a group discussion, we must be prepared to communicate our ideas in ways that others can understand. Being right is not enough; we must also be effective.

Finding Points of Connection

When sharing new ideas, it's helpful to find relatable examples to connect with our audience. Tyson suggests using points of connection that people take for granted to explain complex ideas, a technique that helps in overcoming cognitive biases by making unfamiliar concepts easier to grasp. Finding points of connection is a great way to help someone assimilate new knowledge into our current understanding.

Humor and Body Language

Tyson also recommends humor and body language as essential tools for communication. Humor can break down barriers and engage people, while body language reinforces the message. Effective communication isn't just about what we say; it's about how we say it.

Navigating the World Through Clearer Lenses

We don't navigate the world as it is—we navigate it as we perceive it. Cognitive biases act as filters, shaping our understanding in ways we often don't realize. By recognizing and overcoming these biases, students can approach learning—and life—with greater clarity, effectiveness, and humility.

Understanding these biases not only improves academic performance but also sharpens critical life skills. Neil deGrasse Tyson's lessons offer a roadmap for navigating the world more realistically, fostering better decision-making, and promoting continuous growth.

Cognitive biases are powerful forces in the mind, but we can overcome them by taking a little extra time to recognize the patterns and reevaluate what we think. Take time to slow down, reflect, and approach new knowledge with openness and healthy skepticism. This will not only improve our learning but also help us navigate life more effectively.

THE MEMORY BLUEPRINT
OUR MIND'S STORAGE SYSTEM

Understanding our memory system enhances our learning, problem-solving, and creative abilities. Memory is our ability to store and retrieve information and intersects various fields, including neuroscience, psychology, and biology. Our brain organizes and strengthens the knowledge we accumulate, making us more efficient learners and thinkers.

The Myth of Muscle Memory

First, let's address a common myth: "muscle memory" is a misnomer. Muscles don't store memories. Instead, the neurons controlling those muscles are responsible for memory storage.

When people talk about muscle memory, they're actually referring to the neurons controlling those muscles, which become more efficient with repeated brain commands. Initially, performing a task like learning a new dance move requires deliberate thought and high cognitive load. But over time, the neurons controlling the muscles become more efficient, and these actions become automatic. This is why certain physical actions, like riding a bike or typing, feel second nature after enough practice.

It's not our muscles remembering—it's the efficient use of neurons.

A Closer Look at Memory Types

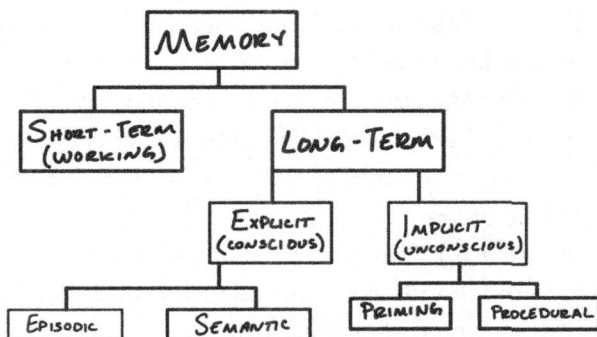

Memory Tree

Working Memory vs. Long-Term Memory

Working memory functions like a small whiteboard, temporarily holding information—such as a phone number we're about to dial or a sentence we just read. But its capacity is limited, usually able to handle around 7 items at a time, and only for about a minute.

In contrast, long-term memory is like a vast library with almost limitless space, capable of storing knowledge for years. The transition of information from our "whiteboard" to the "library" happens mainly in the hippocampus, particularly when we sleep or when strong emotions are involved. These processes help make fleeting information stick.

Emotionally charged events, such as the first day at a new school, are more likely to be stored in long-term memory because the brain prioritizes significant experiences.

Types of Long-Term Memory

- *Explicit Memory:* These are our conscious, intentional recall of facts and experiences, divided into:
    - *Episodic Memory:* This is where we store our personal experience and their context. Like a personal photo album, this holds our autobiographical experiences. It's what helps us recall our last birthday or that one history lesson we'll never forget.
    - *Semantic Memory:* This is our general knowledge bank—where we store facts and concepts like knowing that water boils at 100°C or that Paris is the capital of France.
- *Implicit Memory:* This type of memory operates in the background. It influences our behaviors and thoughts without us even realizing it:
    - *Procedural Memory:* The knowledge of how to do things—like riding a bike or typing on a keyboard. With repeated practice, actions require less conscious effort.
    - *Priming:* When exposure to something influences your response to something else later. For example, seeing a picture of a waterfall might make you more likely to remember the word "cascade" because your brain has been "primed."

Retrieval: Recall & Recognition

Retrieving stored information is just as important as encoding it. Information retrieval primarily occurs through *recall* and *recognition.*

- *Recall:* When you pull information from memory without any cues—like answering an open-ended test question. This requires more effort but demonstrates a deeper understanding.

- *Recognition:* When we recognize the correct answer with a hint or visual aid—like answering a multiple-choice question. Recognition is easier because the options serve as prompts to jog your memory.

A great way to strengthen recall is through repeated self-testing. Practicing retrieval strengthens memory pathways, making recall more efficient and reducing cognitive load over time.

Use It or Lose It: Neural Pruning & Long-Term Potentiation

"The only use of knowledge of the past is to equip us for the present." - Alfred North Whitehead (*An Introduction to Mathematics*)

While our memory system is vast, the brain doesn't keep everything. It is efficient, holding on to what's necessary and pruning what we don't use.

Here's how it works:

- *Neural Pruning:* The brain eliminates infrequently used synaptic connections, optimizing space for essential information. This is why we may forget something if we haven't practiced it in a long time.
- *Long-Term Potentiation (LTP):* The opposite of pruning, LTP strengthens the connections we use most often. The more we practice a skill, the stronger and more efficient these neural pathways become. This is why daily habits like brushing our teeth feel automatic.

To put it simply: the more we repeat an action, the less effort it requires. The brain strengthens the synaptic connections we use often and deletes the stuff we don't use to give more processing power to the useful synaptic connections. This principle underpins skill mastery, whether in calculus or choreography.

Learning something new—whether it's algebra or a new language—can feel challenging at first. Our brains are firing new synapses, and that requires significant effort. But the more we practice, the easier it becomes. Trust in the process. What feels difficult today will eventually become second nature, thanks to the brain's incredible ability to strengthen useful connections.

So, when we're tempted to give up, remember: every time we practice, we're making the next attempt easier. Conversely, if we stop practicing, our brain will prune away those connections to make room for new information.

As the saying goes: use it or lose it.

BECOMING YOU
IDENTITY & SELF PERCEPTION

"Every action you take is a vote for the type of person you wish to become. No single instance will transform your beliefs, but as the votes build up, so does the evidence of your new identity." – James Clear (*Atomic Habits*)

At the heart of who we are lies our identity—a dynamic blueprint that shapes how we view ourselves and navigate the world. Far from being static, our identity drives our habits, decisions, and ultimately, the trajectory of our lives. *Identity Formation* refers to how we see ourselves and how we navigate the world. The choices we make and the habits we cultivate all orbit around the gravitational pull of our perceived identity.

Identity is formed, defended, and shaped. Understanding these ideas is crucial for getting our habits to match with our deepest aspirations.

Identity Defense and Creating New Actions

Identity Defense refers to the unconscious process of preserving our self-concept—the internal narrative we tell ourselves about who we are. This drive for consistency often leads us to align our actions with our perceived identity, even when that identity feels limiting or outdated. We crave consistency, which can lead us to reject opportunities or challenges that conflict with our current self-view.

For example, if we see ourselves as someone who's "bad at math," we might avoid situations that require mathematical skills, not because we're incapable, but because we need to defend that identity. Identity defense is often at the root of why adopting new habits is difficult. If a new habit contradicts our identity, we instinctively resist it to protect our self-image.

- If we see ourselves as an athlete, we are more likely to adopt athletic habits.
- If we see ourselves as a musician, we will naturally gravitate toward playing musical instruments.
- If we see yourself as a lifelong learner, we are more likely to adopt habits that foster continuous learning.

The key to habit formation is not just action, but identity transformation. When we shift our identity, our actions follow effortlessly.

The Many Faces of the Self: Actual, Ideal, and Ought

When we say "I know myself," who are we actually referring to? Our identity is not singular but rather a multifaceted concept. It encompasses several dimensions of self that interact in complex ways to shape who we are.

- *Self-concept:* The sum of how we describe ourselves across time – past, present, and future. This forms the foundation of our identity.
- *Actual Self:* The person we are in reality, with all our strengths, weaknesses, and imperfections. This is the self we experience daily.

- *Ideal Self:* The aspirational version of ourselves. This is the self we strive to become, the one that judges us when we fall short but praises us when we act in alignment with its vision.
- *Ought Self:* The self that others expect us to be. This external expectation, while less powerful than our Ideal Self, still influences our behavior, particularly when we feel societal or familial pressure.

Our identity is shaped by our self-concept, which reflects how we perceive ourselves across time—past, present, and future. This self-concept is multifaceted, encompassing the Actual Self, the Ideal Self, and the Ought Self, each contributing uniquely to our sense of who we are. How we balance these versions of ourselves plays a key role in shaping our identity. When our Actual Self aligns closely with our Ideal Self, we tend to feel more fulfilled and confident. However, when there's a significant gap between who we are and who we aspire to be, that tension can create internal conflict and dissatisfaction.

Bridging the Gap: Self-esteem and Self-efficacy

The distance between our Actual and Ideal selves plays a crucial role in determining our self-esteem. *Self-esteem* is essentially an evaluation of how closely we live in accordance with our Ideal Self. The wider the gap, the lower our self-esteem tends to be. The narrower the gap, the more positive we feel about ourselves.

Raising self-esteem involves clearly defining our Ideal Self and taking consistent actions that align with it. While simple in theory, this process is challenging because it requires constant self-awareness and intentionality. We must frequently ask ourselves, "What would my Ideal Self do in this situation?"

In tandem with self-esteem, *self-efficacy* – our belief in our ability to succeed in specific tasks or areas – plays a significant role in identity formation. Self-efficacy shapes how we approach learning, challenges, and new experiences. Low self-efficacy can make us feel incapable, leading to avoidance of areas where we perceive ourselves as weak.

To build self-efficacy, follow these three steps:

1. Set small, achievable goals.
2. Acknowledge each accomplishment as a significant step.
3. Gradually increase the difficulty of our goals as our confidence grows.

By improving self-efficacy, we create a healthier self-concept and cultivate a belief that we are capable of change.

Learned Helplessness: The Antithesis of Self-Efficacy

"Think of a young elephant tied to a stake in the ground. When it's a baby, the elephant isn't strong enough to pull the stake out, so it eventually stops trying because it learns the effort is futile. As the elephant grows, it gains more than enough strength to pull out the stake, but it remains tied by something as weak as a rope because of what it learned as a baby." – Jim Kwik

This vivid example illustrates *learned helplessness*—a state where repeated exposure to challenges fosters the false belief that we are incapable of overcoming them, even when we possess the ability to succeed. In psychological terms, learned helplessness is the destruction of self-efficacy, and it is a significant barrier to personal growth.

Overcoming learned helplessness requires recalibrating our identity and restoring belief in our abilities. We must break free from self-imposed constraints and recognize that the past does not define our future capabilities. By incrementally boosting self-efficacy, we can rebuild confidence and challenge the mental blocks that limit us.

The Dramaturgy of Life: Front Stage and Back Stage Selves

Sociologist Erving Goffman's *dramaturgical perspective* helps explain how we manage different versions of ourselves in social contexts. According to this view, we have two primary selves:

- *Front Stage Self:* This is the version of ourselves that we present to the world. It's curated for public display, designed to fit social norms and expectations.
- *Back Stage Self:* This is our true, unfiltered self – the person we are when we're alone, free from judgment or societal pressure.

While these distinctions can serve a purpose, living authentically often requires narrowing the gap between the two. When our Front Stage and Back Stage selves are more aligned, we experience higher levels of self-esteem and self-efficacy.

However, it's not necessary to completely merge them. The goal is to cultivate a Back Stage Self that is as strong, confident, and well-polished as our public persona. Doing so allows us to achieve personal goals with integrity and authenticity.

The Path to Identity Transformation

Understanding and developing our identity is crucial for personal growth. It's about navigating the different parts of who we are—our self-concept—and recognizing how things like self-esteem and self-efficacy influence our lives.

Real change happens when we bring our Actual Self closer to our Ideal Self, overcome feelings of learned helplessness, and find a balance between the version of ourselves we show the world (Front Stage) and who we are when no one's watching (Back Stage). By doing this, we can live more authentically and confidently, taking actions that reflect who we truly want to be.

Our identity is not fixed; it evolves with intentional effort, self-awareness, and consistent action. By embracing this process, we unlock the potential for continuous personal growth and transformation. Embracing this process opens the door to ongoing personal growth and self-improvement.

COGNITIVE PROCESSING IN LEARNING

TOP-DOWN VS. BOTTOM-UP

Many people skim through a chapter of a book, understand the general idea, but struggle when it came time to recall the specifics. Or maybe they've memorized every tiny detail for an exam, but couldn't see how it all fit together when faced with real-world application. These challenges reflect two essential processes our brain uses to learn: top-down and bottom-up processing.

These ideas can help us process through new information more efficiently and with greater depth. Instead of relying on one approach and getting stuck, we can master both and transform how we study and learn.

Top-Down Processing: Seeing the Big Picture First

Top-down processing allows us to grasp the bigger picture by drawing on prior knowledge and context. Take the sentence: *Rocky loves to rock on his rcoking chair to rock music.* Even with the typo in 'rcoking,' we effortlessly understand the sentence's meaning. That's top-down processing at work—our brain fills in gaps using context and expectations. This immediate comprehension is top-down processing at work; we see the sentence's overall meaning before recognizing the swapped letters in "rocking." It demonstrates our brain's ability to correct and understand based on context and expectation.

This approach is like standing back to observe a landscape before exploring the details—it's fast and allows us to make sense of new information based on previous knowledge. However, there's a risk here. If we rely too heavily on top-down processing, we may miss crucial details and develop an incomplete understanding. For example, glancing over our notes may give us a general sense of familiarity, but when it's time for the test, we may realize we didn't fully absorb the material.

Bottom-Up Processing: Building Knowledge from the Ground Up

Bottom-up processing, on the other hand, builds understanding piece by piece by focusing on individual details. Revisiting the 'rcoking' example, bottom-up processing helps us notice the misspelling and reconstruct the correct word by analyzing its components.

In learning, this approach involves focusing on the finer points, like solving practice problems to fill gaps in understanding. When we solve a math problem step by step or break down a scientific concept into its parts, we're using bottom-up processing. This method can be powerful for mastering complex subjects but can feel overwhelming if we try to apply it to everything right away.

Striking a Balance

Mastering learning lies in knowing when to toggle between top-down and bottom-up processing. If we only focus on top-down processing, we might gloss over important details. But if we stick strictly to bottom-up processing, we can get bogged down in minutiae and miss the broader context.

When approaching new material, start with top-down processing to establish a mental framework. Familiarize yourself with the overarching structure, themes, and purpose of the content. Then, pivot to bottom-up processing to examine the finer details, filling gaps and solidifying your understanding. Once that's in place, shift to bottom-up processing to dive into the specifics. Ask: Where are my gaps? What details did I miss in my initial review?

This balance can enhance both our understanding and retention, making us more effective learners. Whether we're preparing for an exam, learning a new skill, or just trying to retain more from our daily reading, integrating top-down and bottom-up processing will help us access deeper comprehension at a faster rate. By experimenting with both, we'll discover how to tackle even the most complex subjects with greater ease. Next time you encounter a new concept, start broad and then drill down. First, grasp the big picture to create a roadmap. Then, dive into the details to strengthen your understanding. This balanced approach transforms learning into a more efficient and lasting experience, helping knowledge stick long after the book is closed.

BEYOND COMFORT
CHOOSING DISCOMFORT FOR A LIFE OF MEANING

"If you look for truth, you may find comfort in the end; if you look for comfort, you will not get either comfort or truth, only soft soap and wishful thinking to begin, and in the end, despair." - C.S. Lewis (*God in the Dock: Essays on Theology and Ethics*)

The Illusions of Comfort

Comfort is universally appealing, but it's also deceptively limiting. While it offers temporary relief, it often leads to shortcuts and avoidance of meaningful challenges. The comfortable path lets us indulge in instant gratification, but at the expense of long-term growth and meaningful achievements.

This doesn't mean that success is only achieved through misery and suffering. There is a balance between living a comfortable life and living a meaningful one. However, this balance is not achieved by aiming for comfort; instead, it comes from aiming at truth.

Truth provides the clarity needed to recognize what meaningful success demands. Only by pursuing truth can we accept the challenges required to live a fulfilling life.

Comfort, though tempting, discourages us from confronting failure and stifles the learning process. When our environment perfectly aligns with our expectations, our instinct to grow and absorb new information disappears. Humans are creatures of necessity—we learn when we need to. If everything is comfortable, there's no need to learn, and stagnation creeps in. This stagnation keeps us stuck, far from our full potential.

Choosing the comfortable path often leads us astray and complicates our journey. I've seen this in my own life every time I made decisions solely because they were easy. It's been worthwhile to evaluate my intentions, ensuring that I change to be effective, not just comfortable. Comfort, I believe, comes as a byproduct of being more effective.

"Too many people believe that everything must be pleasurable in life, which makes them constantly search for distractions and short-circuits the learning process." - Robert Greene (*Mastery*)

Nietzsche's Dichotomy: The Last Man vs. The Ubermensch

"The earth has become small, and on it hops the last man, who makes everything small. His race is as ineradicable as the flea-beetle; the last man lives longest." - Friedrich Nietzsche (*Thus Spoke Zarathustra*)

Nietzsche's concepts of the Last Man and the Ubermensch offer a powerful lens through which we can understand our attraction to comfort.

In *Thus Spake Zarathustra*, the prophet Zarathustra preaches to a crowd about his mountaintop reflections on life. He shares his vision of The Ubermensch (or "Overman") and the Last Man. While the crowd awaits a performance of a tightrope walker, Zarathustra's profound words fall on deaf ears.

The Last Man epitomizes mediocrity, choosing ease and security over growth, resulting in a life devoid of creation or deeper meaning. Content with distractions like fancy careers, social events, and trivial pleasures, the Last Man avoids challenges and risks. They consume more than they create and fear confronting the hard truths of life.

In contrast, the *Ubermensch* embraces discomfort, channeling suffering into creativity and growth. This journey is not easy, but it is through this hardship that a meaningful, lasting life is created. The Ubermensch confronts discomfort head-on, channeling suffering into growth and creativity, leaving behind a lasting legacy.

Nietzsche dramatically illustrates this dichotomy with the tightrope walker. While the crowd dismisses Zarathustra's message, the tightrope walker silently performs. The walker, balancing above the abyss, symbolizes the struggle of the Ubermensch— walking the fine line between chaos and order, between comfort and growth.

"Man is a rope stretched between animal and overman—a rope over an abyss." - Friedrich Nietzsche (*Thus Spoke Zarathustra*)

Our existence is precarious, like that tightrope walker. We can drift toward the comfort of the Last Man, or we can choose the challenging path toward the Ubermensch. The Ubermensch's path is difficult, but it's also the one that allows us to create something meaningful.

Zapffe's Four Methods of Coping with Discomfort

Life oscillates between moments of clarity (order) and confusion (chaos). This tension is uncomfortable, but it's also where learning and adaptation happen. To grow, we must accept discomfort rather than flee from it. Comfort lulls us into a false sense of security, preventing us from evolving.

The Norwegian philosopher Peter Zapffe explored this idea

further by identifying four ways people cope with life's inherent discomfort:

- Isolation
- Anchoring
- Distraction
- Sublimation.

These methods, while helping us manage discomfort, can often lead us down the path of the Last Man.

Isolation

Isolation is the act of avoiding anything that causes discomfort. Zapffe described isolation as the 'dismissal of disturbing thoughts or feelings.' Whether it's hitting snooze, avoiding tough conversations, or ignoring opposing views, isolation traps us in a comfort bubble. But in doing so, we miss out on opportunities to learn and grow.

Anchoring

Anchoring is when we rely on familiar structures—whether it's a routine, belief, or group identity—to protect ourselves from complexity. Children anchor to their parents for security, and adults often anchor to their culture, community, or nation. While anchoring offers comfort, it can prevent us from questioning assumptions and challenging the unknown.

Distraction

Modern society thrives on distraction. Zapffe described it as "limiting attention to the critical bounds by constantly enthralling it with impression." Technology, social media, and entertainment reward us for distraction, pulling us away from meaningful engagement with life's challenges. While distraction temporarily numbs discomfort, it stifles our capacity for meaningful learning and creative growth.

Sublimation

Sublimation is the most constructive way to cope with discomfort. It involves transforming suffering into something meaningful —channeling pain and struggle into creativity, purpose, or innovation. This process is characteristic of the Ubermensch. When isolation, anchoring, or distraction fail, sublimation allows us to take life's tragedy and transform it into something beautiful.

Creation is a powerful antidote to life's suffering. Whether through art, innovation, or thought, sublimation channels discomfort into growth and contribution. It is in this act of creation that we discover purpose and transcend the temporary comforts that hold us back.

COMFORT MAY FEEL safe and enticing in the moment, but it often leads us to avoid the very challenges that foster growth and meaning. As C.S. Lewis suggests, when we seek comfort first, we are left with neither comfort nor truth, but wishful thinking and, eventually, despair. True comfort comes as a byproduct of seeking truth and embracing the discomforts along the way.

As Nietzsche illustrated with his concept of the Last Man versus the Ubermensch, we can either settle for mediocrity and security or strive toward greatness by embracing hardship and discomfort. The path of the Last Man may be easier, filled with distractions and shallow pleasures, but it leads to a life void of creation and depth. In contrast, the Ubermensch accepts suffering as a necessary part of growth, transforming it into creativity, legacy, and purpose.

Peter Zapffe's methods of coping with discomfort—whether through isolation, anchoring, distraction, or sublimation—remind us that how we deal with life's challenges shapes the course of our existence. Sublimation, or transforming suffering into creation, allows us to channel discomfort into something lasting and meaningful, making it the most constructive way forward.

By embracing discomfort and resisting the seductive pull of comfort, we unlock the potential for deeper learning, profound personal growth, and a life rich with purpose. The challenge is hard, but the rewards are immense—comfort through truth, and meaning through struggle.

HARNESSING EMOTIONS FOR GROWTH

HOW TO CHANNEL OUR CORE DRIVES FOR LEARNING & TRANSFORMATION

Our emotions are the invisible architects of our actions, shaping how we learn, grow, and navigate challenges in life. Jaak Panksepp, in *Affective Neuroscience*, and Temple Grandin, in *Animals Make Us Human*, offer deep insights into these core emotional systems. Known as the "blue-ribbon emotions"—SEEKING, RAGE, FEAR, PANIC, LUST, CARE, and PLAY—these primal drives influence how we engage with the world and adapt to its challenges. To prevent any confusion, the emotions will be written in all caps.

These emotions are universal, shared across species. The lower regions of the brain that control these impulses are nearly identical in both animals and humans. Stimulating one of these core systems produces the same behavior, whether in a pig or a person. Understanding these emotions can help us leverage their power to learn, grow, and navigate discomfort.

SEEKING: The Drive to Explore and Learn

SEEKING is one of the most important emotions for growth. It's the basic impulse to search, investigate, and make sense of the environment. It is inherently pleasurable, driving curiosity, motivation, and problem-solving.

When we engage our SEEKING system, we actively pursue new knowledge and experiences. This system encourages exploration, which is crucial for intellectual and personal development. Without SEEKING, there is no growth.

Cultivating this emotion is key to stepping out of comfort zones and facing new challenges. A person driven by curiosity will naturally gravitate toward experiences that foster learning, even when those experiences are uncomfortable. SEEKING is the engine of curiosity, driving us to venture into the unknown and achieve personal and professional breakthroughs.

We can actively engage our SEEKING systems by setting small goals to explore something new every day—whether it's learning a new fact, tackling a problem, or trying a different hobby. Curiosity is our most powerful tool for growth—feed it regularly.

RAGE: The Response to Frustration

RAGE evolved as a survival mechanism, originally designed to help our ancestors escape predators. In modern life, RAGE shows up when we encounter obstacles or feel trapped. While RAGE often gets a bad reputation, it can be a useful emotion when directed properly. It helps us break free from limitations or unfair situations.

However, unregulated RAGE can lead to destructive behaviors or cause us to give up when faced with discomfort. The key to growth is learning to recognize frustration and using that energy for constructive action. When frustration arises, instead of letting it defeat us, we can harness it to solve problems or push through challenges.

When frustration builds, pause and ask: 'How can I channel this energy into constructive action?' RAGE becomes a tool for problem-solving rather than a barrier. Frustration is fuel—use it to break through limits, not to be consumed by it.

FEAR: A Double-Edged Sword

FEAR is another core emotion, essential for survival. It activates when we perceive a threat—whether physical, emotional, or social. While FEAR keeps us safe, it can also paralyze us in situations where action is needed. FEAR often arises when we face the unknown or take on new challenges. But growth happens when we face our fears rather than avoid them. By recognizing FEAR as a natural response, we can learn to manage it and transform it into a catalyst for calculated risks and meaningful growth. By reframing fear as a signal that something important is at stake, we can use it as motivation to grow.

When we feel fear about a new challenge, acknowledge it as a normal part of growth. We can ask ourselves, "What can I learn from this situation?" Pushing through fear often leads to the most valuable learning experiences.

PANIC: The Need for Connection

PANIC is the emotional system that triggers anxiety and distress when we experience social separation or loss. This system drives our need for connection and belonging. While PANIC can motivate us to form relationships, it can also lead to anxiety about rejection or abandonment.

In terms of personal growth, PANIC reminds us that strong social support is essential. Surrounding ourselves with people who challenge and encourage us creates a safety net that allows us to take risks and push through discomfort. However, it's also important not to let PANIC drive us into unhealthy dependencies on others.

We can strengthen our support network by nurturing meaningful relationships while cultivating resilience to face challenges independently when necessary. We can use our need for connection as a way to build emotional resilience, but also practice independence by tackling challenges on your own when necessary.

LUST: The Drive for Connection

LUST is tied to reproduction and sexual desire, but it also connects to the broader human need for intimacy and connection. While it may seem less relevant to personal growth, healthy expressions of LUST help us form deep, meaningful bonds, which in turn contribute to emotional well-being.

Healthy relationships, driven by connection and intimacy, can provide the emotional stability that allows us to face challenges and grow.

CARE: The Urge to Nurture

CARE is deeply tied to empathy and the desire to nurture others. This system drives us to protect, care for, and support those we love. Engaging the CARE system encourages selflessness, which fosters emotional growth.

When we care for others, we strengthen our own emotional resilience and deepen our connections. This emotional system reminds us that growth is not only about personal achievement but also about helping others along the way.

Actively seek opportunities to nurture others. Whether through mentorship, teaching, or simply offering support, caring for others strengthens our emotional capacity and helps us grow in the process.

PLAY: The Joy of Learning Through Fun

PLAY is one of the most powerful emotions for growth. It encourages us to take risks, try new things, and explore ideas in a low-stakes environment. PLAY is tied directly to creativity and problem-solving.

Incorporating playfulness into your approach to learning helps make the process enjoyable and sustainable. PLAY fosters a sense of safety that encourages experimentation, creative problem-solving, and the freedom to stretch our abilities without fear of failure. According to Stanford professor, Andrew Huberman, when we play we form neural connections faster.

Make room for PLAY in life, whether it's through hobbies, creative work, or light-hearted experimentation. The more we engage with play, the more flexible and adaptive you become in all areas of life.

Emotional Regulation: Mastering the Core of Growth

To fully harness the power of these blue-ribbon emotions for growth, we need to practice emotional regulation. According to Bessel van der Kolk in *The Body Keeps the Score*, emotional regulation is key to managing discomfort and pushing through life's challenges. Techniques like mindfulness, breathwork, and meditation help recalibrate our nervous system, allowing us to engage with discomfort constructively.

The goal is not to suppress these emotions but to recognize and channel them productively. By doing so, we can use them to propel us forward, rather than allowing them to hold us back.

We can use mindfulness techniques to regularly check in with our emotions. We can ask ourselves, "What am I feeling, and how can I channel this emotion into action?" Breathing exercises and meditation can also help bring balance to intense emotional responses, giving us greater control.

Mastering the Emotional Blueprint for Growth

The blue-ribbon emotions are not just ancient survival systems—they are powerful tools for personal transformation. When we recognize and harness these emotions, they become pathways to exploration, creativity, and growth. True growth emerges not from avoiding discomfort but from embracing it, using our emotions as navigational tools on the journey to transformation. By learning to regulate and channel SEEKING, FEAR, RAGE, CARE, and PLAY, we open up a world of possibilities for growth, learning, and personal evolution.

SHIFTING OUR LOCUS OF CONTROL
THE POWER OF OWNERSHIP

"You can't blame your boss for not giving you the support you need. Plenty of people will say, 'It's my boss's fault.' No, it's actually your fault because you haven't educated him, you haven't influenced him, you haven't explained to him in a manner he understands why you need this support that you need. That's extreme ownership. Own it all."- Jocko Willink (*Extreme Ownership: How U.S. Navy SEALs Lead and Win*)

The Locus of Control: Internal vs. External

The locus of control is a psychological framework that categorizes our perception of control as internal (ILC) or external (ELC).

Internal Locus of Control (ILC) refers to the belief that an individual has the ability to influence the events and outcomes in their life. Someone with an ILC believes their actions shape their future. For example, a student who believes that studying harder, seeking help, or adopting better strategies can improve their grades operates with an ILC.

External Locus of Control (ELC), on the other hand, is the belief that outside forces—such as luck, fate, or the actions of others—determine one's success or failure. In contrast, an ELC places control in the hands of external forces like luck, fate, or other people, often leaving individuals feeling powerless to change their circumstances.

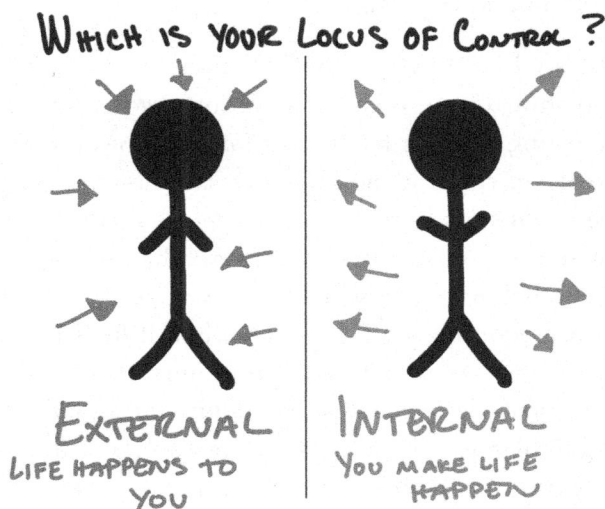

I drew this (if you couldn't tell)

Understanding the Power Within

Embracing an ILC can feel daunting because it forces us to acknowledge that many of the outcomes in our lives—such as our study environment, grades, and stress levels—are the result of our own choices and actions. But rather than feel overwhelmed by this, we can see it as an opportunity.

Recognizing the role of our own actions in shaping our reality is incredibly empowering. It opens the door to change. If we have control, we can initiate solutions tailored to our personal challenges. For example, if we're struggling in a class, adopting an ILC might push us to seek out a tutor, ask better questions, or find resources beyond the textbook to help.

While external factors can influence outcomes, an ILC gives us the freedom to control how we respond and adapt. We aren't helpless passengers in our academic journey—we are in the driver's seat.

From Victimhood to Heroism

Clinging to an ELC might provide temporary relief because it allows us to shift blame. It can cushion our egos when things go wrong, protecting us from feelings of failure. However, over time, an ELC creates a sense of powerlessness. When we believe that nothing we do matters because outside forces control everything, we lose our sense of agency. Even if it is true that outside forces are influencing us, believing that will destroy our agency.

In contrast, adopting an ILC—even when it feels like external factors are at play—empowers us. It positions us to navigate and overcome the obstacles we face. If our grades are slipping, it might be tempting to blame a difficult teacher, but an ILC will push us to ask: What can I do differently? How can I seek extra help or approach the material in a new way?

An ILC allows us to become the hero of our own story. Even when it feels like life is throwing curveballs, we can take action, adapt, and rise above.

Responsibility vs. Fault: Redefining Accountability

"With great power, comes great responsibility." - Uncle Ben (*Spider-Man*)

One of the biggest challenges in adopting an internal locus of control is redefining our relationship with responsibility. Many people equate responsibility with fault, which can make it feel burdensome. But there's a crucial distinction: responsibility is about taking ownership of the present and the future, regardless of whether we are to blame for how things began.

While a situation may not be our fault, it remains our responsibility to address and improve it. This distinction—between fault and responsibility—is where true empowerment begins. For example, if we receive a poor grade, it may be due to an unclear assignment or inadequate instruction. While that's not our fault, our responsibility is to seek out clarity, improve our understanding, and ensure we perform better next time.

Cultivating Personal Growth

In academic life, it's easy to fall into the trap of assigning blame. A bad grade might lead us to point fingers at a teacher's unclear instructions or the difficulty of the material. But adopting an ILC reframes this: instead of asking who is to blame, we ask, "What can I do to change this?"

Adopting this mindset doesn't mean dismissing external hardships. It acknowledges that some challenges—whether they're personal, familial, or institutional—are real and difficult. However, having an internal locus of control means we don't let these challenges define us. We find ways to rise above them.

Instead of focusing on what's wrong, we focus on what can be done. It's not about fault, but about taking charge of our own education, seeking knowledge, and overcoming obstacles. No matter the difficulty, it's our responsibility to learn the curriculum, grow from our mistakes, and excel. This is how personal growth happens—not by finding fault, but by accepting responsibility.

"Losers define themselves by what happens to them. Winners define themselves by what they make happen." - Alex Hormozi

Practical Steps: Shifting Your Locus of Control

Shifting from an ELC to an ILC takes practice and intention.

Here are some steps we can take to cultivate an internal locus of control in your academic life:

1. *Reflect on challenges:* We can identify areas where we feel powerless. Are we blaming external factors for our struggles? What can we do differently to change the outcome?

2. *Focus on solutions:* When faced with a problem, ask yourself, "What can I control in this situation?" Even if external factors are at play, how you respond is within your power.

3. *Take responsibility for our learning:* If we don't understand something, seek help. Use resources like online tutorials, study groups, or extra materials to gain clarity.

4. *Track progress:* Set small, achievable goals, and track progress. Over time, this will build confidence in our ability to influence our outcomes.

Adopting an ILC isn't about taking the blame for everything that goes wrong—it's about recognizing that we have the power to change, adapt, and grow, no matter the circumstances.

HARNESSING HYPNOTIC RHYTHM
THE LAW THAT SHAPES OUR LIVES

"Any thought or physical movement which is repeated over and over through the principle of habit finally reaches the proportion of rhythm. Then the habit cannot be broken because nature takes it over and makes it permanent. It is something like a whirlpool in water...Then it is carried round and round but it cannot escape... Habit establishes one's rhythm of thought, and that rhythm attracts the object of one's dominating thoughts." – Napoleon Hill (*Outwitting the Devil*)

There is an idea that intertwines our deepest drives with the power of habit: *Hypnotic Rhythm*. In his book *Outwitting the Devil*, Napoleon Hill dives deep into this principle, showing us how our thoughts and actions shape the rhythms of our lives, for better or worse.

What is Hypnotic Rhythm?

Hypnotic rhythm is the natural law that turns repeated actions and thoughts into permanent habits, much like gravity keeps us grounded. Hill describes it as a force that eventually takes over our habits, making them automatic and, in some cases, hard to break.

Imagine a whirlpool forming in a river: initially small and barely noticeable, it grows stronger as more water flows into it, pulling everything around into its circular motion. This is how hypnotic rhythm works—it starts with small, repeated actions and thoughts, but over time, it grows into a powerful current that shapes our daily lives.

From Actions to Rhythm

1. *Actions:* Every conscious decision we make starts with a single action. These actions are the building blocks of our habits.
2. *Habits:* When repeated enough times, these actions evolve into habits. Habits feel natural and require less effort to maintain.
3. *Rhythm:* Once habits are deeply ingrained, they become automatic—this is the stage of hypnotic rhythm. The rhythm becomes so strong that it's almost impossible to break free from it without conscious effort.

The Role of Our Drives

Our thoughts, just like our actions, are influenced by hypnotic rhythm. The human drives, as outlined by Josh Kaufman in *The Personal MBA*, play a key role in shaping the rhythms of our thoughts.

- *The Drive to Acquire:* We seek not just material wealth but also knowledge, status, and peace. This drive pushes us to focus our thoughts on what we want to obtain, feeding the rhythm of acquisition.

- *The Drive to Bond:* Our desire for connection shapes our thoughts around relationships, often leading us to align our thinking with societal norms. Understanding this drive can help us break free from conforming thought patterns and focus on our true desires.
- *The Drive to Learn:* Curiosity leads us toward growth, but only if we direct it mindfully. Choosing what we learn determines whether our mental rhythm propels us toward progress or distraction.
- *The Drive to Defend:* While survival instincts are necessary, they can lead to anxiety and fear. Recognizing this can help us reshape defensive thoughts and create a rhythm of courage and resilience.

How to Use Hypnotic Rhythm to Our Advantage

"Nature uses hypnotic rhythm to make one's dominating thoughts and one's thought-habits permanent." – Napoleon Hill (*Outwitting the Devil*)

The secret to success lies in shaping our habits and thoughts before they solidify into a hypnotic rhythm. By consciously guiding our actions and thoughts, we can create rhythms that align with our goals and aspirations. Here's how to get started:

1. *Identify a Key Habit:* Focus on one habit that, if mastered, would significantly improve your life.
2. *Take Small, Consistent Actions:* Break down the habit into small, manageable tasks and repeat them consistently.
3. *Reinforce Positive Thoughts:* Align our thoughts with our goals. Each time a negative thought arises, consciously replace it with a more empowering one.

The Power of Positive Thought Rhythms

Our thought habits are just as critical as our actions. As Napoleon Hill reminds us, our dominating thoughts become permanent through the law of hypnotic rhythm. This means that by cultivating positive, success-oriented thoughts, we can create a rhythm that naturally guides us toward our goals.

HYPNOTIC RHYTHM IS a force that shapes our lives, whether we are aware of it or not. By understanding this law and harnessing it for positive growth, we can shape habits and thought patterns that lead us toward our highest potential. The key is to start small, repeat often, and let the rhythm carry us to success.

FROM DRIFTING TO DIRECTION
ESCAPING AIMLESSNESS WITH PURPOSE

"He who has a why to live for can bear almost any how." - Friedrich
Nietzsche (*Twilight of the Idols*)

Purpose is not merely a luxury; it is essential to human survival. Without it, we drift, and as Napoleon Hill illuminates in *Outwitting the Devil*, drifting is one of the most common yet destructive habits.

Drifting is the act of relinquishing control over one's life, allowing external forces to dictate one's future. When I first read this, I was skeptical. But the more I observed people—and reflected on my own experiences—the more I realized Hill was onto something.

Understanding Drifters

A drifter is someone who lacks clear direction in life. Drifters float through life passively, accepting whatever comes their way without conscious decision-making. Drifters may possess great potential, but they often fail to act on it, caught in a cycle of indecision and complacency. Rather than choosing a path, drifters allow external circumstances to dictate their direction, inevitably inviting chaos.

Drifting isn't always intentional. Many drifters start by choosing comfort over challenge or avoiding difficult decisions. Over time, however, this lack of intentionality leads to frustration, aimlessness, and even despair.

A drifter has many options but none of them are their own.

Napoleon Hill suggests that 98% of people are drifters. While that figure may seem high, upon closer reflection, it does not seem far from the truth. Drifting is dangerously common because it often feels easier than confronting life with purpose. But as Hill emphasizes, there's nothing more dangerous than being aimless. When we don't aim at something, we leave space for something worse instead.

Signs We Might Be Drifting

- Life feels overwhelmingly negative, and none of the options in front of us seem appealing.
- We find ourselves stuck in circumstances that feel unfair or beyond our control.
- Avoidance and denial become our default coping mechanisms.
- We constantly wonder how our life ended up filled with suffering and dissatisfaction.
- A sense of stagnation prevails, with our dreams and aspirations feeling distant or out of reach.

It's important to note that not all difficult situations stem from drifting. External circumstances can be challenging, but our perception of those challenges—and whether we respond actively or passively—makes all the difference. The key is recognizing when we've stopped choosing our path and started merely reacting to life.

Drifting isn't just a personal issue; it's contagious. Being around drifters can pull us into their sphere of aimlessness. It's important to recognize this pattern in others and protect ourselves from being pulled into their orbit.

The Consequences of Drifting

Remaining a drifter is a silent form of failure. Many avoid setting specific goals, fearing the sting of failure, but in doing so, they fail by default. Over time, drifters find themselves asking, "Where did it all go wrong?" The truth is, they avoided aiming at something and allowed themselves to be swept away by life's currents.

The pain of failure is real, but the pain of never trying is far worse. When we drift, we don't just fail—we fail without even knowing why. But by setting clear goals, we at least give ourselves the chance to course-correct.

We ca do ourselves a favor—live with clarity and learn what failure really is. Pretending it doesn't exist doesn't mean it isn't happening.

Yes, failure can hurt, but it hurts far more to hate our existence. If we don't actively create a meaningful life, we'll be handed something much worse.

Counteracting Drifting: The Power of Purpose

The antidote to drifting is purpose. Purpose transcends ambition; it's a calling that pushes us to exceed our limits. It transforms mundane tasks into meaningful pursuits, and it makes life feel worth living.

The best way to stop drifting is to live with a definitive purpose. We must aim at something bigger than ourselves, something that inspires us to bring out our best. With purpose, we transform from passive participants in life to active creators of our reality. Purposeful living doesn't just help us reach our goals—it makes the journey worthwhile.

Being aligned with purpose makes it easier to learn, grow, and stay present in life. When we pursue meaningful goals, even challenging tasks become more engaging. The pursuit of purpose brings fulfillment, as we experience positive emotions when we see ourselves making progress toward our goals.

The Benefits of Living with Purpose

- Purpose gives us determination to keep going, no matter the obstacles.
- We stop making excuses for our current situation and start creating opportunities to improve it.
- Achieving small milestones toward our purpose brings feelings of accomplishment and happiness.
- We become comfortable admitting what we don't know, seeing gaps in our knowledge as chances to grow.
- We take responsibility for our mistakes and stop blaming others.
- Living with purpose inspires others, as they see the clarity and strength we all possess.
- We gain the power to help others, all while relying less on favors for ourselves.
- We no longer need to make excuses for our shortcomings—they simply become areas for improvement.

Finding Our Purpose

"The whole law of human existence consists in nothing other than a man's always being able to bow before the immeasurably great. If people are deprived of the immeasurably great, they will not live and will die in despair. The immeasurable and infinite are as necessary for man as the small planet he inhabits." - Fyodor Dostoyevsky (*The Brothers Karamazov*)

Having a purpose sounds ideal, but how do we find it?

Our purpose often lies within our interests, passions, inclinations, and something greater than ourselves. As Robert Greene explains in *Mastery*, these interests serve as clues to our life's mission. By reflecting on what captures our attention, losing ourselves in our work, and challenging ourselves with new skills, we can discover our authentic purpose.

Here are three strategies I've used to develop a strong and authentic purpose:

1. *Reflect on Interests:* We can pay attention to the activities that naturally draw us in. Our unique inclinations often hold the key to our purpose. These are the things we could lose hours doing and not even notice. For me, it's learning and teaching. We can ask ourselves: "What do you love so much that it makes time disappear?"

2. *Get Lost:* While people often joke about "finding themselves," there's truth in the idea. Letting go of rigid control and allowing ourselves to explore new paths can lead to self-discovery. We cannot be afraid to lose ourselves, especially in our work; it's a sign we're on the right track.

3. *Seek Out Resistance:* Learning something new can be painful, but it's also one of the best ways to discover our purpose. Purpose emerges when we master different skills and use them creatively. Resistance is a sign of growth, and growth brings clarity.

Avoiding False Purposes

"Man would rather have the void as purpose than be void of purpose." - Friedrich Nietzsche (*On the Genealogy of Morality*)

In our quest for meaning, it's easy to chase false purposes—things that seem fulfilling but ultimately lead to dissatisfaction.

Pursuits like money, power, or vanity can seduce us, but they are fleeting and often destructive. False purposes may look appealing in the short term, but they lead to frustration and emptiness in the long run.

Here are a few examples of false purposes I've chased:

- Money
- Vanity and egoism
- Power over others
- Pleasure and intoxication
- Attention

These pursuits may bring temporary satisfaction, but they don't offer lasting fulfillment. They can distract us from our true purpose, but if we align our lives with something greater, we can achieve the best of these things as byproducts, rather than primary goals.

Maintaining Purpose Amidst Life's Turbulence

"Nothing is more creative... nor destructive... than a brilliant mind with a purpose." - Dan Brown (*Inferno*)

Keeping aligned with our purpose requires mindfulness, discipline, and resilience. Life will throw challenges our way, but by staying committed to our purpose, we gain the strength to navigate difficulties. Purpose offers clarity, helping us make decisions that align with our values and goals.

The journey away from drifting toward purposeful living is marked by continuous effort. We must engage deeply with our interests, confront our fears, and embrace our unique path with courage. Purpose is not something we find once and hold onto forever—it's something we cultivate daily. And when we live intentionally, we create a life of meaning and fulfillment, leaving the shadow of the drifter far behind.

THE SPIRAL OF GROWTH

NAVIGATING CIRCUMAMBULATION AND COURSE CORRECTION

Circumambulation and the Quest for the Self

Carl Jung introduced the concept of *circumambulation*, the idea that personal growth doesn't follow a straight line. Instead, it's a spiral or orbit around our ideal self. Each experience, skill, and even failure adds to our development, guiding us closer to who we are meant to become.

> "I began to understand that the goal of psychic development is the self. There is no linear evolution; there is only a circumambulation of the self. Uniform development exists, at most, at the beginning; later, everything points toward the centre. This insight gave me stability, and gradually my inner peace returned." – Carl Jung (*Memories, Dreams, Reflections*)

At first, our development feels linear. We focus on specific skills or goals, thinking they'll take us directly to our desired outcome. But as we go through life, we realize that every skill we acquire and every interest we pursue is part of a larger picture—a journey around the ideal version of ourselves.

When I was younger, I worried that having too many interests would scatter my focus. I repressed my love for music because I believed it didn't align with my goals in medicine. Now I see that every skill and passion contributes to my overall growth, creating a more complete and authentic version of who I am meant to be. Music, once seen as a distraction, is now part of my circumambulation journey, bringing me closer to my highest potential. Additionally, my journey in medicine brought me closer to achieving my potential in education.

The Fool's Journey

In mythology and storytelling, the *fool* is often seen as the precursor to the hero. The fool is someone willing to make mistakes, to learn and grow despite the fear of looking foolish. By taking risks and confronting failure, the fool gathers wisdom, eventually transforming into the hero. Looking like a fool is the cost of entry when seeking mastery.

This metaphor aligns perfectly with the process of circumambulation. We must be willing to take on new challenges, make mistakes, and embrace failure to evolve. Growth doesn't happen in a straight line—it's messy and full of detours, but every step matters. We may start as the fool, but with perseverance, we step closer to becoming the hero of our own lives.

The Liberating Power of Failure

Failure is not just inevitable; it is essential. Every misstep we take helps reveal the areas where we need to grow. Failure is our most honest teacher. It shows us our weaknesses, helping us adjust and improve.

Just as circumambulation leads us around our ideal self, failure redirects us, offering crucial lessons along the way. Rather than something to be feared, failure is a necessary part of this spiral journey.

Course Correction: Learning from Failure

While failure teaches us valuable lessons, it also demands *course correction*. When we encounter setbacks, it's important not just to get back up and keep going, but to reflect on why we failed and how we can adjust. Course correction means taking the time to realign with our goals, just like a ship that constantly adjusts its path to reach its destination.

> "On its way to landing astronauts safely on the surface of the moon, the miracle of modern engineering that was an Apollo rocket was actually on course only 2 to 3 percent of the time. Which means that for at least 97 percent of the time it took to get from the Earth to the moon, it was off course. ... It reached the moon—safely—and returned to tell the tale." – Jeff Olson (*The Slight Edge*)

Like the Apollo missions, we are often off course, but through consistent adjustments, we can still reach our goals. Course correction involves reflecting on our missteps, reassessing our path, and making the necessary changes to move forward with purpose.

Inclinations and Self-Development

In his book *Mastery*, Robert Greene emphasizes the importance of following our natural inclinations. Inclinations are the passions and interests we develop early in life but often ignore as we grow older. Greene suggests that by rediscovering and leaning into these inclinations, we uncover the skills necessary for personal mastery.

Our inclinations are essential in our journey of circumambulation. They lead us toward the experiences and skills that shape our ideal selves. By embracing what naturally excites and inspires us, we fuel the centrifugal force that moves us around the orbit of self-actualization.

I once ignored my inclination toward music, believing it wasn't relevant to my professional goals. Now, I see how every interest plays a vital role in my development. By embracing all of my inclinations, I'm able to pursue a more integrated, fulfilled version of myself.

The Law of Hypnotic Rhythm

Napoleon Hill's *Law of Hypnotic Rhythm* describes how repeated thoughts and actions eventually solidify into habits. Over time, these habits become second nature, shaping our character and guiding our actions. By consciously directing our thoughts and actions toward our goals—and embracing failure as part of the process—we can use this law to our advantage.

> "Any thought of physical movement which is repeated over and over through the principle of habit finally reaches the proportion of rhythm. The habit cannot be broken because nature takes hold of it and makes it permanent." – Napoleon Hill (*Outwitting the Devil*)

As we continue on the path of self-discovery, our repeated efforts and course corrections become ingrained in our character, making the journey easier and more natural over time.

Navigating the Journey

Circumambulation and course correction are not just philosophical concepts; they are practical tools for personal and professional growth. As we move through life, our interests, failures, and inclinations help shape us into the people we are meant to be. Every step—whether forward or backward—brings us closer to our ideal self.

The path to self-actualization is not linear. It's a journey around the self, with each failure, each lesson, and each course correction guiding us toward a more fulfilled and complete version of who we are meant to be. Embrace the journey wholeheartedly, and let every step, no matter how uncertain, lead us closer to our highest potential.

BUILDING AN UNSHAKABLE SELF-RELATIONSHIP
HOW INTEGRITY, GRIT, & ANXIETY SHAPE US

The Most Important Relationship

We often pour significant time and energy into how we relate to the world around us—our work, relationships, and external responsibilities. Yet, we rarely stop to consider the most important relationship of all: the one we have with ourselves.

How we relate to ourselves affects every area of our lives. It shapes our experiences, influences our opportunities, and determines our life satisfaction. While we look outward for fulfillment, the inconvenient truth is that everything we need is already within us. Our ability to face challenges, pursue goals, and navigate life's complexities all stem from how well we know and trust ourselves.

This self-relationship isn't just about introspection—it's about action. We build or break trust with ourselves through the things we do, not just the things we think. Each time we follow through on a commitment, we strengthen our inner bond. When we fail to act or give up too soon, that bond weakens.

We are the only ones who've been with ourselves through every experience, hardship, and triumph. No one knows our full story as intimately as we do. It is through this deep understanding that we form the core of our relationship with ourselves.

Integrity: The Cornerstone of Trust

Integrity is commonly defined as doing the right thing when no one is watching. But when it comes to our self-relationship, integrity takes on a deeper meaning. It's about staying true to our values and commitments, even when the only one watching is ourselves.

Every promise we make to ourselves, whether it's completing a project, hitting a fitness goal, or simply sticking to a routine, either strengthens or weakens our self-trust. When we break these commitments, we create cracks in our integrity. But when we uphold them, we reinforce the belief that we can rely on ourselves. This sense of wholeness and alignment is what gives us peace of mind and personal power.

Think of integrity as the foundation of a house: if it is solid, everything built upon it will stand strong. If it's cracked, the entire structure is at risk of collapsing. The same goes for our lives. When we live with integrity, we become our greatest ally. But when we stray from our commitments, we erode the very foundation of our self-worth.

Living in alignment with our values creates a sense of inner harmony that is irreplaceable. It's more than just doing the right thing—it's about being whole and undivided, knowing that every part of our life is working in service of our greater purpose.

Grit: The Power of Passionate Persistence

While integrity forms the foundation of our self-relationship, grit is what keeps us moving forward. Grit is the ability to persevere with passion and resilience toward long-term goals, even when the going gets tough. It's what separates those who give up from those who push through adversity to reach new heights.

Grit isn't just about working hard—it's about cultivating a mindset of passionate persistence. It's the belief that, with enough effort and time, even the most challenging goals are within reach. And this belief is essential for our self-relationship. Knowing we are capable of enduring difficult situations empowers us. It gives us the confidence to take on bigger challenges, knowing we have what it takes to see them through.

Developing grit requires fostering five key characteristics:

- *Courage* – This doesn't mean eliminating fear but learning to act despite it. To trust ourselves as courageous, we need to recognize our fear, choose the best course of action, and take it.
- **Conscientiousness** – Dependable, achievement-oriented people know they can rise to the occasion because they have done it before. We build self-trust by proving to ourself that we can be reliable and focused on our goals.
- **Endurance** – Life's most valuable rewards often take time. Building a long-term vision and sticking with it strengthens our self-relationship by proving we are someone who follows through, even when the goal seems distant.
- **Resilience** – Optimism, confidence, and creativity help us navigate life's hardships. By knowing ourselves as resilient, we face obstacles not with fear, but with the certainty that we will find a way through.
- **Excellence over Perfection** – Perfectionism can paralyze, but striving for excellence frees us to act. When we know ourselves as someone who puts in our best effort, we move forward without the unrealistic burden of perfection.

By developing these characteristics, grit becomes a protective shield, helping us navigate internal resistance and external challenges. It reassures us that we have the inner strength to endure and succeed, no matter what lies ahead.

The Constructive Role of Anxiety

Anxiety is often viewed as a negative emotion—something to be avoided at all costs. But, like integrity and grit, anxiety plays a critical role in our self-relationship. It can act as a guide, showing us where our most important work lies.

Søren Kierkegaard, the Danish philosopher, described anxiety as a teacher. While it has a demonic side that can overwhelm us, it also has a constructive side that points us toward self-realization. Anxiety highlights the areas of our lives that need attention and growth. It gives us a glimpse into what truly matters to us.

Instead of running from anxiety, we should use it as a tool for self-discovery. When we feel anxious, it's often because we're standing on the edge of something meaningful—a new opportunity, a challenge, or a potential transformation. Embracing this feeling can guide us toward growth and fulfillment.

To harness the power of anxiety, we need to do two things:

- *Take Action Despite Anxiety* – Anxiety doesn't have to be eliminated before we act. In fact, acting in the face of anxiety builds self-trust and resilience.
- *Enhance Articulation* – The more clearly we define the source of our anxiety, the more manageable it becomes. Vague fears paralyze us, but pinpointing the exact cause of our discomfort allows us to focus on addressing the real issue.

Anxiety, when understood and embraced, becomes a powerful motivator. It shows us the path to self-realization and helps us stay on course even when uncertainty looms.

Restoring Integrity Through Action

In life, we inevitably make mistakes, break commitments, and veer off course. When this happens, our integrity—and our relationship with ourselves—can become fractured. But just like the Japanese art of kintsugi, where broken pottery is repaired with gold, we can restore our integrity and come back stronger than before.

Restoring integrity involves a simple process:

1. Acknowledge where we've missed the mark.
2. Understand the impact of our actions.
3. Find ways to make amends or realign with our values.
4. Take action to correct the course.

When we repair our integrity, we not only regain our self-trust but also strengthen it. We become more resilient and more aligned with who we want to be.

Becoming Our Own Ally

The relationship we have with ourselves is the foundation for everything else in life. Through integrity, we build trust; through grit, we find the strength to persevere; and through anxiety, we discover what truly matters.

By nurturing this self-relationship, we become our own greatest ally. We unlock the potential to live a life of purpose, courage, and fulfillment—one that is not defined by external success but by an unwavering commitment to personal growth and self-respect.

In the end, the greatest gift we can give ourselves is the confidence that no matter what life throws at us, we will rise, adapt, and continue moving forward.

THE HIDDEN COST OF BEING GOOD
REPRESSION & SHADOW INTEGRATION

The Good Child Syndrome

In the pursuit of perfection and the ideal self, we often overlook the profound impact of repression, particularly in children who strive to be "good." These "good children" are the ones who seem to do everything right: they finish their homework early, remain quiet and shy, consistently try to help their parents, and have neat handwriting. They are praised for their behavior, and on the surface, they seem to meet the high expectations set for them. But beneath this facade of compliance lies a darker truth.

The real danger of being a "good" child is that no one thinks anything is wrong with them. Adults and caregivers often shift their focus to the more conspicuous troublemakers, leaving the good child unnoticed, even though some degree of trouble is essential for a healthy psyche. These good children, by constantly doing what is expected, repress their own desires and emotions.

Take, for example, a child with a depressed or overwhelmed parent. This child might believe that they must not add to their parent's burdens, so they suppress their needs and emotions, trying to be perfect. Or, perhaps one parent is a violent perfectionist who explodes at any mistake, teaching the child that compliance is a means of survival.

Regardless of the reason, excessive compliance is both unnatural and dangerous. Over time, this repression leads to emotional and psychological consequences, not only in childhood but also later in life.

"When one tries desperately to be good and wonderful and perfect, then all the more the shadow develops a definite will to be black and evil and destructive. People cannot see that; they are always striving to be marvelous, and then they discover that terrible destructive things happen which they cannot understand, and they either deny that such facts have anything to do with them, or if they admit them, they take them for natural afflictions, or they try to minimize them and to shift the responsibility elsewhere. The fact is that if one tries beyond one's capacity to be perfect, the shadow descends into hell and becomes the devil."- Carl Jung (*Visions: Notes of the Seminar Given in 1930–1934*)

The Dangers of Repression

When children develop the need to comply excessively, they begin to repress their emotions and desires for the sake of others. Over time, this repression can manifest in psychosomatic symptoms such as twitches, sudden emotional outbursts, bitterness, or irritability. The child may not even be aware of what is happening because they've lost touch with their feelings.

One of the most insidious outcomes of this repression is that good children may come to believe that their wants and desires are wrong or inappropriate. This detachment from their emotions and bodies can make it difficult for them to form healthy relationships later in life. In some cases, the repression may backfire, and they may rebel, indulging their inner desires in unhealthy ways.

As adults, these former good children may struggle to break

rules or push back against authority, leading to a life of mediocrity and people-pleasing. They are so accustomed to playing by the rules that they lack the flexibility and resilience needed to handle the unpredictability of life. Without the ability to express negative emotions and confront challenges, they remain trapped in a cycle of compliance and repression.

The Shadow: Our Unseen Companion

> "The sad truth is that man's real life consists of a complex of inexorable opposites – day and night, birth and death, happiness and misery, good and evil. We are not even sure that one will prevail over the other, that good will overcome evil, or job defeat pain. Life is a battleground. It always has been, and always will be." - Carl Jung (*Man and His Symbols*)

Swiss psychiatrist Carl Jung warned that the path to wholeness lies not in perfection, but in integrating the shadow—the parts of ourselves that society deems "bad" or "immoral." These rejected aspects of our personality, when repressed, don't disappear. Instead, they grow in power, waiting to surface in unintended and destructive ways.

Jung's concept of the shadow is essential to understanding the plight of the "good child." In striving for goodness and perfection, they ignore their darker impulses, which in turn fester and eventually emerge in destructive ways. By ignoring these aspects of ourselves, we risk unleashing them unexpectedly—often in harmful ways.

The goal, Jung argued, is not to eliminate the shadow but to integrate it. By acknowledging and confronting our less-than-perfect sides, we become more complete and resilient. The wholeness Jung described involves accepting both our capacity for creation and destruction, beauty and catastrophe. Only by wrestling with our shadow can we find true authenticity and freedom.

"By not being aware of having a shadow, you declare a part of your personality to be non-existent. Then it enters the kingdom of the non-existent, which swells up and takes on enormous proportions... If you get rid of qualities you don't like by denying them, you become more and more unaware of what you are, you declare yourself more and more non-existent, and your devils will grow fatter and fatter." - Carl Jung (*Dream Analysis: Notes of the Seminar Given in 1928-1930*)

Practical Ways to Support the "Good Child"

It is crucial for caregivers, parents, and educators to recognize that a child's goodness may mask deeper emotional struggles. Here are some practical ways to support a child who exhibits signs of being overly compliant:

- *Encourage Emotional Expression:* Provide a safe space for the child to express their feelings without fear of punishment or judgment. This can be through conversations, journaling, or creative outlets like art and play.
- *Model Imperfection:* Demonstrate to the child that making mistakes and occasionally breaking the rules is a natural part of life. Emphasize that failure is not something to fear, but a valuable opportunity to learn and grow.
- *Balance Praise and Attention:* Don't only praise children for their compliance. Pay attention to their emotional world, and give them space to challenge and question authority in healthy ways.
- *Help Them Set Boundaries:* Teach the child that it is acceptable to say no, set limits, and prioritize their

needs. This will help them build a sense of autonomy and prevent people-pleasing in the future.

- *Foster Healthy Risk-Taking:* Encourage the child to take small, manageable risks that push them outside of their comfort zone. This could be as simple as trying a new hobby or speaking up in class. The goal is to show them that it's okay to be bold and assertive, even if it leads to failure or rejection.

Integration of the Shadow

As adults, we must also learn to integrate our own shadow—the parts of ourselves that we've repressed or ignored. Shadow integration involves four key steps:

- *Identify the Shadow:* The first and often most difficult step is recognizing the shadow within ourselves. This can be done by paying attention to the traits we most strongly dislike in others, as they often reflect the parts of ourselves we've rejected. Sensitivity to certain remarks or behaviors can also indicate shadowed areas of our psyche.
- *Embrace the Shadow:* Once we've identified the shadow, we must embrace it without judgment. This doesn't mean indulging in destructive behavior, but rather accepting that these darker impulses are part of who we are. By acknowledging them, we reduce their power over us.
- *Explore the Shadow:* Delve deeper into the shadow to understand its origins and its impact on your behavior. This may involve exploring repressed desires, insecurities, or unresolved emotional wounds. As uncomfortable as this process may be, it is essential for growth.

- *Consciously Release the Shadow:* Finally, we must find healthy ways to express and release the shadow. This might involve assertively setting boundaries, standing up for ourselves, or engaging in creative pursuits that allow us to channel our darker impulses in productive ways.

Embracing Wholeness, Not Perfection

Understanding and integrating our shadow is not merely an exercise in self-improvement, but a necessary step towards a balanced and authentic life. The plight of the "good child," who represses their desires in the name of compliance, serves as a powerful reminder of the dangers of striving for perfection. In adulthood, this same repression can manifest as a lack of fulfillment, mediocrity, and emotional numbness.

By embracing our imperfections and integrating the shadow, we unlock a deeper understanding of who we truly are. We allow ourselves to live more authentically, free from the constant pressure to be good or perfect. This journey towards wholeness is challenging but essential for true maturity and fulfillment.

The key to living a more authentic and resilient life is not to strive for perfection, but to accept and integrate all facets of our nature, shadow included. Through this process, we liberate ourselves and set an example of courage and authenticity for those around us.

THE ROLE OF REST
SLEEP & LEARNING

Most of us don't give sleep the credit it deserves, even though it plays a critical role in almost every aspect of our lives. Dr. Matthew Walker is one of the world's leading sleep experts. In his book, *Why We Sleep*, he explains that understanding and improving our sleep can dramatically enhance our learning, health, and overall well-being.

"The best bridge between despair and hope is a good night's sleep."
- Matthew Walker (*Why We Sleep*)

The Importance of Sleep

Sleep is not a luxury; it's a necessity. Just missing an hour or two can throw off our performance, mood, and health. While many believe that the amount of sleep we need decreases as we age, the truth is that adults need 7-9 hours of sleep each night—no exceptions. Sleep is as crucial to our survival as food and water.

The Consequences of Sleep Deprivation

Sleep deprivation isn't just about feeling groggy in the morning. It severely impacts our brain's ability to function. People who are sleep-deprived tend to have a harder time controlling their emotions. That's because a lack of sleep impairs the prefrontal cortex, the part of the brain responsible for decision-making and self-control. Without enough rest, we become more impulsive, sensitive to negative emotions, and less able to think clearly.

Although it is quite often taken as a joke, beauty sleep is a real thing. Sleep deprivation also affects our physical appearance. Studies show that people who get adequate sleep not only look more attractive but also feel healthier and exhibit greater confidence.

But it's not just our brains and looks that suffer. Our immune system, cardiovascular health, and overall life expectancy are all deeply linked to how well we sleep. In fact, losing just one hour of sleep (as during daylight saving time) can increase the risk of heart attacks and strokes by 24%.

Emotional and Cognitive Impact

Ever wonder why everything seems more overwhelming when we're tired? Lack of sleep makes it harder to regulate emotions and respond to stress. Sleep acts as a reset button for our emotional health. It helps us process negative emotions and bounce back from stress. Missing out on sleep, however, makes us more susceptible to mood disorders like depression and anxiety.

More importantly, sleep deprivation can lower our IQ more than alcohol intoxication. If we're pulling an all-nighter for a test or presentation, know that it's doing more harm than good. Proper sleep primes our brains for learning, consolidating memories, and improving cognitive function.

Sleep and Learning: The Mechanics

Sleep isn't just about resting. It's when our brains get to work, organizing and consolidating information from the day. Imagine our short-term memory as a cluttered desk. Throughout the day, we pile on more papers, notes, and ideas. Without sleep, that desk stays cluttered, making it difficult to focus or learn anything new. Sleep, particularly during *memory consolidation*, organizes and files information from our short-term memory into long-term storage.

But there's more to it than just one type of sleep. Let's break down the four phases of the sleep cycle and their specific roles in memory and learning.

Sleep Cycle and Memory

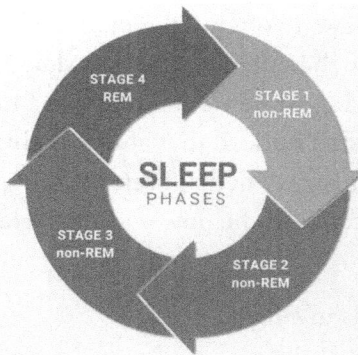

Image from purehempbotanicals.com

1. *Stage 1 (Light Sleep):* This is when we drift in and out of sleep. If we wake up during this stage, we'll feel refreshed, which is why power naps can sometimes work wonders.
2. *Stage 2 (Deeper Sleep):* In this stage, our body temperature drops, and our heart rate slows. It's a transition to deeper sleep, lasting around 20 minutes.

3. *Stage 3 (Deep Sleep):* This is where the magic of *declarative memory consolidation* happens—the kind of memory that helps us recall facts, names, and general knowledge. Deep sleep is essential for learning things that are straightforward or neutral.

4. *REM Sleep (Dream Sleep):* During this stage, our brain is highly active, even though our body remains deeply relaxed. *Procedural memories*—how to ride a bike, play an instrument, or perform a specific skill—are consolidated during REM. If we're learning a new sport or trying to master a skill, REM sleep is where we'll see the most improvement. Interestingly, our brain can repeat these motor skills 30-40 times during a night of REM sleep, which explains why we might wake up better at something than when we went to bed. When we learn something new, it's often difficult at first, but we usually find we're much better at it the next day. This is our brain practicing while we sleep. When I first learned to play the guitar, I noticed that after a night of sleep, I could suddenly play better, even without practicing. This was because of the power of REM sleep.

The Health Benefits of Sleep

Sleep is crucial for more than just learning and memory. It plays a vital role in maintaining overall health.

- *Neurological Maintenance:* While we sleep, the brain cleans itself. The glymphatic system flushes out harmful proteins like beta-amyloid, which can build up and lead to Alzheimer's if not cleared. If we have a family history of Alzheimer's, prioritizing sleep can be a protective measure.
- *Hormonal Health:* For men, sleep directly affects testosterone levels. Men who sleep less than 5 hours a

night have testosterone levels comparable to someone 10 years older. That's not all—sleep deprivation affects fertility for both men and women.

- *Cardiovascular Health:* Our heart also needs rest. Sleep helps regulate blood pressure and reduce the risk of heart attacks and strokes. Missing just an hour of sleep can lead to serious health consequences, which is why it's crucial to maintain a consistent sleep schedule.

Societal Impacts: Rethinking Sleep

Our society often undervalues sleep. People boast about how little sleep they get, as if it's a badge of honor. But the truth is, sacrificing sleep makes us less productive, not more. Teenagers, in particular, are often the victims of this perspective. High schools typically start too early, ignoring the fact that teens have a naturally shifted circadian rhythm. Starting school later could significantly improve academic performance and mental health.

We also underestimate the dangers of sleep deprivation. Driving or performing tasks without enough sleep can be more dangerous than being under the influence of alcohol. Sleep-deprived drivers have slower reflexes, making them more likely to cause accidents.

Practical Tips for Better Sleep

We know why sleep is important, but how do we improve it? Here are some simple, actionable steps to boost your sleep quality:

- *Manage Our Sleep Environment:* Avoid blue light exposure from screens an hour or two before bed. Blue light disrupts melatonin production, delaying sleep onset and reducing sleep quality. Try dimming the lights and using night mode on our devices to minimize this effect.

- *Watch What We Eat and Drink:* Caffeine can stay in our system for up to 14 hours, affecting our ability to fall asleep. Alcohol, while it might make us feel sleepy, disrupts the quality of our sleep, especially REM stages. Avoid these substances close to bedtime for better rest.
- *Keep Cool:* Our body temperature needs to drop slightly for us to fall asleep. Taking a warm shower before bed helps the body release heat, priming it for sleep. Keep our bedroom cool to facilitate deeper, more restorative sleep.
- *Stick to a Sleep Schedule:* Our bodies thrive on consistency. Going to bed and waking up at the same time every day, even on weekends, helps regulate your circadian rhythm, making it easier to fall asleep and wake up refreshed.

Sleep is not just a passive activity; it's a powerful force that influences nearly every aspect of our lives. From improving our cognitive function and emotional well-being to maintaining our physical health, sleep is essential for optimal performance. There are deep connections between sleep, learning, and overall well-being. When we prioritize sleep and make small adjustments to our environment and habits, we can learn faster, perform better, and live healthier lives.

The benefits of proper sleep go beyond just feeling rested. It enhances our memory, sharpens our decision-making, and protects our health in ways that are often undervalued in modern society. Yet despite its profound impact, sleep is often the first thing we sacrifice when life becomes busy.

It's time to rethink how we approach sleep. Instead of viewing it as something to cut down on, we should view it as a critical investment in our long-term health and success. With simple changes—such as managing our sleep environment, sticking to a schedule, and avoiding harmful habits like late-night screen use or caffeine—we can significantly improve our sleep quality and, in turn, our quality of life. After all, a good night's sleep may be the most effective and accessible tool we have for achieving our goals and thriving in our daily lives.

NEUROTRANSMITTERS & LEARNING

THE CHEMICALS OF HUMAN BEHAVIOR, MENTAL HEALTH, & LEARNING

How Chemical Messengers Shape Learning, Mood, and Daily Life

Neurotransmitters may sound complicated, but they play a huge role in our daily lives. Think of them as the brain's text messages, sending signals between cells to control everything from our mood and sleep to our ability to learn and make decisions. We can boost our mental clarity, sharpen our ability to learn, and enhance our mental well-being by understanding how these chemical messengers work.

What Are Neurotransmitters?

Our brains are made up of billions of neurons, and these neurons communicate across gaps called synapses. Neurotransmitters act as messengers, carrying signals from one neuron to another. Every time we think, feel, or learn something new, neurotransmitters are at work, creating and strengthening connections in our brain.

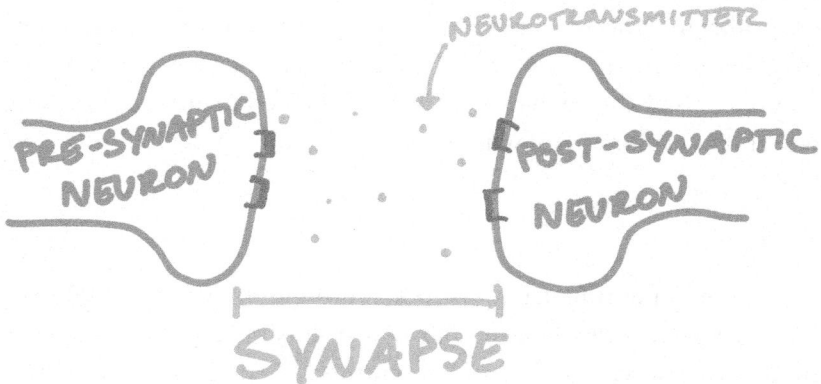

I drew this (if you couldn't tell)

Here's a breakdown of the primary neurotransmitters that are key to learning and everyday functions:

Norepinephrine (Adrenaline)

This neurotransmitter gears us up for action, triggering the body's fight-or-flight response. Norepinephrine, also known as adrenaline, is released when we face a threat or something unexpected. It increases heart rate, sharpens focus, and prepares the body for movement. In learning, adrenaline helps us stay alert when we need to pay attention to something important.

Dopamine

Dopamine is our brain's reward chemical. It motivates us to pursue goals by making challenges seem more achievable and less tiring. Think about the excitement we feel after finishing a difficult task—that's dopamine giving us a sense of accomplishment. It reinforces behaviors, so if we study hard and do well on a test, dopamine makes it more likely that we'll study hard again in the future.

But dopamine works both ways. It can reinforce negative behaviors too. For example, if someone lies to cover up harmful habits, like substance abuse, and then experiences a dopamine release, they're more likely to lie again in the future. This is why dopamine is often called the molecule of "more"—whether it's good or bad, we tend to want more of what releases it.

Serotonin

While dopamine drives us to achieve more, serotonin helps us enjoy what we already have. This neurotransmitter is linked to feelings of calmness, safety, and contentment. When we pet our dog, serotonin is released, making us feel good about the moment. It's essential for mood stability, sleep, and even digestion.

Importantly, serotonin makes us feel safe, which is critical for learning. Without enough serotonin, we can feel anxious or stressed, making it harder to focus and absorb new information.

GABA

Gamma-aminobutyric acid (GABA) is the brain's calm-down signal. It reduces neural activity, promoting relaxation and focus. GABA helps filter out distractions, allowing us to concentrate on what really matters. Without enough GABA, our brain may become overstimulated, making it difficult to focus or remain calm under stress.

Acetylcholine

Acetylcholine is the neurotransmitter that helps us zero in on a task. It sharpens focus, improves memory, and keeps us motivated. When we encounter a problem or something that grabs our interest, acetylcholine helps us pay attention long enough to solve it. Think of it as the brain's spotlight, highlighting important details so that we can store them in our memory.

Acetylcholine is released after norepinephrine signals to the brain that something is wrong. It helps us focus on figuring out the solution, making it crucial for learning and attention.

OTHER IMPORTANT NEUROTRANSMITTERS:

- *Glutamate:* The main excitatory neurotransmitter involved in learning and memory.
- *Histamine:* Plays a role in the sleep-wake cycle and the body's response to allergens.
- *Endorphins:* Natural pain relievers that also promote feelings of pleasure.
- *Anandamide:* Helps regulate appetite, motivation, and pleasure.
- *Adenosine:* Promotes sleep and reduces arousal, acting as a natural calming agent.

How Diet Impacts Brain Chemistry

What we eat can influence our neurotransmitter levels. Here are some dietary choices that can affect our brains:

- *Fasting:* Short-term fasting increases norepinephrine and dopamine, which can make us feel more alert and improve our ability to learn. However, fasting for too long may impact our ability to retain information.
- *Carbohydrates:* Eating carbs triggers serotonin release, which promotes feelings of calm and well-being. This can create a safe mental space for learning.
- *Eggs, Nuts, and Nicotine:* These substances are known to increase acetylcholine production, improving focus and attention.

Neurotransmitters and the Learning Process

Our brains aren't always learning. We only learn something when our brain encounters something frustrating or experiences high emotional intensity. There is a specific release of neurotransmitters that facilitates learning in our brains. It can be thought of in three steps:

1. *Epinephrine (Adrenaline)* is released when we first realize we don't understand something. It's that uncomfortable feeling of frustration or confusion that signals the brain to pay attention. This signals to our brain that we need to learn something new.
2. *Acetylcholine* then helps us focus on solving the problem, directing our brain's energy to find a solution.
3. Finally, *Dopamine* is released when we make progress or achieve a goal, reinforcing the effort and helping solidify new neural connections.

Meanwhile, serotonin keeps us calm enough to stay focused, while GABA blocks unnecessary distractions, allowing us to learn effectively.

Why Winners Keep Winning: A Dopamine Insight

Research has shown that winners tend to keep winning because of increased activity in the brain's frontal cortex, which helps convert stress into forward motion. The brain's response to success enhances performance, making it easier to build on previous achievements.

Dopamine also plays a role here. When we experience success, it reinforces the behaviors that led to that success, making us more likely to repeat them.

.   .   .

NEUROTRANSMITTERS ARE the unsung heroes of how we think, feel, and learn. By understanding how these chemical messengers work, we can optimize our brain function, manage stress, and improve our learning abilities. Additionally, small changes in diet and daily habits can go a long way in enhancing our mental clarity and well-being.

NEUROPLASTICITY & FOCUS
THE KEY TO LIFELONG LEARNING

"Live as if you were to die tomorrow. Learn as if you were to live forever." – Mahatma Gandhi

Our brains are more like sculptors than machines, reshaping themselves constantly with each new experience and challenge. Neuroplasticity, the brain's remarkable ability to reorganize itself, allows us to adapt, learn, and grow throughout our lives. However, this reshaping doesn't happen automatically; certain conditions trigger the brain to change.

Neuroplasticity is not a continuous process. Instead, it occurs when we encounter failure, experience intense emotions, repeat actions, or find ourselves off balance. Some neural pathways are strengthened while others fade, depending on our focus and effort. At times, this transformation happens gradually, while in other moments, a single event can forever alter the way our brains function.

For adults, learning doesn't involve growing new neurons but rather reshaping the ones we already have. While some systems, like autonomic functions, are difficult to change, voluntary systems are more accessible, enabling us to acquire new skills, rewire habits, or lessen the emotional weight of grief.

The Brain-Behavior Relationship

The brain is the control center of behavior, capable of adapting to new experiences by modifying its neural pathways. Every time we engage in activities that push us out of our routine, we challenge the brain to adjust and evolve.

To harness this adaptability, we must step outside our comfort zones and confront failure. This act of pushing ourselves beyond what we know is what prompts neuroplasticity to take effect. Without challenges, the brain has no reason to change.

Learning Through Failure: The Emotional Steps of Learning

Contrary to the belief that learning happens best in a state of flow, true learning occurs through failure. While flow represents the brain executing what it already knows, neuroplasticity is sparked when we attempt something unfamiliar and fail.

Frustration & Epinephrine

Failure is not a dead end but a starting point. When we fail, the brain releases epinephrine and cortisol—stress hormones that signal something isn't working. This stress primes the brain to be open to change, unlocking the learning process. Without failure, we lack the drive for improvement.

We can increase epinephrine levels and stimulate alertness through sleep, caffeine, strong emotions like love or hate, or accountability measures like deadlines. The frustration arising from failure is a powerful trigger, signaling to the brain that it's time to adapt. Embrace frustration—it's our brain's way of telling us that we're about to learn something new.

Focus & Acetylcholine

Once epinephrine kicks in, the brain releases acetylcholine, the neurotransmitter responsible for focus. The brain doesn't initially know what the problem is, only that something needs to be fixed. If we concentrate on the source of frustration, acetylcholine helps us zoom in on the issue, giving us the chance to solve it.

To enhance acetylcholine and improve focus, we can practice visual focus techniques. Looking at a specific point for a sustained period trains the brain to concentrate. Mental focus follows visual focus. Unfortunately, many people avoid frustration and focus instead on distractions, missing the opportunity to solve the problem.

Reward & Dopamine

As we make progress and correct mistakes, dopamine—the brain's reward chemical—comes into play. Dopamine reinforces behaviors by rewarding close approximations to success. The closer we get to solving a problem, the more dopamine is released, encouraging us to keep going.

This dopamine release is subjective; different people respond to different stimuli. By learning to associate dopamine with the act of making errors, we can transform mistakes into exciting opportunities for growth. However, the same mechanism can work against us if we avoid challenges, training the brain to seek escape rather than perseverance.

This biochemical feedback loop—frustration, focus, and reward—is essential for learning. Without failure and frustration, there can be no progress. The more we focus on the problems that initially frustrate us, the more we grow and improve.

Other Triggers of Neuroplasticity

Highly emotional or traumatic events can trigger neuroplasticity, sometimes creating lifelong memories. While our nervous systems are designed for survival, intense experiences compel the brain to pay extra attention. This hyper-focus leads to long-lasting neural changes, but these effects can be managed and restructured through processes like therapy, meditation, or deliberate learning practices.

Surprise, both good and bad, also stimulates neuroplasticity. Unexpected events force the brain to adapt quickly, preparing for future uncertainties. Neuroplasticity is further consolidated during sleep, where the brain strengthens neural circuits activated during learning. Non-sleep deep rest (NSDR) techniques and meditation can mimic this effect, enhancing the brain's ability to adapt and learn even outside of sleep.

Age and Plasticity

There is a myth that as we age, we get "stuck in our ways." Regardless of age, our brains remain capable of change. Younger people, especially those under 25, exhibit remarkable plasticity, spending more time in learning states and adapting quickly to new environments. Their nervous systems naturally embrace change without sacrificing old neural pathways.

In adults, neuroplasticity still happens but requires more deliberate effort. Adults must be willing to sacrifice old habits or ways of thinking to make room for new learning. This process starts with recognition—the prefrontal cortex alerts the brain that something important is happening and deserves attention. Short, intense learning sessions can help adults maximize their brain's potential for change, especially when highly motivated or facing survival-based challenges.

The Ultradian Cycle for Focus

The ultradian rhythm is a concept from chronobiology. It is a cycle that repeats throughout a 24-hour day. Ultradian rhythms are shorter cycles that occur multiple times throughout the day and regulate hunger, thirst, and heart rate.

The ultradian rhythm lasts about 90 minutes and provides a practical framework for organizing learning sessions.

The cycle starts with difficulty focusing, followed by a peak focus period, and ends with the mind wandering, which signals that it may be time to take a break.

People typically have trouble focusing when they start a task, but this is a normal part of the cycle and not a signal that we can't concentrate. We can use the ultradian rhythm to plan periods of productivity and learning.

Strategies for Enhancing Focus and Neuroplasticity

Engage in Learning Bouts

Plan learning sessions when we are most alert, using short bursts of focused effort. We can aim for intervals of 7 to 23 minutes, depending on our capacity to focus. The first few minutes may feel uncomfortable as our brain ramps up, but pushing through this initial phase is crucial for deep learning.

Manage Emotional and Physical States

Learning requires a balance of stress and calm. If we're too stressed, breathing techniques like the double inhale-exhale can calm the nervous system by reducing excess carbon dioxide. Alternatively, if we're too relaxed, practices like hyperoxygenation can raise stress levels, boosting our focus. Visual focus exercises—

focusing our gaze on a small object for a sustained period—can also sharpen mental concentration.

Novel Physical Experiences

Engaging the vestibular system, which governs balance, can enhance neuroplasticity. Activities that challenge your balance, like yoga, cycling, or gymnastics, stimulate the brain's plasticity centers, opening new pathways for learning.

WHEN WE UNDERSTAND the mechanisms behind neuroplasticity and actively engage in practices that promote it, we can continuously evolve and adapt. Whether it's through managing frustration, improving focus, or challenging ourselves physically, we have the tools to shape our brains for a lifetime of learning and growth.

The key to lifelong learning is to embrace challenges, use our body's natural rhythms, and make failure a friend, not an enemy. Through intentional practice and a deeper understanding of how our brains respond to new experiences, we can unlock the transformative power of neuroplasticity, no matter our age or background.

FINDING FLOW
MASTERING FOCUS & PEAK PERFORMANCE

"The best moments in our lives are not the passive, receptive, relaxing times... The best moments usually occur if a person's body or mind is stretched to its limits in a voluntary effort to accomplish something difficult and worthwhile." - Mihaly Csikszentmihalyi (*Flow: The Psychology of Optimal Experience*)

Occasionally, we become so immersed in a task that time seems to melt away. Maybe we've experienced this while playing an instrument, working on a project, or even during a conversation where hours felt like minutes. This powerful mental state is known as *flow*. When in flow, we're completely absorbed in what we're doing, and nothing else seems to matter. It not only feels good but also makes us highly productive. The good news is that flow isn't something that just happens by chance—we can learn to enter this state more often.

What is Flow?

Flow is a state of deep focus, where we're fully engaged and enjoying the task at hand. Psychologist Mihaly Csikszentmihalyi, who coined the term, described it as a time when we're so involved in an activity that we keep going simply because it feels good. Think of a painter losing track of time while creating a masterpiece, or an athlete who is "in the zone" during a game. Flow has eight main characteristics:

- Absolute concentration
- Clear focus on our goals
- Time seems to speed up or slow down
- We feel rewarded by the experience itself
- The task feels effortless
- The challenge is just right—difficult but not overwhelming
- Our actions become almost automatic
- We feel comfortable and in control of what we're doing

When we're in flow, everything seems to click. We can work at our highest potential, often without even realizing it. The world fades away, and it's just us and the task at hand.

The 4 Stages of Flow

According to Steven Kotler, author and founder of the Flow Research Collective, there are four stages that help us reach flow. These stages are like climbing a mountain—each one brings us closer to the peak, where flow happens.

Struggle

This is the initial stage, and it often feels like anything but flow. It's the tough uphill climb where we're trying to get started. Whether we're beginning a workout, diving into research, or brainstorming, we might feel as if we're forcing ourselves to focus. The key here is persistence—getting past the struggle is essential to reaching flow.

Relaxation

After struggling to get started, it's time to take a step back. This could be as simple as taking a walk, doing some deep breathing, or stretching. This phase is like pausing halfway up the mountain to catch your breath. Relaxation helps us recharge and prepares our brains for the next stage.

Flow

This is where the magic happens. Once we've pushed through the struggle and recharged, we reach flow. We're completely absorbed in the task, and everything feels automatic. Time flies by, and we're doing our best work. It's like being on a smooth section of the trail, where every step feels natural.

Consolidation

After the flow stage, we may feel a sense of letdown. It's normal. Our brain is consolidating everything we've accomplished. This is when we need to rest and let our brain process before the next round of flow. Like reaching the peak of the mountain, we take a moment to appreciate the view before heading back down.

Why Flow Feels So Good: The Role of Dopamine

One reason flow feels so incredible is dopamine—a powerful brain chemical that makes us feel happy and motivated. When we're in flow, our brain releases a flood of dopamine, which rewards us with feelings of pleasure and satisfaction. It's like the brain's way of saying, "Keep going, this feels amazing."

In addition to dopamine, other chemicals like norepinephrine (which sharpens focus) and endorphins (which reduce pain and enhance euphoria) play a role. This cocktail of brain chemicals not only helps us stay in flow longer but also makes us crave it. This is why flow can feel addictive—we want to keep coming back to this rewarding state.

Flow is About Doing, Not Learning

It's important to understand that flow involves using what we already know, not learning something new. When we're in flow, we're putting our existing skills into action. We're not figuring things out or learning new techniques; instead, we're operating at peak performance using the knowledge and abilities we've already mastered.

For example, a musician in flow isn't learning a new song—they're playing one they know by heart. Flow occurs when the challenge is just right—enough to keep us engaged but not so difficult that we need to pause and learn. Learning happens outside of flow, during the practice stage. Once we've developed new skills, we can return to flow to apply them effortlessly.

How to Find Flow

Flow doesn't happen by chance. We can take specific steps to make entering this optimal state easier.

- *Plan for Enough Time:* Flow takes time. It usually kicks in after 20–30 minutes of focused work, so set aside a solid block of uninterrupted time for the task at hand.
- *Eliminate Distractions:* Create a space where we can focus by turning off our phones, closing unnecessary tabs, and using noise-canceling headphones if needed.
- *Do Something We Love:* It's easier to find flow when we're working on something we enjoy or that has personal meaning. Passion drives focus.
- *Have Clear Goals:* Even a small, clear goal can help guide

our focus and lead us into flow. We need to know what we're trying to accomplish.

- *Challenge Ourselves (But Not Too Much):* Make sure the task is challenging enough to keep us engaged but not so difficult that we feel overwhelmed. The sweet spot is where effort meets ability.

The 3 Enemies of Flow

Just as there are ways to find flow, certain factors can block it. Here are three major enemies to watch out for:

- *Multitasking:* Trying to juggle multiple tasks prevents us from fully focusing on any one thing. Research shows that multitasking not only reduces productivity but also makes it harder to enter flow. Our brain needs sustained attention to reach this state.
- *Stress:* When we're preoccupied with stress, it's tough to focus. If there's something pressing on our minds, we need to deal with it before starting the task. However, if it's not urgent, we can set it aside and focus on the task at hand—stress can wait.
- *Fear of Failure:* Perfectionism and fear of failure are huge blockers to flow. If we're too focused on doing things perfectly, it's hard to let go and fully immerse ourselves in the moment. Mistakes are part of growth. Letting go of the need for perfection allows us to tap into creativity and productivity.

FLOW IS a powerful mental state that allows us to be both productive and deeply satisfied with what we're doing. When we understand the stages of flow, take steps to minimize distractions, and recognize the barriers that can prevent us from finding it, we can access this rewarding state more often. Whether we're working on a creative project, tackling an important task, or exercising, flow is within reach—ready to elevate our work and make it feel effortless.

THE RESILIENT MIND

HOW THE AMCT SHAPES LEARNING, WILLPOWER, & AGING

Sometimes we experience a rush of focus right before tackling a difficult problem. This can happen when we are preparing for an exam or pushing through a tough workout. That heightened state of readiness comes from a part of the brain called the anterior midcingulate cortex, or AMCT. The AMCT plays a crucial role in how we approach life's challenges, influencing our ability to learn, exercise willpower, and even how we age.

The Role of the AMCT in Learning and Willpower

The AMCT, a part of a broader brain region known as the anterior cingulate cortex (ACC), acts as the brain's challenge-response center. It is activated when we face difficult tasks, signaling the need for more focus and effort. This region is involved in both cognitive functions (like attention, problem-solving, and error monitoring) and emotional regulation (managing how we feel about those tasks). In essence, the AMCT helps us persevere when the going gets tough.

When we repeatedly engage in challenging tasks, the AMCT

doesn't necessarily "grow" in size but becomes more efficient and functionally connected. This is a form of neuroplasticity, where brain regions develop stronger connections and improve their overall performance. Just as a muscle becomes stronger with repeated use, the AMCT improves in its ability to handle difficult cognitive and emotional tasks over time.

However, if we avoid challenges or give up too easily, the AMCT doesn't get the "exercise" it needs. Over time, such avoidance may weaken the AMCT's ability to handle challenges, much like how unused muscles lose strength.

Learning Through Challenge

One of the most critical times the AMCT is activated is right before we take on something difficult. It prepares our brain and body to focus, get ready for effort, and stay mentally sharp. This can be thought of as a mental 'warm-up' signaling readiness.

Interestingly, as we improve at handling a particular challenge —such as learning a new skill or mastering a tough task—the AMCT requires less effort. The brain adapts and becomes more efficient, so the level of AMCT activation decreases as we become more comfortable and proficient at that task. This is part of how our brains optimize and make once-challenging tasks feel easier with practice.

Willpower and the Will to Life

Willpower is a critical component of success, and it is closely tied to the function of the AMCT. When we stick with difficult tasks and persevere through challenges, the AMCT plays a key role in maintaining our focus and determination. However, it doesn't work alone—other parts of the brain, such as the prefrontal cortex, also contribute to willpower by helping us make decisions and regulate our impulses.

Over time, regular engagement in challenging tasks not

only strengthens our willpower but also enhances our resilience. This aligns with philosopher Friedrich Nietzsche's concept of the "will to life," the fundamental drive to overcome obstacles and thrive. Individuals with a well-developed AMCT, and the corresponding cognitive networks, may display a stronger will to push through difficulties and achieve their goals.

The AMCT and Super Agers

One of the most fascinating aspects of the AMCT is its potential link to aging. Researchers have identified a group of people known as *super agers* who maintain sharp cognitive function well into their later years. Interestingly, these individuals tend to have larger and more active anterior cingulate cortices (of which the AMCT is a part) compared to the average person.

While we cannot say that the size of the AMCT alone determines how well someone will age, there is evidence that regularly engaging in cognitively and emotionally challenging tasks throughout life may help keep the brain robust. Super agers often engage in mentally challenging activities—such as learning new skills, solving puzzles, or staying socially active—which strengthen the AMCT and other critical brain areas, potentially preventing cognitive decline.

What Makes the AMCT Stronger or Weaker?

Just like a muscle, the AMCT can become more efficient—or lose its edge—depending on how much we engage it. Here's what contributes to its resilience or decline:

Growth Factors

- *Engagement with Difficult Tasks:* Regularly challenging ourselves increases the functional efficiency and connectivity of the AMCT, making it better at helping us focus and persevere.

- *Learning to Appreciate Challenges:* When we face difficult tasks and learn to appreciate the growth they offer, the AMCT becomes even more efficient at handling future challenges.

Shrinking Factors

- *Avoidance of Challenges:* If we shy away from hard tasks, the AMCT doesn't get the stimulation it needs, potentially weakening over time.
- *Chronic Stress:* Moderate, manageable stress can enhance the brain's performance, including that of the AMCT. However, chronic stress—especially without periods of recovery—can impair the function of the brain regions that work alongside the AMCT, reducing its overall effectiveness in managing challenges.

Embracing the AMCT's Power

The AMCT is a remarkable part of the brain, responsible for helping us rise to challenges, grow through them, and build mental resilience. By regularly engaging in tasks that push us outside our comfort zones and managing stress in healthy ways, we can train our AMCT to work more efficiently. This not only enhances our ability to learn and persevere but also has long-term benefits for maintaining cognitive sharpness as we age.

Through neuroplasticity, the brain adapts to the demands we place on it. Stimulating the AMCT through challenging tasks develops its functional capacity, enabling us to tackle future challenges with greater ease. And the benefits don't stop at learning and willpower—they extend into how well we age. The "super-ager" phenomenon highlights the importance of maintaining a healthy, active brain through consistent mental and emotional engagement.

. . .

EMBRACING CHALLENGES, appreciating their growth potential, and managing stress constructively are essential strategies for nurturing a strong, resilient AMCT and, by extension, a powerful and adaptable brain.

THINK LIKE AI, LEARN LIKE HUMANS
WHAT MACHINES CAN TEACH US ABOUT MASTERY

A rtificial Intelligence (AI) offers us a fascinating glimpse into the mechanics of learning. While AI doesn't learn exactly as humans do, its processes of training, inference, and feedback provide valuable insights that can inspire us to approach learning and skill-building in new ways.

Training: The Power of Practice and Patience

Training is the first phase in developing AI. AI requires vast amounts of data and computational power to identify patterns and make sense of information. In a way, this mirrors how humans learn—we need practice, time, and focus to master new skills.

For instance, think of a student learning to read. The student spends hours going over words and sentences, gradually improving. Similarly, AI processes vast data sets repeatedly to learn, but unlike humans, it doesn't "understand" concepts—it recognizes patterns. This brute-force repetition is necessary for both AI and human learning, but the human brain also engages with the material on a deeper level, forming connections and gaining deeper understanding.

While AI's training is computationally heavy, requiring significant power and time, human learning, though slower, involves not just memory and recognition but also emotional and intellectual engagement. Both processes demand substantial effort and persistence, but the return on investment is tremendous. Once trained, applying the knowledge becomes easier for both humans and AI.

Inference: Applying Knowledge with Efficiency

Once an AI model has been trained, it enters the *inference* stage, where it uses its learned data to make decisions or predictions. For example, after processing thousands of images of cats, AI can now recognize a cat in a new picture with ease. The computational power needed for inference is much lower than for training, but it still requires some resources.

For humans, this is like mastering a skill—once we've spent time learning to read, play a musical instrument, or solve math problems, using that skill becomes less effortful. The heavy lifting happens during the learning phase, but applying knowledge becomes smoother and more natural with practice.

This is a key lesson for us: while learning requires significant time and energy, applying what we've learned later takes much less effort. Both AI and humans demonstrate this efficiency in the application of knowledge.

Key Lessons from AI for Human Learning

Here are four crucial takeaways we can learn from AI's training process:

Practice is Fundamental to Mastery

AI must process large amounts of data repeatedly before it can make accurate predictions. Similarly, humans require practice and repetition to improve at any skill, whether it's learning to read, playing an instrument, or mastering a sport. While the initial learning phase is energy-intensive, it is an investment that pays off later when the skill becomes second nature.

Diverse Inputs Enhance Learning

AI performs best when it is trained on varied types of data. The more diverse the input, the better it can generalize and make accurate predictions. For humans, diverse experiences—such as trying new activities, reading different books, or learning from different perspectives—enrich our understanding and enable us to make creative connections.

For example, I like to apply the culinary concept of *mise en place* (having everything in its place) from cooking to my music production process. By organizing tools and sounds before starting to create, I find myself working more efficiently. This shows how diverse inputs can help us discover new approaches to problem-solving.

Applying Knowledge Reduces Cognitive Load

Once AI is trained, using what it has learned is far less demanding than the training process. Similarly, once we've mastered a skill, applying it becomes less mentally taxing. This is why practice is so important—what starts out as difficult and energy-consuming eventually becomes easier and automatic.

Understanding that the effort required to learn a new skill diminishes after mastery can help us persist through the early, challenging phases of learning. The reward is fluency, where applying knowledge becomes effortless.

Feedback Fuels Improvement

AI continually improves when it receives feedback on its predictions. Humans, too, benefit greatly from feedback, whether it comes from teachers, peers, or the results of our own efforts. Feedback allows us to course-correct and refine our skills, and this iterative process is essential for growth.

Constructive feedback, even when it points out mistakes, is one of the most effective ways to improve quickly. In fact, embracing feedback is crucial for continuous development, whether in academics, sports, or professional life.

Learning as an Investment

The parallels between AI and human learning remind us that while the initial stages of learning are energy-intensive and often challenging, they are crucial investments in our future. AI's brute-force training may seem mechanical, but the same principles apply to us: persistence, practice, and feedback are essential for mastering any skill. And just like AI, once we've internalized a skill, using it becomes almost effortless.

The AI process shows us that learning doesn't just get easier with time—it becomes more powerful. Mastery is within reach for those willing to put in the work, and once that work is complete, applying knowledge becomes second nature.

BOOK REFERENCES & RECOMMENDATIONS

FOR MINDFUL LEARNING

"It's not about the book, it's about the book the book leads you to."
- Austin Kleon (*Steal Like an Artist*)

Book References & Recommendations

Distinguishing Knowledge from Wisdom: The Foundations of Being a Better Learner

- "The Republic" by Plato
- "Nicomachean Ethics" by Aristotle
- "The Collected Works of Jean Piaget" by Jean Piaget
- "Wisdom, Intelligence, and Creativity Synthesized" by Robert J. Sternberg
- "The Power of Habit" by Charles Duhigg
- "The 48 Laws of Power" by Robert Greene
- "The Obstacle Is the Way" by Ryan Holiday
- "Letters from a Stoic" by Seneca
- "Bloom's Taxonomy of Educational Objectives" by Benjamin Bloom

The Pareto Principle: The 80/20 Rule in Learning

- "The 80/20 Principle" by Richard Koch
- "Deep Work" by Cal Newport
- "Atomic Habits" by James Clear
- "Essentialism" by Greg McKeown
- "Make It Stick" by Peter C. Brown, Henry L. Roediger III, and Mark A. McDaniel
- "The Four-Hour Workweek" by Tim Ferriss
- "First Things First" by Stephen R. Covey, A. Roger Merrill, and Rebecca R. Merrill
- "Outliers" by Malcolm Gladwell
- "The Practicing Mind" by Thomas M. Sterner
- "Flow" by Mihaly Csikszentmihalyi

Eat the Frog: Mastering Cognitive Load

- "Cognitive Load Theory" by John Sweller
- "The Power of Habit" by Charles Duhigg
- "The Practicing Mind" by Thomas M. Sterner
- "Thinking, Fast and Slow" by Daniel Kahneman
- "Atomic Habits" by James Clear
- "The Personal MBA" by Josh Kaufman
- "Eat That Frog!" by Brian Tracy

The Urge to Feel Special: Cognitive Biases in Learning

- "Thinking, Fast and Slow" by Daniel Kahneman
- "Scientific Thinking & Communication)" by Neil deGrasse Tyson (course)
- "The Black Swan" by Nassim Nicholas Taleb
- "The Demon-Haunted World" by Carl Sagan
- "12 Rules for Life" by Jordan Peterson
- "The Art of Thinking Clearly" by Rolf Dobelli
- "You Are Not So Smart" by David McRaney

The Memory Blueprint: Our Mind's Storage System

- "The Brain That Changes Itself" by Norman Doidge
- "Thinking, Fast and Slow" by Daniel Kahneman
- "Moonwalking with Einstein" by Joshua Foer
- "Make It Stick" by Peter C. Brown, Henry L. Roediger III, and Mark A. McDaniel
- "The Art of Memory" by Frances A. Yates
- "An Introduction to Mathematics" by Alfred North Whitehead

Becoming You: Identity & Self Perception

- "Atomic Habits" by James Clear
- "Mindset" by Carol S. Dweck
- "The Power of Habit" by Charles Duhigg
- "The Self Illusion" by Bruce Hood
- "Limitless" by Jim Kwik

Cognitive Processing in Learning: Top-Down vs. Bottom-Up

- "Thinking, Fast and Slow" by Daniel Kahneman
- "Make It Stick" by Peter C. Brown, Henry L. Roediger III, and Mark A. McDaniel
- "The Organized Mind" by Daniel J. Levitin
- "A Mind for Numbers" by Barbara Oakley
- "How We Learn" by Benedict Carey

Beyond Comfort: Choosing Discomfort for a Life of Meaning

- "Thus Spoke Zarathustra" by Friedrich Nietzsche
- "The Last Messiah" by Peter Zapffe
- "Mastery" by Robert Greene
- "God in the Dock" by C.S. Lewis

Harnessing Emotions for Growth: How to Channel Our Core Drives for Learning & Transformation

- "**Affective Neuroscience: The Foundations of Human and Animal Emotions**" by Jaak Panksepp
- "**Animals Make Us Human**" by Temple Grandin
- "**The Body Keeps the Score**" by Bessel van der Kolk

Shifting Our Locus of Control: The Power of Ownership

- "**Extreme Ownership**" by Jocko Willink and Leif Babin
- "**Man's Search for Meaning**" by Viktor E. Frankl
- "**The 7 Habits of Highly Effective People**" by Stephen R. Covey
- "**The Locus of Control**" by H. M. Lefcourt
- "**Mindset**" by Carol S. Dweck
- "**Dare to Lead**" by Brené Brown
- "**Spider-Man**" The Marvel Comics

Harnessing Hypnotic Rhythm: The Law That Shapes Our Lives

- "**Outwitting the Devil**" by Napoleon Hill
- "**The Personal MBA**" by Josh Kaufman

From Drifting to Direction: Escaping Aimlessness with Purpose

- "**Thus Spoke Zarathustra**" by Friedrich Nietzsche
- "**Twilight of the Idols**" by Friedrich Nietzsche
- "**Outwitting the Devil**" by Napoleon Hill
- "**Man's Search for Meaning**" by Viktor E. Frankl
- "**Mastery**" by Robert Greene
- "**The Power of Now**" by Eckhart Tolle
- "**Atomic Habits**" by James Clear
- "**The Brothers Karamazov**" by Fyodor Dostoyevsky
- "**On the Genealogy of Morality**" by Friedrich Nietzsche

- "The Purpose Driven Life" by Rick Warren
- "Inferno" by Dan Brown
- "The War of Art" by Steven Pressfield
- "The 7 Habits of Highly Effective People" by Stephen R. Covey
- "The Hero with a Thousand Faces" by Joseph Campbell
- "Digital Minimalism" by Cal Newport

The Spiral of Growth: Navigating Circumambulation and Course Correction

- "Memories, Dreams, Reflections" by Carl Jung
- "Mastery" by Robert Greene
- "Outwitting the Devil" by Napoleon Hill
- "The Slight Edge" by Jeff Olson

Building an Unshakable Self-Relationship: How Integrity, Grit, & Anxiety Shape Us

- "Maxims and Reflections" by Johann Wolfgang von Goethe
- "Outwitting the Devil" by Napoleon Hill
- "Integrity" by Henry Cloud
- "Mastery" by Robert Greene
- "Grit: The Power of Passion and Perseverance" by Angela Duckworth
- "The Meaning of Anxiety" by Rollo May
- "Civilization in Transition" by Carl Jung
- "The Gay Science" by Friedrich Nietzsche
- "The Hero with a Thousand Faces" by Joseph Campbell
- "Extreme Ownership" by Jocko Willink and Leif Babin
- "The Six Pillars of Self-Esteem" by Nathaniel Branden

The Hidden Cost of Being Good: Repression & Shadow Integration

- "Visions: Notes of the Seminar Given in 1930–1934" by Carl Jung
- "Archetypes and the Collective Unconscious" by Carl Jung
- "Dream Analysis: Notes of the Seminar Given in 1928-1930" by Carl Jung
- "Man and His Symbols" by Carl Jung
- "The Laws of Human Nature" by Robert Greene
- "Self-Reliance" by Ralph Waldo Emerson
- "Thus Spoke Zarathustra" by Friedrich Nietzsche
- "The Gay Science" by Friedrich Nietzsche
- "Maxims on Life and Character" by Johann Wolfgang von Goethe

The Role of Rest: Sleep & Learning

- "Why We Sleep" by Dr. Matthew Walker
- "The Body Keeps the Score" by Bessel van der Kolk
- "Practice with Sleep Makes Perfect" (study) by Matthew P. Walker et al.

Neurotransmitters & Learning: The Chemicals of Human Behavior, Mental Health, & Learning

- "The Molecule of More" by Daniel Z. Lieberman and Michael E. Long
- "Dopamine Nation" by Anna Lembke
- "Behave" by Robert Sapolsky
- "The Biology of Belief" by Bruce H. Lipton
- "Why We Sleep" by Matthew Walker
- "The Brain That Changes Itself" by Norman Doidge
- "Limitless" by Jim Kwik
- "Neurotransmitter Networks" by Olivier Pichon and Christel Bastide
- "Spark" by John J. Ratey

- "The Upward Spiral" by Alex Korb

Neuroplasticity & Focus: The Key to Lifelong Learning

- "The Brain That Changes Itself" by Norman Doidge
- "Behave" by Robert Sapolsky
- "The Power of Habit" by Charles Duhigg
- "Peak" by Anders Ericsson and Robert Pool
- "Atomic Habits" by James Clear
- "The Talent Code" by Daniel Coyle
- "Limitless" by Jim Kwik
- "Spark: The Revolutionary New Science of Exercise and the Brain" by John J. Ratey
- "Deep Work" by Cal Newport
- "Neuroplasticity" by Philippe Douyon

Finding Flow: Mastering Focus & Peak Performance

- "Flow"by Mihaly Csikszentmihalyi
- "The Art of Impossible" by Steven Kotler
- "Stealing Fire" by Steven Kotler and Jamie Wheal
- "Deep Work" by Cal Newport
- "Atomic Habits" by James Clear
- "Grit" by Angela Duckworth
- "The Power of Now" by Eckhart Tolle
- "Peak" by Anders Ericsson and Robert Pool
- "The One Thing" by Gary Keller and Jay Papasan

The Resilient Mind: How the AMCT Shapes Learning, Willpower, & Aging

- "Neuroplasticity" by Norman Doidge
- "The Practicing Mind" by Thomas M. Sterner
- "Grit" by Angela Duckworth

- "The Longevity Project" by Howard S. Friedman and Leslie R. Martin
- "The Upside of Stress" by Kelly McGonigal
- "The Telomere Effect" by Elizabeth Blackburn and Elissa Epel

Think Like AI, Learn Like Humans: What Machines Can Teach Us About Mastery

- "Deep Learning" by Ian Goodfellow, Yoshua Bengio, and Aaron Courville
- "The Practicing Mind" by Thomas M. Sterner
- "Grit" by Angela Duckworth
- "Range" by David Epstein
- "Outliers" by Malcolm Gladwell
- "Peak" by Anders Ericsson and Robert Pool
- "Make It Stick" by Peter C. Brown, Henry L. Roediger III, and Mark A. McDaniel

4

ELEVATING OUR STUDY GAME
TECHNIQUES AND STRATEGIES

LEARNING = UNDERSTANDING + REMEMBERING

HOW WE MAKE, STRENGTHEN, AND SUSTAIN CONNECTIONS

"Give a person an idea, and you enrich their day. Teach a person how to learn, and they can enrich their entire life." - Jim Kwik (*Limitless*)

I magine preparing for an important exam. We've read and reread our notes, yet key concepts still feel out of reach. What if the issue isn't with us, but rather that we haven't been shown how to truly learn?

The foundations of learning involve genuinely understanding and remembering information. Once we understand these principles, we can apply them to every area of our lives. Many of these ideas will be expanded on in other chapters.

The Formula for Learning

Learning = Understanding + Remembering

Learning is more than memorizing facts. It's about understanding (making new connections) and remembering (strengthening and maintaining those connections). Both are essential for lifelong learning.

Understanding: Making New Connections

Receptive vs. Expressive

Understanding is not a passive process; it is an active one involving both receptiveness and expressiveness. In this context, *receptive* means taking in information through listening, reading, or observing. It's the stage where we gather new ideas, facts, and insights. However, merely collecting information is insufficient for deep understanding. It's like having the pieces of a puzzle without knowing how they fit together.

To truly understand, we need to move into the *expressive* phase, where we explain or demonstrate what we've learned. Expressive means using what we've absorbed by speaking, writing, or teaching it to others. This step forces us to organize our thoughts and spot gaps in our knowledge. Applying what we learn to new situations deepens our understanding and helps us see how different ideas connect. By being both receptive and expressive, we turn information into lasting knowledge that we can use in various areas of life.

Apprehension vs. Comprehension

Understanding has two phases: *apprehension* (taking in information) and *comprehension* (making sense of it).

Think of it like assembling a puzzle: apprehension is gathering all the pieces, while comprehension is fitting them together to reveal the full picture.

Apprehension is when we're still learning, feeling uncertain because we don't fully grasp the concept yet.

Comprehension is when everything clicks—we confidently

understand the material because we've integrated it with what we already know.

"It is one thing to remember, another to know." - Seneca (*Letters from a Stoic*)

Comprehension transforms information from something we merely recall to something that becomes a part of us.

A Gradual Process: The Information Processing Model

How does the brain handle all this? George Armitage Miller's *Information Processing Model* explains how we process, store, and retrieve information. Learning transfers information from short-term memory (what we just read or heard) to long-term memory (what we retain for life).

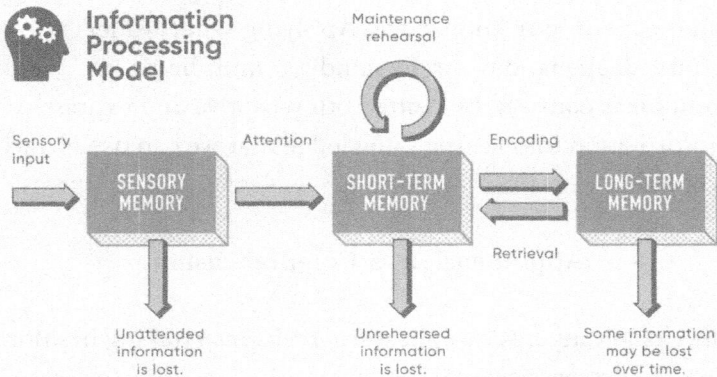

Image from learnupon.com

Similarly, *Bloom's Taxonomy* emphasizes that higher levels of thinking—like creating or evaluating—result in deeper learning than just memorizing facts. But to get higher levels of thinking, we first need a solid foundation of knowledge.

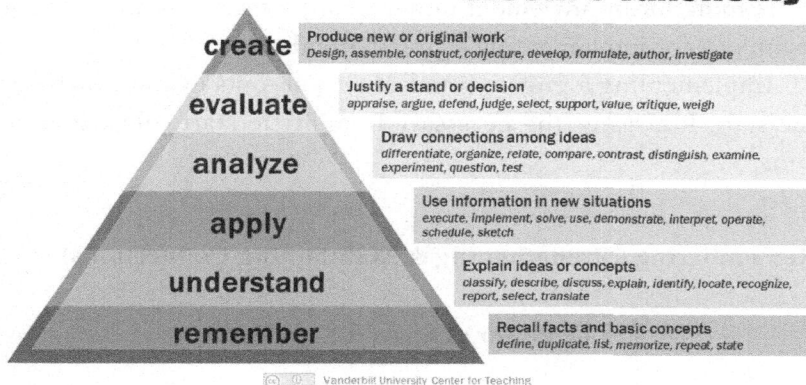

Image from cft.vanderbilt.edu

The Myth of Learning Styles

Many people believe they have a distinct learning style, such as being a "visual learner," but research shows everyone benefits from a variety of learning methods. Rather than relying on one style, it's better to mix techniques like reading, practicing, and teaching others.

While different people may have *preferences* for how they learn, everyone can learn from these methods. A "visual" learner can attempt to teach others rather than try to learn everything through visual aids. I prefer to learn by audio-visual means, but I have a bias for audio. However, my own experience has shown me that practicing and teaching others are much more efficient and effective methods for learning.

Learning is an active process, not a passive one.

Embracing a Growth Mindset

Carol Dweck describes a growth mindset as the belief that abilities can be developed through effort and learning, as opposed to a fixed mindset that sees abilities as innate.

At first, we may not be skilled, but over time, we improve.

Aiming for improvement rather than perfection is an excellent technique for implementing a growth mindset.

Implementing a growth mindset also permits us to be awful at the start. It gives us the necessary humility to start compounding wins.

Remembering (Strengthening & Maintaining Connections)

The Power of Spaced Repetition

Our brains are wired to forget things that don't seem important. But through *spaced repetition*, we can trick our brains into thinking information is crucial. This method works by reviewing material at increasing intervals, helping us move it from short-term memory to long-term memory.

Here's how it works:

1. *Learn Something New:* Start with a new idea or fact.
2. *Review After a Short Time:* Revisit the material after a day or two.
3. *Review Again Later:* Come back to it after a week, then again after longer intervals.
4. *Keep Reviewing:* Continue to space out our reviews as time goes on.

Spaced repetition mimics how we naturally strengthen connections in the brain, making it easier to recall information when needed.

Strengthen and Maintain Neural Pathways

We can strengthen newly formed neural pathways through two key methods:

1. *Practice Regularly:* Consistent practice reinforces neural connections, ensuring the information sticks.
2. *Use Multiple Senses:* The more senses we engage while learning, the more pathways we create. For example, when learning a language, practice speaking, listening, reading, and writing. The more connections we form with new information, the easier it becomes to retain.

Think of it like driving to the store. The first time we go, we need a map. But after several trips, we remember the way automatically. This is how memory works—repetition builds a well-worn path in our brain.

To maintain those pathways, we can stay engaged with the material by applying it in different contexts and leading a healthy lifestyle. Nutrition, sleep, and exercise are essential for overall brain health and memory retention.

The Harder We Work, The More We Remember

Effortful learning is more effective. When we actively engage with material through methods like practice and teaching, we make stronger neural connections. This is why active learning— like solving problems or explaining concepts—trumps passive activities like listening to lectures. However, our brains can roughly handle about three hours of intense mental activity. After three hours, our effectiveness significantly decreases until we rest.

Focus for Remembering

Concentration is key to solidifying new connections. To improve focus:

- *Eliminate distractions:* Create a quiet space to concentrate.
- *Set clear goals:* Break tasks into small, manageable goals.
- *Take breaks:* Short breaks help prevent mental fatigue and keep our focus sharp.

Practical Tips for Applying What We've Learned

Now that we've explored the science behind understanding and remembering, here are three practical strategies we can use make our learning stick:

- *Use spaced repetition:* Schedule regular review sessions to strengthen our memory.
- *Teach someone else:* Explaining a concept to another person helps solidify our understanding.
- *Embrace effort:* Don't rush to understand everything at once. Focus on the process, and remember that comprehension comes with time and practice.

Understanding and remembering are the twin pillars of learning. First, we take in new information (apprehension), then fully understand it (comprehension). Using techniques like spaced repetition, active learning, and maintaining focus helps strengthen these connections. Embracing a growth mindset and effortful learning ensures that the more we practice, the more we remember —and the easier learning becomes.

By understanding how learning works, we can make the process more efficient, ultimately enhancing every aspect of our lives.

THE POWER OF ASKING QUESTIONS
OUR PICKAXE TO GET EVERYTHING WE WANT

"Often, all that stands between you and what you want is a better set of questions." - Tim Ferriss

After college, I realized how transformative asking the right questions can be. Tim Ferriss, in his book *Tribe of Mentors*, says that everything we want is in other people's heads, and that questions are our pickaxe to dig them out. He believes his success stems from asking better questions.

This idea resonated deeply with me because I had spent years struggling with unanswered questions—ones that never seemed to bring me closer to the solutions I sought.

I used to ask:

- Why am I always getting the short end of the stick?
- How come I'm not being rewarded for doing the right thing?
- Is this all there is to life?
- Will it ever get easier?
- What's the point of understanding complicated things if no one cares?

- When will I have sacrificed enough?
- How do I make more money?
- Why do I keep making bad choices?

I realized that the problem wasn't in the harsh answers I was receiving—it was in the questions themselves. The questions I had been asking were setting me up to fail. When I learned to ask better, more focused questions, my perspective shifted, and the answers became clearer.

Improve my questions, improve my life.

This shift gave me a newfound sense of power and hope. The better my questions became, the better my outcomes. I stopped asking "Why am I getting the short end of the stick?" and started asking "What can I do to improve this situation?" That small tweak changed everything.

When we ask questions, our minds immediately begin finding answers.

Asking ourselves tough questions can be uncomfortable, but once we do, our minds begin searching for answers. This happens automatically—it doesn't matter who asks the question. Whether it's a simple, "What do I want for dinner?" or a life-altering question like, "What do I want my life to mean?" our brains will start working toward answers.

And when those questions are purposeful, they can change everything.

How to Ask Better Questions

"Judge a man by his questions rather than his answers." - Voltaire

So, how do we improve the questions we ask? The key is to make them specific and actionable. Broad, vague questions can often lead us to dead ends or answers that don't provide clarity. The more specific the question, the easier it is to answer—and the more useful the answer will be.

For example, asking, "What is your favorite movie?" might lead to a long pause and a hesitant answer. However, asking, "What movie do you most recommend people watch?" is easier to answer because it narrows down the field. The person is no longer scanning all their memories but is instead focusing on something more specific—what they would recommend to others. And once we have that answer, it's actionable: we can watch the movie they recommend, and it's likely to be something worth our time.

The order in which we ask questions matters. Good questions asked in the wrong order can lead to misleading answers. I've found that starting with smaller, easier-to-answer questions often leads to more honest, meaningful responses when I later tackle the harder ones.

Questions Shape Our Thinking

The questions we ask ourselves shape our perspectives and shape our thinking. The questions we ask ourselves can send us spiraling out of control or help us stay focused and grounded.

Here are some of the important questions I now ask myself:

- What do I want to change, and how will I know when I have?
- What would this look like if it were easy?
- What am I avoiding just because I know the answer is painful?
- How can I make my 10-year plans happen in 6 months?
- What am I not saying that needs to be said?
- What's being told that I'm not hearing?
- What actions do I need to take today?
- What am I unwilling to feel?
- Whose expectations am I trying to fulfill? My own or someone else's?

- What would make today great?
- How could I have made today even better?

What Else Can Questions Do?

Questions don't just help us find answers; they help us think differently, break old patterns, and challenge our assumptions. Research backs this up.

Chouinard (2007) demonstrated that children ask questions to resolve gaps in their knowledge, thereby driving their cognitive development. This means that asking questions isn't just a way to get new information—it's a way to understand what we don't know. Questions can precisely target the areas where we lack clarity, pushing us toward growth.

Another study by Bonawitz et al. (2020) found that children often change their answers when a knowledgeable person asks a neutral follow-up question, even without offering new information. This demonstrates that simply being asked a question can shift our thinking. Sometimes, the question alone is enough to change our perspective.

Flammer (1981) proposed that questions address gaps in our knowledge and serve as a mechanism for cognitive change. The act of asking questions can, by itself, drive us toward achieving our goals—sometimes without even acquiring new information.

These studies reinforce what I've come to understand: great questions unlock new perspectives, drive change, and shape our futures.

A Final Thought

"What you seek is seeking you." - Rumi

Questions act as bridges between where we are and where we want to be. If we learn to ask the right questions—of ourselves and others—there's no limit to what we can achieve.

STUDY REFERENCES:

- Chouinard, M. M. (2007). Children's questions: a mechanism for cognitive development. *Monographs of the Society for Research in Child Development.*
- Bonawitz, E., et al. (2020). The power of neutral follow-up questions. *Journal of Experimental Child Psychology.*
- Flammer, A. (1981). Toward a theory of question asking. *Psychological Review.*

LEARNING NEW THINGS
CONSTRUCTING KNOWLEDGE

"Learning is deeper and more durable when it's effortful. Learning that's easy is like writing in sand, here today and gone tomorrow." - Peter C. Brown, Henry L. Roediger III, and Mark A. McDaniel (*Make It Stick*)

Building Knowledge, One Brick at a Time

Learning is like building with LEGO bricks. Each concept we learn is a piece, and how we connect them forms our understanding. But knowing where and how to place those pieces is key to creating something solid. This chapter will guide us through the process of gathering, assembling, and locking in our knowledge so it sticks.

The Four Levels of Competence

Learning is a journey that happens in steps. Picture it like climbing a ladder with four rungs, each representing a different level of competence:

1. *Unconscious Incompetence:* At this stage, we don't know what we don't know. It's like not knowing we can't ride a bike because we've never tried. We're unaware of the skill gap.

2. *Conscious Incompetence:* This is when we realize what we don't know. Maybe we've seen others ride bikes and recognize that we haven't learned how yet. The gap becomes clear.

3. *Conscious Competence:* We've now learned how to ride a bike, but we have to focus on every step. It takes effort to balance, steer, and pedal all at once. We're competent but only when we're actively thinking about it.

4. *Unconscious Competence:* Finally, we reach the point where riding a bike becomes second nature. We can hop on and ride without even thinking about it. The skill has become automatic.

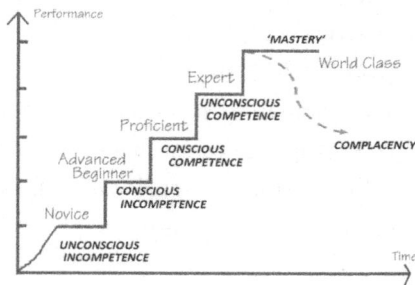

Image from Minh Do at Medium

The goal of learning is to progress from unconscious incompetence—where we're unaware of what we don't know—to unconscious competence, where we perform a skill with ease and confidence.

Two Stages of Learning

As we learn, we pass through two important stages:

1. *Apprehension:* This is the initial stage where we start to gather information. Imagine it like looking at the pieces of a puzzle without knowing exactly how they fit together yet. We're aware of the pieces, but the full picture isn't clear.
2. *Comprehension:* At this stage, everything starts to click. The pieces of the puzzle fit together, and we can see the whole picture. We not only recognize the individual pieces, but also understand how they connect and make sense.

When learning something new, it's helpful to first focus on collecting all the pieces—this corresponds to the apprehension stage. Then, with practice and study, we work our way to comprehension, where everything falls into place.

For example, when learning to cook, we might start by gathering basic skills like chopping vegetables or sautéing. At first, we're just going through the motions (apprehension), but with time, we start to see how those skills combine to create complex dishes (comprehension).

It's important to be patient in the early stages. Rarely does anyone fully understand something immediately. By breaking down learning into apprehension and comprehension, we can take the pressure off and focus on making progress at our own pace.

Three Techniques to Make Learning Stick

Learning isn't just about understanding—it's about remembering. To help information stick, use these three proven techniques:

Association

This is linking new information to something we already know. This helps the brain create a mental "hook" to hold on to. For example, if we're learning about photosynthesis, we might connect it to a memory of a plant we grew in our backyard.

The more connections we make to new information, the easier it becomes to recall. Think of learning as adding new bricks to an existing structure; each brick fits better when it's supported by others.

Emotion

We remember things better when they are tied to emotions. Whether it's excitement, happiness, or even frustration, emotional experiences leave a lasting imprint. Think about how vividly we remember failing a test or a sports game—those emotionally charged events help the brain prioritize what to remember.

High emotional states—such as excitement or joy—can enhance memory. On the flip side, stress can impair it. So when learning, try to attach positive emotions to the experience to reinforce it in our mind.

Location

Our brains are wired to remember places easily—a skill developed for survival. By associating new information with specific locations, we provide our brain with another "road" to follow during recall.

For instance, if we're trying to memorize facts for an exam, we can imagine placing each fact in a different room of our house. When it's time to recall the information, we can mentally walk through our house, and we'll be able to retrieve each piece more easily.

How to Learn New Information (Actionable Steps)

Here are some practical, actionable steps to help us retain new information more effectively:

- *Read and Pause:* When we're reading, take time to stop and reflect on what we've learned. After each section, we can ask ourselves:
  - What are the key concepts I just read?
  - Can I explain this in my own words?
    - Writing these answers down will solidify our understanding. Don't just think about them— writing forces us to engage with the material actively.
- *Close the Book:* After reading, close the book and we can test ourselves. Can we remember what we learned without looking? Testing ourselves helps strengthen our memory by forcing our brains to retrieve information, which improves retention.
- *Focus on Active Learning:* Learning is most effective when it's active. Instead of passively reading more words, we can ask ourselves questions, explain concepts to someone else, or create flashcards. Active learning significantly strengthens our understanding.
- *Handwrite Notes:* While typing may seem faster, handwritten notes improve retention. Learners who handwrite notes understand and remember the material more deeply than those who type them.

The Power of Sleep in Learning

Finally, don't forget the importance of sleep in the learning process. After learning something new, getting a good night's sleep is critical. Sleep helps our brain transfer information from short-term to long-term memory.

During sleep, particularly during REM and Stage 3 sleep, our brain consolidates memories—this is the stage when newly formed connections are strengthened. That's why getting enough sleep after a study session is key to making sure the information sticks.

Learning is a process. Collect the pieces, create connections through association, emotion, and location, and remember to test yourself regularly. Learning is not just about gathering information; it's about building something strong, lasting, and automatic.

OUTSMARTING THE FORGETTING CURVE
REMEMBERING WHAT'S IMPORTANT

"Memory is not a warehouse, but a garden. What we focus on grows, and what we neglect fades." - Peter C. Brown, Henry L. Roediger III, and Mark A. McDaniel (*Make It Stick*)

How Our Brain Retains Information

Sometimes, we learn something new and forget it the next day. This happens to everyone and it's not just about having a bad memory. It's a natural process our brain uses to filter information—a phenomenon psychologists have studied for over a century. This process is called the *Forgetting Curve*.

What Is the Forgetting Curve?

The Forgetting Curve was discovered by a 19th-century German psychologist Hermann Ebbinghaus. It shows that we forget information over time unless we actively recall it. When we first learn something, we are prone to forgetting it quickly unless we revisit the information. But here's the key: each time we recall it, we slow down the forgetting process, making the information stick better in our long-term memory.

Think about a simple fact like 2+2=4. Most of us don't need to think about this—it's automatic. But when we first learned it, our brain created a new neural pathway, one that wasn't strong at first. Like a barely visible hiking trail, the more we used it, the clearer the path became over time. Over time, as we practiced and recalled this information, the neural pathway strengthened, becoming as smooth as a paved road in our brain.

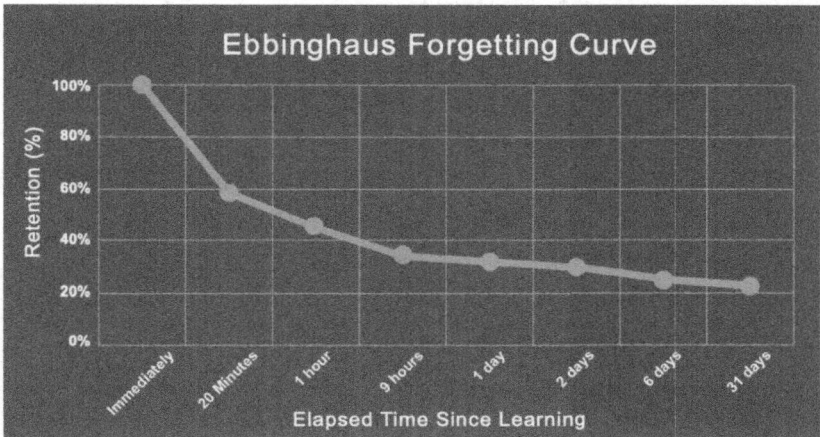

Image from amplifire.com

Our memory behaves in predictable ways. Within an hour, we can forget about 50% of what we've learned, and after 24 hours, nearly 70% is gone. However, there's a way to combat this rapid decay: active recall and spaced repetition.

Why Is Our Brain So Good at Forgetting?

Our senses take in up to 11 million bits of information every second. If our brain tried to process all of it at once, we'd be completely overwhelmed. So, like a highly efficient filter, our brain lets in only the most relevant bits, while the rest fades into the background.

Forgetting serves as a necessary survival mechanism. Imagine if our brain held onto every tiny piece of information—it would clog up our mental processing. By filtering out what it deems "unnecessary," the brain protects itself from overload. This is why forgetting plays a crucial role in maintaining mental clarity.

How Our Brain Decides What to Remember

Our brain is constantly deciding what to keep and what to discard. It's like a gardener pruning a plant, trimming away the weaker branches so the stronger ones can flourish. This process is called *neural pruning.* The more we use certain pieces of information, the more our brain deems them important. The less we use them, the more likely they are to be cut away.

Think of it this way: if we frequently recall a fact or skill, our brain assumes it is important for survival and strengthens the neural pathway. But if we don't use it, the brain prunes that pathway, making room for more frequently used information.

Strengthening Our Memory & Overcoming the Forgetting Curve

Ebbinghaus also suggested that memory is like a muscle that can be strengthened with practice and people with stronger memory could retain information longer, thus slowing the rate at which they forget. He called this concept the *Strength of Memory.* It suggests that the better we get at learning and recalling information, the less effort we need to put into remembering things over time.

Active recall and spaced repetition are powerful techniques that can help us combat the Forgetting Curve. Active recall involves trying to remember information without looking at notes, while spaced repetition requires reviewing information at increasingly spaced intervals.

For example, if we're studying for a test, passively reading notes won't help. Instead, we can quiz ourselves on the material regularly, spacing out the reviews over time. This method strengthens the neural pathways connected to the information, helping you retain it for the long term.

Overcoming The Curve

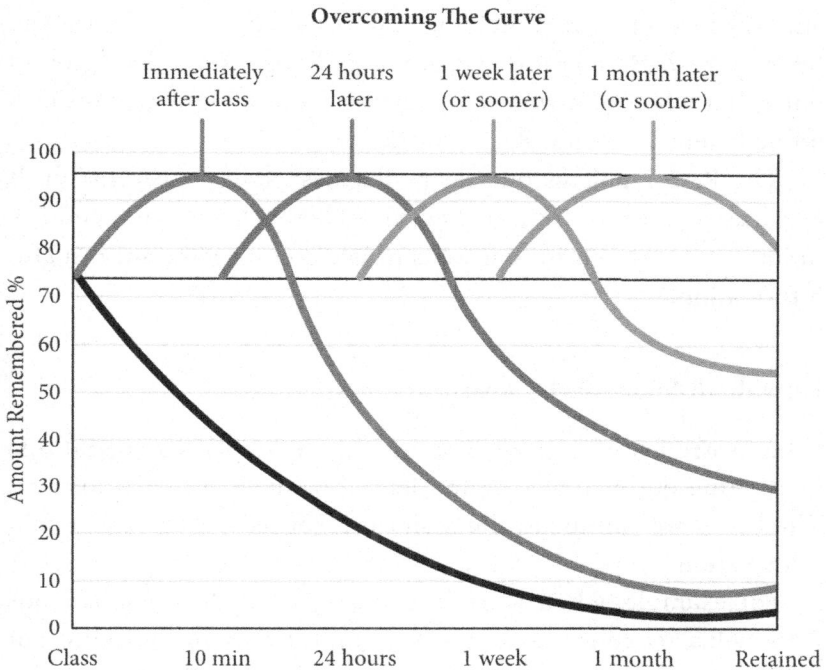

Image from nappiuk.com

There is a natural decline in memory retention if no active recall or repetition occurs. However, each repetition of recall slows down memory loss, leading to better retention over time.

This process applies to more than just classroom facts—it can help master any skill. By periodically revisiting what we've learned, whether it's playing the piano or practicing a language, we can retain and sharpen those skills over time.

The Reticular Activating System (RAS): Filtering What's Important

Now that we've covered the Forgetting Curve, let's talk about a part of the brain that plays a crucial role in learning and memory retention: the *Reticular Activating System (RAS)*.

The RAS acts as a bodyguard for our brain, filtering out noise and distractions while helping us focus on what's important. Imagine being in a crowded room, full of chatter and background noise, but when someone says our name, our attention snaps to it immediately. That's our RAS at work.

The RAS regulates our sleep, alertness, and concentration. It also uses a process called *habituation*—where it filters out repetitive, unimportant stimuli so that we can focus on new and meaningful information.

How the RAS Helps Us Learn

When we're learning something new, the RAS plays a critical role by filtering out distractions and letting us focus on what matters. The better we can focus, the easier it is for us to learn and retain information.

For example, when we're learning a new skill or subject, our RAS helps us concentrate on that information by blocking out other distractions. This makes it easier to store new information in our memory and prevents our brain from being overwhelmed by unnecessary stimuli.

The RAS and the Forgetting Curve: Working Together to Boost Learning

The RAS is also essential when it comes to overcoming the Forgetting Curve. When we use active recall and spaced repetition, we're essentially signaling to the RAS that this information is important. Each time we review a piece of information, the RAS pays closer attention to it, helping us commit it to memory.

In this way, the RAS acts as a gatekeeper, ensuring that what's truly valuable is stored and reinforced in our brains. It's like a helpful assistant, prioritizing the information we need to focus on and ignore distractions. By combining the power of the RAS with techniques like active recall and spaced repetition, we can significantly improve our memory and learning capacity.

. . .

IN TODAY'S FAST-PACED WORLD, it might feel like memory works against us, but with the right tools, we can align with our brain's natural processes to retain more information. By understanding the Forgetting Curve and using the RAS to our advantage, we can sharpen our memory, enhance our learning, and stay ahead in whatever we choose to master.

ACTIVE RECALL & SPACED REPETITION
THE PERFECT PAIR

Active Recall: A Powerful Way To Learn

Imagine spending hours reading a textbook, feeling confident that we've absorbed the information. Then, the day of the test arrives, and suddenly our mind goes blank. Frustrating, right? That's because reading or highlighting isn't enough to make the material stick. Our brains need something more: a method that strengthens our ability to remember by challenging it to actively recall information.

What is Active Recall?

Active recall is a powerful technique that challenges the brain to retrieve information from memory without relying on external cues. It's not about reading or recognizing the correct answer from a list; it's about trying to remember the information on our own. Dr. William Klemm from Texas A&M University states that most students don't realize how critical it is to force themselves to recall information. By doing so, we reinforce the mental pathways that store that knowledge.

Think of active recall as exercise for the brain. Just as muscles grow stronger with resistance training, our memory strengthens when we make it work harder to retrieve information. In his book *Make It Stick*, Peter C. Brown explains two key reasons why active recall is so effective:

1. It reveals gaps in our understanding, highlighting areas that need more attention.
2. It strengthens memory connections, making future recall easier.

Why is Active Recall Important?

Active recall engages our brain in a way that other study methods don't. Each time we successfully retrieve information, we reinforce neural pathways in the brain, making future recall easier. It's similar to building a muscle—the more we exercise it, the stronger it becomes. Research shows that the best learning happens when we challenge ourselves to recall information multiple times over a period of time.

Minimum Effective Dose (MED)

The Minimum Effective Dose (MED) is the smallest amount of effort needed to achieve the desired result. Picture boiling water— we need just enough heat to make it boil, and adding more doesn't speed up the process. The same principle applies to learning. When we apply the MED to studying, it means we focus on the most efficient techniques—like active recall—to maximize our learning without wasting time or energy.

When studying, avoid doing more for the sake of it. We can use the MED to make our studying efficient. Active recall is one of the best ways to meet the MED, giving us better results in less time.

How to Use Active Recall

Here are some practical ways to incorporate active recall into our studying:

- *Practice Problems:* Solving problems forces us to recall information. The harder the problem, the more effective the recall.
- *Free Response Questions:* These are especially effective because they don't give us any hints. We must retrieve the information entirely from memory.
- *Fill-in-the-Blank Questions:* These are a step down from free response but still challenge our recall because they provide only partial context.
- *Multiple-choice Questions:* Although not as effective, we can improve multiple-choice questions by asking ourselves additional questions about each answer option.
- *Running Through Information in Our Heads:* As a quick, easy method, we can ask ourselves questions and mentally try to recall the answers during a walk or break.
- *Creative Projects:* Applying what we've learned in a project forces us to recall and use the information in new ways, strengthening your understanding.
- *Explaining to Someone Else:* If we can explain a concept to a five-year-old, it demonstrates true understanding. This is a powerful way to test and strengthen our recall.
- *Flashcards:* One of the best tools for active recall. Write questions on one side of the card and answers on the other. Regular self-testing strengthens our memory.
- *Connecting to Our Life:* Relating new information to personal experiences makes it easier to recall later. We remember things better when they feel meaningful.

- *Review Questions:* Reviewing questions at the beginning and end of our study sessions reinforces what we've learned.
- *Maximizing Each Question:* Don't settle for just knowing the answer. Understand the reasoning behind the correct answer, why other choices are wrong, and how the question could be asked differently.

Spaced Repetition: A Smart Way to Study

Active recall works best when combined with another powerful technique: spaced repetition. While active recall strengthens our memory, spaced repetition ensures we review the material at strategic intervals, helping our brain retain information over the long term.

What is Spaced Repetition?

To understand spaced repetition, we have to understand Hermann Ebbinghaus' Forgetting Curve. Refer to the previous chapter for a deeper look at Ebbinghaus' Forgetting Curve. Essentially, we forget new information unless we actively review it. The more we recall information, the slower we forget it. Spaced repetition takes advantage of this by helping us review information just as we're about to forget it, making each recall more effective.

Think of learning as building a brick wall. Each piece of information is a brick. We lay down a layer, then wait for the mortar to dry before adding another. If we rush and stack too many layers too quickly, the structure will crumble. Our brains work similarly: it needs time between study sessions to solidify the connections between pieces of information.

Why is Spaced Repetition Important?

Spaced repetition strengthens the brain's memory connections by introducing time gaps between study sessions. This makes each recall attempt harder, but the payoff is that the memory becomes much more durable. When we space out our reviews, we tell our brain that the information is important and needs to be remembered for the long term.

Techniques for Spaced Repetition

The Leitner System

This is a simple but effective system using flashcards. We sort our cards into groups based on how well we know the material. If we answer a card correctly, it moves to a group that we review less frequently. If we get it wrong, it goes back to a group that we review more often. This allows us to focus on the material we struggle with while reviewing the easier content less frequently.

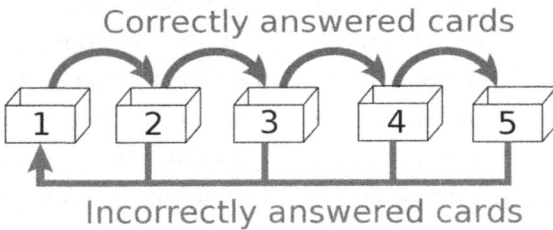

Image from wikipedia.org

We can do variations of the Leitner System as well. Instead of returning the incorrect answer to Box 1, we can return the question to the previous box.

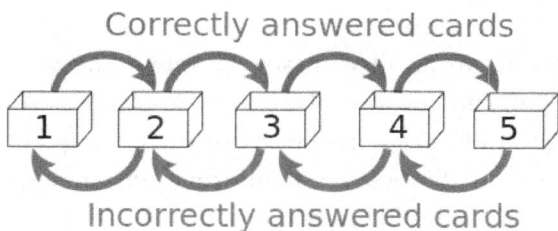

Correctly answered cards

Incorrectly answered cards

Image from wikipedia.org

The first variation is more efficient, but the second variation can work well too.

The frequency of reviewing each box depends on our study schedule. For example, let's say we have an exam in a month. Maybe we review Box 1 daily, Box 2 every other day, Box 3 every three days, Box 4 once a week, and Box 5 every two weeks. Maybe the last few days before the exam, we review all of the information regardless of what box they are in.

Anki

Anki is a digital flashcard app that employs the Leitner system and offers customizable features. We can adjust the difficulty levels, and the app decides when to show us each card again, helping you focus on the most challenging content.

Why Spaced Repetition is Efficient

Spaced repetition saves time and enhances memory retention. Just like we wouldn't train our muscles every day to avoid overtraining, we shouldn't overload our brain with too much studying at once. Spacing out study sessions gives our brain time to build stronger connections between pieces of information, making our study sessions both shorter and more effective.

. . .

BY COMBINING active recall with spaced repetition, we'll not only retain more information but also spend less time studying. The quality of our study time matters more than the quantity. Active recall sharpens our ability to retain information, while spaced repetition ensures long-term memory retention.

PEAK LEARNING STATES
OPTIMIZE OUR STATE, ENHANCE OUR LEARNING

How Our State Influences Learning

Think back to a moment of full energy and focus—learning likely felt effortless and smooth. In contrast, studying while feeling tired or distracted can make concentration a real challenge. This difference lies at the heart of *state-dependent learning*, meaning that the physical and mental state we're in deeply influences how well we learn and recall information.

When we sit up straight, feel alert, and stay engaged, our brain works more effectively than when we slouch, feel tired, or become disengaged. Our posture, for example, directly affects our cognitive state. Sitting like we're ready to learn primes our brain for focus, while poor posture can lead to reduced oxygen flow to the brain and decreased concentration.

Beyond our physical state, emotions also play a crucial role. Negative emotions, such as stress or fear, can make memories more vivid because the brain is wired to remember potential threats for survival. This is why failure, while uncomfortable, is often one of the best teachers—it comes with a strong emotional charge, which helps cement the experience in our memory.

Understanding this means we can actively shape our learning environment and mental state to enhance memory and comprehension.

The Science Behind State-Dependent Learning

When we're alert, areas like the prefrontal cortex—responsible for complex thinking and decision-making—are highly active. In contrast, when we're tired or stressed, cortisol, a stress hormone, floods our system, impairing memory retrieval. This interplay between brain chemistry and mental state explains why long-term learning is most effective when we are in an optimal state of focus and calm.

The amygdala, which processes emotions, also plays a key role in memory. Strong emotions, whether positive or negative, activate the amygdala, helping to encode experiences into long-term memory. This is why emotionally charged experiences, such as a major failure or even a thrilling success, tend to stick with us. Our brain prioritizes these memories because they feel important for survival or growth.

State-Dependent Learning & Active Learning

State-dependent learning is closely tied to *active learning*, as both emphasize the importance of engagement through emotional involvement, physical posture, or mental focus.

- *Enhanced Focus:* Active learning requires a state of alertness. Adopting a focused posture—like sitting up straight—improves concentration and makes learning more effective.
- *Emotional Engagement:* Active learning involves interacting with the material by asking questions, testing

yourself, or discussing it with others. These activities trigger emotions that make the information more memorable.

- *Physical State:* Learning activities such as note-taking or teaching others engage the body and mind. Physical actions, like writing or using hand gestures, strengthen memory and understanding.

By aligning our physical state, emotional engagement, and mental focus, we can significantly improve how we learn.

How to Optimize Our Learning State

Optimizing our learning state is all about creating the right conditions for our body and mind to absorb information more effectively. Here are a few simple, actionable strategies:

- *Adopt a Good Posture:* Sitting or standing up straight helps us stay alert and focused by increasing oxygen flow to our brain. Good posture signals to the brain that what we are learning is important.
- *Manage Emotions:* Emotions like curiosity, excitement, or even challenge make learning more engaging. Cultivate a positive or curious emotional state when tackling new information.
- *Stay Physically Active:* Incorporate movement into our learning. Walk around while reciting information, use gestures to explain concepts, or even switch locations to keep our brain engaged.
- *Create an Optimal Learning Environment:* Adjust the lighting, reduce distractions, and ensure our study space is organized to promote focus and calm.
- *Use Breathing Techniques:* Deep breathing before and during study sessions can help reduce stress and increase focus by delivering more oxygen to our brain.

Combining these strategies with active learning techniques can make study sessions more effective and enjoyable.

Active vs. Passive Learning

Let's dive deeper into how *active learning* compares with *passive learning*, and why active engagement is more effective for memory retention.

Passive learning occurs when we receive information without much interaction. We may listen to a lecture, read a textbook, or watch a video, but we're not actively engaging with the material.

Characteristics of Passive Learning

- Lower engagement, with the learner being more of a spectator.
- Less retention of information over time.
- Surface-level understanding, without a deep grasp of underlying concepts.

Examples of Passive Learning

- Listening to a lecture without taking notes.
- Reading a textbook without stopping to reflect.
- Watching an educational video without interacting or reflecting on the content.

Active learning, on the other hand, requires participation in the learning process by interacting with the material, questioning it, and applying it.

Characteristics of Active Learning

- Higher engagement, keeping us focused on the task.

- Better retention of information because we're interacting with the material.
- Deep understanding, where we see connections and understand complex ideas.

Examples of Active Learning

- Summarizing key points in our own words after reading.
- Creating and answering questions about the material.
- Using flashcards or practice quizzes to test ourselves.
- Discussing what we've learned with others to reinforce understanding.
- Explaining the material to someone else, which strengthens our grasp of the concepts.

Which is Better?

Active learning helps with deeper understanding and retention by encouraging critical thinking and responsibility for the material. While passive learning can be useful for getting an initial overview, combining it with active techniques generally leads to better outcomes.

Passive learning is ideal for an initial grasp of material (apprehension), while active learning is key for deeper understanding (comprehension).

Here's why active learning promotes better comprehension:

- *Sustained Interest:* Engaging with the material keeps us interested and motivated.
- *Long-Term Memory:* Actively working with information helps transfer it to long-term memory.
- *Critical Thinking:* Active learning encourages us to think critically and make connections between ideas.
- *Ownership of Learning:* We become more responsible and invested in the learning process.

How to Make Learning Active

To make learning more active and improve comprehension, consider these six actionable strategies:

- *Take Notes by Hand:* Writing by hand forces us to process the information deeply, leading to better retention.
- *Summarize in Our Own Words:* Paraphrasing material helps solidify our understanding.
- *Engage in Discussions:* Talk about what we're learning with others. Study groups or casual discussions can help reinforce key ideas.
- *Ask Questions:* Be curious and challenge the material. Seek out answers to any uncertainties we have.
- *Teach Someone Else:* Teaching is one of the most powerful ways to deepen our understanding.
- *Use Practice Tests:* We can test ourselves regularly to see what we know and identify any gaps in our knowledge.

By becoming aware of how our mental and physical state influences learning, and combining that with active learning strategies, we can maximize both comprehension and retention. With a few adjustments to learning posture, emotional state, and engagement, our study sessions can become more effective—and even enjoyable.

11 STUDY METHODS
PROVEN STUDY TECHNIQUES FOR BETTER GRADES &LESS STRESS

"All truly wise thoughts have been thought already thousands of times; but to make them truly ours, we must think them over again honestly, until they take root in our personal experience." - Johann Wolfgang Von Goethe (*Torquato Tasso*)

A ctive recall and spaced repetition are powerful principles for learning efficiently, reducing stress, and improving grades. In this chapter, I'll share specific study methods that align with these principles and how to adapt them to suit individual learning styles.

The focus isn't on which method we use—it's on how well we apply the principles. Experiment with these techniques, mix and match, and adapt them to our needs. My goal is to provide a toolkit of study strategies, enabling us to develop a personalized system.

"As to methods there may be a million and then some, but principles are few. The man who grasps principles can successfully select his own methods. The man who tries methods, ignoring principles, is sure to have trouble." - Harrington Emerson (*The Twelve Principles of Efficiency*)

1. Modifying the Pomodoro Technique and Understanding Attention Span

Despite its name, tomatoes have no connection to this technique. *Pomodoro*, which means tomato in Italian, refers to the tomato-shaped timer that Francesco Cirillo used when he created this study technique.

How to Use the Pomodoro Technique

The Pomodoro Technique is simple yet effective. Here's how it works:

1. Choose a task we need to complete.
2. Set a timer for 25 minutes.
3. Work on the task until the timer goes off.
4. Take a 3-5 minute break.
5. Repeat this process four times.
6. After four sessions, take a longer break of 15-30 minutes.
7. Repeat as needed.

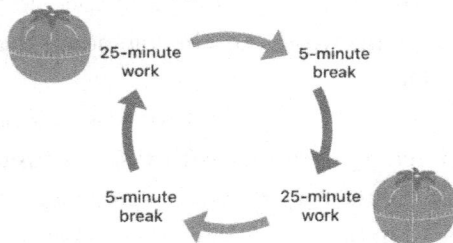

Image from theforestscout.com

Each 25-minute session is called a *Pomodoro*. After a few Pomodoros, we've likely made significant progress, but taking those small breaks helps reset our focus. I use this method to get started on tasks that feel overwhelming because telling myself I only need to work for 25 minutes is much easier than expecting to work for hours.

My Pomodoro Variation

However, breaks can sometimes interrupt my flow. I modify the technique by adjusting the length of each session based on my attention span. On days when I can focus for longer, I stretch a Pomodoro to match my focus level, often working for an hour or more before taking a break. Other times, when I feel mentally drained, a 10-minute Pomodoro is all I can manage.

Key Tip: We can adjust the length of our Pomodoros to match our attention span.

Finding Our Attention Span

To find our ideal Pomodoro length, we can try timing ourselves when we start a task and see how long it takes before we naturally want to take a break. Average these times over several sessions to determine our optimal focus length.

For me, it's often around an hour, but on tough days, it can be shorter. Experiment and modify the technique to fit our needs. This flexibility ensures that we can always make progress, even on low-energy days.

Pomodoro and Learning

Jim Kwik, a well-known brain coach, explains that the Pomodoro technique leverages the *primacy* and *recency effects*—the principle that we remember the first and last parts of a session better than the middle. By taking regular breaks, we create more beginnings and endings, boosting our memory retention.

Pomodoro can make studying feel manageable and productive, especially when we adapt it to our attention span.

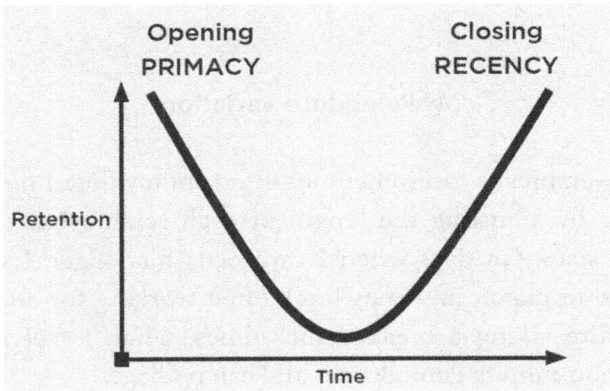

Image from rapidbi.com

2. The Feynman Technique (Explain Like I'm 5)

Named after the physicist Richard Feynman, this technique is all about understanding by simplification. When I first started tutoring, I noticed that my understanding of math was improving rapidly. At the time, I thought it was just because I was practicing more, but over the years, I realized that constantly explaining concepts in simple terms was the key to my progress.

The Feynman Technique works in four steps:

1. *Choose a Concept:* Pick a topic we want to learn deeply.
2. *Teach It to a 5-Year-Old:* Try explaining the concept in simple terms as if we were teaching it to a child. This forces us to confront gaps in our understanding.
3. *Identify Gaps and Review:* Notice where we struggled to explain or oversimplified. Go back to our sources and fill in these gaps.
4. *Simplify and Use Analogies:* Refine our explanation further, using analogies to make it even clearer.

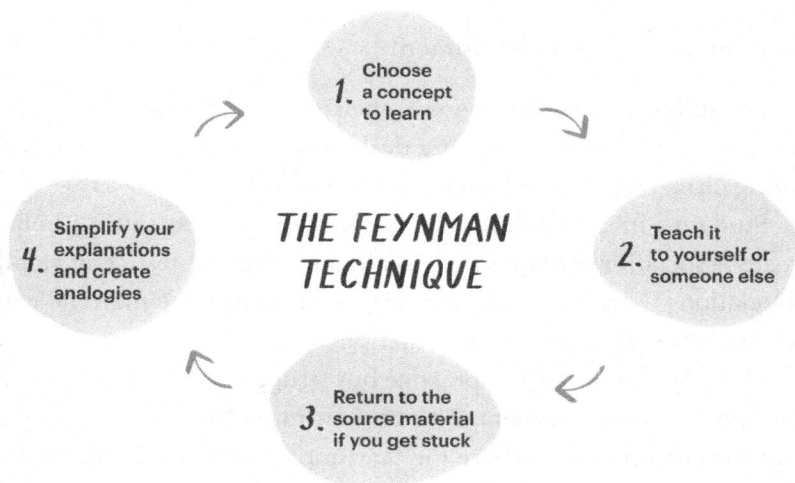

Image from todoist.com

This technique works because it forces us to actively engage with the material and identify areas where our understanding is incomplete. When we can explain a topic simply, we truly know it.

If we don't have someone to explain the concept to, write it down. Writing forces us to clarify our thoughts, and reading it back later will help solidify the concept in your memory.

3. Incorporate Concepts into Everyday Speech

Another powerful way to reinforce learning is by casually incorporating new concepts into our daily conversations. This practice strengthens neural pathways associated with these ideas, improving memory retention.

We can slide the concepts into everyday speech to make them a natural part of our thinking. This is something I do regularly, and though it might make me seem nerdy at times, it's worth it for the learning benefits.

Talking about new ideas in our conversations doesn't just help us remember—they become part of our lived reality, shaping how we think and interact with the world.

4. Simulate the Test Environment

When studying, simulate the test environment as closely as possible. This can include sitting at a desk, using similar materials, and timing ourselves as we would on the actual test.

Studying in an environment similar to the test setting helps create associations that can be recalled during the test. The small associations we make while learning (or studying) the material can be cues when recalling the information later.

Many students excel in practice but struggle during tests due to the different environments. The human mind makes associations with the surroundings where the learning takes place. Some of the neural connections necessary to recall the information may be tied up with specific elements of the environment in which we learned something. For example, a student may be more likely to remember math concepts in their math class than at home.

When the test environment differs significantly from the practice environment, the unfamiliarity can trigger anxiety and affect performance.

There are two reasons why different test environments could lead to test and performance anxiety:

- As mentioned earlier, the mind constantly associates learning with the environment. When studying in a familiar place, such as home, the mind creates associations with that setting. However, the test environment, often a classroom, is different and that difference can lead to anxiety.
- The brain prefers operating in familiar (orderly) environments where outcomes are predictable. A test in an unfamiliar (chaotic) environment can disrupt this sense of order, leading to anxiety and poor performance.

Students can improve their performance by simulating the test environment during study sessions. This approach reduces the unfamiliarity and anxiety associated with the test setting, helping create strong mental associations that aid in better recall and application of knowledge during tests.

5. No-Stakes Practice

No-stakes practice involves engaging in activities without the fear of severe consequences, fostering a relaxed learning environment. This approach allows individuals to make mistakes and learn from them, ultimately leading to mastery.

Here are a few benefits of no-stakes practice:

- *Freedom to Make Mistakes:* Practicing without serious consequences offers the freedom to make mistakes. These mistakes become valuable learning opportunities, lighting the path to mastery. The absence of pressure encourages experimentation and creativity.
- *More Approachable:* A relaxed attitude toward practice makes difficult subjects more approachable. When learners understand that making mistakes is part of the process and not something to fear, they become more willing to attempt new challenges. This mindset shift can significantly improve learning outcomes.
- *High-Yield Lessons:* Trial runs with no stakes often result in high-yield lessons. The freedom to try and fail without repercussions allows for deeper engagement with the material and more profound learning experiences. With no-stakes practice, we can more easily identify gaps in understanding and prior knowledge.
- *Practical Applications:* No-stakes practice can be applied in many different contexts, such as studying, drafting papers, or creating music. For instance, a "no-stakes" Pomodoro technique sets a definite time for focused practice, allowing for creativity and learning without the pressure of doing things perfectly the first time.

- *Encourages Growth Mindset:* By allowing ourselves to be beginners and make mistakes, growth, and improvement become natural outcomes. This strategy helps in academic subjects as well as creative and professional endeavors.

No-stakes practice is a powerful strategy promoting learning through a relaxed, consequence-free environment. This approach encourages experimentation, creativity, and a deeper understanding of the material, leading to mastery and growth.

6. The Leitner System

The Leitner System is an efficient method for reviewing flashcards based on spaced repetition. Here's how it works:

- Start with all flashcards in Box 1.
- When we answer a flashcard correctly, move it to the next box.
- Review the boxes at increasing intervals—Box 1 every day, Box 2 every other day, Box 3 weekly, and so on.
- If we get a flashcard wrong, move it back to Box 1.

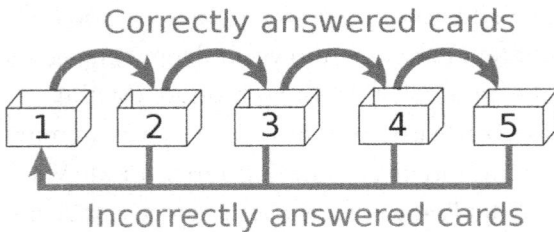

Correctly answered cards

1   2   3   4   5

Incorrectly answered cards

Image from wikipedia.org

Apps like Anki automate this system, simplifying progress

tracking and optimizing review sessions. The Leitner System integrates active recall and spaced repetition, helping you remember information more effectively.

Modifications for Flexibility

The Leitner System can be adapted to upcoming exams or deadlines. For example, if an exam is approaching, the review intervals can be shortened (e.g., studying Box 3 every three days instead of every week).

This requires careful planning and using a study calendar to track review schedules.

Additionally, incorrect answers must not always be returned to Box 1. Incorrect answers can be shifted one box over if deadlines are not urgent. However, returning incorrect answers to Box 1 is the most efficient method of reviewing using this system.

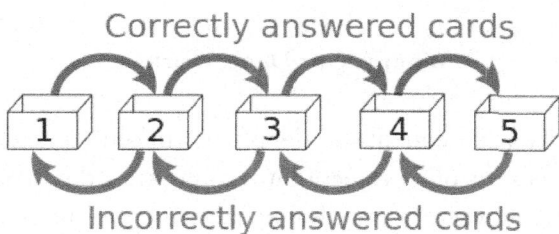

Image from wikipedia.org

7. Practice "Deep Work" & Utilize Flow

Cal Newport's concept of *deep work* refers to focused, distraction-free effort that pushes our cognitive abilities to their limits. Deep work is often challenging but produces valuable results.

Deep Work vs. Shallow Work

Cal Newport defines deep work as:

"Professional activities performed in a state of distraction-free concentration that push your cognitive capabilities to their limit. These efforts create new value, improve your skill, and are hard to replicate."

Deep work involves the most challenging aspects of a task or project, often avoided due to their difficulty.

Conversely, "shallow work" consists of:

"Noncognitively demanding, logistical-style tasks, often performed while distracted. These efforts tend not to create much new value in the world and are easy to replicate."*

Shallow work includes activities like emails, meetings, and text messages. While completing shallow work can feel productive, it rarely results in significant accomplishments or value creation.

What is Our Deep Work?

To identify what constitutes deep work in our context, consider the tasks or aspects of a project that we find most daunting or aversive. This aligns with the psychological principle that confronting what we fear or find repulsive can lead to significant personal and professional growth.

The story of the Holy Grail also illustrates this principle. In the legend, seekers of the Grail must enter the part of the forest that appears darkest and most frightening to them. Deep work is found in the areas we are most reluctant to explore.

Once we've identified our deep work, the challenge becomes doing it. Since deep work demands intense focus and pushes cognitive limits, it requires significant mental resources. Achieving a state of *flow* is crucial for deep work.

Flow

Achieving a state of *flow*—when we are fully immersed in a task —helps make deep work more enjoyable and productive. To get into flow, minimize distractions, focus on one task at a time, and work for extended periods without interruption.

This concept extends beyond study skills. Seeking out and engaging in deep work in any area of life can unlock new opportunities and lead to personal growth. By confronting and overcoming challenges, we reap the rewards of achievement, akin to a hero defeating a dragon and claiming treasure.

8. Record Distractions

When distractions arise during deep work, keep a *distraction list*. Writing down intrusive thoughts lets us offload them mentally and return to them later. This strategy helps maintain focus and keeps us on track.

9. Avoid Pseudo-Productive Habits

Some study habits feel productive but aren't effective. Be cautious of activities like re-reading chapters, over-highlighting, or rewriting notes without purpose. These actions can waste time without significantly improving understanding.

The Pareto Principle, often called the 80/20 rule, posits that 80% of outcomes stem from 20% of causes. For example, 80% of business sales often come from 20% of customers. We can see this distribution in many places. We can apply the Pareto Principle to identify and focus on the 20% of actions that produce 80% of results.

10. Focus on Topics, Not Time

Studying isn't about how long we spend, but how well we understand the material. Consider the amount of topics covered instead of measuring our study sessions by how long we spent on them. The goal is comprehension, not time logged.

Time is our most valuable resource—it cannot be replenished. So why waste it on inefficient study methods? By focusing on the quality of our study sessions and using effective techniques, we can achieve better results in less time.

We can shift our focus from "How many hours did I study?" to "What did I learn today?" Quality of study always outweighs quantity.

11. Interleaving Practice

Interleaving is a technique where we mix up the topics we study. Instead of spending hours on one subject, alternate between different topics to challenge our brain and improve retention.

Interleaving helps students perform better because it makes the brain work harder to retrieve information. Interleaving prevents our brain from taking shortcuts. When we repeatedly study the same topic, our brain becomes efficient at recalling that information in a specific context. However, it doesn't help much to apply the knowledge in varied situations. Interleaving forces the brain to constantly switch gears, enhancing our ability to apply concepts flexibly.

As a teacher, I've observed the benefits of interleaving firsthand. When my students work on a single topic, they might understand the steps but struggle to know when to apply the concept. Interleaving helps bridge this gap, making students more adept at recognizing and using the right strategies in different contexts.

. . .

LEARNING IS a journey shaped by both the principles we follow and the methods we choose to apply. By grounding our study habits in the powerful techniques of *active recall* and *spaced repetition*, we can significantly enhance our efficiency, reduce stress, and master new concepts more effectively. Regardless of the method, the key is to experiment with different strategies and adapt them to our own needs.

Remember, it's not about the quantity of time we spend studying, but the quality of our focus and the methods we use. We can use these methods to develop a system that fits us personally, leading to greater success with less effort.

In the end, it's about creating a learning process that works for us—a system built on principles that can evolve and grow with us, just as we evolve and grow through our learning experiences.

11 MORE STUDY METHODS

MORE METHODS FOR INTENTIONAL LEARNING

The Importance of Principles Over Methods

"Hard work is not always something you can see. It is not always physical effort. In fact, the most powerful form of hard work is thinking clearly. Designing a winning strategy may not look very active, but make no mistake: it is very hard work. Strategy often beats sweat." - James Clear (*Atomic Habits*)

Using study methods without understanding their core principles is like using tools without knowing how they work—it wastes both time and energy. Once we grasp the principles, we can adapt, combine, and personalize strategies to create a study system tailored to our needs.

Let's break down these 11 study methods, and understand how the principles behind them can help us learn more effectively. This chapter is a continuation from the previous.

1. Scope the Subject

Before diving into a new subject, it's crucial to understand the bigger picture. *Scoping the subject* is about mapping out what we already know and identifying gaps in our understanding. It's like planning a route before a road trip—it prevents us from getting lost.

Methods of Scoping the Subject

- *Mind Mapping:* Create a visual map to organize knowledge and identify gaps.
  - For example: when studying cell biology, start with "Cell Biology" in the center. Branch out into "Cell Structure," "Cell Function," "Cell Division," and "Cellular Respiration." List what we know under each and pinpoint areas for improvement.
- *Skimming the Textbook:* Quickly browse chapters, highlighting unfamiliar terms. This helps us target our focus.
  - For example: skim through a chapter on the American Civil War, noting key terms like "Gettysburg" and "Emancipation Proclamation." These become our learning targets.
- *Reviewing Syllabi or Exams:* Reviewing old exams or the course syllabus gives insight into which topics to prioritize.
  - For example: in a calculus syllabus, list topics like "Limits," "Derivatives," and "Integrals" and note what we remember versus what's new.

Scoping the subject is beneficial because it clarifies what to focus on, reduces distractions, and outlines study priorities, ultimately saving time in the long run. We can easily implement scoping the subject in our net study session by just taking five minutes to create a quick mind map, skim the textbook, or review the syllabus.

2. Build Knowledge Frames

Knowledge frames help simplify complex concepts by breaking them down into manageable parts. Think of them as a skeleton—adding layers of detail over time creates a solid understanding.

Creating a Knowledge Frame

Let's use the flow of blood through the heart as an example. Instead of memorizing each step by brute force, simplify the process:

1. *Simplify the System:* Imagine the heart as a box with four chambers—two atria and two ventricles. Blood flows in through the atria and out through the ventricles.
2. *Add Details Gradually:* Add valves and pathways like the tricuspid valve and pulmonary artery. Use mnemonics, such as "Try it before you buy it," to remember that blood passes through the tricuspid valve before the bicuspid.

When we apply building knowledge frames to other concepts, the steps are the same. Simplify the concept, then gradually add details. Building knowledge frames is great because it makes memorization easier by organizing complex ideas and we can build a deeper understanding by building gradually. The next time we come across a challenging topic, we can start broadly and add details as we learn.

3. Clearly Articulate Failure and Success

"When things cannot be defined, they are outside the sphere of wisdom, for wisdom knows the proper limits of things." - Seneca (Letters from a Stoic XCIV – On the Value of Advice)

Learning becomes less stressful when we define what success and failure look like. Setting clear intentions and boundaries allows us to measure progress and stay on track. Not only do we experience dopamine releases as we move towards our goals, but having specific targets also helps us stay on track.

Setting Clear Goals
Define specific objectives go beyond just "spending time" on a subject.

Here are some examples of how to articulate success and failure in different situations:

- Regarding practice questions:
  - *Goal:* Complete practice questions covering specific topics until we can do them without mistakes.
    - *Failure:* Struggling to complete the problems or making frequent mistakes.
    - *Success:* Consistently solving problems correctly without errors.
- Regarding completing chapters:
  - *Goal:* Finish studying one chapter of new information per day.
    - *Failure:* Not completing the chapter within the day.
    - *Success:* Complete the chapter and understand the content thoroughly.
- On quantitative goals:
  - *Goal:* Complete a set number of practice problems, such as 20 problems, in a study session.

- *Failure:* Completing fewer than 20 problems or getting many wrong.
- *Success:* Finishing all 20 problems and understanding the solutions.

Knowing when we've succeeded or failed helps keep us motivated and focused. This principle applies outside studying too. Defining success in any pursuit provides direction and focus. Before we start our next study session, we can clearly define what success and failure look like for that topic.

4. Breakdown Past Papers, Exams, and Essay Plans

Old exams and essay plans are some of the most effective tools for preparation. They show us exactly what to expect, reducing uncertainty and anxiety.

The Value of Old Exams

Reviewing old exams reveals the types of questions, wording, and key themes to focus on. If past papers aren't available, practice tests at the end of textbook chapters are useful alternatives.

Essay Plans

When writing essays, look at old papers. Ask:

- How is the paper structured?
- What are its strengths and weaknesses?

While plagiarism is unethical, drawing inspiration from others is entirely acceptable. In Austin Kleon's *Steal Like an Artist*, he discusses the uniqueness of each individual and how it affects our ability to imitate. Kleon suggests that trying to copy another's work will inevitably result in a new creation influenced by individualism. I believe this is true. By allowing ourselves to be influenced by our surroundings, we naturally influence the world around us. When looking over old papers, mimic as much as possible. Steal the concepts, plans, and ideas, but let your voice shine through and make them your own.

5. Work Until the Point of Diminishing Returns

"The last 10 percent of performance generates one-third of the cost and two-thirds of the problems." - Norman R. Augustine (*Augustine's Laws*)

The *Point of Diminishing Returns* is when the effort we're putting in no longer yields meaningful progress. Understanding when to stop is just as important as knowing when to push harder.

The 90% Solution

Aim for 90% mastery and then move on. The last 10% often requires disproportionate effort and time. It's more efficient to reach a solid understanding and move forward rather than striving for perfection in every detail. That being said, if what we are doing requires 100% level mastery, then it may be worth taking on the extra cost.

6. Avoid Multitasking

Contrary to popular belief, multitasking is a myth. What we call multitasking is really *task-switching*, which prevents deep, focused work.

Why Multitasking Doesn't Work

Switching between tasks distracts our brains, making it harder to focus on any one task. True productivity comes from deep work, which requires uninterrupted attention.

For example, if we're switching between writing an essay and scrolling through social media, our brain can't focus on either, leading to lower-quality work.

By focusing on one thing for an extended period, we'll not only complete tasks faster but with higher quality. During our next study session, we can turn off notifications and focus solely on one task for at least 30 minutes. Avoid switching contexts to allow deep focus.

7. Use Maintenance and Elaborative Rehearsal

There are two types of rehearsal when it comes to memory: *Maintenance* and *Elaborative Rehearsal*.

Maintenance Rehearsal

This is great for quick memorization but doesn't transfer information to long-term memory. Think of how we memorize a phone number briefly and forget it immediately after using it.

Elaborative Rehearsal

This type of rehearsal involves connecting new information to what we already know. It's more effortful but much more effective for long-term learning.

For concepts we need to remember long-term, focus on elaborative rehearsal. Find meaningful connections to what we already know.

8. Account for Spill Days

Life rarely goes exactly as planned, so it's important to account for the unexpected by scheduling *Spill Days*—days where we catch up on tasks we didn't finish. Tasks often take longer than expected, and unforeseen events frequently arise.

Why Spill Days Matter

If something comes up and throws off our schedule, a Spill Day can help us stay on track without the stress of piling up incomplete tasks. I regularly schedule Spill Days into my plans because things regularly don't go according to plan.

9. Schedule Around Our Body's Natural Rhythms

Our bodies follow natural rhythms like *circadian rhythms*, which govern sleep and wake cycles. Understanding and working with our body's rhythms can significantly boost productivity.

Working With Our Rhythms

Plan our most mentally demanding work during our peak energy hours. For most people, this is in the morning or early afternoon. Leave less demanding tasks for when our energy levels naturally dip. We can figure out what our rhythms are by paying attention to our energy levels throughout the day or throughout the month. We can schedule difficult tasks during high-energy periods and lighter tasks when we naturally feel more tired. When we schedule around our rhythms, we reduce the need for willpower.

Personally, I've noticed that I do my most challenging work best in the morning. I try to save my simple repetitive tasks for later in the day.

10. Create a Guiding Environment to Minimize Willpower

Our environment can either make our work easier or harder. A well-designed environment minimizes distractions and reduces the need for willpower. It's helpful to have a space that is specifically designated for work.

Design a Guiding Environment

Set up a space that's optimized for focus. Eliminate distractions, keep tools and resources within reach, and ensure our space is conducive to productivity. When our spaces are optimized for functionality, we drastically reduce the friction to get things done.

We can turn our spaces into a guided environment by taking a look at our workspace. What distractions can we remove? How can we optimize it for more focus and less friction?

Creating a guiding environment reduces the need for willpower by making it easier to stay on task. Minimizing distractions and optimizing our workspaces can enhance productivity and make our goals more achievable. While everyone's optimal environment will look different, the key is to design spaces that support and guide us toward our objectives with minimal resistance.

Maintaining a helpful environment involves keeping it clean and organized. I try to take a few minutes after I finish working to reset the space so it doesn't become another barrier to my goals.

11. Use Mnemonic Devices to Remember

Mnemonic devices help us remember complex information by associating it with something easier to recall.

Types of Mnemonic Devices

- *Acronyms:* create a word from the first letters of a series of words. For example, NASA stands for National Aeronautics and Space Administration.

- *Acrostics:* form a sentence where each word starts with the first letter of each piece of information you want to remember. For example, "Every Good Boy Deserves Fudge" helps music students remember the notes on the lines of the treble clef (E, G, B, D, F).
- *Rhymes:* create a catchy, memorable pattern, like "In 1492, Columbus sailed the ocean blue."
- *Alliteration:* repeats the same initial consonant sounds in words, like "Peter Piper picked a peck of pickled peppers."
- *Chunking:* breaks down large amounts of information into smaller, more manageable units. For example, we might remember a phone number as 123-456-7890 instead of 1234567890.
- *Imagery and Visualization:* Creating vivid mental images related to the information helps improve recall. For instance, to remember a grocery list, we might visualize a giant carrot dancing with a loaf of bread.
- *Method of Loci:* Also known as the memory palace technique, this method involves associating items to be remembered with specific physical locations in a familiar place. For example, imagine placing items around our house as we walk through it in our mind.
- *Peg Systems:* involves associating numbers with words that rhyme or sound similar, creating an easy-to-remember list. For example, one is a bun, two is a shoe, three is a tree, etc.

Mnemonics are great because they enhance our memory, increase learning speed, reduce cognitive load, and are more enjoyable. Whenever I need to memorize a new fact, I create a mnemonic device to solidify it in memory.

. . .

THE KEY TAKEAWAY is that understanding the "why" and "how" behind these methods enables us to study smarter, not harder. Ultimately, it's about creating a learning process tailored to our needs —a system grounded in principles that evolve alongside us and our learning experiences. We can apply them thoughtfully, experiment, and refine our approach to become a more efficient, strategic learner.

HOW TO BEAT PROCRASTINATION
UNDERSTANDING SELF-REGULATION & PROGRESS

"You cannot escape the responsibility of tomorrow by evading it today." - Abraham Lincoln

We've all been there—staring at a growing to-do list, feeling the weight of each unchecked box. We know we should get started, yet something holds us back. Procrastination isn't merely about avoiding tasks—it's a struggle with ourselves. The good news? There are strategies to overcome it, and by understanding why we procrastinate, we can take control of our time and lives.

Why We Procrastinate

Procrastination often stems from avoidance. We might avoid tasks because they feel overwhelming, or maybe we're uncertain about the outcome. It's not laziness; it's a defense mechanism. At its core, procrastination is a self-regulation issue—an inability to manage our emotions, focus, and impulses. We tend to rely on external pressures like deadlines to push us into action, but this external motivation isn't sustainable.

By understanding the underlying causes of procrastination, we can shift our approach. The goal is to improve our self-regulation and find internal reasons to act.

Discovering Our "Why"

One of the most powerful tools to combat procrastination is understanding our "why." When we know the deeper reason behind a task, it becomes easier to follow through. Motivation is deeply personal; finding the right internal motivator makes all the difference.

I remember a student who once told me he didn't see the point of studying Shakespeare. To him, it was irrelevant and confusing. But when I explained that Shakespeare's characters are reflections of people we encounter in real life, something clicked. He realized that by understanding these characters, he could better understand human behavior. Suddenly, his "why" shifted, and he was motivated to dive into the text. A week later, he was leading discussions in class, finding connections between the story and his own experiences.

"He who has a why to live can bear almost any how."- Friedrich Nietzsche (*Twilight of the Idols*)

When our motivation aligns with our personal values, procrastination loses its power. A compelling internal 'why' is far more effective than any external deadline.

Systems to Stay on Track

Once we find our "why," we need to create systems to help us stay on course. Different tools work for different people, so it's important to find what resonates with us.

- *Checklists:* Writing down everything we need to do and checking off tasks as we go can create a sense of accomplishment and momentum.
- *Calendars:* Scheduling tasks and setting deadlines in advance helps prevent last-minute panic.
- *Task Managers:* Apps or tools like Reminders, Todoist, Trello, or Google Keep can help us organize tasks and prioritize them based on urgency.

Prioritizing with Chunking and Batching

To better manage our tasks, we can divide them into smaller, more manageable parts. This helps prevent the feeling of being overwhelmed and keeps us moving forward.

- *Chunking:* Large tasks can be overwhelming, but when we break them into smaller pieces, they become more manageable. For example, writing a term paper might seem daunting, but writing just one paragraph is much more approachable.
- *Batching:* Grouping similar tasks together can save us time and mental energy. Instead of doing laundry daily, set aside one day a week to get it all done. This way, we focus on one type of task at a time, reducing decision fatigue.

Taking Baby Steps to Overcome Procrastination

When tasks feel overwhelming, we can fall into the trap of inaction. To combat this, we can break tasks into smaller steps. Small steps lead to small wins, which compound over time and build towards bigger successes.

Completing smaller tasks helps take the weight off our minds. The *Zeigarnik Effect* is a psychological phenomenon that suggests people remember uncompleted or interrupted tasks better than completed ones. Our minds are inclined to continue thinking about unfinished tasks, which can create a mental reminder to complete them. By breaking tasks into smaller, manageable parts and achieving them, we can reduce mental clutter and increase our sense of accomplishment, making it easier to stay motivated and productive.

Behavior Change: Small Steps Lead to Big Results

When it comes to changing behavior, there are three primary methods: having an epiphany, changing our environment, or taking small steps. While epiphanies are rare and environment changes can be challenging, taking small, manageable steps is a powerful tool. Small, incremental changes compound over time, leading to lasting success.

Aim for Incremental Progress

Progress is progress, no matter how small. I've come to believe that incremental progress is the only kind of progress that exists. Whether we're working on a major project or learning a new skill, it's the tiny, consistent actions we take each day that add up.

Consider athletes, musicians, or even successful entrepreneurs. Their success doesn't happen overnight—it's the result of daily, often unnoticeable, small improvements. Each small task completed gives us a sense of achievement, creating a success spiral that keeps us moving forward.

Start a Ritual

"The secret of getting ahead is getting started." - Mark Twain

Often, the most challenging part of any task is just starting. Creating a starting ritual can help overcome that initial inertia. For example, Mel Robbin's 5-second rule—counting down from five and immediately starting the task—can help us push through that resistance.

However, it's essential to ensure that our rituals don't become another form of procrastination. The key is to use them as a tool to launch into action, not as a way to delay.

Adequately Prepare (The 25% Rule)

Preparation is a critical yet frequently overlooked step. By spending time getting ready before we dive into a task, we can increase our effectiveness significantly. *The 25% Rule*: adequate preparation requires 25% of the time spent preparing. For instance, if we have a one-hour meeting, we can spend 15 minutes prepping for it. This preparation can make us two to three times more effective and help us avoid wasting time later.

Break and Set Milestone Deadlines

Breaking larger assignments into smaller chunks and setting milestone deadlines can keep us on track. This method ensures we're not overwhelmed by the enormity of a project and helps us manage our workload more effectively. For example, if we have a major project due in a month, setting weekly goals can make the process feel more manageable.

PROCRASTINATION IS a challenge we all face, but it's not insurmountable. By discovering our 'why,' establishing systems, dividing tasks into smaller parts, and taking incremental steps, we can transform procrastination into productivity. Small progress is still progress—and it might even be the only kind of progress.

Begin with a simple ritual, prepare thoroughly, and divide tasks into achievable milestones. By doing so, we can manage our time more effectively, remain on track, and achieve our goals with greater efficiency.

MASTERING THE ART OF NOTE-TAKING

8 METHODS TO HELP US RETAIN & APPLY KNOWLEDGE

"He listens well who takes notes." - Dante Alighieri

Taking notes isn't just about writing down what we hear; it's about processing, organizing, and making sense of information. When we take notes, we internalize information by translating it into our own words and thought patterns. This personalization helps us understand, remember, and apply what we've learned.

Why Note-Taking Matters

"The ultimate advantage of taking notes is that they customize the information you need to retain to your vocabulary and your mode of thinking. At their best, notes allow you to organize and process information in a way that makes it most likely that you can use this information afterward." - Jim Kwik (*Limitless*)

Whether we're a student or a lifelong learner, finding the right note-taking method is crucial. Some methods are better suited to different types of material or learning styles. Let's explore 8 effective note-taking methods, their strengths, and when to use each one.

1. Outlining

Outlining is one of the simplest and most popular ways to take notes. By listing main ideas as bullet points and indenting subpoints underneath, we create a clear and organized structure. This method is especially useful for subjects like history or philosophy, where information builds on itself in a hierarchical way.

- *Best for:* Subjects with clear structures, like history, philosophy, or psychology.
- *Pros:*
  - Easy to organize information
  - Helps visualize relationships between ideas
- *Cons:*
  - Challenging to maintain in fast-paced lectures
  - Can lead to mindless copying if overdone

2. Mind Mapping

Mind mapping is especially beneficial for learning visually. Start with the main idea in the center of the page, and branch out with related subtopics. This method helps us visually see how ideas are connected, making it ideal for brainstorming or understanding complex, interconnected concepts.

- *Best for:* Brainstorming, problem-solving, or synthesizing ideas (e.g., creative writing, project planning).
- *Pros:*
  - Encourages creativity
  - Provides a clear visual representation of ideas
- *Cons:*

- ◦ Can become messy if not well-organized
- ◦ Time-consuming to create in real time

3. The Boxing Method

The boxing method involves grouping related notes into individual boxes. It's great for subjects where the relationships between concepts are crucial, like biology or business strategy. By organizing related points visually, we can easily see how ideas connect, making it easier to review.

- *Best for:* Subjects with clearly defined sections or categories (e.g., biology, business, or textbooks).
- *Pros:*
  - ◦ Clear visual representation of grouped information
  - ◦ Keeps notes neat and organized
- *Cons:*
  - ◦ Not suitable for unstructured lectures
  - ◦ May oversimplify nuanced connections between ideas

4. The Slides Method

Many students use the slides method in college. Printing out lecture slides and annotating them allows us to focus more on the professor's words rather than frantically copying everything verbatim. However, this method can lead to passive learning if we rely too heavily on the slides without processing the information.

- *Best for:* Lectures with prepared slides, especially in fact-heavy courses like science or engineering.
- *Pros:*
  - ◦ Saves time during lectures
  - ◦ Allows us to focus on listening and understanding
- *Cons:*

- Encourages passive learning
- Can lead to missing out on key details not included in the slides

5. Cornell Notes

The Cornell method is a structured approach that divides our paper into three sections: questions, notes, and a summary. This system promotes active learning by encouraging us to think critically about the material and engage with it during review sessions. It's a fantastic method for retaining and recalling information over time.

- *Best for:* Subjects that require critical thinking and review (e.g., law, social sciences).
- *Pros:*
  - Structured for efficient review
  - Encourages active engagement with the material
- *Cons:*
  - Requires effort to summarize and generate questions
  - Limited space for detailed notes

6. The Flow Method

The Flow Method is all about creativity and flexibility. Instead of rigidly following a structure, we can write, doodle, and draw as ideas come to mind. This method is ideal for visualizing complex ideas and seeing connections between them, which is useful for subjects like anatomy or design.

- *Best for:* Subjects that require big-picture thinking and visual representation (e.g., anatomy, design).
- *Pros:*
  - Encourages creative thinking
  - Simplifies complex ideas through visuals

- *Cons:*
  - Can be disorganized
  - Requires a solid understanding of the subject to be effective

7. The Charting Method

Charting organizes information into a table or chart, making it easy to compare and contrast facts, figures, or concepts. This method is especially helpful for subjects like math or science, where data and comparisons are critical.

- *Best for:* Comparing facts or concepts (e.g., statistics, biology, economics).
- *Pros:*
  - Clear visual comparison of information
  - Reduces excessive writing and aids active recall
- *Cons:*
  - Time-consuming to create
  - Not suitable for unstructured or abstract subject

8. Systematic Consolidation & Expansion

This method focuses on summarizing and expanding our notes to reinforce learning. *Systematic Consolidation* shrinks notes into smaller summaries, forcing us to prioritize key information. *Systematic Expansion*, on the other hand, involves expanding our notes into larger creative projects, like blog posts or videos, which deepens our understanding.

Systematic Consolidation

In college, I used this method by shrinking my notes to fit on one notecard for closed-book exams. The process of deciding what to include not only helped me learn the material but also solidified it in my memory. This method worked so well that for some exams I didn't even need to use the notecard.

- *Best for:* Reviewing for exams, summarizing key points for quick recall.

Systematic Expansion

As a tutor, I would expand my notes into blog posts or teaching materials. This method helped me fill gaps in my understanding and articulate concepts clearly to others, deepening my mastery of the subject.

- *Best for:* Deepening understanding through creative projects.

My Personal Workflow for Note-Taking

When I come across ideas worth remembering, I quickly jot them down in my iPhone's Notes app for convenience. To keep everything organized, I use tags related to the topic for easy retrieval. Later, I transfer these notes into *OneNote*, where I organize them into notebooks, sections, and pages. This process allows me to see how new information fits into my existing knowledge base, creating stronger neural connections.

Recently, I've started using Notion to better organize and expand ideas into larger projects, including blog posts, videos, and books. This process not only helps me understand each idea better but also turns my notes into something valuable to others.

Handwritten vs. Typed Notes: Which is Better?

Research shows that *handwritten notes* are better for retention than typing. When we write by hand, we engage more of our brain, which leads to deeper processing of information. In a study by

Princeton and UCLA, students who took notes by hand remembered more and performed better on conceptual questions than those who used laptops.

For subjects like math or science that require deeper understanding, handwriting is the better option. However, for subjects where speed and volume matter, such as the humanities, typing can be more efficient.

When to Use Each Note-Taking Method

Choosing the right method depends on our goals and the subject matter. If we're in a concept-heavy class like math or science, try the Flow Method or handwriting. For fact-heavy subjects like history or biology, Cornell Notes or Charting may be more effective.

Tips for Effective Note-Taking

"If you take notes with a goal in mind, every note you take will have relevance." - Jim Kwik *(Limitless)*

- *Clarify the purpose of our note-taking:* Different contexts demand tailored methods. If we had a bigger purpose for collecting the information, then all the notes we take are relevant.
- *Listen for key points:* Don't write down everything—focus on what matters.
- *Use our own words:* This helps with retention.
- *Consolidate notes periodically:* Shrink our notes into a smaller space for more effective recall.
- *Avoid highlighting:* It may feel productive, but it's not as effective as active note-taking methods. Highlighting ends up creating more work than not.

Layering Notes: A Secret to Mastering Content

Layering our notes—revisiting them multiple times with a different purpose each time—allows us to engage more deeply with the material. Each time we layer, we refine our understanding and retention.

NOTE-TAKING IS a skill that improves with practice. Experiment with different methods, and soon, we'll find the approach that works best for us. The best method for note-taking is to be clear on why we are collecting the information in the first place. I never cared to take notes until I got serious about writing books — suddenly I naturally wanted to capture every piece of information in sight.

HOW TO READ TEXTBOOKS EFFECTIVELY
LEARNING WITH PURPOSE & EFFICIENCY

"To be better equipped for the tests that the year will bring — read a textbook. To prepare for the tests that life will bring — read a book." - Mokokoma Mokhonoana

Remember the night before a final exam? Flipping through hundreds of pages, hoping the right answer would magically stick in our brain? It's a struggle most students know too well. But there's a better way to tackle textbooks, and that's what this chapter is all about.

Textbooks are a different beast compared to regular books. They're designed to teach us facts and principles, not entertain us. For example, *The Fundamentals of Chemical Engineering* differs wildly from *Man's Search for Meaning*. Textbooks are packed with information we need to understand and remember, which makes them feel intimidating and hard to read. But with the right strategies, they become much easier to handle.

If we're reading a textbook to pass an exam, this is the right place. If we're reading one for pleasure, feel free to ignore this chapter.

Finding a Clear Purpose

Humans are goal-oriented creatures. To stay motivated, we need to know *why* we're reading something. Looking at a huge textbook with the vague idea of "learning everything" can be overwhelming. Instead, we need a clear, focused purpose to make the process manageable and rewarding.

Here's how to create that purpose:

1. *Scan the Textbook First:* Before diving in, flip through the pages. Notice any images, charts, or phrases that stand out. This helps us get a broad sense of the material. Focus on unfamiliar concepts and transform them into questions.
2. *Review the End-of-Chapter Questions:* If the textbook includes questions at the end of each chapter, start there. This helps us know what to focus on when we read. If there is no quiz, review the chapter summary and turn it into questions instead.
3. *Read the Bold Print:* Bold print highlights the most important ideas. Skim these first to grasp the main concepts quickly before diving into the details.
4. *Read the First and Last Sentences:* The first sentence introduces the key idea, and the last one wraps it up. This gives you a quick understanding of what each paragraph is about.

The Main Goals of Reading a Textbook

When reading textbooks, keep three goals in mind:

1. *Get the Correct Information:* Make sure we're studying the right content.
2. *Retain the Information:* Ensure that we remember the information for the long haul.

3. *Spend Less Time:* Textbooks can be tedious, so learning how to read them efficiently is key.

Techniques for Effective Reading

Here are some methods that will help us test our understanding and make reading easier:

- *Answer the Questions:* We can use the end-of-chapter questions to test ourselves as we go. Write out the main ideas in our own words—this ensures we really understand the material. If we can explain a concept simply, we are on the right track.
- *Evaluate the Text:* When was this textbook published? Older textbooks may miss out on newer research or developments in the field. Make sure the information is still relevant.
- *Summarize to Teach:* Try explaining the material as if we were teaching it to a 5-year-old. Simplifying concepts not only helps us understand them but also reinforces our memory.
- *Practice Active Reading:* Engage with the text by using the methods we've covered. Ask questions, summarize ideas, and test ourselves regularly. Active reading keeps our brain engaged, which improves both comprehension and retention.
- *Determine Our Focus:* Are we reading for main concepts or small details? Focus on learning the big ideas first, then dive into the details. This way, we'll build a strong foundation that helps us understand the more complex parts of the text.

Extra Tips for Textbook Success

- *Try a Pomodoro Session:* The Pomodoro technique is straightforward but effective. Work for 25-30 minutes, then take a break. This makes it easier to start reading and keeps us motivated through longer sessions.
- *Reward Ourselves:* After finishing a tough section or completing a study session, we can give ourselves a small reward—whether it's a snack, a break, or something fun. This will help prevent burnout and keep us motivated over time.
- *Use Mnemonics to Memorize:* Mnemonics are a fantastic way to memorize difficult information. Create acronyms, rhymes, or silly phrases to help the information stick. For example, "ROY G. BIV" helps remember the colors of the rainbow (Red, Orange, Yellow, Green, Blue, Indigo, Violet).
- *Use Spaced Repetition:* This technique involves reviewing material at gradually increasing intervals. Spacing out reviews helps move information from short-term to long-term memory. Try reviewing new material the next day, then again after three days, and once more after a week.
- *Visualize the Material:* Turn complicated concepts into diagrams, mind maps, or sketches. Visual aids help organize information and can be easier for our brain to remember than text alone.

Wrapping It All Up

Reading textbooks may never feel as relaxing as reading our favorite novel, but it becomes much more manageable when we use the right methods. The key to success in reading textbooks is having a clear purpose when we read. Start by scanning the textbook, checking the questions, and focusing on the most important parts.

Keep the three main goals in mind: get the right information, retain it for the long term, and spend our time wisely. Practice active reading, summarize in our own words, and decide whether we're focusing on big ideas or the finer details. Don't forget to use extra techniques like the Pomodoro method, rewards, and memory aids to make the process easier and more enjoyable.

Reading is like working out—it takes time and consistent effort to get better. Just like training our bodies, reading textbooks is a skill that improves with practice. Stick with it, and soon, we'll find that reading becomes less of a chore and more of a valuable tool for learning. The more we practice these techniques, the more confident and efficient we'll become.

By focusing on purpose, engaging actively with the material, and using proven techniques, we'll not only pass our exams—we'll become a better learner for life.

WHY MEMORY MATTERS
HOW TO KEEP IT FIT

The Power of a Trained Memory

"There's no such thing as a good memory or a bad memory, only a trained memory or an untrained memory." - Jim Kwik (*Limitless*)

Imagine walking into an important exam and feeling like everything we've studied is slipping away. We've all been there—that moment of panic when our memory feels like a sieve. But what if memory could be trained, strengthened like a muscle, ensuring we never feel unprepared again? Keeping our brains in shape is as vital as maintaining physical fitness. Without mental challenges, our minds weaken, leaving us unfocused and forgetful. But why is memory so crucial, and how can we improve it?

Why Memory Matters

Memory is our constant companion. It helps us navigate every part of our lives, from daily routines to complex problem-solving. Think of a computer with limited storage or an inability to remember basic functions—it would be frustratingly slow. Our brains work the same way.

A strong memory allows us to perform everyday tasks efficiently, learn new things, and solve problems more effectively. It doesn't just help us remember facts—it fuels creativity, decision-making, and expertise.

Memory is a Foundation for Learning

"Memorization is discipline for the mind. Much needed in an age when so many minds are lazy, distracted, have little to think about, or think sloppily. Memorization helps train the mind to focus and be industrious." - William R. Klemm (*Memory Power 101: A Comprehensive Guide to Better Learning for Students, Businesspeople, and Seniors*)

He also reminds us:

"No, you can't always 'Google it.' Sometimes you don't have access to the internet. Not everything of importance is on the web (and a great deal of irrelevant trash will accompany any search)."

Memorization exercises our minds, training them to focus and work harder. While we have access to endless information online, relying on external sources for everything can weaken our cognitive abilities. Memory gives us immediate access to knowledge without distractions.

Memory Builds Understanding

When we commit things to memory, we can think more clearly and connect new information to what we already know. Memory builds context, which helps us understand concepts deeply rather than just surface-level details. The more we remember, the more we can learn. Becoming an expert in any field without retaining foundational knowledge would be impossible.

How to Improve Our Memory

So, how can we improve our memory? A simple mnemonic that I learned from Jim Kwik's book *Limitless* is MOM:

- *M: Motivation*
- *O: Observation*
- *M: Methods*

Let's break down each part:

M: Motivation

We are more likely to remember information when we feel motivated. Think of it this way—if someone offered us $5,000 to remember a phone number, we'd be much more likely to remember it than if there was no incentive.

Motivation is about finding value in what we're trying to remember. We can ask ourselves, *Why is this important to me?* When we tie new information to our goals or values, it sticks better.

O: Observation

Most memory problems aren't because we can't retain information—they occur because we weren't paying attention in the first place. Be present and focus on what we want to remember. We can improve our observation by practicing mindfulness or playing games that train our attention.

M: Methods

Using the right techniques can make memorization much easier and more enjoyable. Let's explore a few effective methods:

Rote Memorization (and When It's Useful)

Rote memorization involves repeating information over and over until it sticks. While this can be tedious, it's sometimes necessary—think of memorizing vocabulary or math formulas. But it's inefficient when applied broadly because it only engages a small part of our brain.

One way to enhance rote memorization is through associations. For example, the Baker/baker Paradox shows that people remember occupations better than last names because we can connect more with professions. In a study, people were shown pictures of faces with names and faces with occupations. The participants could remember the professions easier than the names because we could make more connections with occupations. People remembered the job "baker" more quickly than the name "Baker" because the job made us think of bread, baking, and other related ideas. These connections help our brains remember better. So, creating associations can make it easier to remember information.

Turn Facts into Stories

People can remember stories far more easily than isolated facts. If we need to memorize something, try turning it into a narrative. Stories engage us emotionally and help us create vivid images in our minds, making them easier to recall.

For example, if we're trying to remember historical dates, we can imagine ourselves as part of that history. Create a story where we're interacting with the key figures or events. This brings the information to life and locks it into our memory.

Use Visualization

Our brains are wired for images. We think in pictures, dream in pictures, and much of our brain's processing power is devoted to visual information. We can leverage this by creating mental images of the information we want to remember.

Let's say we're trying to memorize a list of items. Instead of simply repeating the list, visualize each item in an unusual way. For example, if we need to remember to buy milk, eggs, and bread, imagine a giant milk carton dancing with eggs while they're all eating slices of bread. The sillier and more outlandish the image, the better it will stick.

Spaced Repetition

Another effective technique is spaced repetition, where we review information at increasing intervals. Instead of cramming everything in at once, we revisit it over time, which reinforces the memory and helps move it from short-term to long-term storage.

Keep Our Brain in Shape

Keeping our brains in shape is just as essential as staying physically active. A strong memory helps us in every aspect of life, from performing daily tasks to mastering new skills. By staying motivated, observing carefully, and using the right methods—such as creating associations, telling stories, and visualizing information—we can train our memory to be stronger, sharper, and more reliable. Just like working out at the gym, practice and consistency will bring improvement.

MEMORY IS NOT A FIXED TRAIT—IT'S something that can be trained and improved. The more we work on it, the better it gets, and the more we'll be able to use it to our advantage in learning, work, and life.

ADVANCED STUDY METHODS
TECHNIQUES FOR HIGHER LEVEL LEARNERS

"The best moments in our lives are not the passive, receptive, relaxing times. The best moments usually occur when a person's body or mind is stretched to its limits in a voluntary effort to accomplish something difficult and worthwhile." - Mihaly Csikszentmihalyi (*Flow*)

Ever crammed for an exam, only to forget everything the next day? I know I have. But what if there's a better way to learn—one that not only helps us retain information but actually makes studying more enjoyable?

Revisiting Basic Study Methods

Before diving into the more advanced strategies, let's quickly cover a few of the fundamental study methods that can make a significant difference. We may already be familiar with some of these, but they're crucial building blocks for mastering new information.

Time Management Techniques

- *Modifying the Pomodoro Technique:* Work for 25 minutes, then take a 5-minute break. Adjust the time based on our attention span to avoid burnout and boost focus.
- *No-Stakes Practice:* Study without worrying about mistakes. This reduces stress and helps identify gaps in our knowledge. It's like practicing a sport—low pressure, but high payoff.
- *Work Until the Point of Diminishing Returns:* Stop studying when we feel that the information is no longer sticking. There's no sense in pushing when our brain has hit its limit for the day.
- *Account for Spill Days:* Life happens. Plan for extra days in our schedule to cover unexpected delays. If nothing goes wrong, consider it bonus time to rest or get ahead.

Memory and Retention Techniques

- *The Feynman Technique (ELI5):* Explain concepts as if teaching a 5-year-old. This reveals gaps in our understanding, making it easier to fill them.
- *The Leitner System:* Use flashcards and spaced repetition to prioritize what we don't know, while reviewing what we do know less frequently.
- *Use Mnemonic Devices:* Rhymes, acronyms, and visual cues help us remember tricky information. Think of mnemonics like mental shortcuts.

Cognitive Techniques

- *Deep Work & Flow:* Focus intensely on one task at a time to reach a state of flow. This is where learning feels seamless, and we perform at our peak.
- *Interleaving Practice:* Mix different subjects or topics

while studying. This forces our brain to adapt, improving retention.

- *Simulate the Test Environment:* Practice in conditions that mimic our test day. This helps our brain prepare for the actual experience, reducing stress and improving performance.
- *Avoid Multitasking:* We all think we can juggle tasks, but our brains work best when focusing on one thing at a time.
- *Create Knowledge Frames:* Build a mental map of the topic before diving into details. Having an overview helps us connect new information with what we already know.

Reflective Techniques

- *Articulate Failure and Success:* Reflect on what went right or wrong during our study sessions. This way, we know what to focus on next time.
- *Break Down Past Papers:* Analyze old tests and assignments to spot patterns. Understanding the structure can give us an edge for future exams.
- *Incorporate Concepts into Everyday Speech:* Find ways to use what we're learning in conversations. It strengthens our understanding and helps make the material stick.

Advanced but Accessible Methods

Some of these basic techniques—like *Interleaving Practice* and *Building Knowledge Frames*—might seem a bit challenging at first, but trust me, they're worth the effort. Start small and notice how much they can improve our retention and understanding.

Advanced Study Methods

Now that we have a solid foundation, let's dive into advanced study techniques. These strategies are more complex, but they will significantly enhance our learning process.

Frontloading

Frontloading means completing as much work as possible early on to build a strong foundation. This leaves us more time later to reinforce and refine what we've learned.

When I tried this in college, it transformed my study process. Here's why:

- I spent more time deepening my learning, rather than just building initial connections.
- I capitalized on my motivation, which is strongest at the start of a semester.

Frontloading might feel intense at first, but it allows us to focus more on review later in the course—when others are scrambling to learn new material.

Multiple Coding (Dual Coding)

Dual Coding means combining verbal and visual information to improve retention. But it doesn't stop there—we can take it further by engaging multiple senses and encoding methods.

For example, when we combine:

- *Visual Encoding* (diagrams, charts) with
- *Auditory Encoding* (lectures, discussions) and
- *Kinesthetic Encoding* (hands-on activities),

the brain builds stronger connections, making learning more efficient.

Each encoding method taps into different pathways in the brain, helping us remember information longer and with less effort. This strategy works best when we intentionally mix different methods to solidify our understanding.

Metacognition: Thinking About Thinking

Metacognition is all about being aware of how we learn and thinking about our thinking process. This skill helps us reflect on what's working and what's not, allowing us to adjust our strategies as needed. Here are a few benefits of developing our metacognition :

- *Self-Awareness:* We'll understand our strengths and weaknesses, helping us focus our efforts more effectively.
- *Goal Setting:* Setting clear, specific goals directs our focus and efforts.
- *Self-Regulation:* We can monitor our learning progress and adapt strategies to improve retention.

Here are a few practical methods we can do to develop our metacognition:

- *Ask Questions:* We can regularly ask ourselves questions like, "What do I already know about this?" or "What's my plan for solving this?"
- *Keep a Learning Journal:* Writing down our goals, strategies, and reflections helps track our progress and spot areas for improvement.
- *Teach Others:* Explaining what we've learned helps solidify our understanding and exposes any gaps in our knowledge.

Cognitive Load Management

Our brain, like a muscle, can only handle so much at once. *Cognitive Load Management* helps us avoid mental overload by pacing our learning and gradually building up knowledge.

One simple trick? *Maximize the Signal-to-Noise Ratio*—eliminate distractions and focus only on what's essential. It's like clearing the clutter so our brain can focus on what matters most.

Focused and Diffuse Modes of Thinking

Learning is more effective when we alternate between focused work and relaxed thinking. In *Focused Mode*, our brain zeroes in on specific tasks, like solving math problems. In *Diffuse Mode*, our brain relaxes, making creative connections between ideas.

Here's how it works:

- *Focused Mode:* Best for detail-oriented tasks like studying for an exam or solving problems.
- *Diffuse Mode:* Best for creativity and integrating new information. Activities like walking or doodling can trigger this mode.

Switching between these modes helps solidify learning and can even lead to breakthroughs when we're stuck on a difficult problem.

STUDYING EFFECTIVELY ISN'T JUST about spending hours in front of a textbook. By using foundational techniques and then layering on advanced strategies, we can turn studying into a process that is not only more efficient, but also more enjoyable.

Learning is a skill we can develop. The more we understand how our brain works, the better we'll get at mastering new information. So, take what resonates with us from these techniques, and start experimenting to find what works best for our unique learning style.

CREATING A STUDY PLAN

ACHIEVING OUR LEARNING GOALS WITH A PERSONALIZED STUDY PLAN

"Clarity about what matters provides clarity about what does not."
- Cal Newport (*Deep Work*)

Know the Principles and Pick What Works

Creating a study plan is like going to the gym: the best plan is the one we stick to.

If we plan to study for eight hours straight, it might feel overwhelming, and we might not stick to it. Instead, we should plan for what we can and want to do. Study plans that are written down and suit our strengths and preferences are more likely to succeed.

Here are six steps to craft a study plan that works for us:

1. Assess Learning Preferences

Understanding how we learn best can make all the difference in creating a study routine that we'll actually follow.

Identify Learning Preferences

- Visual
- Auditory
- Kinesthetic
- Reading/Writing

We may find that we learn best through visual aids, while others might prefer listening to lectures or writing things down. The key is to combine multiple modalities. For example, if we prefer visual learning, we can focus on diagrams, charts, and videos that explain the concept. But we can also reinforce that by writing about the visuals or listening to a podcast on the same topic.

Reflect on Past Study Habits

Take a moment to think about what has worked and what hasn't in the past:

- What study methods helped us the most?
- Which ones were ineffective?
- When did we feel motivated to study, and when did we avoid it?

Once we understand these patterns, we can design a plan that aligns with what makes studying easier for us. A great question to ask is, "What would a study session look like if it were easy?"

Understand Duration, Path, Outcome

Our brains naturally process tasks by breaking them down into three parts:

- *Duration:* How long will it take?
- *Path:* What steps are involved?
- *Outcome:* What happens when it's done?

If we can clearly answer these questions for each study session, our brain will encounter less resistance when starting the task.

2. Set Clear, Achievable Goals

Let Go of Perfection

Let's stop aiming for perfection. Perfect potential is something we dream up, but in reality, it often paralyzes us. By focusing on what we can achieve today—no matter how small—we'll make more consistent progress.

Embrace the SMART Goals Framework

A good study plan starts with practical goals. We can use the SMART goals framework to guide us in setting realistic, achievable objectives:

- Specific
- Measurable
- Achievable
- Relevant
- Time-bound

Here's how to break it down:

- **Specific:** We should clearly define what we want to achieve. For instance, instead of saying, "I want to study chemistry," we can say, "I want to review Chapter 3's equations."
- **Measurable:** Goals need to be trackable. How much will we study, and how will we know we've succeeded?
- **Achievable:** Are our goals realistic given the time and resources we have? If we only have two hours, let's not aim to finish an entire chapter.
- **Relevant:** Our goals should align with our broader academic objectives.

- **Time-bound:** Every goal should have a deadline. Instead of "I'll study this week," we can set a time limit, like "I'll finish these problems by 4 p.m."

Balancing Short-Term and Long-Term Goals

Short-term goals give us quick wins that build momentum, while long-term goals provide vision and direction. Balancing them is essential for making steady progress without losing sight of the bigger picture. One way to do this is by linking short-term efforts directly to long-term outcomes, such as studying an hour daily (short-term) to achieve a high grade by semester's end (long-term).

Regularly reviewing and adjusting these goals will help us stay on track.

3. Create the Study Schedule

Time Management

Time management is the backbone of a good study plan. Here's how we can make the most of our time:

- *Plan Study Times During Peak Alertness:* Some of us work best in the morning, others at night. We need to know when we're most alert and schedule our toughest study tasks during those times.
- *Balance Study with Other Commitments:* If we neglect our other obligations, it can weigh on our minds during study sessions. By scheduling time for both work and leisure, we can stay mentally clear.
- *Use Time Pressure to Our Advantage:* Setting a deadline creates urgency. For example, if a test is four weeks away, we can map out how often we need to review material leading up to it.

Breaks and Rest

Breaks aren't just a luxury—they're essential. They help prevent burnout and keep our minds sharp. Scheduling regular breaks helps us remember more, prevents burnout, and gives our brain a chance to recharge.

During the breaks we can move around, stay hydrated, or do something we enjoy. I usually schedule a few short breaks, but if I end up in flow I don't stop myself.

4. Implement Evidence-Based Study Strategies

Effective study strategies are the key to maximizing our learning. We should focus on methods that are backed by research and proven to enhance memory retention, such as:

- *Active recall:* Test ourselves frequently on what we've learned.
- *Spaced repetition:* Review material in intervals to help with long-term retention.

For more ideas, we can explore detailed study strategies in previous chapters.

5. Monitor Progress and Make Adjustments

Self-Assessment and Reflection

Regular self-assessment is crucial. We should set aside time each week to ask:

- What went well?
- What was challenging?
- How can we improve?

These questions help us reflect on our progress and adjust our study plan to keep moving forward.

Quizzes and Tests

Frequent practice tests allow us to see what we've mastered and where we need more work. Testing ourselves keeps us accountable and gives us feedback on how effective our study plan is.

Seeking Feedback

Sometimes, we're too close to our work to see clearly. Getting feedback from friends, classmates, or instructors can provide valuable insights. They may notice gaps or offer advice that hadn't occurred to us. Listening to their input and using it to refine our approach will keep us on the path to improvement.

6. Prepare for Common Challenges

Study plans are never perfect. Procrastination, burnout, and distractions are real hurdles, but we can develop strategies to overcome them.

Combating Procrastination

Procrastination often arises when tasks feel too big or unclear. We can fight this by:

- Breaking tasks into smaller steps.
- Setting a timer (Pomodoro Technique) to focus in short bursts.
- Using temptations as rewards: If we study for an hour, we get to watch our favorite show. (This is what I do)

Preventing Burnout

To prevent burnout, we need to recognize the signs early—like constant fatigue or loss of interest—and take action:

- Take regular breaks.
- Get enough sleep and exercise.
- Practice mindfulness or relaxation techniques.

Reducing Distractions

Creating a distraction-free environment is key to maintaining focus. We can do this by:

- Choosing a quiet, well-lit study spot.
- Turning off notifications.
- Using focus apps or noise-canceling headphones.

THE BEST STUDY plan isn't the one that looks perfect on paper—it's the one we can stick to (and the one that's written down). We'll face challenges, but if we stay flexible, monitor our progress, and adjust as needed, we'll see improvement over time. Like going to the gym, the key is consistency. Step by step, we'll get stronger and closer to our academic goals.

CREATING THE PERFECT STUDY ENVIRONMENT
DESIGNING OUR STUDY SPACE FOR SUCCESS

"Environment is the invisible hand that shapes human behavior. Small changes in our surroundings can lead to big shifts in how we work and study." - James Clear (*Atomic Habits*)

Having a good study environment is crucial for effective learning and productivity. A well-designed study space minimizes distractions, keeps us comfortable, and promotes focus. Proper lighting, comfortable seating, and an organized area can significantly enhance our ability to concentrate and retain information. So how do we create the perfect study environment?

How Screens and Close-Up Viewing Affect Our Focus

Our bodies react differently to things that are close up than to things that are far away. This is especially important to remember with screen time. Staring at screens for long periods can make our eyes work harder and increase stress levels.

When we examine things closely, we may feel more focused, but this also releases higher levels of cortisol, the stress hormone.

To combat this, we can take breaks by looking at things farther away. This helps relax our eyes, reduces stress, and may even prevent or reverse nearsightedness (myopia).

Lighting That Boosts Focus

When we're studying, the right lighting makes all the difference. Here's what we need to know:

- *Bright, white light* reduces eye strain and keeps us alert— perfect for reading and writing.
- *Natural light* from windows is the best for our eyes and mood. If possible, study near natural light sources.
- *Low light in the evening* signals our brain that it's time to wind down, making it easier to fall asleep.

Blue light, the kind emitted by screens, is helpful in the morning when we need a boost of alertness. However, at night, too much blue light can interfere with our sleep. It's best to avoid screens before bed to protect our sleep quality.

Should We Listen to Music While Studying?

Music can be a helpful tool for studying—if we choose the right kind. Dr. E. Glenn Schellenberg's *arousal-and-mood hypothesis* suggests that music may improve our mood and help us focus. Baroque music, like that composed by Bach or Handel, creates a calm, focused atmosphere that helps with concentration.

However, lyrics can distract us because our brains naturally try to decode the meaning of words. Music without lyrics, like classical or ambient music, is ideal for studying, as it allows us to stay focused without splitting our attention.

Minimize Distractions for Maximum Focus

A quiet, organized study space is key to staying focused. Turning off electronic devices or enabling "Do Not Disturb" mode helps minimize distractions. If thoughts or distractions come up, we can keep a small notepad nearby to offload them, clearing our mind for more important tasks.

Many high-performing students prefer smaller rooms with minimal decorations and good lighting. The fewer distractions around us, the easier it is to focus.

Comfortable Seating to Stay Focused Longer

Comfort is essential for long study sessions. Having an ergonomic chair supports good posture and prevents fatigue or discomfort from taking up cognitive load. An ergonomic chair helps us sit straight with our feet flat on the floor, which is great for our back and neck. Additionally, taking regular breaks helps maintain blood flow and prevents stiffness.

Temperature Matters

Temperature can greatly affect our ability to focus. If the room is too hot or too cold, it becomes distracting. A cooler room generally helps us stay awake and alert, while a warmer room can make us feel relaxed or even sleepy. We can adjust by dressing for the room's temperature to stay comfortable throughout our study session.

Organized Spaces Minimize Stress

A tidy, organized study space reduces mental clutter and stress. When everything has its place, we don't have to waste time looking for materials, which means we can focus fully on studying. Spending just a few minutes tidying up at the end of each session allows us to return to a clean, organized space next time.

Fresh Air and Plants: Breathing Life into Our Study Space

Good air circulation is essential for maintaining a fresh, energizing study environment. Opening a window or using a fan can help keep the air fresh, and adding plants to the room not only improves air quality but also creates a calming atmosphere.

Plants naturally purify the air and increase oxygen levels, which helps us stay focused and relaxed. Having a few plants in visible places can enhance our mood and help us concentrate.

How Colors Influence Mood

The colors in our study space can significantly impact our mood and focus. Blues and greens are especially helpful for creating a peaceful, focused environment. Blue helps us stay calm and clear-headed, while green can boost our mood and reduce stress.

We can combine these calming colors with neutral tones, such as white or gray, to maintain a balanced, distraction-free atmosphere.

Personalize Our Space, But Stay Focused

Personalizing our study space can help keep us motivated. Items like vision boards, motivational quotes, or reminders of our goals can inspire us while we work. However, we should be careful not to overdo it—too much personalization can become a distraction. Regularly updating decorations keeps the space fresh and exciting.

Creating a Guiding Environment: Reducing the Need for Willpower

Our environment plays a huge role in our productivity. When things get tough, it's easy to lose motivation. One of the most effective ways to stay consistent is by creating a guiding environment. A guiding environment supports our goals and reduces the need to rely on willpower. Designing our study space to minimize distractions and encourage productivity makes it easier to stick to our study habits.

Establishing a routine also helps. When our bodies know what to expect, they go on autopilot, reducing the effort it takes to get started.

CREATING the ideal study environment takes a bit of thought and planning, but it pays off by making studying more enjoyable and effective. Everyone's ideal setup will be different, but the key is to design a space that minimizes distractions, supports our focus, and guides us toward success with minimal resistance.

THE BEST & WORST FOODS FOR STUDYING
UNDERSTANDING WHAT FUELS OUR BRAIN

Foods That Help with Studying

"What's good for your heart is also good for your brain. The foods you eat influence your risk of cognitive decline and can boost brain health at any age." - Sanjay Gupta (*Keep Sharp*)

What we eat during study sessions has a direct impact on how well we focus, retain information, and stay energized. By choosing brain-boosting foods, we can set ourselves up for a productive and focused study session. Here are some great options to keep in mind:

- *Blueberries:* These little powerhouses are rich in vitamins and antioxidants that can improve memory and concentration. They're a perfect snack to help us stay sharp for long hours.
- *Nuts:* Almonds, walnuts, and peanuts are packed with healthy fats and protein that provide sustained energy. They also contain vitamin E, which protects our brain from oxidative stress and helps us think clearly.

- *Dark Chocolate:* A small amount of dark chocolate can elevate our mood and boost alertness. It contains both caffeine and antioxidants, which help improve blood flow to the brain and keep us mentally engaged.
- *Whole Grains:* Oatmeal, whole-grain bread, and brown rice release energy slowly, keeping us full and focused over time. This steady energy helps us avoid the distractions of hunger during study sessions.
- *Leafy Greens:* Spinach, kale, and broccoli are rich in vitamins like K, which supports brain health and cognitive function. These greens help our brains stay sharp and healthy.
- *Fish:* Fish like salmon, trout, and sardines are rich in omega-3 fatty acids, which are excellent for improving brain function. Omega-3s support clear thinking and better concentration, making fish a great study food.

Foods That Hurt Studying

While some foods fuel our brains, others can hinder our ability to concentrate and stay focused. It's important to be mindful of what we eat to avoid feeling sluggish or distracted. Here are some foods to watch out for:

- *Sugary Snacks:* Though candy, cookies, and soda give us a quick energy boost, they often lead to an energy crash. That crash can leave us feeling tired and distracted, making it harder to focus on our work.
- *Fast Food:* Burgers, fries, and pizza might taste good in the moment, but they tend to make us feel sluggish and unfocused afterward.
- *Energy Drinks:* While energy drinks are loaded with caffeine and sugar, they can make us jittery and anxious. Over time, they might disrupt our concentration instead of helping it.

- *Highly Processed Foods:* Chips, packaged snacks, and instant noodles often contain unhealthy fats and preservatives that slow us down mentally, making it harder to stay focused on our studies.

Making Studying Fun with Food

The best study snacks not only fuel our brains but also help us enjoy the process of studying. Eating foods that take time to snack on can help us pace ourselves, keeping us at our desks longer and improving our concentration. Here are some ideas to make studying more enjoyable with food:

- Choose snacks that make us happy. When we feel good about what we're eating, studying becomes a more positive experience.
- Try foods that take time to eat, like apple slices with peanut butter, a small bowl of nuts, or a few pieces of dark chocolate. These snacks are not only delicious but also keep us energized and focused for longer periods.

It's okay to enjoy occasional treats from the "Foods That Hurt Studying" list if they make our study session more enjoyable. The key is balance—by mixing healthy options with occasional indulgences, we can stay productive and still enjoy the experience.

WHAT WE EAT while studying can have a major impact on how well we learn, retain information, and stay focused. By choosing brain-boosting foods like blueberries, nuts, dark chocolate, whole grains, leafy greens, and fish, we can improve our mental performance and make studying more enjoyable. While it's okay to indulge in sugary snacks or fast food occasionally, keeping those choices balanced with healthier options will help us avoid feeling sluggish or unfocused.

When we incorporate these foods into our study routine, we can turn studying into a more positive and productive experience, ensuring that we stay energized and ready to take on any challenge.

STAYING FOCUSED
STRATEGIES FOR MAINTAINING ATTENTION

"Concentration is at the heart of all human success and endeavor."
- Dandapani

Learning to Concentrate

Concentration is a skill we can learn and improve with practice; yet, many of us have unknowingly become experts at distraction. Our minds often jump from one thought to another—exacerbated by technology—making it challenging to focus on a single task for long. Imagine how different things might be if we practiced concentration for just a few minutes each day, deliberately training our focus instead of reinforcing distraction.

Dandapani, a Hindu priest and former monk, describes concentration as keeping our awareness on one thing for an extended period. He compares it to holding a glowing ball of light in our minds, keeping that light focused on a single point. When our attention starts to wander, we can use willpower to bring the light back to where we want it. Concentration isn't about rigid control—it's about consistently guiding our awareness back when it drifts.

By doing this, we can actually change the structure of our brains. Research from the Max Planck Institute shows that practicing focus can increase the gray matter in our anterior cingulate cortex (ACC)—the part of our brain responsible for focus and emotional regulation. In contrast, multitasking, something many of us do regularly, has been shown to shrink this same region. So, by training ourselves to concentrate, we're not only improving our mental clarity but also physically reshaping our brains in a positive way.

The Impact of Visual Stimuli on Focus

Our mental focus is deeply connected to where we direct our visual attention. Simply put, what we see impacts what we think about, and the sharper our visual focus, the better our mental concentration.

This connection stems from the way our brain processes sensory input. The brain's visual cortex, which is responsible for understanding what we see, is closely tied to areas that manage attention and cognitive control. When we visually focus on one specific thing, such as reading a book or looking at a screen, our mental resources are directed toward understanding and processing that information. Conversely, when our eyes dart from one thing to another—glancing at a phone, scanning a room, or jumping between tabs on a computer—our mind follows, fragmenting our attention and making it harder to concentrate.

A study from Princeton University supports this link. Researchers found that the more visual stimuli we're exposed to at once, the more our brain has to fight to decide what to focus on. This battle for attention dilutes our mental focus, making it harder to process information deeply. Essentially, the more we try to see and take in simultaneously, the more overwhelmed and distracted we become.

This is why cluttered environments or spaces with excessive visual noise can hinder our concentration. When our surroundings pull our eyes in multiple directions, our mental focus suffers, constantly shifting between different stimuli. On the other hand, reducing distractions in our visual field—such as working in a clean, organized space or turning off unnecessary screens—helps our brain concentrate on the task at hand.

In essence, when we direct our visual focus toward one thing, we give our brain permission to allocate all its mental energy there too. This is why focusing our eyes on a single task—whether it's reading, writing, or even practicing mindfulness—can help us sharpen our mental focus and deepen our engagement.

When we are intentional with where we look, we become more intentional with how we think, improving our ability to concentrate and boosting productivity.

Calming a Busy Mind

In today's fast-paced world, we rarely give ourselves time to pause and think. Author and consultant, Juliet Funt, calls this "white-space," the moments between busyness when we can reflect and strategize. We can use this whitespace to calm our minds and regain clarity. It's like giving our brains the oxygen they need to function creatively and efficiently.

Research from University College London shows that people who multitask frequently tend to have less gray matter in their ACC, which impairs their ability to focus and manage emotions. However, studies also suggest that when we practice focusing, we can increase the gray matter in this region, improving our ability to concentrate.

Interruptions are another major obstacle to focus. Research from the University of California, Irvine, shows that while 82% of interrupted work gets completed the same day, it takes an average of 23 minutes and 15 seconds to fully refocus after an interruption.

This delay adds up, making it crucial to manage our interruptions wisely.

Three Ways to Calm Our Minds

- *Breathe:* Dr. Andrew Weil's 4-7-8 Method helps activate the body's relaxation response.
  ○ Exhale completely through our mouth, making a whoosh sound.
  ○ Close our mouth and inhale quietly through our nose for four counts.
  ○ Hold our breath for seven counts.
  ○ Exhale completely through our mouth for eight counts.
  ○ Repeat this cycle three more times for a total of four breaths.
- *Handle Stressful Tasks First:* Tackling the most stressful tasks early can free up mental space. These tasks often weigh on our minds, so addressing them first can help us feel more in control.
- *Schedule Distracted Time:* Knowing that we have designated time for distractions can make it easier to focus in the present. Planning breaks for non-essential activities allows us to concentrate more effectively during work time.

Tips for Staying Focused While Studying

- *Set Clear Goals:* Knowing exactly what we want to achieve in each study session can help us stay on track.
- *Take Regular Breaks if Struggling:* Techniques like the Pomodoro Technique (25 minutes of studying followed by a 5-minute break) can help keep us fresh. However, if

we're in a flow state, it's best to ride that wave for as long as possible.

- *Eliminate Distractions:* Turning off notifications and finding a quiet space can dramatically improve our ability to focus.
- *Stay Organized:* Keeping our study space tidy and preparing all materials before starting can reduce friction and help us maintain momentum.
- *Use Active Learning Techniques:* Engaging with the material by summarizing, questioning, or teaching it to others deepens our understanding and keeps us actively involved.
- *Stay Hydrated and Eat Healthy Snacks:* Drinking water and eating brain-boosting snacks like nuts and fruit can help fuel our concentration.
- *Set a Timer:* Tracking our study sessions with a timer can help us be mindful of how long we're genuinely focused versus how long we're sitting at the desk. This awareness helps us become more intentional with our time.
- *Practice Mindfulness:* Short mindfulness exercises before studying can help calm pre-task anxiety. By examining our internal state for a few minutes, we can work through feelings of resistance, making it easier to start. While mindfulness doesn't eliminate these feelings, it helps us acknowledge and manage them.
- *Review and Recap:* Regularly reviewing what we've learned helps reinforce the material and gives us a sense of accomplishment, especially when we've set clear study goals.
- *Get Enough Sleep:* Fatigue has a significant impact on concentration. Quality sleep, particularly REM sleep, is crucial for feeling rejuvenated and ready to tackle the next day.
- *Stay Positive and Reward Ourselves:* Celebrating small achievements can keep us motivated. Small wins build

up over time, and acknowledging them sends a signal to our brain that we're on the right track.

Concentration is a skill we can practice and improve, yet many of us have trained ourselves to be distracted instead. By understanding the importance of focus and implementing small, actionable strategies—like setting clear goals, practicing mindfulness, and using the Pomodoro technique—we can reclaim our attention and direct it toward the things that matter most. Whether we're studying, working, or simply trying to manage daily life, the ability to concentrate will empower us to achieve our goals more effectively and improve our overall well-being.

DEALING WITH BURNOUT
WITHOUT COMPROMISING PRODUCTIVITY

Finding Joy in Work and Rest

Burnout is a state we reach when we push ourselves too hard for too long, especially on tasks that feel draining rather than fulfilling. Burnout rarely occurs all at once; it is something that slowly creeps in over time. Burnout also occurs when we lose agency, or at least perceived agency. When we feel like we aren't in control of our actions, burnout tends to creep in faster.

But what if the key to avoiding burnout isn't just working less, but *working differently*? When we love what we do, work can feel more like play, fueling us rather than depleting us. In fact, working on things that feel like play to us (but might feel like work to others) could be one of the best ways to prevent burnout.

However, even when we find joy in our work, rest is essential. To thrive, we need time to recharge, reflect, and adjust when things aren't working. Here's how we can manage burnout and still get things done.

Reward Ourselves After a Day of Work

One of the simplest ways to maintain our energy is to give ourselves something to look forward to after a hard day's work. Just as we might reward a dog for good behavior, rewarding ourselves at the end of the day boosts our motivation to dive in again tomorrow.

These rewards don't have to be extravagant. Maybe it's 20 minutes watching our favorite show, taking a walk in the park, or enjoying a quiet moment with a cup of tea. Small, intentional rewards not only make us feel good but also reinforce positive habits—making it more likely that we'll tackle the next day with renewed energy.

Methods to Handle Burnout

Burnout is more than just physical exhaustion; it's about feeling disconnected from joy and purpose. We can tackle it from several angles—physical, mental, and social—to restore balance and stay engaged.

Physical Strategies

- *Mindfulness and Meditation:* Taking time to sit quietly and focus on our breathing can help reset our minds. Just like rebooting a computer when it's sluggish, a short pause can clear mental clutter and leave us feeling refreshed. Research shows that mindfulness can reduce stress and improve emotional well-being.
- *Physical Activity:* Moving our bodies, whether through a brisk walk, a run, or a favorite sport, can give us more energy and improve sleep. Exercise not only strengthens muscles but also enhances our ability to cope with life's challenges.
- *Sleep Hygiene:* Sticking to a consistent sleep schedule can work wonders. Going to bed and waking up at the same time every day helps our bodies and minds recover.

Creating a peaceful bedtime routine ensures we wake up ready to tackle the day.

- *Healthy Diet:* What we eat affects how we feel. A balanced diet of fruits, vegetables, lean proteins, and whole grains fuels both our physical and mental performance. When we nourish our bodies, we set ourselves up to perform at our best.

Mental Strategies

- *Relaxation Techniques:* Incorporating deep breathing, stretching, or yoga into our routine can ease physical tension and quiet mental stress. These simple practices help us feel more grounded and resilient.
- *Job Crafting:* If possible, we can adjust our work duties to better align with what we enjoy and excel at. Reshaping our roles to align with our strengths can transform draining tasks into energizing ones.
- *Engaging in Hobbies:* Hobbies provide a true mental break because they engage our minds in different, enjoyable ways. Whether it's painting, gardening, or playing an instrument, hobbies can recharge us in ways that work cannot.
- *Time Management:* Planning our days, setting small goals, and scheduling regular breaks can help prevent feelings of overwhelm. Effective time management allows us to navigate our to-do lists without burning out.
- *Seek New Perspectives:* Sometimes, it's not the workload itself but our perspective on it that drains us. By challenging limiting beliefs and reframing challenges as opportunities, we can shift from feeling powerless to feeling empowered. Often, burnout is more about our mindset than the actual demands placed on us. Additionally, we can ask ourselves, "How can I give myself more choice in the matter?"

Social Strategies

- *Social Support:* We are social creatures, and when we feel isolated, burnout can creep in. Spending time with loved ones or connecting with people who share our interests can remind us that we're not alone in our struggles. Talking to friends or family about our challenges can lighten the emotional load.
- *Professional Help:* Sometimes, we need outside support to cope with stress. Speaking with a therapist or counselor can offer new strategies for managing burnout and help us find fresh perspectives.
- *Setting Boundaries:* One of the most important tools for preventing burnout is learning to say "no" when necessary. By setting boundaries and not overcommitting ourselves, we protect our energy and make space for what truly matters.
- *Reducing Work Hours:* If we're feeling overwhelmed, it might be time to scale back. Taking a few days or even a week off to recharge can restore our motivation and energy. This isn't a permanent solution, but a strategic pause can prevent longer-term exhaustion.
- *Regular Breaks:* It's easy to push ourselves to work non-stop, but taking short breaks throughout the day is essential. Even stepping away for a few minutes can help us refocus and recharge, preventing burnout from creeping in.

BURNOUT IS a common experience in a world that often prizes constant productivity. But we're not machines—we need rhythms of rest and work to function at our best.

Think of how lions operate. They hunt intensely for short bursts, then rest deeply to recover. We, on the other hand, often try to sustain high levels of work for long stretches without a break, expecting continuous productivity. But our most creative and productive moments come when we balance periods of deep work with meaningful rest.

Preventing burnout isn't just about avoiding exhaustion. It's about building a life that balances work with joy, intensity with rest, duty with choice, and productivity with play. By taking care of our minds, bodies, and relationships, we can not only prevent burnout but also thrive, finding purpose and fulfillment in both our work and our lives.

SOLO STUDYING VS. GROUP STUDYING
OUR LEARNING TRIBE

"Surround yourself with good people who complement the areas where you are weak." - Jocko Willink (*Extreme Ownership*)

We've got an exam on the horizon. We've learned all the theories and techniques, built our perfect study environments, figured out how to manage our time, and even tackled test anxiety. Then just as we think we're set, a classmate asks, "Do you want to join our study group?"

Before we answer, we need to understand some key differences between solo studying and group studying to decide what works best for us.

Solo Studying

Benefits of Solo Studying

- *Fewer Distractions:* When we study alone, distractions are minimized. This helps us focus deeply and get more done.

- *Control Over Study Environment:* We can study whenever and wherever it suits us. Midnight at McDonald's? Sure, why not?
- *Flexibility:* We can take breaks whenever we want and spend as much time as we need on challenging topics without feeling rushed.
- *Focus on Weak Areas:* Solo studying allows us to target the topics we find difficult, rather than waiting for others to catch up.

Drawbacks of Solo Studying

- *Less Motivation:* It can be hard to stick to a study schedule when there's no one around to keep us accountable.
- *Risk of Inaccuracy:* Without others to check our work, we might not realize when we've misunderstood something. Without external feedback, there's a chance we could be reinforcing incorrect information.

When to Study Solo

"To believe your own thought, to believe that what is true for you in your private heart is true for all men,—that is genius." - Ralph Waldo Emerson (*Self-Reliance*)

We should consider solo study sessions if:

- The group is too chatty or tends to get off-topic.
- The group keeps rescheduling, and we're struggling to find consistency.
- The group's level of understanding is very different from ours. If they're way ahead or way behind, it might be better for us to go it alone.

Studying solo can be a powerful exercise in self-reliance. As

Emerson suggests, it helps us trust our instincts and build confidence in our own thinking.

Group Studying

Benefits of Group Studying

- *Discussion Enhances Learning:* Engaging in discussions with others helps us grasp and retain information better.
- *Immediate Feedback:* In a group, if we don't understand something, chances are someone else does and can explain it.
- *Increased Motivation:* Being around focused, driven people can push us to stay on track—assuming they're just as dedicated as we are.
- *Reduced Anxiety:* Studying with others can calm our nerves and remind us that we're all in this together.
- *Teaching as Learning:* Explaining concepts to others is one of the best ways to reinforce our own understanding.

Drawbacks of Group Studying

- *Potential for Distractions:* It only takes one unfocused person to derail the group.
- *Less Flexibility:* We're limited by the availability of others. Syncing schedules can be tough, especially when everyone has outside commitments.
- *Slower Progress:* Group study can move at a slower pace as time may be spent catching others up or reviewing basics.

When to Study in Groups

"In the crowd one feels no responsibility, but also no fear." - Carl Jung (*Archetypes and The Collective Unconscious*)

Group studying works best when:

- Our classmates are high-performers and highly motivated.
- We have a solid understanding of the material and are looking to review or refine our knowledge.

Jung's insight highlights a potential pitfall of group studying: we can sometimes lose individual responsibility in the comfort of the group. That's why it's important to make sure our study group is focused and on track.

What to Look for in a Study Partner or Group

- *Similar Goals:* It's important that everyone wants the same kind of study session—productive, focused, and efficient.
- *Same Test Date:* Studying with people who are preparing for the same exam ensures that everyone is on the same timeline.
- *Complementary Strengths and Weaknesses:* It helps to study with someone who excels in areas where we struggle, and vice versa.
- *Similar Study Habits:* If we're structured, it's best to pair up with someone who is too. Misaligned habits can lead to frustration.
- *Resource Sharing:* Finding study partners with access to resources we might not have can improve the quality of our prep.
- *Accountability:* The right partner will help keep us motivated and on track.

- *Comfort Level:* We need to feel comfortable asking questions and making mistakes within the group.

My Personal Experience with Study Groups

Group studying saved me in organic chemistry but sank me in physical chemistry. In organic chemistry, I partnered with someone who knew far more than I did and had better study resources. Their knowledge and guidance accelerated my learning, and I performed much better as a result. I wouldn't have passed the class without him.

On the flip side, in physical chemistry, I found myself in a group where we all believed we were nailing the material. But we fell into the trap of confirmation bias, reinforcing each other's misunderstandings. We were convinced we were prepared, but we all ended up failing the exam. That experience has taught me a hard lesson about the importance of choosing the right study group.

Bottom Line

Both solo and group studying offer benefits, but the choice depends on what we need to accomplish. If we have a lot of ground to cover or need to dive deep into challenging material, solo studying or working with just one person might be best. On the other hand, if we're reviewing content or need a little extra motivation, group study can be a great option.

In the end, the best study method is the one that works for us. Whether it's late-night solo flashcard sessions or energizing group discussions, the goal is always the same: to keep those neurons firing and prepare ourselves as best we can.

CONQUERING TEST & PERFORMANCE ANXIETY
FACING FEAR & BUILDING CONFIDENCE

"I'm just not a good test taker."

How many times have we said this or heard others say it? The room is silent, the air thick with tension. Our hearts race as we stare at the test paper, the words blurring. It's easy to feel like we're powerless in these moments, but here's the truth: it's not that we're "just not good test takers." It's that anxiety is tricking our brains. And once we understand it, we can conquer it.

Why Anxiety?

Test and performance anxiety can be terrifying, but we can beat it. First, let's understand why we get anxious in the first place.

Our brains are always on the lookout for danger. When they perceive a threat, they immediately try to solve it. This constant effort to prepare for every possible worst-case scenario can easily turn into anxiety.

Anxiety stems from our minds trying to prepare us for everything—whether it's a panther attack, an economic crash, embarrassing ourselves in front of a class, or all of them at once. Our brains work overtime to solve problems that may never even happen. We feel anxious because we're trying to solve every possible problem at once, and that's impossible.

When we can't find a solution, our brains go into overdrive, triggering the body's stress responses. Our bloodstream releases with cortisol and adrenaline, which are helpful in the short term but harmful if they become chronic. This is why anxiety, especially when prolonged, can be so draining on both our minds and bodies.

But these stress responses aren't entirely bad—they're great for spotting potential threats. In education, we can use our anxiety as a signal to check if we're prepared. The difference between unnecessary anxiety and useful anxiety lies in our habits.

How much have we prepared for the challenge in front of us?

Coping with Anxiety

"Anxiety is the dizziness of freedom." - Søren Kierkegaard *(The Concept of Anxiety)*

A lot of our test anxiety comes from not knowing what to prepare for. One of the first steps in beating anxiety is understanding why it arises and then taking steps to address the problems head-on.

When anxiety strikes, many of us freeze. It can feel impossible to move when the weight of our anxiety sets in. Freezing is part of our stress response. If we want to overcome this, we need to define what exactly we're anxious about.

Our minds are problem-solvers, and when the problem isn't clear, anxiety takes over. Conquering anxiety means defining it. One useful approach is Tim Ferriss's *Fear Setting Exercise*. By identifying the worst-case scenario and working to either improve it or limit its downside, we take control of our anxiety.

"We suffer more in imagination than in reality." - Seneca *(Letters from a Stoic,* Letter XII)

Once we know what needs to get done, the anxiety melts away. Clarity turns vague fears into manageable tasks. For this reason, *checklists* are one of the most powerful tools we can use. They break down big, intimidating goals into small, actionable steps. Dr. Atul Gawande's *The Checklist Manifesto* beautifully illustrates how simple lists can help us get things done right.

Breaking down our tasks into small, simple steps helps reduce anxiety.

Another way to cope with anxiety is to shorten our timeframes. When stress is high, it helps to focus on smaller and smaller chunks of time. Instead of worrying about what's happening next year, month, week, or day, focus on just the next few moments.

When stress feels overwhelming, focusing on just the next three seconds can help. Breaking things down this way gives us a sense of control, even during the most stressful times.

"By knowing yourself, your anxiety will push you forward instead of stopping you." - Jordan Peterson

We can also cope with anxiety through self-knowledge. When we know ourselves—our strengths, our weaknesses, our triggers— we can use anxiety as a motivator rather than letting it hold us back. Anxiety often comes from uncertainty, but self-awareness helps reduce that uncertainty. By understanding what makes us anxious and why, we can prepare better and respond with confidence rather than fear.

For example, if we know that tests make us anxious because we fear failure, we can focus on developing strong study habits and practice tests to feel more in control. This way, anxiety becomes a signal to prepare more thoroughly, not a barrier to success.

Self-awareness transforms anxiety into a stepping stone, helping us channel it as a motivating force. The more we know ourselves, the more we can channel anxiety as a force that propels us forward.

Yerkes-Dodson Law

The Yerkes-Dodson Law describes the relationship between stress and performance. It shows that while too much stress can hurt our performance, we actually need some stress to do our best. Too little stress, and we may not be motivated enough to perform well. The key is finding the right balance.

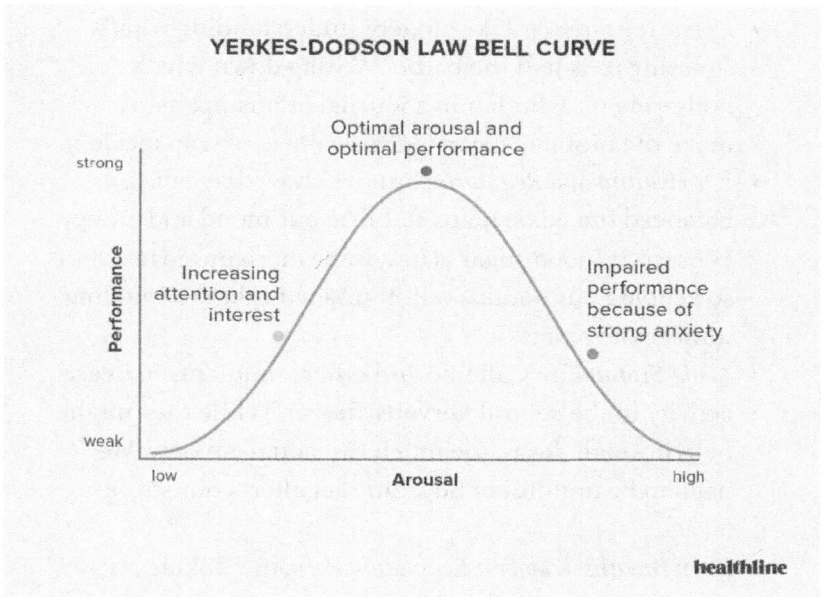

Graph from healthline.com

Understanding this curve helps us realize that not all stress is bad. In fact, we can use stress to our advantage, but only if we manage it well.

Stress Management

"Stress is a result of a lack of structure." — Touré Roberts

To manage stress, we need to keep the good stress (eustress) while letting go of bad stress (distress). Here are some practical methods for managing stress effectively:

- *Entering Sleep-like Brain States:* Activities like meditation, running, deep breathing, or even showering can get our minds into a relaxed, sleep-like state, which helps to calm the nervous system.
- *Define the Stressor:* Like anxiety, understanding what's stressing us is half the battle. Writing down what's bothering us, whether in a journal or an app, helps make the problem clear. Once we see it, we can tackle it.
- *Eat Healthy and Regularly:* Studies show that eating a balanced breakfast helps stabilize our mood and energy. When our blood sugar is low, we're more prone to stress, so keeping our bodies well-nourished is key to avoiding unnecessary stress.
- *Avoid Stimulants:* Caffeine and other stimulants increase activity in the central nervous system. While they might help in small doses, too much can add to anxiety. We need to be mindful of how our diet affects our stress levels.
- *Deep Breaths Trigger a Relaxation Response:* Taking six deep breaths, with longer exhales than inhales, signals our bodies to relax, activating the parasympathetic nervous system.

We need some stress to perform at our best—it's about finding the right balance.

Confidence and Anxiety

Confidence plays a crucial role in overcoming anxiety. If we don't believe we can succeed, our anxiety will increase. Confidence gives us a fighting chance. But how do we build confidence?

The tricky part about confidence is that we need to *prove* to ourselves that we can do something before we start feeling confident. Instead of trying to talk ourselves into it, we need to take action and get small wins.

Learning something new—anything—is a great way to build confidence. Whether it's a hobby, a new skill, or a challenging subject, watching ourselves grow helps us believe in our abilities. Confidence comes from evidence that we are capable.

By focusing on small wins and building solid habits, we develop genuine confidence over time.

Last Thoughts on Anxiety

"I am an old man and have known a great many troubles, but most of them never happened." — Mark Twain

"There is nothing so wretched or foolish as to anticipate misfortunes. What madness it is in expecting evil before it arrives!" — Seneca (*Letters from a Stoic*, Letter XIII)

These two men, from different centuries, remind us that most of our worries are imagined. We suffer more in our minds than we do in reality. So, instead of letting anxiety take over, we need to focus on the present and remind ourselves that not all of our thoughts are true or useful.

Currently, in my workspace, I have a quote posted that says "You believe things that are not true." I keep it up as a reminder that not all of my thoughts are to be taken seriously, or taken as truth.

Stoic philosophy offers great insights into managing anxiety. Books like *Letters from a Stoic* or *On the Shortness of Life* by Seneca provide timeless wisdom for navigating stressful situations. I frequently look to the stoics when I feel anxiety taking hold over my decisions.

Life is full of challenges, but learning how to perform under pressure is a skill we can develop. Whether in school, work, or any other area of life, anxiety doesn't have to hold us back. With deliberate practice and the right strategies, we can conquer anxiety and perform at our best.

Everyone can become a great test-taker—it just takes preparation, clear goals, and learning to manage our stress effectively.

SUBJECT SPECIFIC STRATEGIES
TECHNIQUES FOR EACH CLASS

uccess looks different in every subject, and while we may excel in one area, other subjects often require different techniques to thrive. As we navigate through various disciplines—math, science, writing, history, and more—it's essential to understand the strategies that work best for each one. This chapter draws from my own experiences and insights from expert educators to give us a starting point for success in every class.

At the core, no matter the subject, success with learning comes from the same principles: staying organized, practicing regularly, and engaging deeply with the material. The specific strategies might differ, but the mindset remains the same.

Writing & Classes that Require Writing

Writing is Rewriting

Always start with an outline. Even if we think we can jump straight into writing, an outline helps organize our thoughts and makes the process smoother.

Know what the teacher is looking for. We need to be clear about the grading criteria and expectations. This helps us focus on the right elements and prioritize what's important.

Even experienced writers use outlines! Writing is a process of revision, and our first draft is just the beginning. As we rewrite our ideas, they become clearer and more refined with each revision. This book went through 7 full revisions before I published it for the first time. With each revision, my messages become clearer and easier to understand.

Research with a Goal

Research with purpose. Before we dive into sources, we need to know what we're looking for. This saves time and ensures that our research stays focused.

Make connections between what we're studying and how it fits into the real world. For example, if we're researching climate change, let's think about how it impacts our daily lives. This makes the material more relevant and easier to remember.

Math Classes

We need regular practice. Math is a subject that rewards consistency. Regular practice helps us reinforce our skills and discover patterns in problem-solving. Using techniques like active recall and spaced repetition can help solidify our understanding of concepts over time.

It's crucial to focus on understanding the "why" behind formulas and procedures. Simply memorizing processes or formulas will make it easier to mix up concepts and create anxiety. When we grasp the reasoning, it becomes much easier to apply it to new problems.

Diagrams, graphs, and other visual tools make complex math concepts easier to understand. As visual creatures, we remember concepts better when they are presented visually.

Common Mistakes

Memorizing formulas without understanding them can lead to errors in application.

Skipping steps in problem-solving makes it harder to spot mistakes.

Better Strategies

Don't hesitate to ask for help. Teachers, classmates, or tutors can clarify tricky concepts, and it's always beneficial to seek out support from someone who has recently learned the material.

Work through examples step-by-step, even if they seem simple. Writing down every step helps us see the process clearly. When we are learning, it's better to write down every single step, no matter how trivial.

Science Classes

Like math, science requires consistent practice. Whether we're solving problems or conducting experiments, regular practice builds familiarity with the material.

Hands-on experiments allow us to apply theoretical knowledge in a tangible way. These experiences make the material come alive and deepen our understanding.

Relating scientific concepts to real-life situations helps us see their applications. For example, understanding chemical reactions becomes more meaningful when we consider how they impact the food we cook or the environment around us.

Mnemonics can be lifesavers for remembering complex information. For instance, to recall the order of planets in the solar system, we might use a funny sentence like "My Very Educated Mother Just Served Us Nachos." The sillier, the better!

Common Mistakes

Overlooking small details can lead to misunderstandings in experiments or theories. Science is all about precision.

Cramming the night before won't help us retain information in the long run.

Better Strategies

Similar to math, rather than memorize things — seek understanding of fundamental principles. When we understand the principles, we can solve most science problems and derive most scientific concepts.

Review notes and questions regularly, and try to engage with the material consistently over time rather than all at once.

Study groups can help us clarify difficult concepts, but we should make sure they're actually productive for our learning.

History Classes

Visual timelines help us track important events and understand their order. Creating them ourselves reinforces our knowledge much better than simply printing one out.

Understanding the causes and effects of historical events helps us see the bigger picture and how history shapes our present.

Engaging with primary sources gives us insight into the context and mindset of the time, offering a richer understanding of historical events.

Common Mistakes

Focusing only on memorizing dates without grasping the significance of the events.

Ignoring different perspectives or failing to consider the broader context of events.

Better Strategies

Relating historical events to current issues helps make them more relevant and easier to remember.

Discuss historical events with others to explore multiple perspectives.

World Language Classes

Regularly practicing speaking improves our pronunciation and fluency. It can feel awkward at first, but the more we speak, the more natural it becomes.

Listening to music, watching movies, and reading in the language helps us get used to its rhythms and expands our vocabulary.

Flashcards are great for memorizing vocabulary and phrases. By focusing on the most commonly used words, we can speed up our progress.

Common Mistakes

Being afraid to make mistakes. We'll learn faster by trying, even if we stumble along the way.

Relying too much on textbooks without engaging with native speakers or real-life materials.

Better Strategies

Aim to make mistakes. The most mistakes we make, the better we get. Practicing this with native speakers is a great way to develop conversational skills. They can inform us when we make a mistake and we can practice in real time.

Use language learning apps for extra practice and exposure to the language in daily life.

Art Classes

Trying different tools, materials, and techniques can inspire creativity. Visiting galleries or studying famous works gives us new ideas and fresh perspectives.

Common Mistakes

Not practicing regularly can hinder our growth as artists.

Ignoring feedback from instructors may cause us to miss opportunities for improvement.

Better Strategies

Keep a sketchbook to document ideas and practice new techniques.

Actively seek constructive criticism to grow as an artist. Constructive criticism is not a statement of our value as people but of the decisions and work we produce. Constructive criticism helps us improve; without it, we stagnate.

Physical Education

Just like in other subjects, regular practice is key to improving our fitness and physical skills.

Common Mistakes

Failing to warm up properly can lead to injury.

Neglecting hydration and nutrition makes it harder to stay energized and healthy.

Better Strategies

Set personal fitness goals to track our progress and stay motivated.

Joining sports teams or clubs can keep us active and engaged with others.

Music Classes

Like all other classes, regular practice is essential to improving our skills. Whether it's learning an instrument or developing our voice, consistent effort helps us progress.

Common Mistakes

Not practicing scales and other basics can slow our development.

Ignoring music theory limits our understanding of the music we play.

Better Strategies

Take private lessons if possible to get personalized guidance.

Participate in ensembles or bands to gain experience performing with others.

Online Classes

Online classes have their own unique challenges, but with the right strategies, we can succeed in this environment.

Common Mistakes

Assuming the class will be easy because it's online.

Ignoring the course's technical requirements.

Procrastinating on assignments or losing motivation.

Better Strategies

Set up a dedicated study space and create a schedule to stay organized.

Use technology to stay connected with classmates and teachers. Participating in discussions and asking for help when needed will keep us on track.

Stay motivated by focusing on our long-term goals and reminding ourselves of why we're pursuing our studies.

IN THE END, success across all subjects—whether it's math, science, writing, or art—comes down to a few universal principles: staying organized, practicing regularly, and seeking help when we need it. By sticking to these principles, we can overcome any challenge that any class throws at us. It's not about mastering every subject effortlessly, but about adopting the right strategies and consistently putting in the effort to improve.

BECOMING AN EXPERT AT STANDARDIZED TESTS
TACKLING BIG EXAMS

S tandardized tests are unique. They don't just assess what we know but also how well we can take the test itself. For example, studying for the SAT isn't just about mastering high school subjects; it's about understanding the SAT format, pacing, and question style. The same is true for AP/IB Tests, GMAT, MCAT, NCLEX, NREMT, USMLE, TOEFL, CSET, LSAT, and many others.

We're not just studying for tests—we're training for them. Here's a guide to mastering standardized tests that goes beyond just memorizing facts:

Step 1: Know the Test

Learn the Format

Before diving into the content, we need to understand the structure of the test. This includes knowing the types of questions, the number of sections, and how much time we have for each part. For example: Are there multiple-choice questions, essays, or practical components?

Understand the Scoring

Each test has its own scoring system. Some tests penalize wrong answers, while others don't. Knowing how our test is scored can help us decide whether to skip questions or take educated guesses.

Step 2: Study Strategies

Focus on Content

Once we understand the format, we need to identify the subjects we'll be tested on. Using high-quality study materials is key. The best study resources often come from the people who create the test. They understand the topics, the question style, and the level of difficulty.

For instance, if we're preparing for the MCAT, the materials from the Association of American Medical Colleges (AAMC) will be the most aligned with the actual test.

Practice, Practice, Practice

Full-length practice tests are invaluable. They give us a sense of the actual test day experience—everything from timing to pacing ourselves through each section. But we don't need to do a full-length test every time. Start with one to gauge where we stand, then periodically take full tests to assess our growth.

After each practice test, it's essential to analyze our results. Are there patterns in the mistakes? Is there a particular type of question we struggle with? This analysis helps us refine our study focus.

Learn Test-Taking Strategies

Different types of questions require different strategies. We need to develop approaches to handle multiple-choice questions, essays, or logic problems effectively. Practice managing our time so we can finish every section within the allotted time. Each exam has its nuances, and the strategies will vary accordingly.

Step 3: Psychological Preparation

Build Confidence

One of the most powerful tools we have in our test-taking arsenal is confidence. We need to believe in our ability to succeed. Instead of imagining everything that could go wrong, let's visualize ourselves conquering the test. Studies show that this kind of positive visualization can improve performance.

Manage Stress

Stress is natural but how we manage it makes all the difference. Incorporating relaxation techniques like deep breathing or mindfulness into our study routine can help calm nerves. Also, getting enough sleep, especially in the days leading up to the test, is crucial. Lack of sleep can hurt our performance just as much as lack of preparation.

Use Anxiety as a Tool

It's normal to feel anxious when preparing for a big test. But instead of seeing anxiety as a sign that we're unprepared, let's view it as a reminder of how much we care. It can push us to study smarter and take the preparation seriously. If anxiety becomes overwhelming, it might be a signal that more preparation is needed. If we've done the work, our anxiety will be manageable.

Step 4: Resources and Tools

Study Guides and Books

The best resources often come from the test creators themselves. But don't hesitate to use other reputable study materials. Sometimes, different perspectives can make difficult concepts easier to understand. Still, when it comes to question style and structure, the materials from the test's authors are often the most reliable.

Online Resources

There's a wealth of online platforms and apps that offer practice questions, mock tests, and study groups. These can be valuable tools, especially when we want quick, on-the-go practice or explanations.

Tutors and Prep Courses

If we need extra help, a tutor or a prep course can make a big difference. But even without spending a lot of money, we can still score well by being diligent and using free resources.

Step 5: General Tips for Success

Have a Regular Study Schedule

Consistency is key. Having a regular study schedule reduces the amount of willpower needed to get started. By studying in manageable chunks over time, we can avoid burnout and retain information better.

Use Active Learning Techniques

Passive reading isn't enough. Techniques like flashcards, summarizing information in our own words, or teaching concepts to someone else can dramatically improve retention.

Maintain a Healthy Lifestyle

Taking care of our bodies is just as important as studying. Eating a balanced diet, exercising, and getting enough sleep will keep our brains sharp and ready for the challenge.

Step 6: Make a Game Plan

Commit to a Test Date

Setting a firm test date early on is crucial. Many of us make the mistake of studying until we feel "ready" and only then picking a date. But that's risky. Without a set deadline, procrastination can take over, and we may never feel "ready enough." Choose a date and let that be the anchor for our study plan.

Plan Based on the Date

Once we have a date, we can work backward to create a study plan. This is where techniques like spaced repetition come in handy. Spreading out our study sessions over time helps with long-term retention. Grab a calendar and write down when the sessions will happen.

Use the Best Resources

Stick to high-quality materials, especially those from the test creators. While it's helpful to explore other resources for different explanations, nothing beats practicing with materials that mirror the actual test.

Execute with 'Open-to-Goal' and 'Finisher Soup'

When it comes to executing our study plan, having clear goals for each session can make a huge difference. A concept I like to apply is "*Open-to-Goal.*" Set a clear goal for each study session, whether it's reviewing all incorrect questions from the previous session or mastering a specific topic like glycolysis. Once the goal is reached, the session is over. American entrepreneur, Alex Hormozi, used to run his highest performing gyms with this method. The athletic trainers would work from when the gym opened until they reached their goal of X sales per day. If they reached their goal by noon, their shift was over. If it took until 11 PM to get their goal, then that is how long they worked. "Open-to-Goal" is about working until the goal is reached. This can get challenging, but this method guarantees we accomplish what we intend.

Then there's the idea of "*Finisher Soup.*" The number one most important aspect of a winner's diet, is "Finisher Soup." Winners finish what they start. No matter what. When things don't go according to plan, we pivot and adjust. Failure is not about things not going perfectly—it's about giving up on the plan. Sticking to our plan is how we find success. "Open-to-Goal" is not stopping until we accomplish the goal. "Finisher Soup" is about being committed to finishing no matter the circumstances.

Jonny Kim is a prime example of this mindset. By age 40, he became a Navy SEAL, a Harvard-trained surgeon, and a NASA astronaut. His secret? He didn't consider himself special. He simply made plans and stuck to them. We, too, can achieve great things by following through, even when it's tough.

Final Thoughts

Preparing for standardized tests isn't just about mastering content. It's about mastering ourselves. By combining focused study strategies, psychological resilience, and consistent execution, we can walk into any test with confidence. Believe in the process, trust our preparation, and know that success is within our reach—one goal at a time.

BOOK REFERENCES & RECOMMENDATIONS
FOR ELEVATING OUR STUDY GAME

"It's not about the book, it's about the book the book leads you to."
- Austin Kleon (*Steal Like an Artist*)

Book References & Recommendations

Learning = Understanding + Remembering: How We Make, Strengthen, and Sustain Connections

- **"Limitless"** by Jim Kwik
- **"Mindset"** by Carol S. Dweck
- **"The Genius in All of Us"** by David Shenk
- **"The Talent Code"** by Daniel Coyle
- **"Make It Stick"** by Peter C. Brown, Henry L. Roediger III, and Mark A. McDaniel
- **"The Brain That Changes Itself"** by Norman Doidge
- **"Atomic Habits"** by James Clear
- **"Deep Work"** by Cal Newport
- **"Grit"** by Angela Duckworth

- **"Range"** by David Epstein
- **"Letters from a Stoic"** by Seneca

The Power of Asking Questions: Our Pickaxe to Get Everything We Want

- **"Tribe of Mentors"** by Tim Ferriss
- **"Letters from a Stoic"** by Seneca
- **"Limitless"** by Jim Kwik
- **"The Power of Now"** by Eckhart Tolle
- **"Awaken the Giant Within"** by Tony Robbins
- **"The Four-Hour Workweek"** by Tim Ferriss
- **"Man's Search for Meaning"** by Viktor Frankl
- **"The Art of Asking"** by Amanda Palmer
- **"The Book of Questions"** by Gregory Stock

Learning New Things: Constructing Knowledge

- **"Make It Stick"** by Peter C. Brown, Henry L. Roediger III, and Mark A. McDaniel
- **"The Four Stages of Competence"** by Noel Burch
- **"Mindset"** by Carol S. Dweck
- **"The Feynman Lectures on Physics"** by Richard Feynman
- **"Atomic Habits"** by James Clear
- **"The Talent Code"** by Daniel Coyle
- **"Peak"** by Anders Ericsson and Robert Pool
- **"The Art of Learning"** by Josh Waitzkin
- **"Why We Sleep"** by Matthew Walker

Outsmarting the Forgetting Curve: Remembering What's Important

- **"Memory"** by Hermann Ebbinghaus

- **"Make It Stick"** by Peter C. Brown, Henry L. Roediger III, and Mark A. McDaniel
- **"Deep Work"** by Cal Newport
- **"The Talent Code"** by Daniel Coyle
- **"Atomic Habits"** by James Clear
- **"The Art of Learning"** by Josh Waitzkin
- **"The Brain That Changes Itself"** by Norman Doidge
- **"Why We Sleep"** by Matthew Walker

Active Recall & Spaced Repetition: The Perfect Pair

- **"Make It Stick"** by Peter C. Brown, Henry L. Roediger III, and Mark A. McDaniel
- **"How We Learn"** by Benedict Carey
- **"Atomic Habits"** by James Clear
- **"Deep Work"** by Cal Newport
- **"The Talent Code"** by Daniel Coyle
- **"The Art of Learning"** by Josh Waitzkin
- **"Limitless"** by Jim Kwik
- **"A Mind for Numbers"** by Barbara Oakley
- **"Ultralearning"** by Scott H. Young
- **"Learning How to Learn"** by Barbara Oakley and Terrence Sejnowski

Peak Learning States: Optimize Our State, Enhance Our Learning

- **"Make It Stick"** by Peter C. Brown, Henry L. Roediger III, and Mark A. McDaniel
- **"Limitless"** by Jim Kwik
- **"The Talent Code"** by Daniel Coyle
- **"The Art of Learning"** by Josh Waitzkin
- **"Deep Work"** by Cal Newport
- **"Atomic Habits"** by James Clear
- **"Mindset"** by Carol S. Dweck

- **"Grit: The Power of Passion and Perseverance"** by Angela Duckworth
- **"How We Learn"** by Benedict Carey
- **"Ultralearning"** by Scott H. Young

11 Study Methods: Proven Study Techniques for Better Grades & Less Stress

- **"Torquato Tasso"** by Johann Wolfgang Von Goethe
- **"The Twelve Principles of Efficiency"** by Harrington Emerson
- **"Deep Work"** by Cal Newport
- **"Make It Stick: The Science of Successful Learning"** by Peter C. Brown, Henry L. Roediger III, and Mark A. McDaniel
- **"Limitless"** by Jim Kwik
- **"Atomic Habits"** by James Clear
- **"The Feynman Lectures on Physics"** by Richard Feynman
- **"The Talent Code"** by Daniel Coyle
- **"Ultralearning"** by Scott H. Young
- **"The Pareto Principle"** by Richard Koch
- **"The Power of Habit"** by Charles Duhigg
- **"A Mind for Numbers"** by Barbara Oakley

11 More Study Methods: More Methods for Intentional Learning

- **"Atomic Habits"** by James Clear
- **"Deep Work"** by Cal Newport
- **"Steal Like an Artist"** by Austin Kleon
- **"Augustine's Laws"** by Norman R. Augustine
- **"I Will Teach You to Be Rich"** by Ramit Sethi
- **"Letters from a Stoic"** by Seneca

- **"Make It Stick"** by Peter C. Brown, Henry L. Roediger III, and Mark A. McDaniel
- **"The Feynman Lectures on Physics"** by Richard Feynman
- **"The 80/20 Principle"** by Richard Koch
- **"The Four-Hour Workweek"** by Tim Ferriss
- **"The Power of Habit"** by Charles Duhigg

How to Beat Procrastination: Understanding Self-Regulation & Progress

- **"Twilight of the Idols"** by Friedrich Nietzsche
- **"Limitless"** by Jim Kwik
- **"Atomic Habits"** by James Clear
- **"The Checklist Manifesto"** by Atul Gawande
- **"Essentialism"** by Greg McKeown
- **"The 5 Second Rule"** by Mel Robbins

Mastering the Art of Note-Taking: 8 Methods to Help Us Retain & Apply Knowledge

- **"Limitless"** by Jim Kwik
- **"Make It Stick"** by Peter C. Brown, Henry L. Roediger III, and Mark A. McDaniel
- **"The Pen Is Mightier Than the Keyboard"** (Study) by Pam A. Mueller and Daniel M. Oppenheimer
- **"The Art of Note-Taking"** by Jim Kwik (or similar works that discuss note-taking strategies)

How to Read Textbooks Effectively: Learning with Purpose & Efficiency

- **"Confessions of a Misfit"** by Mokokoma Mokhonoana
- **"The Fundamentals of Chemical Engineering"** (Author varies by edition)

- **"Man's Search for Meaning"** by Viktor E. Frankl
- **"Limitless"** by Jim Kwik
- **"Atomic Habits"** by James Clear

Why Memory Matters: How to Keep It Fit

- **"Limitless"** by Jim Kwik
- **"Thank You Brain, For All You Remember"** by William R. Klemm
- **"Keep Sharp"** by Sanjay Gupta
- **"Memory Power 101"** by William R. Klemm

Advanced Study Methods: Techniques for Higher Level Learners

- **"Limitless"** by Jim Kwik
- **"Surely You're Joking, Mr. Feynman!"** by Richard P. Feynman
- **"A Mind for Numbers"** by Barbara Oakley
- **"Thinking, Fast and Slow"** by Daniel Kahneman
- **"The Art of Learning"** by Josh Waitzkin
- **"Flow"** by Mihaly Csikszentmihalyi
- **"Moonwalking with Einstein"** by Joshua Foer

Creating A Study Plan: Achieving Our Learning Goals with a Personalized Study Plan

- **"Limitless"** by Jim Kwik
- **"Atomic Habits"** by James Clear
- **"Make It Stick"** by Peter C. Brown, Henry L. Roediger III, and Mark A. McDaniel
- **"The Power of Habit"** by Charles Duhigg
- **"Deep Work"** by Cal Newport
- **"The 7 Habits of Highly Effective People"** by Stephen R. Covey
- **"Mindset"** by Carol S. Dweck

- "Grit" by Angela Duckworth

Creating the Perfect Study Environment: Designing Our Study Space for Success

- "Limitless" by Jim Kwik
- "Deep Work" by Cal Newport
- "Atomic Habits" by James Clear
- "The Power of Habit" by Charles Duhigg
- "Make It Stick" by Peter C. Brown, Henry L. Roediger III, and Mark A. McDaniel

The Best & Worst Foods for Studying: Understanding What Fuels Our Brain

- "Brain Food" by Lisa Mosconi
- "The Mind-Gut Connection" by Emeran Mayer
- "The End of Alzheimer's" by Dale Bredesen
- "Genius Foods" by Max Lugavere
- "How Not to Die" by Michael Greger
- "Keep Sharp" by Sanjay Gupta

Staying Focused: Strategies for Maintaining Attention

- "Focus" by Daniel Goleman
- "A Minute to Think" by Juliet Funt
- "Deep Work" by Cal Newport
- "Atomic Habits" by James Clear
- "The Power of Now" by Eckhart Tolle
- "The Willpower Instinct" by Kelly McGonigal
- "The Miracle of Mindfulness" by Thich Nhat Hanh

Dealing with Burnout: Without Compromising Productivity

- **"The Power of Full Engagement"** by Jim Loehr and Tony Schwartz
- **"Atomic Habits"** by James Clear
- **"The Burnout Cure"** by Julie de Azevedo Hanks
- • **"Burnout"** by Emily Nagoski and Amelia Nagoski
- **"The Joy of Work"** by Marie Kondo
- **"Essentialism"** by Greg McKeown
- **"The Art of Rest"** by Claudia Hammond
- **"Rest"** by Alex Soojung-Kim Pang

Solo Studying vs. Group Studying: Our Learning Tribe

- **"Extreme Ownership"** by Jocko Willink and Leif Babin
- **"Self-Reliance"** by Ralph Waldo Emerson
- **"Archetypes and The Collective Unconscious"** by Carl Jung
- **"The Art of Learning"** by Josh Waitzkin
- **"The Power of Collaboration"** by Thea Singer

Conquering Test & Performance Anxiety: Facing Fear & Building Confidence

- **"The Concept of Anxiety"** by Søren Kierkegaard
- **"The Checklist Manifesto"** by Dr. Atul Gawande
- **"Letters from a Stoic"** by Seneca
- **"On the Shortness of Life"** by Seneca
- **"Fear Setting Exercise"** by Tim Ferriss (from *Tools of Titans*)
- **"Beyond Good and Evil"** by Friedrich Nietzsche
- **"The Antidote"** by Oliver Burkeman

Subject Specific Strategies: Techniques for Each Class

- **"The Checklist Manifesto"** by Dr. Atul Gawande
- **"Letters from a Stoic"** by Seneca

- "On the Shortness of Life" by Seneca

Becoming an Expert at Standardized Tests: Tackling Big Exams

- "The Checklist Manifesto" by Atul Gawande
- "Letters from a Stoic" by Seneca
- "On the Shortness of Life" by Seneca
- "MCAT Official Guide" by Association of American Medical Colleges (AAMC)
- "The Official SAT Study Guide" by The College Board

5

NAVIGATING ACADEMIC SUCCESS

STRATEGIES AND MINDSETS FOR THRIVING IN ACADEMIA

THE ANATOMY OF A CLASS

SYLLABUS MASTERY, TIME MANAGEMENT, AND ACADEMIC SUCCESS

"Clarity about what matters provides clarity about what does not."
- Cal Newport (*Deep Work*)

Know What Makes Our Class Tick

Every class is unique, and every teacher has a different style. To succeed, we need to understand what's important in each class. This comes down to figuring out our Key Performance Indicators (KPIs)—the factors that go into our grades. Do tests carry the most weight? Are assignments more important? Some classes might prioritize tests, while others give more credit for participation or projects. It's up to us to uncover this and plan accordingly.

Understanding the Grade

If we want to reach our desired grade, we need to understand how it's calculated. Take time to break down the grading system so we can focus our energy where it matters most. This way, we can master the material while still having time for the things we enjoy outside of class. Most of this information will be in the syllabus, but if it's not clear, we should always ask.

The Importance and Power of the Syllabus

The syllabus is like a map for our classes—it lays out the path to success. Knowing it inside out helps us navigate assignments, deadlines, and expectations with ease. Think of it like knowing the rules of a game: once we understand them, we can play to win. During the first week of class, often called "syllabus week," many students relax or socialize, but the wisest students use this time to prepare.

Breaking Down the Syllabus

The syllabus contains all the critical information we need to succeed. It tells us the grading breakdown, important deadlines, and class policies. By understanding these details, we can find opportunities to excel. For example, knowing when assignments are due helps us plan our time better, and understanding how much an assignment is worth might lead us to prioritize it—or skip it—based on our other commitments.

Example Syllabus Breakdown

Here's a simple example of what a syllabus might include:

- *Grading Policies:* 40% Tests, 30% Homework, 20% Projects, 10% Participation
- *Important Dates:* Test 1 - Sept 15, Project Due - Oct 1
- *Major Assignments:* Weekly Homework, Monthly Projects

Knowing this breakdown, we can plan our efforts accordingly. If we're falling behind, focusing on tests or catching up on missing homework could make the most significant impact on our grade. Scheduling important deadlines in our planner or calendar also ensures we don't double-book ourselves and can stay on top of things.

Know What Supplies We Need

Being prepared is key to staying organized and ready to learn. Knowing what supplies we need—whether it's books, notebooks, calculators, or other tools—allows us to focus on the material. For instance, I couldn't afford to buy textbooks for every class in college. But after reviewing my syllabi, I found that not all of my classes required textbooks, which allowed me to save money and still succeed. By making informed decisions, we can avoid unnecessary expenses and focus on what's essential.

Extra Credit: The Secret Weapon

Never underestimate the power of extra credit. It can be our secret weapon for boosting grades, often with less effort than regular assignments. Picture our grade as a pie: each extra credit piece makes that pie bigger. Extra credit can sometimes offer more value than regular assignments, especially if those assignments don't count much toward the final grade. Always keep an eye out for extra credit opportunities.

Ask for Help When Needed

We should never be afraid to ask for help, whether it's from a teacher, tutor, or classmate. Clarifying confusing topics early can prevent problems down the line. Most teachers appreciate when students take initiative and seek help—it shows we care about doing well.

Take Advantage of Office Hours

Office hours are a great opportunity to get extra help or clarification on assignments. They're usually listed in the syllabus, but if not, asking about them on the first day is a great way to show initiative. We can use this time to build a relationship with our teacher and get personalized advice.

Stay Organized

Keeping our notes, assignments, and materials organized will save us time and reduce stress. Whether we prefer physical folders or digital tools, the key is easy access. If we can find what we need in less than a minute, then our system is working well. Staying organized also helps us manage our time better, especially when exams or major assignments are approaching.

Prioritize Tasks

Once we understand the grading breakdown and our syllabus, it's easier to prioritize tasks. Tackling the most critical assignments first ensures that we make the best use of our time. Even if we run out of time for less important tasks, we'll have completed the essentials.

Use a Planner

Tracking assignments, tests, and deadlines in a planner or calendar is one of the simplest ways to stay organized. Whether we prefer a digital or physical planner, the key is consistency. I like using digital planners because they sync across all my devices, but some people prefer the tactile feel of a paper planner. Try different methods and find what works best for our personal workflows.

Set Realistic Goals

Setting achievable goals for each class can keep us motivated and on track. Whether it's completing several assignments a week or aiming for a specific grade, having clear goals gives us direction. Personally, I set deadlines in my calendar and plan out specific times to complete tasks.

UNDERSTANDING our classes and how they work is the key to thriving. By knowing what makes each class tick, breaking down the syllabus, being smart about supplies, seeking extra credit, asking for help, staying organized, and prioritizing our tasks, we can excel. The effort we put in and how we manage our time will lead to better results. Anything critical—like grading breakdowns, deadlines, and office hours—can usually be found in the syllabus, and if not, it's up to us to ask about it on the first day.

HOW TO ACT IN CLASS
CLASSROOM ETIQUETTE AND ENGAGEMENT

"The difference between who you are and who you want to be is what you do." - Charles Duhigg (*The Power of Habit*)

Starting a new class can be both exciting and daunting, but how we conduct ourselves can significantly impact our success. Whether we aim to impress our teacher, make friends, or stay on top of our studies, knowing the best ways to behave in class can help us reach our goals. Below are some practical tips on everything from where to sit to how to manage our workload and build strong relationships with classmates and instructors:

Sit in the Second Row

Choosing the right seat in class can make a big difference in how well we engage. Sitting in the back often feels too removed from the action, while sitting in the front can sometimes make us feel like we're drawing too much attention. The second row strikes a great balance—it keeps us engaged and helps us blend in while still being noticeable.

However, the key is finding a seat where we can pay the most attention. If we need specific accommodations, like sitting closer to the board because of hearing or vision issues, we should prioritize those needs. In my experience, sitting near the front helps me stay focused, and I've observed that students who sit in the first two rows tend to perform better. But remember, the most important thing is choosing a seat where we can participate fully and comfortably.

Arrive Early and Be Consistent

Getting to class early and sitting in the same spot each time can do wonders for our routine. It helps reinforce what we've learned and shows our instructors that we're serious about the class. Consistency in where we sit and when we arrive helps us mentally prepare for each lesson. Plus, it can positively affect how instructors perceive us—distinguishing ourselves from the crowd makes it easier to build relationships and ask for help when needed.

Learn from Everyone

We should strive to learn from everyone, not just our instructors. Judging others isolates us and limits potential opportunities. For example, I once misjudged a classmate in my Organic Chemistry class because he seemed uninteresting, only to later find out that he had a deep understanding of the material. He ended up being integral to me passing the class.

Being open to learning from everyone, regardless of their initial impressions, allows us to build valuable connections and grow in unexpected ways. After all, we're all in this learning journey together, and everyone has something to offer.

Get to Know Classmates

Our classmates can be some of the most important people we meet. Not only can they become friends, but they can also help us with notes, clarify concepts, and collaborate on assignments. Building good relationships with them is beneficial both academically and socially.

Many of the most rewarding relationships in my life started in the classroom. By being open and approachable, we can make connections that enhance our learning experience and potentially extend beyond the classroom.

Frontload the Work

Whenever possible, frontload the work at the beginning of the term. This means completing as many assignments as we can in the first few weeks, which gives us more time for reviews, projects, and relaxation later on. By doing this, we create flexibility in our schedule and can take breaks when needed without feeling behind.

This strategy isn't always feasible in every class, especially if we have external responsibilities, but even starting a little early can provide a huge advantage. The more we can accomplish early on, the more control we have over our workload throughout the term.

Pre-Screen Lectures or Lessons

Pre-reading or pre-screening the material before class is a game-changer. When we do this, we prime our brain—through the reticular activating system—to notice key points and make deeper connections during the actual lecture. Understanding the purpose of each class ahead of time makes the material more meaningful and easier to follow.

Even if we only skim the material, this habit can significantly enhance our comprehension and retention during class.

Ask Questions

Asking questions is one of the most effective ways to learn. Not only do questions clarify confusion, but they also show the instructor that we're engaged and curious. Questions act like a pickaxe, helping us dig deeper into the material and unlock understanding.

Many of us hesitate to ask questions out of fear of looking foolish...

> "The man who asks a question is a fool for a minute, the man who does not ask is a fool for life." - Confucius

It is better to be perceived as a fool than to actually be one.

Learning to ask high-level questions can build goodwill with instructors and ensure we never miss important information. Asking questions is not a sign of weakness—it's a mark of someone who is getting better.

Identify People of Interest

In every class, there are key people we should pay attention to: the instructor, the teaching assistant (TA) or instructional assistant (IA), and the most dedicated students. These people can become invaluable resources throughout the term.

Sometimes, it's easier to relate to or get help from a TA or IA, especially if they explain concepts in a way that resonates with us. For example, in my Organic Chemistry 2 class, the TA was the person who truly helped me grasp the material. While my professor for that class was amazing, I learned more of the details from the TA. Similarly, identifying the most dedicated students—those who are serious about the class—gives us a reliable study group and improves our own performance.

Reflect on Our Actions

Taking time to reflect on how we behave in class can lead to major growth. For instance, a former student of mine, Max, refused to turn in assignments because he disliked his teacher. He realized that he was not turning in his work because he did not like how his teacher treated him. He didn't feel respected and his response was to defy all instructions. In the end, he realized his stubbornness hurt no one but himself and started to turn in his work.

Self-reflection helps us avoid these kinds of self-sabotaging behaviors. If we ever find ourselves holding back from succeeding out of spite or frustration, it's important to pause and reconsider. Reflection only takes a moment but often leads to more personal growth than any other tactic we employ. All of my biggest wins in life have come from self-reflection.

SUCCESS in the classroom isn't just about showing up—it's about actively engaging, building strong relationships, and developing habits that support long-term learning. Whether it's choosing the right seat, asking meaningful questions, or frontloading our work, each action we take moves us closer to mastering the material and maximizing our educational experience. Learning is a journey, and how we approach each class shapes our path. By staying open to growth, reflecting on our actions, and connecting with those around us, we set ourselves up not only for academic achievement but also for personal development that will serve us well beyond the classroom. Every class is an opportunity to grow, adapt, and move closer to our goals, if we let it.

ORGANIZATIONAL FRAMEWORKS
WORKING SMARTER, NOT HARDER

"Rowing harder doesn't help if the boat is headed in the wrong direction." – Kenichi Ohmae (Organizational Theorist)

Working hard is ineffective if we're not focusing on the right things. In this chapter, we'll explore how to work smarter, not harder, by building systems that help us prioritize what truly matters.

Organizing Physical & Digital Files

Productivity starts with understanding our situation. To do that, we need to organize our resources—both physical and digital—so we know exactly what we're dealing with. Let's begin with the basics of file organization.

Organizing Physical Files

Keeping physical files in order is essential for reducing clutter and maintaining focus. Here's a simple approach:

- Use file boxes, an inbox, and folders to sort documents.
  - Keep one inbox for new or incoming files.
  - Use as many folders or boxes as needed to stay organized.
- Consider turning physical files into digital copies using a scanner or a smartphone app. This reduces physical clutter and makes searching for documents easier.

By doing this, we create an environment that helps us think clearly and access the materials we need without wasting time.

Organizing Digital Files

Just like our physical files, digital files need a system. One effective method is *branching*, which helps us create a structured hierarchy of folders and subfolders—much like the branches of a tree. Here's how we can set it up:

1. *Start with Broad Categories:* Begin by creating top-level folders for the main areas of our life:
   - *Work*
   - *School*
   - *Personal*
2. *Create Subfolders:* Within these broad categories, create subfolders for specific tasks or subjects. For example, under *School*, we could have:
   - *Assignments*
   - *Class Notes*
   - *Projects*
3. *Break Down Further:* For complex topics, we can continue breaking them down into even more specific subfolders. For example, under *Assignments*, we might have:
   - *Math*
   - *Science*

- *English*
4. *Use Clear Naming Conventions* When naming files, we should use descriptive and consistent names. Including dates or version numbers makes it easier to track changes and updates. For example:
   - Math_Assignment1_2024-07-16
   - Science_Project_Final_V1
5. *Regular Maintenance* Periodically, it's important to review our folders and clean up outdated files. This keeps the system efficient and prevents digital clutter from building up. If we don't practice regular maintenance, these systems could cause more problems than we started with.
6. *Backup the Files:* Always have a backup system—whether it's cloud storage or an external hard drive—to protect our files from accidental loss.

By implementing this branching system, we streamline our workflow, making it easy to find what we need when we need it.

Inbox Zero: Clearing Digital Clutter

An overflowing inbox can create stress and distraction. Enter *Inbox Zero*, a method that helps us manage our inbox by keeping it as close to empty as possible. But this practice isn't just for email—it can be applied to any kind of task list or incoming messages. Here's how we can achieve it:

1. *Set Aside Time:* Designate specific times of day to check and process emails or tasks.
2. *Process, Don't Just Check:* When opening an email, decide what to do with it right away. Don't just read and leave it sitting there.
3. *Use the 4 D's:*
   - *Delete:* Get rid of irrelevant messages.

- *Delegate:* If someone else can handle it, forward it to them.
- *Defer:* If it requires more time, move it to a calendar or folder for later.
- *Do:* If it takes less than two minutes, complete the task immediately.
4. *Unsubscribe:* Regularly unsubscribe from newsletters and spam that clutter our inbox.
5. *Use Filters:* Organize emails with filters that automatically sort messages into folders.
6. *Utilize Tools:* Tools like email management apps can help us sort, prioritize, and automate tasks.

While some may find Inbox Zero unnecessary, it can dramatically reduce mental load and improve focus by keeping our inbox clean and our tasks manageable.

Things in Their Place: The Power of Organization

Mise en place is a practice chefs use to keep everything in the right place before cooking. This principle can be applied to our workspace, ensuring that everything has its place. The benefits go beyond neatness:

- *Increased Efficiency:* Knowing where everything is saves us time, allowing us to focus on tasks without distraction.
- *Reduced Stress:* A cluttered space leads to a cluttered mind. Organizing our environment can significantly reduce the stress that comes from searching for misplaced items.
- *Enhanced Productivity:* An organized space helps us maintain focus and get more done in less time.
- *Improved Accuracy:* When everything is in its place, we're

less likely to misplace important documents or tools, leading to fewer mistakes.

- *Facilitates Collaboration:* A well-organized workspace makes it easier for others to find what they need, improving teamwork and efficiency.
- *Better Time Management:* We waste less time searching for things, giving us more time to dedicate to important tasks.
- *Professional Appearance:* A tidy space presents a professional image, whether it's to colleagues, clients, or visitors.

By keeping things in their place, we create a system that's easy to maintain and supports both our focus and productivity.

Checklists: Doing Things Right, Every Time

Checklists aren't just for grocery shopping—they're vital tools in high-stakes fields like aviation and healthcare. As an EMT, I relied on checklists to ensure I gathered all the necessary information from patients. Pilots use them because they understand that their memory and judgment can sometimes be unreliable. In our own work, checklists can help us stay on track and ensure critical steps aren't overlooked.

How to Make a Good Checklist

1. Identify when the checklist needs to be used.
2. Keep the wording simple and clear.
3. Limit the checklist to 5-9 items to avoid overwhelming ourselves.
4. Focus on "killer items"—the most crucial steps that must not be missed.
5. Test the checklist in real-world situations to refine and improve it.

Checklists are living documents, meant to be updated and improved as our environment changes. By using them, we make sure that important tasks are completed correctly every time.

Eliminate Daily Annoyances

We often face small, recurring issues that drain our energy—what some call "death by a thousand paper cuts." By identifying and eliminating these daily annoyances, we free up our mental resources for more important tasks.

Ask ourselves, "How can I remove this problem forever?" Fixing these little issues leads to big improvements in the long run.

Create Systems That Eliminate Decisions

The goal of any good system is to reduce the number of decisions we need to make. Whether we use Notion, Google Sheets, or simple reminders, the tool isn't as important as the system itself. The best systems eliminate multiple decisions with just one setup, allowing us to focus on the work that matters.

Staying Organized Over the Long Term

Staying organized requires consistency. The key is to make our systems *easy to use* and *simple to maintain*.

- *Keep It Simple:* The more complex a system, the less likely we are to use it. By labeling items clearly and minimizing steps, we make it easier to maintain.
- *Regular Cleaning:* Just as clutter builds up over time, our systems will naturally decay (thanks to entropy). Scheduling regular *entropy management sessions*—times when we review and clean up our systems—helps ensure that they continue to function smoothly. Whether it's once a week or once a month, these sessions prevent overwhelm and help keep things running efficiently.

. . .

BY ORGANIZING OUR FILES, managing our inbox, adopting checklists, and creating systems that eliminate unnecessary decisions, we can dramatically reduce stress and improve our productivity. Working smarter, not harder, is about focusing on what matters, and by keeping our lives organized, we can free our minds for more important tasks. The key is maintaining these systems over time, so we stay on track and continue to thrive in both our personal and professional lives.

THE MAGIC OF SCHEDULING
HOW TO TAKE CONTROL OF OUR TIME AND LIFE

"Focus on being productive instead of busy." - Tim Ferriss (*The 4-Hour Workweek*)

L earning something new often takes longer than expected, even when we anticipate the challenges. Here's the truth: that's okay. If we don't accomplish everything we planned, there's no need to be hard on ourselves. The key is to plan effectively and give ourselves grace along the way.

Mastering Our Schedule

Scheduling our time is one of the most powerful tools we have. By organizing our tasks, we separate the mundane from the meaningful and ensure uninterrupted time for what matters most. This strategy is rooted in the idea that willpower is a finite resource, and we have the most of it in the morning, making it the perfect time for focused work.

Strategic Future-Thinking

The trick is to think ahead without getting overwhelmed. When we schedule our time, we need to think about the near future—1-2 weeks is a good range. When we're stressed, it's best to shorten that timeframe to just a few days, or even one day if necessary. This allows us to stay focused and flexible without being consumed by anxiety about the long term.

People often fall into depression by dwelling on the past and into anxiety by thinking too far into the future. By scheduling mindfully, we can manage our present with a clear eye on what's coming up, without losing ourselves in what's too far away.

Time Management Tips

1. *Get a Blank Calendar:* Whether it's for school, work, or life in general, start by marking all the important dates. For school, we'll go through our syllabus; for life, we'll input big priorities first. Smaller tasks come after.
2. *Assign Due Dates and Work Times:* As soon as we get assignments or tasks, we'll note the due dates and schedule time to work on them. This way, nothing gets left until the last minute.
3. *Use the Calendar as a To-Do List:* When we list tasks on our calendar, it helps us see when we'll actually get them done, keeping us accountable.
4. *Listen to the Calendar:* Sticking to our schedule can be tough, but it's worth it. The best schedule is the one we follow.
5. *Keep a General To-Do List:* As new tasks pop into our heads, we'll jot them down and add them to the calendar later.
6. *Schedule Fun First:* Enjoyment is a priority, not an afterthought. Scheduling time for activities we love—

whether spending time with family or pursuing hobbies —helps us stay balanced and motivated. While it may seem like "scheduling" in fun may ruin it, it allows us to be present in the moment and have something to look forward to.

My Journey with Scheduling

Before I learned the power of scheduling, my life was chaotic. I often forgot tasks, double-booked myself, or became overwhelmed by the mountain of responsibilities. But everything changed when a friend gave me a simple piece of advice: "Schedule everything."

At first, it felt a little rigid. But soon, my life began to flow smoothly. I was a college student with a packed schedule—juggling classes, two jobs, and a busy social life—but I never missed a commitment, never forgot an assignment, and rarely felt stressed. In fact, just putting tasks into my calendar gave me a sense of accomplishment, knowing that I'd follow through.

Over time, though, I learned an important lesson. When I stuck to my calendar, I felt on top of the world. But when I drifted from it, stress and overwhelm crept back in. Now, whenever I feel that familiar sense of anxiety, I know it's time to check in with my schedule and realign with my priorities.

The Chaos of No Schedule

At first, the idea of a schedule felt like a mental prison. It seemed like something adults used to prove they had it all together. But I soon discovered that a schedule wasn't tyrannical—it was liberating. A well-planned schedule adds value to life, lightening our mental load and freeing us to enjoy the present moment while still preparing for the future.

Building a Useful Schedule

Designing Our Day

We need to be proactive, not reactive, with our time. By scheduling peak performance hours for our most important work, we set ourselves up for success. For example, my brain works best between 11 AM and 2 PM, so I block that time for deep, focused tasks.

At the end of each day, I like to reflect on what I've accomplished and plan for the next day. When I wake up with a clear plan, I'm able to live intentionally, not improvisationally. This doesn't mean we have to be busy every minute; sometimes I even schedule downtime. The goal is to spend our time on purpose, not accidentally.

Make the Schedule for Someone We Care About

Jordan Peterson suggests we make a schedule as if designing it for someone we care about. This means balancing obligations with enjoyment, and being realistic about what we can accomplish. A schedule isn't about being overly productive—it's about creating a life that works for us, one we can sustain without burning out.

Schedule Fun Too

Including fun activities in our schedule is essential. When we have something to look forward to after completing a task, we're more focused and productive. For example, my ideal day includes a slow morning, productive work in the afternoon, and time in the evening with my kids. This balance keeps me energized and fulfilled.

Effective Scheduling Tips

Start with High-Priority Events

Always begin by scheduling the most important events. This ensures we have enough time for the tasks that truly matter.

Plan Everything to the End

Half-baked plans lead to overwhelm. When we schedule with a clear end in mind, we know what we're working toward and can celebrate the finish line.

Schedule Tasks Immediately

As soon as we're aware of a task, we'll add it to our calendar. This prevents us from forgetting and ensures the work gets done.

Be Specific

We reduce decision-making and procrastination by being specific about when and where we'll complete tasks. For example, if I know I'll work at 2 PM at my desk, I'm less likely to avoid it. The more decisions we make ahead of time, the fewer excuses we'll have.

Schedule Time for Managing Chaos and Ensuring Recovery

Life gets messy, and entropy is inevitable. We'll build in time to manage disorder—whether it's cleaning up our physical space or catching up on tasks that slipped through the cracks. This also means scheduling downtime for recovery, so we can recharge and perform at our best.

· · ·

SCHEDULING IS a skill that takes time to master, but it's well worth the effort. By taking control of our time, we can manage our tasks more effectively and create a life that balances work, play, and rest. Remember, our schedule is supposed to work for us, not the other way around.

SETTING HEALTHY BOUNDARIES
CREATING SPACE FOR WHAT TRULY MATTERS

"People who matter don't mind and people who mind don't matter." - Bernard Baruch

S etting boundaries is essential for maintaining our well-being, empowering us to live intentionally and with respect. Without boundaries, we risk burnout, resentment, and losing sight of our own needs. Healthy boundaries teach others how to treat us and ensure that we are honoring ourselves in all areas of life.

Many of us struggle with setting boundaries because saying "no" can feel uncomfortable. We fear disappointing others, being misunderstood, or creating conflict. But without boundaries, we lose control over our time, energy, and emotions, often leading to frustration or burnout. Setting boundaries is not about pushing people away; it's about making space for what truly matters to us.

Know Our Limits

The first step to setting healthy boundaries is knowing our own limits. It's important to reflect on our needs, values, and priorities, so we can understand what we can and cannot tolerate. Setting healthy boundaries starts with us, not others.

Writing down our limits in different areas—whether at work, in relationships, or during personal time—helps us evaluate our boundaries more objectively. When our boundaries are only in our heads, they can feel unclear, making them harder to understand or enforce.

Say No Quickly and Gently

Saying no can be one of the toughest challenges in boundary-setting, but it's essential. When we need to decline an offer or request, it's helpful to do so politely and with gratitude. For instance, we might say, "Thank you for thinking of me, but I'm going to have to decline this time." This shows appreciation while firmly setting our boundary.

However, the easiest "no" is often a quick one. The longer we delay, the more complicated or burdensome the "no" can become.

Communicate Clearly

Clear communication is crucial when setting boundaries. We must use straightforward and concise language so that our boundaries are easy to understand. Good communication falls on the speaker, not the listener, so it's up to us to make sure we're being as clear as possible.

Using "I statements" is a great way to frame boundaries from our own perspective. For example, saying, "I need some time alone after work" is more effective than, "You never give me space." The focus remains on our needs without sounding accusatory.

Setting Boundaries with Technology

Boundaries aren't just necessary in our relationships with people; they're also important when it comes to managing our time and attention, especially with technology. Screens can consume much of our focus, and we often find ourselves pulled into endless scrolling.

One effective strategy for reducing screen time is turning our phones to greyscale. Companies invest billions into making apps and websites visually appealing, and turning off the bright colors helps reduce the urge to engage with our devices. By switching to greyscale, we might find ourselves less drawn to our phones, potentially reducing screen time by 30-40%.

Creating Boundaries by Saying No to Categories

Rather than saying no to specific requests, we can set boundaries by saying no to entire categories. For example, setting a rule like "no phones after 8 PM" or "no sweets during the week" helps create clear, consistent boundaries. It's easier to follow these guidelines than to make decisions on a case-by-case basis.

We can use this same technique at work. For instance, we might tell colleagues, "I check my email once daily in the morning," which sets a clear boundary. This way, everyone knows what to expect, and we avoid the pressure of constantly responding to messages.

Setting Boundaries Requires No Effort from Others

The best boundaries are the ones that don't require anything from other people. For instance, if we decide to spend Sunday afternoons without plans, this boundary doesn't require anyone else to change their behavior. It's a simple, personal choice that gives us space without creating conflict.

We can also use this approach in parenting. Instead of asking a child to stop watching TV, for example, we might say, "I'm going to turn off the TV in a few minutes." The boundary is set, and we remain in control of its enforcement, without needing the other person's cooperation. In this example, the boundary is set and requires no effort on her part, and I am in control of the boundary enforcement. All the effort is in my court.

I use this as a teacher as well. I let my students know that if they keep acting out, I will do ____. I rarely tell *them* to stop acting out. I just let them know what *I* am going to do. This works every time.

Enforcing Consequences

If we want others to respect our boundaries, we need to follow through and consistently enforce them. If someone oversteps, it's important to remind them of the limits and take appropriate action when necessary.

Consistency is key. If we've told someone that we don't take calls after 9 PM, we should follow through by not answering the phone after that time. By sticking to our boundaries, we show others that they're important and non-negotiable.

A "No" is a Bigger "Yes" to Something Else

When we say no to something, we're actually saying yes to something else that matters more. While it may feel difficult to say no, we're ultimately making room for the things that align with our goals and values.

We often avoid saying no because we don't want to reject others, but we fail to consider that saying yes to someone else can mean saying no to ourselves. What do we want to say yes to in our lives? What are the big things that matter? When we're clear on those answers, saying no becomes easier, because we're saying yes to ourselves.

Set Physical Boundaries

Physical boundaries can help reinforce emotional and social limits. If we need time alone, for example, being in a separate room can give us the space we need. Rearranging our living and working spaces to support our boundaries can make it easier to stay aligned with them.

Emotional Boundaries

Setting emotional boundaries requires us to recognize our emotional limits and avoid situations that drain us. Sometimes, not being around certain environments is the best way to maintain our emotional well-being.

It's also important to remember that we are not responsible for other people's feelings. Boundaries are for our benefit, not others. If someone needs to set their own limits, they are responsible for doing so. Everyone is responsible for their own boundaries.

Respecting Others' Boundaries

Just as we expect others to respect our boundaries, we must be mindful of theirs. Encouraging open communication around boundaries can help make them a social norm, rather than something taboo.

Reevaluate Regularly

Boundaries are not static; they change as we grow and our circumstances evolve. It's important to regularly reassess our boundaries to ensure they're still serving us and adjust them as necessary. The boundaries we set at 18 may not serve us when we're 28, and that's okay. Regular reflection helps keep our boundaries dynamic and aligned with our current needs.

By setting healthy boundaries, we can manage our time more effectively, reduce stress, and create a life that aligns with our values. The best boundaries require no effort from other people and give us space to say yes to what matters. Those who truly care about us will respect our limits, and by saying no to what doesn't serve us, we make room for the things that do.

BASICS OF SYSTEMS
GALLS' LAW & COMPONENTS OF SYSTEMS

"Every system is perfectly designed to get the results it gets." - Josh Kaufman (*The Personal MBA*)

The Push for Hyper-Personalization

We live in a world where almost everything can be personalized—workouts, diets, sleep routines, even the mattress we sleep on. But before we get lost in the allure of customization, it's easy to forget that most people are mostly the same. Before we dive into the world of expensive personalization, the real question is: do we have the fundamentals down?

Many of us spend years searching for the "perfect" solution but rarely ask ourselves, "How can I become someone with the perfect solution?" We move from one personalized product to the next without mastering the basics. In our search for quick fixes—especially personalized ones—we sometimes forget that the simplest, foundational systems often yield the best results.

Once we master the basics, we earn the right to customize and personalize. We have to beware of premature personalization.

Whether it's a workout routine, diet, financial advice, or sleep hygiene, we can make significant progress by simply applying the basics. As the saying goes, success is relentless execution of the basics.

Systems Are Everything

Systems are everywhere, both inside and outside of us. Our bodies are systems made up of organs, chemical reactions, and energy flows. Every cell, organelle, and molecule is part of a system, and this pattern extends all the way down to the subatomic level and below.

On a larger scale, we see systems in our neighborhoods, cities, countries, and even the entire planet. Systems can be as vast as galaxies or as small as a single conversation. Businesses, for example, are complex systems operating within even larger systems—markets, industries, and societies.

When we understand systems as an abstract idea, we can apply this knowledge to almost any field. Personally, I've used my understanding of systems across different areas—from chemical engineering to music, mathematics, medicine, social dynamics, education, economics, and even gaming. Most systems share similar parts, can be analyzed in the same way, and follow similar rules.

Whether we are learning, working, or improving any aspect of our lives, the concept of systems gives us a powerful framework for thinking and solving problems.

Gall's Law

"A complex system that works is invariably found to have evolved from a simple system that worked. The inverse proposition also appears to be true: a complex system designed from scratch never works and cannot be made to work. You have to start over, beginning with a simple system." - John Gall (*The Systems Bible*)

Gall's Law teaches us that every complex system started as a simple system that worked. Take smartphones as an example: they started as simple devices for phone calls. Over time, features like texting, music, and internet browsing were added, evolving into the complex systems we rely on today. But had we tried to build smartphones as they are now from the start, they never would have worked.

This principle applies across all areas of life. Whether we're developing work systems, designing diets, or managing finances, we should always start with the simplest version that works. As we go, we can add complexity as needed.

In my own life, I've applied Gall's Law to everything from my family's financial systems to my exercise and diet routines. Each of these systems started with basic, manageable actions, and only after mastering those basics did I start adding complexity. This approach allowed me to avoid getting overwhelmed and helped ensure the systems worked well from the beginning.

Components of a System

In his book *The Personal MBA*, Josh Kaufman breaks down systems into essential components. He says that each system will have the same 5 core components, but there are more components that can be analyzed to help create or improve a system.

The core 5 components in every system are:

- *Inputs:* Resources that enter the system. These could be money, raw materials, energy, or time.
- *Processes:* Actions or steps that transform inputs into outputs. These are the operations that take place within the system.

- *Outputs:* The results or products that come from the system, which could be goods, services, or information.
- *Feedback:* Information from the system's output that can be used to adjust inputs or processes. Feedback helps improve system performance over time.
- *Environment:* The external context within which the system operates. It includes everything outside the system that can impact how it functions, like market conditions, regulations, or societal norms

Understanding the following components helps us design, analyze, and improve any system, regardless of what it does:

- *Flow:* The movement of resources through the system—what comes in and what goes out.
- *Stock:* A reserve of resources, like money in a business or food in a kitchen.
- *Slack:* The amount of resources available as extra stock. This can be good or bad, depending on the system.
- *Constraints:* The barriers that prevent the system from achieving its goals.
- *Feedback Loops:* When the output of a system becomes an input, either reinforcing (positive feedback) or reducing (negative feedback) the system's behavior.
- *Autocatalysis:* A system where the outputs feed back into the inputs, like reinvesting profits into a business.
- *Environment:* Everything outside the system that can affect it. No system exists in isolation.
- *Selection Test:* Conditions in the environment that determine whether a system succeeds or fails.

While these concepts might seem abstract, they apply to almost every system we create in life. We might not consider every component at the beginning, but understanding them allows us to refine and improve over time.

For example, when I started developing my diet and exercise systems, I didn't worry about every component right away. I focused on simple habits, like regular movement and balanced nutrition. Over time, I layered in more personalized elements as the basics became routine. On the other hand, when my family built our financial system, we carefully considered constraints, slack, and feedback loops from the start. Each system will require different levels of attention to its components at different stages, but the process always begins with simplicity.

The Power of Simple Systems

Gall's Law reminds us that success is born from simplicity. Whether we are learning new skills, developing habits, or managing any aspect of our lives, starting with simple systems allows us to grow and adapt over time. The challenge isn't in finding the perfect system or solution right away—it's in starting small, building on what works, and gradually adding complexity.

By understanding the fundamental components of systems, we can create strong, adaptable structures for any part of our lives. When we master the basics, we can personalize, refine, and grow these systems as we evolve.

Start simple. Build a foundation that works. Then, and only then, personalize and customize as needed.

ANALYZING & IMPROVING SYSTEMS
EXAMINING EXISTING SYSTEMS

"If we are unhappy, it's because our system is broken." - Brandon Turner (*The Book on Rental Property Investing*)

T hink about the systems that shape our everyday lives. If our car breaks down on a busy road, our instinct is to identify which part of the system failed. Similarly, when things go wrong in our lives, it often means a piece of the larger system needs adjustment.

Analyzing and improving systems might seem complicated, but it's a skill we can all master. Once we learn to break systems into simpler parts and measure their effectiveness, we can make thoughtful improvements.

How to Analyze Systems

Deconstruction

When tackling complex systems, we begin by breaking them down. Gall's Law teaches us that all complex systems evolve from simpler ones. By identifying triggers (what starts the system) and endpoints (what stops it), we can map smaller parts and their connections.

Creating flowcharts or diagrams can make this process clearer, revealing inefficiencies or areas where things might go wrong.

Measurement

A key part of analysis is understanding the data a system produces. Measurement is the act of collecting this data. Just as measuring blood glucose can tell us about someone's health, tracking relevant data can provide insight into a system's performance.

Measurement is the first step toward improvement because without understanding what's happening, we can't know where to start.

Key Performance Indicators (KPIs)

While measuring is important, too much data can become overwhelming. We should focus on 3-5 essential Key Performance Indicators (KPIs) that give us the clearest understanding of how the system is functioning. Prioritizing these indicators prevents us from getting bogged down in unnecessary details.

Garbage In, Garbage Out

The quality of what we put into a system directly affects the quality of what comes out. Just like using fresh ingredients makes a better meal, improving the inputs to a system will lead to better outputs.

Tolerance

Every system has a range of tolerance—a space where it operates normally. Some systems are flexible and can handle a lot of variability, while others are more rigid. Understanding tolerance helps us recognize when systems operate smoothly or begin to falter.

Analytical Honesty

We all have biases that can cloud our judgment. To get a clear picture of a system, it's important to be honest and objective. Sometimes it's helpful to bring in an outsider to assess the system, as they may spot things we might overlook due to personal attachment.

Context

Data on its own doesn't mean much without the context to give it meaning. Understanding past performance and future projections helps us make sense of current measurements and informs us about whether a system is functioning well or needs adjustment.

Sampling and Margin of Error

When analyzing systems, we often rely on sampling—using a small part of the output to represent the whole. We must ensure our sample is random to avoid bias, and keep in mind that every sample comes with a margin of error, showing how much the sample might differ from the entire system. The more samples we take, the smaller that margin of error becomes.

Ratios and Correlation

Ratios, like Return on Investment (ROI), help us compare different variables. They give us a clear picture of how different aspects of a system relate to one another. Similarly, correlation shows when two variables are related, but we must remember: correlation does not imply causation.

How to Improve Systems

Once we've analyzed a system, it's time to look at ways to improve it. Optimization isn't about drastic overhauls—it's about incremental, thoughtful adjustments that create meaningful improvement over time.

Intervention Bias

It's human nature to want to make changes to feel like we're in control. But before jumping in to "fix" something, it's wise to consider what might happen if we did nothing at all. Often, unnecessary changes only add complexity without solving the root issue.

Optimization and Refactoring

When optimizing a system, it's best to focus on one variable at a time. Trying to change too many things at once can lead to confusion—we won't know what caused the improvement (or failure). By adjusting a single variable, we can track the direct impact of that change and make clearer decisions moving forward.

In some cases, we might also want to "refactor" the system—rearranging the process to make it more efficient while still achieving the same result. For example, a programmer might reduce the number of lines of code to make a program run faster.

The Critical Few

The Pareto Principle teaches us that 20% of our input produces 80% of the output. By identifying the few critical inputs that create the most significant results, we can focus our efforts where they matter most and see substantial improvements.

Diminishing Returns

After a certain point, more effort stops yielding more results. This is the law of diminishing returns. Instead of aiming for perfection, we should aim to get 85% of the problem right and then move on to other tasks.

Removing Friction

Friction is anything that slows down a process or makes it more difficult. By removing friction, we increase efficiency. Amazon Prime is a great example of a system designed to remove friction—its simplicity makes purchasing easy, which is a major reason customers keep coming back.

Automation

Automating a system can be a powerful way to increase efficiency, but we should be mindful that automation magnifies both strengths and weaknesses. We must ensure a system is running smoothly before introducing automation, or we risk automating inefficiencies.

Checklists and SOPs

Checklists help us complete complex tasks without missing critical steps. A simple checklist can be the difference between a job done perfectly and one riddled with mistakes. Standard Operating Procedures (SOPs) also ensure that everyone involved follows the same process, keeping things consistent and efficient.

Cessation and Resilience

Sometimes, the best way to improve a system is to stop certain processes altogether. After testing a hypothesis and weighing the outcomes, we may find that cessation is the best course of action.

Resilience is also crucial—systems should be built to withstand change and unpredictability. Stress testing, which involves pushing the system to its limits, can help us identify vulnerabilities and make the necessary improvements to strengthen the system.

Experimentation

Finally, frequent experimentation is key to ongoing improvement. By experimenting with different variables, we gain new insights and can continue optimizing over time. Think of it as playful trial and error—a way to keep learning and refining.

SYSTEMS ARE at the heart of everything we do. When we learn how to analyze and improve them, we not only fix what's broken but also set the stage for sustained growth and success. Whether we're looking at our personal habits, a business process, or even relationships, understanding the components and optimizing them step-by-step is the pathway to lasting change.

Continuous experimentation and learning are essential to keeping any system running smoothly. By applying these principles, we can ensure our systems serve us better, making life more efficient and, ultimately, more fulfilling.

CREATING SYSTEMS
SIMPLIFYING OUR LIVES

"Systematize Everything, and Find Peace" - Brandon Turner (*The Book on Rental Property Investing*)

Why Create Systems?

Most of us set goals with good intentions, but we often find ourselves losing momentum due to decision fatigue and inefficiency. This is where systems come in. Goals are great for setting direction, but sustainable results come from systems.

When we focus on goals alone, we're forced to make a series of choices that require constant attention and energy. These repeated decisions can be exhausting, even when we've accomplished similar goals before. Creating systems simplifies this process, making it easier to handle regular tasks and maintain progress.

Systems allow us to make fewer decisions and free up valuable energy for other things. Similar to time, our energy is limited and nonrenewable, so conserving it by using systems can have virtually infinite returns. Systems increase efficiency, making success less about willpower and more about consistent action.

Why Systems Over Goals?

While goals are important, they often depend too heavily on motivation, which can fluctuate. Systems, on the other hand, create habits that turn progress into something automatic, regardless of how we feel on any given day. Systems build discipline into our lives and make success inevitable.

Think of it this way: goals give us direction, but systems build the road that takes us there. Without systems, we can easily get lost, distracted, or overwhelmed along the way.

How to Create Systems

"If you want to build a system that works, the best approach is to build a simple system that meets the environment's current selection tests first, then improve it over time. Over time, you'll build a complex system that works." - Josh Kaufman (*The Personal MBA*)

Creating a system doesn't have to be complicated. In fact, the best way to start is by building a simple system and adding complexity as needed. Attempting to create something too elaborate from the beginning often leads to failure.

Here's a simple approach we can follow:

1. *Identify the task* we want to systematize.
2. *Break it into steps* and perform it at least once to understand the process.
3. *List each step* and look for areas of improvement.
4. *Create a simple checklist* or routine to follow each time.
5. *Test and refine* the system over time.

The goal is to make the task easier every time we repeat it. Once we understand the steps, we can improve them to make the system efficient. But remember, systems are rarely perfect right away—

they need testing and adjustment through experimentation. The key is to make small improvements over time, just like building a habit.

Signs of an Effective System

A truly effective system has several key qualities:

- *Fulfills its functionality:* It does what it's supposed to do.
- *Has solid infrastructure:* It's organized and easy to maintain.
- *Connects well with other systems:* It integrates seamlessly with other parts of our life.
- *Is versatile and adaptable:* It can adjust to changes over time.
- *Is reliable:* It consistently produces results.
- *Offers long-term benefits:* The benefits far exceed the initial investment.

While not all systems need to meet every one of these criteria, these qualities are the mark of a great system that's built to last.

Checklists: Simple but Effective Systems

Checklists are one of the simplest forms of systems, but they're also incredibly effective. In *The Checklist Manifesto*, Dr. Atul Gawande shows that checklists can outperform even highly trained professionals' instincts in high-stakes environments.

- *Normal and Non-Normal Checklists:* Normal checklists are for everyday situations, while non-normal checklists are used for emergencies or unusual circumstances.
- *Two Types of Checklists: Do-confirm* lists are used to double-check tasks. We do something, then confirm we

did it. While *read-do* lists guide us step-by-step, like a recipe. We read what to do, then do it.

Effective checklists are specific, concise, and user-friendly, reminding us of crucial steps without unnecessary details. A well-designed checklist clarifies priorities, making even complex processes easier to manage. However, checklists with too many steps can be more trouble than they're worth so be sure to focus on the critical few.

A Few Systematic Principles

The Matthew Effect

"For to everyone who has will more be given, and he will have abundance; but from him who has not, even what he has will be taken away." - Gospel of Matthew (25:29)

Success breeds success, and failure breeds failure. This principle reminds us that actions compound over time, whether positive or negative. When creating systems, small wins can lead to exponential growth in the long run.

Pareto Principle (The 80/20 Rule)

Eighty percent of a system's output comes from twenty percent of its input. Focusing on this critical input maximizes time and effort. When building systems, identifying and optimizing these critical few tasks will help us achieve the majority of our results with minimal effort.

Parkinson's Law

Work expands to fill the time allotted for it. This principle teaches us that when we give ourselves less time to complete a task, we tend to get it done faster. When creating systems, setting finite deadlines can help us stay efficient and avoid unnecessary delays. The same applies to other resources—allocating less can often lead to more creative and effective solutions.

The Best Systems Are the Ones That Work

Ultimately, the best system is the one that motivates us to take action. Whether it's a study routine, a workout plan, or a daily schedule, systems should be simple, effective, and tailored to our needs. Over time, we can adjust and refine these systems to ensure they continue to serve us well.

Creating systems is about making life easier and more productive. Start small, experiment, and refine. Simplifying processes frees us from decision fatigue, conserves energy, and increases our chances of success. The journey of building systems is one of continuous improvement—and that's what makes it so powerful.

So, what part of our lives can we simplify with a system today? Pick one small area—whether it's meal prep, our morning routine, or our exercise plan—and create a simple system that we can refine over time. With each experiment, we'll move closer to a life that runs more smoothly and efficiently, with less effort.

By FOCUSING ON SYSTEMS, not just goals, we can achieve more with less energy and avoid burnout. Systems make success repeatable and sustainable, freeing us from relying on fleeting motivation. We can begin with something simple and build from there—experiment, adjust, and enjoy the peace that systems bring into our lives.

WINNING OVER TEACHERS
BUILDING POSITIVE RELATIONSHIPS AND GETTING THE HELP WE NEED

"People prefer to say yes to those they know and like." - Robert Cialdini (*Influence*)

Teachers Are People Too

Have we ever wondered how to get our teachers or professors to say yes to our requests? Maybe we need an extension, extra help, or a letter of recommendation, but asking can feel a bit intimidating. The good news is, teachers are human too, and they respond well to many of the same things that motivate all of us.

In my years as a teacher, I've learned that building relationships and approaching requests thoughtfully can go a long way. So, how can we make our requests more likely to be met with a yes?

Ways to Get Professors/Teachers to Say Yes to Our Requests

Reciprocity

We've all experienced how doing something kind for someone often results in kindness returned. This is reciprocity at work—when we do something nice, people tend to respond in kind. For teachers, this could mean offering help when they need it, showing appreciation for their effort, or even engaging in class discussions. These small gestures can set the stage for a positive interaction when we need their support later.

Commonality/Authority

We tend to agree with people who we feel understand us or know what they're talking about. Finding common ground with our teacher, whether it's sharing a similar interest in the subject or simply showing respect for their expertise, can go a long way. When a teacher feels that we appreciate their knowledge, they're more likely to be inclined to help when we ask for it.

Commitment and Consistency

People are creatures of habit. Once someone says yes to a request, they're more likely to say yes again in the future. If a teacher has helped us in the past, like reviewing a draft or answering a question after class, they're more likely to do it again—especially if we followed through on their advice the first time.

Building a Good Relationship with Our Teacher

The best way to ensure that our requests are met with a yes is to build a positive relationship with our teachers or professors. Teachers are trained to connect with students, but that relationship goes both ways. When we take initiative and engage meaningfully, the classroom experience becomes more rewarding for everyone. As a teacher, I always appreciate when students introduce themselves, actively participate, and show genuine interest in their learning.

Introduce Ourselves

A simple introduction can help us stand out. After the first class, let's take a moment to say hello, tell our teacher a bit about ourselves, and share why we're interested in the subject or what we hope to learn. A friendly introduction can lay the foundation for future positive interactions.

Speak Up

Participating in class isn't just about getting good grades—it's about showing that we care. Teachers appreciate students who ask questions, share thoughts, or contribute to discussions. It makes us more than just another face in the crowd, and when the time comes for something like a recommendation letter, it's much easier for teachers to write one if they know us well.

TEACHERS, like anyone else, respond to kindness, respect, and genuine connection. By practicing reciprocity, finding common ground, and showing commitment, we can make our requests stand out. But it all starts with building that authentic relationship—introducing ourselves, speaking up, and showing that we're invested in the learning process. Not only does this increase the chances of getting a "yes," but it also creates a more enjoyable, supportive learning environment for everyone. After our next class, take a moment to introduce ourselves to the teacher or contribute to the discussion with a thoughtful question. Small actions like these can lead to big rewards.

APPROACHING TEACHERS FOR HELP
GETTING THE MOST FROM OUR EDUCATORS

Have we ever been too nervous to ask for help, even when we're stuck on something important? We're not alone. Knowing how to ask for help is essential when learning something new, and it can be the key to success in our academic journey. Here's a guide to help us make the most of our time with our professors and teachers:

1. Identify What We Don't Understand

Before approaching our teacher, it's important to reflect on what specifically is causing confusion. This is called identifying our knowledge gap. For instance, if we're working on a math problem and don't understand why a particular equation is used, we should jot down the steps we do understand and highlight the part that doesn't make sense. The more specific we are, the easier it is for our teacher to help us.

Try the Feynman Technique. If we can explain a concept simply to someone else, we're on the right track. If not, we've identified a gap in our understanding.

2. The 15-Minute Rule

Before asking for help, we should spend at least 15 minutes trying to solve the problem on our own. During that time, it's helpful to write down everything we've attempted. This not only helps us engage more deeply with the material but also shows our teacher exactly where we're struggling.

Let's say we're stuck on a chemistry problem. After 15 minutes of reviewing our notes and re-reading the problem, we still can't solve it. Now, when we ask our professor, we can say, "I tried reviewing the lecture notes and checked examples in the textbook, but I'm not seeing how this reaction leads to the product."

3. Don't Be Afraid to Ask Questions

We've all heard the saying "there's no such thing as a stupid question," but asking can still feel intimidating. It's okay to feel embarrassed—what's important is that we overcome that feeling. The regret of not understanding the material is often worse than the fleeting discomfort of asking a question.

I remember sitting in a huge lecture hall during my freshman year of college. I was confused, but too shy to ask for clarification. Later, when I tried the assignment, I regretted not raising my hand. That one moment of hesitation cost me hours of frustration.

4. Be Respectful and Professional

When we seek help, it's always best to be polite and professional. Address our educators using the correct titles such as "Professor" or "Dr." if appropriate, and express our gratitude for their time. This act of respect fosters positive relationships and smoother future interactions.

5. Take Advantage of Office Hours and Appointments

We shouldn't wait until the last minute to seek help. Professors hold office hours specifically to assist students, so we should take advantage of this time. If our schedule conflicts with their office hours, we can always ask to set up a separate meeting. Being proactive shows that we care about our learning and respect their time.

6. Come Prepared

Whenever we ask for help, it's important to come prepared. This means bringing any relevant materials—our notes, textbooks, and any work we've done on the problem so far. Preparation makes it easier for our teacher to assist us effectively.

7. Follow Up After We Get Help

After we receive help, we should take the time to review what we've learned and try to apply it. If we're still confused, it's okay to ask for clarification again. Learning is an ongoing process, and asking for help more than once is part of that process.

8. Use Multiple Resources

If we're still struggling, it can be helpful to explore other resources like study groups, tutoring centers, or online forums. Different perspectives can often make complex topics easier to understand.

9. Embrace a Growth Mindset

We shouldn't be discouraged by setbacks. Mistakes are part of the learning process, and with perseverance, we'll improve. Believing in our ability to learn and grow helps us face challenges as opportunities to improve rather than as roadblocks.

. . .

WHEN WE APPLY THESE STRATEGIES, we can approach our professors and teachers for help in a way that maximizes our chances of success. The next time we feel stuck, we should remember that asking for help is not a sign of weakness—it's a powerful step toward mastering the material. So let's embrace our confusion, ask the right questions, and take control of our learning journey. Our future selves will thank us.

EFFECTIVE WRITTEN & VERBAL COMMUNICATION
THE SOURCE OF SOUND THINKING & THE IMPORTANCE OF ITERATIONS

"If you can think, speak, and write, you are absolutely deadly. Nothing can get in your way. That's why you learn to write. It's not to put your thoughts down on paper. It's to reorient your mind, and when you're articulate, you can navigate the world. You can think things through, communicate, and persuade. Writing makes you precise, and precision in thought and speech is everything." - Jordan Peterson

Reading and Writing: Two Sides of the Same Coin

Ever notice how reading a powerful story can spark the desire to write something of our own? That's because reading and writing are deeply intertwined, like two sides of the same coin. Reading absorbs ideas; writing refines and expresses them. Think of reading as the input of verbal communication and writing as the output. Critical reading requires sifting through information to retain only what's essential. The challenge lies in discerning what's important, which demands attention, awareness, and existing knowledge.

Verbal communication—the use of words to convey meaning—

is a cornerstone of human interaction. Whether spoken or written, it's more than just exchanging information. Effective communication requires us to articulate clearly, listen actively, strike the right tone, and always consider our audience.

Why Writing Matters

Writing isn't just about putting words on paper; it's a sophisticated form of thinking. When we write, we give structure to our thoughts, allowing us to perceive the world more clearly and make wiser decisions. Without this level of thought, especially with difficult issues, we run the risk of making mistakes that could harm us or others. By writing about important matters, we understand the causes of potential harm and reshape our thinking to avoid it.

In essence, writing is thinking. If we struggle to write well, it's likely because our thoughts aren't yet fully developed. The act of writing forces us to refine and organize our ideas, making abstract concepts more tangible. In this way, we grow as thinkers.

Navigating Two Worlds: Tangible and Intangible

We exist in two worlds simultaneously: the tangible world and the world of words. The tangible world, explained by the hard sciences, is the physical reality we interact with daily—gravity pulling us down, the sharpness of a knife, the heat of the sun. These are undeniable forces that shape and influence our lives in obvious ways. But equally important, and perhaps less obvious, is the world of words. Words shape how we perceive, think, and act within that physical world.

For example, let's take the difference between teachers and students. On a molecular level, teachers are no different from students. Perhaps they have shorter telomeres, degrees, and credentials, but they are no different on a molecular level. What makes teachers different from students, is the language. The word teacher lets everyone know how that person will act in that situation, they may take attendance, give a lecture, but they aren't going to sit down and wait for instruction. Students, on the other hand, are no different from the teachers on a molecular level. What makes them different is the label, the word. So when a student walks in a classroom, they know that they will sit at a student desk and learn from the teacher.

Similarly, in the relationship between a boyfriend and girl-friend. If a friend told you that they just went on a date with someone else, we would be happy for them. If our girlfriend told us they just went on a date with someone else, we wouldn't be so happy. Words define relationships, resolve conflicts, and build emotional bonds. They give shape to the intangible aspects of our interactions, coloring the world we live in.

In both examples, the tangible world influences us, but words help us shape, navigate, and interpret that world.

When we are effective writers, we can more precisely craft our world around us. We can change how people act and how the world forms around us. The pen is indeed mightier than the sword.

Tips for Writing Effectively

So writing is thinking and it controls our existence. So how do we become better writers? This requires consistent practice and close attention to our word choices. Here are a few practical tips:

- *Be Specific:* Use precise, specific language rather than vague or general terms. For instance, instead of writing, "The weather was bad," we might write, "Heavy, swirling clouds darkened the sky, and a bitter wind bit at exposed skin." Being more specific allows us to craft our world in a more precise manner.
- *Identify Value:* As we read articles or books, we can note the words that carry the most value. What phrases stand out? Why did the author choose those words? By analyzing language in this way, we sharpen our own word choices.

- *Rewrite, Then Rewrite Again:* No one's first draft is perfect. Writing is rewriting, and every revision sharpens our message. The point of a first draft is to get something written, not to get it right. We get things right in future iterations of the piece.
- *Be Mindful of Everyday Speech:* The words we use in daily conversations should be clear and intentional. The language we use every day has the most impact in our lives because that is how we will perceive the world. Do our words capture our message accurately?

How to Be a Better Editor

Once we've written our thoughts down, the real work begins: editing. This process is crucial and often more important than the initial writing. This is when we get things right. This is where we accurately capture the world around us. Editing allows us to view our work with fresh eyes, ensuring our message is as clear as possible.

Here are some strategies to help us become better editors:

- *Take a Break:* Stepping away from our piece for 24-48 hours gives us a fresh perspective when we return to it.
- *Change the Format:* Altering the font, color, or size can help us see the text differently, which can make errors stand out.
- *Vary Sentence Length:* Just as Gary Provost beautifully demonstrates below, variation in sentence length creates rhythm and flow. Short sentences convey urgency. Longer sentences build momentum and intensity.
- *Disassociate from Our Ideas:* It's important not to be overly attached to our writing. By treating our words as if they were written by someone else, we can be more objective in our editing. We are not our words, but our words can become us.

Writing has a rhythm that can either lull the reader into monotony or draw them in with energy and variation.

"This sentence has five words. Here are five more words. Five-word sentences are fine. But several together become monotonous. Listen to what is happening. The writing is getting boring. The sound of it drones. It's like a stuck record. The ear demands some variety. Now listen. I vary the sentence length, and I create music. Music. The writing sings. It has a pleasant rhythm, a lilt, a harmony. I use short sentences. And I use sentences of medium length. And sometimes, when I am certain the reader is rested, I will engage him with a sentence of considerable length, a sentence that burns with energy and builds with all the impetus of a crescendo, the roll of the drums, the crash of the cymbals–sounds that say listen to this, it is important." - Gary Provost (*100 Ways to Improve Your Writing*)

Expanding Our Vocabulary

Expanding our vocabulary isn't just about learning new words—it's about expanding our thinking, understanding, and perceptions. When we have the right words to describe our emotions or experiences, they lose some of their hold on us. We gain clarity and the ability to express ourselves more fully, which also helps us understand others more deeply.

The more words we know, the better we control our emotions. For example, when toddlers don't have words for certain feelings or situations, they scream and act out what they are feeling. The same is true for adults that do not have a strong vocabulary. Expanded vocabulary keeps our irrationality in check. It also gives us a wider net, so to speak, to capture and understand the world around us. Additionally, when we have an expanded vocabulary, we can also more intentionally craft the world around us with higher precision allowing us to live more of the life we choose.

A fun way to practice this is by playing a mental game while driving. We can pick an object—say, a tree—and think of as many synonyms or descriptions as we can before passing it. By challenging our minds in this way, we naturally expand our language skills.

Overcoming Communication Barriers

Effective communication goes beyond simply having the right words in the right order. We must also be aware of potential barriers, such as cultural differences, language limitations, and emotional obstacles. Recognizing these barriers allows us to adjust our language so that our message is clearer and more easily understood.

To avoid miscommunication, it's essential to know our audience. Who are we speaking or writing to? Understanding this shapes everything from word choice to tone and delivery. The responsibility of clarity falls on us as communicators, not the recipient. If our audience doesn't understand us, it's on us to adjust, simplify, or explain differently.

Meaning, who ever is communicating is responsible for the other people to understand. Of course, there are people who do not listen, but when we take on this perspective, we can fine tune our communication abilities to speak to all people at all levels of understanding. The more competent we are, the more simply we can explain something.

The Role of Feedback

Feedback is essential in refining our communication skills. It tells us if our message is landing as intended. Feedback isn't about being "good" or "bad"—it's about clarity. Sometimes, when we identify too closely with our ideas, it's easy to shut down to feedback. But if we keep an open mind, feedback becomes an opportunity to sharpen our message and make it more accessible to others.

Consistency and Depth in Writing

As we continue to write, David Perell suggests that our focus should evolve. Initially, consistency is key—we need to develop the habit of writing regularly. But as we gain more experience, the emphasis shifts toward depth. At this stage, it's less about writing every day and more about refining and publishing only our best ideas, especially those that will stand the test of time.

Depth comes from consistent practice and sound judgment, but the road to depth is paved with consistency.

MASTERING WRITTEN and verbal communication is essential for personal and professional success. Writing is the highest form of thinking, and sound thinking only emerges from sound writing. Writing also determines what we can understand, perceive, and experience by shaping the intangible world around us. By understanding the intimate connection between reading and writing, expanding our vocabulary, and refining both our writing and editing skills, we can communicate our ideas more clearly and persuasively. Communication isn't just about exchanging information; it's about ensuring our message is understood and resonates with our audience. As we continue to improve our communication, we'll find ourselves building stronger connections and achieving our goals more effectively.

ESSENTIAL STUDY TOOLS & APPS
A PHILOSOPHY ON INVESTING IN TOOLS

Spend Wisely on Daily Essentials

Our daily habits shape a significant part of our lives, and so do the tools we rely on. That's why investing in high-quality items for the things we use every day is more than just a smart choice—it's a way to enhance our well-being. Whether it's a sturdy backpack for long school days or reliable tech, these essentials aren't just conveniences; they help us stay focused and improve our overall quality of life.

In a world where we're constantly bombarded with new products and upgrades, knowing when to invest and when to hold off is crucial. Spending wisely isn't just about managing money—it's about making intentional decisions that support the lives we want to live.

New Purchases vs. Upgrades

When we think about our spending, it's easy to get caught up in upgrades. The newest version of something can feel exciting, but I've found that new purchases often bring more value than constant upgrades. By waiting until something is genuinely falling apart before upgrading, we get the most out of the items we already have. This not only helps us save money but also teaches us to appreciate the longevity of our possessions.

Avoiding Gear Acquisition Syndrome (G.A.S.)

We've all been there—believing that if we just had better gear, we'd be able to perform better. This is the essence of Gear Acquisition Syndrome (G.A.S.). While sometimes new tools can help, most of the time, we can solve about 95% of our problems with what we already have. Recognizing the difference between a true need for new equipment and a desire to upgrade for the sake of it is important in managing our finances and staying focused on our goals.

Learning on a Budget

During college, I didn't have much money to spend on fancy supplies. I remember sticking to the bare necessities: a five-subject notebook, a few pencils, and a scientific calculator. Even though it seemed minimal, this approach worked because the goal of learning isn't about showing off with the best gear—it's about getting the ideas into our heads. If I had to go back to school today, I'd likely stick to the same essentials, though I'd add flashcards into the mix for better active recall.

This minimalistic mindset allowed us to focus on what truly matters in learning, and it's a strategy that still applies. We don't need flashy gear to learn effectively.

Invest in a Good Backpack

One thing I've learned over time is that investing in a quality backpack can make a big difference. I once relied on cheap bags, and the strain they caused, combined with wear and tear, made school days unnecessarily difficult. When I finally invested in a well-made backpack, everything improved—my posture, my comfort, and even my mindset throughout the day.

For those of us who still rely on notebooks, a five-subject one works well. And for those who can afford to go digital, investing in a tablet with note-taking apps can streamline our learning experience even further.

15 Things in Every College Student's Backpack

Creating a checklist for what to carry with us in our backpacks can save us a lot of headaches. While I believe that the essentials—a backpack, notebook, pencils, and a calculator—are often enough, having a few other items handy can make college life smoother. Here's a list of useful things I've noticed many college students carry:

- Laptop
- Pens and Pencils
- Notebooks or Binders
- Scientific Calculator
- Textbooks
- Laptop Charger
- Phone Charger
- Headphones or Earbuds
- Tissues
- Chapstick
- First Aid Kit
- Mints or Gum
- Pocket Notebook
- Reusable Water Bottle
- Healthy Snacks

Noteworthy Apps & Services

In today's digital world, apps play a crucial role in how we learn and manage our academic lives. Over time, we've found several that work well for both students and educators alike. To future-proof this advice, it's important to remember that it's not the specific app that matters, but the function it serves. While some of these apps may eventually be replaced by new ones, it's the purpose of the tool that we should focus on when looking for alternatives.

Here are some of the most useful ones that I found. The apps with an asterisk are what I find the most useful in my life:

- *Notability* - best for handwritten note-taking on a tablet
- *Anki & plugins* - for active recall and spaced repetition
- *Streaks* - habit tracker for building consistency
- *Forest* - gamifies focus to help us stay productive
- *Google Calendar* - essential for scheduling
- *OneNote/Evernote* - versatile note-taking apps
- *Google Drive* - for file storage
- *Apple Notes* - simple but effective for quick notes
- *Apple Reminders* - great for task management
- *ChatGPT* - large language model
- *Google Docs/Sheets/Slides/Forms* - useful for writing, spreadsheets, presentations, and data collection
- *Adobe Scan* - pocket scanner for creating PDFs
- *Chegg* - textbook rentals and answer guides
- *Quizlet* - great for building active recall question banks
- *Khan Academy* - educational videos on almost any subject
- *Interfolio* - academic portfolio management
- *Desmos* or *Wolfram Alpha* - for online scientific calculations
- *Zoom* - web video calls for online classes
- *Google Classroom* - content management for schoolwork

- *Notion* - database manager for organizing notes and tasks

SPENDING WISELY on daily essentials is about more than just saving money—it's about making choices that enhance our well-being and support our goals. By prioritizing new purchases over unnecessary upgrades, we can avoid falling into the trap of G.A.S. and focus on what truly matters. Learning doesn't require the fanciest tools— just the right mindset and a few essential items. When we invest in a good bag, minimizing our gear, and using helpful apps, we can build a lifestyle that supports both academic success and overall happiness.

HOW TO DO RESEARCH
IN 7 SIMPLE STEPS

"If you steal from one author, it's plagiarism; if you steal from many, it's research." - Wilson Mizner (American Playwright)

Why Research Matters

Research isn't just for students—it's a skill we use in everyday life. Whether we're deciding what car to buy, figuring out how to improve our health, or exploring a career change, strong research skills help us make informed decisions. In fact, mastering research is like developing a superpower: it allows us to turn any question into an answer, any problem into a solution. High school and even college often don't teach research skills well, but we can learn them with practice.

What Is Research?

"A research problem is simply the gap between what we know and what we need to know to solve a problem that we care about." -

Wayne C. Booth, Gregory G. Colomb, and Joseph M. Williams *(The Craft of Research)*

At its core, research is all about answering questions in pursuit of truth. We look for answers in books, academic papers, articles, and other sources. Once we've found the information, we often write an essay or give a presentation on what we've learned. Knowing how to do research not only helps us in school but also equips us to solve problems and make informed decisions throughout life.

Some people think research is only valid if it's done at elite universities, but that's not true. We can find valuable information anywhere by following a few simple rules. Relying solely on what prestigious institutions say would leave us waiting forever for consensus. Instead, we can seek answers from many sources and remain open to changing our perspectives if we discover we're wrong

Good research balances our perspective between dogma and skepticism. In the right amounts both are necessary, but when we lose this balance we find ourselves conflicting with reality and experience unnecessarily hardship.

The 7 Steps of the Research Process

Research becomes more manageable when we break it down into steps. Here are the seven main steps:

1. *Find a Topic*
2. *Refine Our Topic*
3. *Find Key Sources*
4. *Take Notes on Our Sources*
5. *Create Our Paper or Presentation*
6. *Do Additional Research (As Needed)*
7. *Cite Our Sources*

Let's go deeper with each step:

1. Find a Topic

We start by finding a clear topic. Without it, our research will be scattered and unorganized. A great way to find a topic is by creating a mind map:

- Take a large piece of paper and a pen.
- Draw an oval in the center and write a broad topic inside it.
- Draw lines from the oval to smaller ovals with more specific ideas.
- Repeat this until we have 3-5 good topic ideas.

For example, if we're interested in social media, we could branch out into ideas like "social media and mental health," "comparison culture," or "social media detoxes." From there, we choose the idea that seems most interesting or has the most potential sources.

We don't need to make a mind map in order to find a topic. We can find a topic simply by exploring what is interesting to us.

2. Refine The Topic

"Without a clear question, you won't know where to begin, and you will write in circles. With a question, you can read, experiment, and draft with a purpose." - Kate L. Turabian (*A Manual for Writers of Research Papers, Theses, and Dissertations*)

Once we have our ideas, it's time to narrow them down. Spend about 15 minutes researching each one using a library catalog, databases, or Google Scholar. We want a topic that has plenty of credible sources, like journal articles, books, or reliable websites. If one topic has more sources, that's a good sign. If we're unsure, asking a teacher or professor for guidance can help.

Typically, when we first explore ideas, they are general and not clearly defined. Through diving deeper into a topic, we can see the different nuances that exist and explore with more precision.

3. Find Key Sources

Now that we've refined our topic, we'll likely have a lot of sources to choose from. To avoid feeling overwhelmed, focus on 3-5 key sources. These should provide a variety of perspectives and help us dive deeper into the topic. As we're selecting sources, it's important to think critically: who wrote this? What's their agenda? Is the information up-to-date? Where did they get their information? Choosing high-quality sources will set a strong foundation for our research.

4. Read and Take Notes

Once we have our sources, it's time to read actively. This means skimming the material first, then diving in deeper, writing down questions, and underlining key ideas. Taking breaks to rest our minds can help us focus better, and we should summarize our notes in a program like Apple Notes or Notion to keep things organized.

For books, we don't need to read cover to cover—focusing on relevant chapters will save time. Check the bibliography of any source for more potential reading materials.

5. Create the Paper or Presentation

It's easy to fall into the trap of endlessly researching, but at some point, we have to stop gathering information and start writing. The role of good research is so other people can learn what we learned. This is usually accomplished through a presentation of some kind. In my case, my presentation is this book. This book is an attempt to communicate my own research done with learning and education.

A good rule of thumb is to spend about 30 minutes of research per page of the final paper. So, if we're writing a 10-page paper, we should spend roughly five hours researching. This guideline helps avoid procrastination and keeps us from getting stuck in the "I don't know enough yet" phase.

If we only started writing when we knew everything, we'd never get anything done.

6. Do Additional Research (As Needed)

As we write, we might find that we're missing some information or need clarification on a particular point. That's okay! I know this happened countless times while writing this book. We can take note of what we need, continue writing, and do a quick follow-up on those details later. The key is to stay focused on our topic and not get sidetracked by unrelated ideas.

7. Cite Sources

"To make an impact as a writer, you need to do more than make statements of your own position. You must also present those statements as a response to what others have said." - Gerald Graff and Cathy Birkenstein *(They Say / I Say)*

Citing sources is essential to avoid plagiarism and give credit to the authors whose work helped us. Tools like Zotero can be lifesavers, tracking our references and generating citations in the correct format. With just a click, Zotero can create a full bibliography, saving us tons of time at the end of the project.

Critically Analyzing Studies

To take our research to the next level, we also need to know how to evaluate the quality of the studies we come across. Peter Attia's

Studying Studies series offers practical and effective frameworks for critically assessing scientific studies.

Not All Studies Are Equal

The type of study—whether it's observational or a randomized controlled trial (RCT)—matters. Observational studies can show associations (e.g., people who drink coffee might have lower rates of heart disease), but they don't prove cause and effect. RCTs are the gold standard because they directly test cause-and-effect relationships under controlled conditions.

Prioritize RCTs when possible, but be cautious with studies that only show correlations.

Watch for Confounders

Confounding variables are factors that can affect the results without being considered. For example, if a study shows that people who exercise more live longer, but doesn't account for other factors like diet, the results could be misleading. We need to be aware of these confounders when interpreting studies.

Always ask if the study accounted for other possible influences on the results.

Absolute vs. Relative Risk

Many studies report relative risk to make findings sound more dramatic, but it can be misleading. For example, if a diet reduces heart disease risk by 50%, but the original risk was only 2%, the new risk is still 1%—a small absolute change.

Look for both absolute and relative risk when interpreting a study's findings.

The Importance of Sample Size

A study's sample size (how many participants it had) is crucial for reliable results. Studies with small sample sizes can produce inaccurate results due to a lack of statistical power. Larger sample sizes generally lead to more reliable findings.

Publication Bias and the File Drawer Problem

Publication bias is where only studies with positive or interesting results get published, while studies with negative or inconclusive results are often left out. This creates an incomplete picture of reality.

Be mindful that not all studies—especially those with less exciting results—make it into the public eye.

RESEARCH IS a powerful tool that helps us answer questions and solve problems, whether we're working on a school project or making important life decisions. By following a simple process and critically evaluating the quality of the information we gather, we can turn our research into something valuable and insightful. Each time we practice these skills, we build a stronger foundation for the future. So let's dive into our topics, trust our research process, and make informed choices that will benefit us long after the project is done.

BOOK REFERENCES & RECOMMENDATIONS
FOR NAVIGATING ACADEMIC SUCESS

"It's not about the book, it's about the book the book leads you to."
- Austin Kleon (*Steal Like an Artist*)

Book References & Recommendations

The Anatomy of a Class: Syllabus Mastery, Time Management, and Academic Success

- **"The Checklist Manifesto"** by Atul Gawande
- **"Essentialism"** by Greg McKeown
- **"Atomic Habits"** by James Clear
- **"Getting Things Done"** by David Allen
- **"Deep Work"** by Cal Newport

How to Act In Class: Classroom Etiquette and Engagement

- **"Atomic Habits"** by James Clear
- **"Mindset"** by Carol S. Dweck

- **"How to Win Friends and Influence People"** by Dale Carnegie
- **"The Power of Habit"** by Charles Duhigg
- **"Thinking, Fast and Slow"** by Daniel Kahneman
- **"Grit"** by Angela Duckworth
- **"The Art of Learning"** by Josh Waitzkin
- **"The 7 Habits of Highly Effective People"** by Stephen R. Covey
- **"Deep Work"** by Cal Newport
- **"The One Thing"** by Gary Keller

Organizational Frameworks: Working Smarter, Not Harder

- **"The Checklist Manifesto"** by Atul Gawande
- **"Atomic Habits"** by James Clear
- **"Getting Things Done"** by David Allen
- **"Essentialism"** by Greg McKeown
- **"The 4-Hour Workweek"** by Tim Ferriss

The Magic of Scheduling: How to Take Control of Our Time and Life

- **"Atomic Habits"** by James Clear
- **"Getting Things Done"** by David Allen
- **"The 4-Hour Workweek"** by Tim Ferriss
- **"12 Rules for Life"** by Jordan Peterson
- **"Deep Work"** by Cal Newport
- **"The One Thing"** by Gary Keller and Jay Papasan

Setting Healthy Boundaries: Creating Space for What Truly Matters

- **"Boundaries"** by Dr. Henry Cloud and Dr. John Townsend
- **"Essentialism"** by Greg McKeown

- "The Power of No" by James Altucher and Claudia Azula Altucher
- "The Courage to be Disliked" by Ichiro Kishimi and Fumitake Koga
- "Daring Greatly" by Brené Brown
- "The Subtle Art of Not Giving a F*ck" by Mark Manson
- "The 5 Second Rule" by Mel Robbins

Basics of Systems: Galls' Law & Components of Systems

- "The Personal MBA" by Josh Kaufman
- "The Systems Bible" by John Gall
- Analyzing and Improving Systems: Examining Existing Systems
- "The Personal MBA" by Josh Kaufman
- "The Book on Rental Property Investing" by Brandon Turner

Creating Systems: Simplifying Our Lives

- "The Book on Rental Property Investing" by Brandon Turner
- "The Personal MBA" by Josh Kaufman
- "The Checklist Manifesto" by Dr. Atul Gawande
- "Gospel of Matthew" from the New Testament in the Bible

Winning Over Teachers: Building Positive Relationships and Getting the Help We Need

- "Influence" by Robert Cialdini
- "How to Win Friends and Influence People" by Dale Carnegie
- "The Art of Asking" by Amanda Palmer
- "Drive" by Daniel H. Pink

- **"The Like Switch"** by Jack Schafer
- **"Made to Stick"** by Chip Heath and Dan Heath

Approaching Teachers for Help: Getting the Most from Our Educators

- **"The Feynman Technique"** by Richard Feynman
- **"Mindset: The New Psychology of Success"** by Carol S. Dweck
- **"The Art of Asking"** by Amanda Palmer

Effective Written & Verbal Communication: The Source of Sound Thinking & The Importance of Iterations

- **"12 Rules for Life"** by Jordan Peterson
- **"The Personal MBA"** by Josh Kaufman
- **"100 Ways to Improve Your Writing"** by Gary Provost
- **"The Elements of Style"** by William Strunk Jr. and E.B. White
- **"On Writing Well"** by William Zinsser
- **"The War of Art"** by Steven Pressfield

Essential Study Tools & Apps: A Philosophy on Investing in Tools

- **"The Life-Changing Magic of Tidying Up"** by Marie Kondo
- **"Atomic Habits"** by James Clear
- **"Digital Minimalism"** by Cal Newport
- **"The Power of Habit"** by Charles Duhigg
- **"Essentialism"** by Greg McKeown

How to Do Research: In 7 Simple Steps

- **"How to Write a Lot"** by Paul J. Silvia

- **"The Craft of Research"** by Wayne C. Booth, Gregory G. Colomb, and Joseph M. Williams
- **"They Say / I Say"** by Gerald Graff and Cathy Birkenstein
- **"A Manual for Writers of Research Papers, Theses, and Dissertations"** by Kate L. Turabian
- **"Zotero: A Guide for Librarians, Researchers, and Educators"** by Jason Puckett
- **"Studying Studies"** by Peter Attia (series of blog posts)

6

INTEGRATIVE GROWTH

PERSONAL AND BEYOND

WHY READING MATTERS
HOW READING CAN CHANGE LIVES

The Power of Reading

Imagine having access to the thoughts and experiences of the greatest minds throughout history—reading gives us that access. It's a superpower that helps us learn, grow, and see the world through others' eyes. But, like all skills, it takes time and effort to enjoy its rewards. Before we can get lost in a great book or absorb life-changing lessons from someone else's story, we need to learn how to read in a way that opens up our minds.

My Journey with Reading

I didn't always love reading. In middle school, I struggled with comprehension tests and often felt like I was missing something everyone else seemed to grasp. Although I enjoyed reading as a child, I avoided it as much as possible by the time I was a teenager. It felt as though the world of words was closing itself off to me. This avoidance made me miss out on a lot, and for years, I convinced myself that my life experiences were enough.

It wasn't until after college that I realized just how crucial reading is. I started to see that books offered access to a vast range of perspectives and insights, far beyond what I could learn from my own life alone. Reading became a way to live hundreds of lives, learning lessons from different people, places, and times—all without leaving home. It has since become the key to improving every part of my life—business, teaching, finance, and relationships. Reading has helped me grow both inside and out.

The Superpower of Reading

"The ability to learn faster than your competitors may be the only sustainable competitive advantage." - Eric Jorgensen (*The Naval Almanack*)

We live in an era with more information than ever before. According to Eric Schmidt, the former CEO of Google, more information is created in just a few days than in the entire history of civilization up until 2003. This makes our world incredibly competitive, and those who can keep up with the latest information have a clear advantage.

Studies show that those who read regularly tend to do better in life. Readers are more likely to secure better jobs, earn higher incomes, and access greater opportunities. Reading is like a workout for our brain—it keeps our mind active, improves memory, focus, and imagination. It also helps us understand other people's lives and experiences, making us more empathetic and aware of the world around us.

Challenges to Reading

Reading isn't always easy, and a few common challenges can slow us down or frustrate us:

- *Regression:* This happens when our eyes keep going back to reread the same line. It might feel like it helps us understand better, but it actually slows down our reading and disrupts comprehension. By practicing focus and keeping our eyes steady, we can reduce regression over time.
- *Outdated Skills:* Reading is a skill, and like any skill, it can be improved. Often, we think that reading well is something we should automatically know how to do, but it's a practice we need to refine. We don't need a high IQ to be good readers—we just need the right techniques and regular practice.
- *Subvocalization:* That little voice in our heads that reads along with us can slow us down. We all learned to read aloud as kids, and that habit can stick with us. But our brain can understand words much faster than we can speak them. Learning to read without relying on that inner voice can speed up our reading while improving comprehension.

Many of us read so slowly that we lose focus, and a bored mind struggles to stay engaged. The key is to train our brain to read with more concentration and focus.

Learning to Love Reading

The most important thing about reading is to enjoy it. The best way to build a reading habit is to start with what excites us.

> "Read what you love until you love to read." - Naval Ravikant

This piece of advice was a game-changer for me. Once I stopped forcing myself to read "important" books and focused on reading what genuinely interested me, reading became a joy, not a chore. Reading is not a race. The best books are meant to be savored, not rushed through. It's not about how many books we finish, but about the ideas and lessons we take from them. If we start a book and don't enjoy it, there's no harm in putting it down and moving on to something else. The goal is to keep learning, and sometimes that means skipping ahead to something more captivating.

Most people read very little—perhaps only a few minutes a day, if at all. But if we make reading a regular habit, even just for a few minutes each day, we'll be ahead of most. Over time, reading will become something we look forward to, opening up new worlds of knowledge and experience.

THE CALL TO ADVENTURE
A PATH WE ALL CAN TAKE

"It is only in our decisions that we are important." - Jean-Paul Sartre (*Being and Nothingness*)

There comes a time when we live in a world we know very well. Everything feels normal, familiar, and life goes on as it always has. But then, without warning, we hear a call—an invitation to go on an adventure. It might be as dramatic as Harry Potter discovering he's a wizard or as subtle as a growing curiosity about a new path in life. Like Neo in *The Matrix*, we stand at a crossroads: we can either take the red pill and leap into the unknown, or remain in the safety of our ordinary world.

The call to adventure, whether grand or small, challenges us to step beyond the comforts of what we know. But answering it isn't always easy. It demands courage, and it requires us to leave behind what's familiar. When we decide to take that leap, extraordinary things begin to happen. We meet guides and mentors—like Mr. Miyagi in *The Karate Kid*—who teach us new skills and help us face challenges we never thought we could handle. Along the way, we discover strength and abilities we didn't know we had. In fact, we often find powers deep within ourselves that were waiting to be unlocked.

Mentors, Growth, & Struggle

On every adventure, we meet people who help us along the way. Sometimes these mentors offer wisdom or teach us skills, but other times, they appear as experiences that shape and grow us. This is where we begin to change. We step into roles we weren't sure we could fill, and we learn to trust our instincts. But let's be honest— this journey is not all fun and games.

Look at Abraham, who left behind his country, his people, and even his father's household to follow a still, small voice calling him into the world. That voice didn't lead him to an easy life. He faced famine, war, and family problems. At times, Abraham likely questioned whether following the call was the right decision. After all, who would willingly choose to endure all that?

But it's in these struggles that we find our deepest growth. The call to adventure doesn't lead us toward ease or comfort. Instead, it brings us into conflict, into hardship, where we are forced to grow. Just like Abraham, we may doubt ourselves along the way. We may ask, "Why did I embark on this journey?" But the struggles and challenges are where the true meaning of the adventure is found.

Trials and Tribulations: The Crucible of Change

As we face obstacles, we begin to change. We learn, we grow, and we become stronger. This is the heart of every adventure: the challenges shape us into who we are meant to be. Like Dorothy facing the Wicked Witch in *The Wizard of Oz,* we come face to face with our greatest trials. These moments test us, push us to our limits, and reveal our true character.

The hardest parts of the journey often make us question if we're on the right path. We might feel frustrated, disappointed, or even lost. But it's precisely in these moments of difficulty that we grow the most. We are forced to dig deep, to find strength we didn't know we had. This is where life becomes truly meaningful.

Bringing Back the Treasure

When we finally overcome these trials, we return to our ordinary world, but we are no longer the same. We come back with something special—a treasure. It might be wisdom, strength, or a deeper understanding of who we are and what we're capable of. This treasure is not just for ourselves. We bring it back to share with others, enriching the world around us with the lessons we've learned on our journey.

So why do we go on these adventures? Because it's through them that we become the best versions of ourselves. Every challenge, every hardship, every moment of doubt is part of the process of growth. We return not only with new skills and knowledge but with a deeper sense of purpose.

> "Life is C between B and D." - Jean-Paul Sartre (*Being and Nothingness*)

Our life is all about the choices we make between birth and death. It's in these choices—the choice to answer the call to adventure—that we find our true potential.

The Power of Choice: Following Curiosity

Sometimes, we don't even know why something interests us—it just does. It's a curiosity, a pull toward something unknown. And that curiosity is often the spark that ignites our adventure. It's not always easy to follow it, though. In fact, it's often incredibly challenging. But it's in these struggles that we find the most meaning and purpose in life.

When we embrace these challenges, we learn to trust ourselves and others. Doing the hard things strengthens us, increases our capabilities, and opens up new possibilities. Each adventure, whether big or small, teaches us something valuable. And it's through these lessons that we continue to grow.

> "What calls us out into the world, however—to our destiny—is not ease. It is struggle and strife. It is bitter contention and the deadly play of the opposites. It is probable—inevitable—that the adventure of our life will frustrate, disappoint, and unsettle us. But that is where the deep meaning that orients us and shelters us is to be found." - Jordan Peterson (*Beyond Order*)

A Life Worth Living

When we hear the call to adventure—whether it's something big like moving to a new city or something small like picking up a new hobby—remember that this is our chance to grow. This is the adventure of our lives, and it's exactly what we are built for.

The call to "What could be?" makes life exciting and full of possibilities. It leads us into the unknown, where we discover the most valuable treasures of all: our strength, our wisdom, and our purpose. The adventure is where we find the life worth living, but only if we choose to answer the call.

REWRITING OUR STORY
HOW CHANGING OUR NARRATIVE LEADS TO GROWTH & FULFILLMENT

How do we change who we are?

How do we tackle problems that feel bigger than us?

Who decides what a "proper" education is?

Who am I to design my own education?

These are questions many people ask when embarking on self-education. How we approach these questions can either trap us in limiting beliefs or unlock a world of possibilities. Let's look at these questions from a perspective that empowers rather than restricts us.

Chuck Palahniuk's "Let's Take a Break" Theory offers a powerful framework for this shift in thinking. It operates on several key assumptions:

1. *Time:* People today have more free time than ever before, no longer needing to spend their days in survival mode.
2. *Education:* We have unparalleled access to information, more than any generation in history.
3. *Technology:* The tools for creation, expression, and dissemination—like the internet—allow everyone to be their own multimedia channel.

4. *Dissatisfaction:* Many people are unhappy with the repetitive, overused narratives they've seen in media, leading them to say, "I'm going to do it myself."

5. *Experience:* At some point, we all "take a break" to reflect on our lives. We check the boxes of success but find our stories fragmented and incomplete. Baby boomers, in particular, wonder if their life's story will ever be understood by their descendants.

Palahniuk argues that our current culture lacks a unifying, overarching narrative. People have small stories—many of them distractions from what truly matters. But we now have the ability to create a *new* metanarrative that aligns with our values and goals. I like to believe that this new narrative doesn't have to conflict with existing ones; it simply gives us a fresh perspective to see the world.

Changing the metanarrative can have transformative effects. For example, instead of reacting to a global oil shortage, we could adopt a narrative where cars are no longer necessary. This approach doesn't just solve the problem—it makes the problem irrelevant.

When we change our story, we change everything.

Let's revisit those questions:

How do we change who we are?

We change our story.

How do we solve problems that feel bigger than us?

We realize our potential is bigger than those problems and educate ourselves to bring that potential to life.

Who are we to decide what a proper education is?

We are the best judges of our own education, because the journey is unique for everyone.

Who am I to design my own education?

We are the creators of our lives, and to shape the life we want, we must create our own education.

Setting the Stage for Change

It's not enough to want change—we need tools and systems to guide us.

"An intelligent man cannot seriously become anything; only a fool can become something."- Fyodor Dostoevsky

We can overthink our path to change. It's about simplifying the process and starting somewhere.

I break the change process into two parts:

1. *Setting the Stage:* Knowing what we want to change into.
2. *Overcoming Resistance:* Navigating the inevitable pushback from our minds and habits.

Two Mindsets

When it comes to setting the stage, people typically fall into two categories:

- *Group 1:* People who think they need to change *everything*. They don't see themselves as capable and resist taking on new challenges.
- *Group 2:* People who think they need to change nothing. They believe they already know everything and are often blinded by arrogance

Most of us land somewhere between these two extremes.

To find the right balance, we can ask ourselves: How much do I really need to change?

If we lean toward Group 1, we likely have more tools and knowledge than we think. Our goal should be to *optimize what we already know.*

If we lean toward Group 2, it might be time to reevaluate our values and question whether they're still serving us. Is everything truly perfect in our lives?

But before we make any changes, we can ask ourselves: *"If I were to change and get the result I want, what would that do for me?"*

This question helps us focus in on the real motivation behind our desire for change.

Often, it's not about achieving the goal itself (like getting good grades or building a certain physique)—it's about what achieving the goal gets us. Once we understand this, we can streamline our focus on the most meaningful changes.

Overcoming Resistance

Change is hard because our habits and tendencies are often survival strategies we developed in childhood. Letting go of these patterns can feel like losing a part of ourselves. Resistance is normal, and negative emotions don't mean we're on the wrong path —they mean we're on the right one.

There are three common types of resistance, according to Ramit Sethi:

- *What-If-ing:* Our brains love to invent worst-case scenarios, but these are often just distractions.
- *Slicing the Pie:* Excuses like "I don't have time" or "I can't afford it" prevent us from making progress. Instead, focus on finding ways to *make* time or resources.
- *Alibi-Hunting:* Looking for obscure reasons to justify inaction—what Sethi calls "Special Snowflake Syndrome"—stops us from ever starting.

When we face resistance, mantras and affirmations can help override negative thought patterns, but there are also more practical tools. Tim Ferriss suggests six ways to build habits and engineer compliance when logic fails us:

1. *Make it Conscious:* Be aware and intentional about your new habits.
2. *Make it a Game:* Reward yourself after completing five sessions of a new habit.
3. *Make it Competitive:* Create accountability by adding a competitive element.
4. *Make it Small and Temporary:* Start with small, manageable goals.
5. *Lower Your Standards:* Set the bar low enough to guarantee progress.
6. *Keep Things Simple:* Complexity can come later—start with something easy.

The Reality-Possibility Exchange

"You can be anything you want, just not everything you want." - David Allen

One of the most challenging aspects of adulthood is trading the endless *possibility* of what we could be for the *reality* of who we actually are. As children, we imagine becoming astronauts, doctors, or superheroes. As adults, we realize we can't be everything—we must choose or we may not want to be any of those things.

I believe one of the biggest markers between children and adults is the ability to trade possibility for reality. Adults inherently have less potential to manifest than children, which often drains them of their energy. I believe this is why kids seem so full of life while adults can be a little more dreary.

We are in love with potential and possibility. They are the lifeblood of our souls, but making this exchange is essential for growth. We have to let go of the fantasy of being everything in order to fully commit to becoming something. This isn't about settling—it's about focusing our energy to create something meaningful.

We are in love with what could be and the realities of what is usually fails in comparison to the potential we see in things.

Peter Pan: A Cautionary Tale

A great example of the dangers of not participating in the Reality-Possibility Exchange is outlined in the classic story, Peter Pan. Peter Pan is a character who epitomizes the refusal to grow up and face the realities of life.

Peter Pan is not just a whimsical figure, but is a representation of raw potential, much like children who can become anything. His name, Pan, means everything. Emphasizing the symbolism that children can be anything.

Peter Pan lives in Neverland, where no one ever have to grow up or do anything. Pan lives as king of the Lost Boys also known as King of the Losers. Many people who recall the movie, tend to forget that the Lost Boys are characters at all. Refusing to make the exchange will surround us with losers who are easily forgettable

But why does Peter Pan not want to grow up?

Pan's perspective on adulthood is shaped by his experiences and observations of Captain Hook. Hook is Pan's example of what an adult is and Pan sees Hook as cruel and mean. Pan doesn't want to be cruel and mean, so he decides he doesn't want to grow up. He doesn't want to exchange his possibility for reality.

This is the *wrong* conclusion.

There are behaviors and beliefs that adults have that may seem cruel and mean from the perspective of a child, but are not.

However, Pan does have a point. Hook is kind of a jerk...but why?

Captain Hook has lost a hand to the only thing he is afraid of. The infamous crocodile with a clock in its stomach. The crocodile represents time. As we get older, time takes parts of us. Just like the crocodile took a part of Hook. Time is a scary monster that many adults spend their days actively running away from. The truth is, one day that monster will get us.

Adults respond differently to this fate. Some allow this to corrupt them and they develop cruelty and resentment. I believe Captain Hook is like this. He is handling the realities of time in a cruel way and it's no surprise that Pan doesn't want to be like him.

However, if adults can accept their fate with grace, they could inspire children to want to grow up. I believe this is the way to properly engage with the Reality-Possibility Exchange.

There is another character in the movie, Wendy. She initially shares Pan's reluctance to grow up, but realizes through her perilous adventures that embracing adulthood and its responsibilities is a fulfilling journey, a realization that Pan never comes to. As a consequence of not wanting to grow up, Pan loses his opportunity at a real relationship with Wendy and is left with Tinkerbell as his companion. Tinkerbell is the representation of the unattainable fantasy partner. She is silent and over-sexualized, which is a stark contrast to the fulfilling reality of mature relationships.

Refusing to grow up will destroy our chances at real mature relationships.

Pan quite often loses his shadow. In the movie, Pan's shadow literally disconnects from him and causes all sorts of trouble. This represents his inability to integrate his shadow. This lack of shadow integration represents the inner turmoil of those who refuse to mature.

Refusing to grow up will cause us to trip over ourselves. We will become our own worst enemy.

Peter's eternal childhood in Neverland, while seemingly idyllic, is a cautionary tale about the pitfalls of refusing the reality-possibility exchange necessary for true growth and fulfillment.

～

NOT WANTING to trade our possibilities for reality can stop us from accomplishing so many things. We don't get to choose whether or not we get to sacrifice. But, we do get to choose what our sacrifice is.

It's easy to trick ourselves into thinking that we are only holding

. on to our possibility by not dedicating ourselves to something, but in actuality, we are trading our potential for failure.

I see this all the time with teenagers that I teach. They believe that if they do not try, then they cannot fail. The reality is that we are failing, we just don't know we are failing. When we try and fail, then we have an opportunity to learn. When we don't try at all, we fool ourselves into thinking we are without error.

We must make the trade, it's better to decide what we are trading rather than be a drifter and take whatever life gives us.

To create meaningful change, we must be willing to trade reality for possibility. We have to choose our sacrifices rather than letting life choose them for us. Failing to do so keeps us stuck in a cycle of unfulfilled potential.

Some questions to help guide us when trying to rewrite our story and create the future we desire:

- What unique contribution can you offer the world?
- What steps can you take to start sharing it?

Or, more an easier one:

- What do you want to *be* in the world?

THE ART OF PATIENCE
THE SECRET WEAPON FOR ACHIEVING GOALS, SUCCESS, & HAPPINESS

"When you begin to embrace the process of working toward your goal and forget about how long it is going to take to get there, you'll find peace and joy in the journey." - Thomas M. Sterner (*The Practicing Mind*)

The Power of Patience

In a world obsessed with instant results, it's easy to feel like success is slipping through our fingers. Every day, we're bombarded with stories of overnight success, quick wins, and instant gratification. But what if the secret to achieving our goals wasn't about speed, but about our ability to slow down? What if the key to a fulfilling, successful life is patience?

Researchers from the University of California, Berkeley, have uncovered a compelling truth: those who practice patience not only make more progress toward their goals but also experience deeper satisfaction when they reach them. This is especially true when our goals are challenging. Patience isn't just about waiting—it's about persevering, steadily moving forward while we wait for the results to unfold.

But the benefits of patience don't stop there. Emotionally, patience can helps us feel more grounded and connected. People who embrace patience report lower levels of depression, stress, and anxiety, while experiencing more gratitude and a greater sense of abundance. They feel more connected to others and find joy in the journey, even when it's difficult. This mindset is especially powerful when we're building something big—whether it's a business, a passion project, or a lifelong dream.

The Discipline of Patience

"Success is the product of daily habits—not once-in-a-lifetime transformations." - James Clear (*Atomic Habits*)

So how do we cultivate patience in a fast-paced world? The key lies in discipline and building systems that support consistent effort. Patience isn't passive; it's not just sitting back and waiting for things to happen. It's about what we do while we wait, and how we stay focused on the process rather than obsessing over the outcome.

"Patience is doing something else in the meantime." - Alex Hormozi

This highlights the importance of maintaining our momentum —using the waiting period as an opportunity to grow, learn, and refine our skills. By staying engaged with the process, we create an environment where progress becomes inevitable, but more importantly, we don't get in our own way by acting impatient.

"Patience is not about how long you have to wait, but how you behave while you're waiting." - Allan Looks (*Patience*)

Often, we may feel like we need to "become" more patient, as if it's something outside ourselves. But as Thomas M. Sterner explains in *The Practicing Mind*, all the patience we need is already within us. We just need to tap into it. Sterner describes patience as *"quiet perseverance"*—a calmness that allows us to handle everything from minor frustrations, like traffic jams, to major challenges, like navigating difficult conversations or pushing through setbacks.

Taming Our Minds

"Realize deeply that the present moment is all you ever have. Make the Now the primary focus of your life." - Eckhart Tolle (*The Power of Now*)

One of the most critical steps in developing patience is becoming aware of our thoughts. Impatience often arises from letting our minds spiral into worries, fears, and what-ifs. Most of what we worry about never actually happens. When we let go of the mental clutter and focus on the present moment, we create space for patience. Instead of stressing about when we'll achieve our goals, we can stay engaged in the process, knowing that progress will naturally come as a result.

"I've had a lot of worries in my life, most of which never happened." - Mark Twain

By recognizing that our minds tend to overcomplicate the future, we can learn to focus on the here and now. This not only reduces anxiety but also strengthens our ability to stay patient and persistent.

Enjoying the Journey

"The end of a melody is not its goal" - Friedrich Nietzsche (*Human, All Too Human*)

Another critical aspect of patience is letting go of the pursuit of perfection. Life is constantly evolving, and so are we. This means that there's no such thing as a perfect outcome—we're always growing, learning, and improving. The sooner we embrace this idea, the sooner we can focus on enjoying the process of growth rather than obsessing over flawless results.

In *The Practicing Mind*, Sterner shares a story about a musician who spent years practicing piano, only to feel unfulfilled despite his high level of skill. The musician was trapped in the pursuit of perfection, constantly striving for an impossible ideal. It wasn't until he shifted his focus to enjoying the act of learning and creating music that he found true happiness. His story teaches us that patience isn't about waiting for the "perfect" moment or achievement—it's about embracing the journey, finding joy in the process, and trusting that progress will come.

The Transformative Power of Patience

> "Everything can be taken from a man but one thing: the last of the human freedoms—to choose one's attitude in any given set of circumstances, to choose one's own way." - Viktor Frankl (*Man's Search for Meaning*)

When we practice patience, we not only move closer to our goals, but we do so with less stress and greater fulfillment. Patience reshapes how we view success—not as a destination to be hurried toward, but as a journey to be savored. It encourages us to remain grounded in the present, focused on what we can control, and calm in the face of uncertainty.

By cultivating patience, we create a mindset that allows us to enjoy every step of the process, no matter how long it takes. We begin to trust that our goals will come to us in time, and we stop rushing through life. Whether we're building a career, mastering a skill, or deepening relationships, patience reminds us that progress happens one step at a time.

In the end, patience isn't just a virtue—it's a powerful tool for living a fulfilling life. It teaches us to stay focused on the process, trust the journey, and embrace every moment along the way. So, the next time we feel impatient or frustrated, let's remind ourselves: progress comes not to those who hurry, but to those who persist. With patience, we might just find that success arrives faster than we expect—not because we rushed, but because we trusted the process and stayed the course.

RESPONSIBILITY
CREATING OUR OWN OPPORTUNITIES

Why Responsibility Matters

Many of us shy away from responsibility, but it's actually opportunity in disguise. When we take responsibility for something, we gain the power to improve it. By stepping up, we don't just help the world around us; we also transform ourselves.

> "When we take responsibility for something, we are imbued with great power to make things better." - Jim Kwik (*Limitless*)

Taking responsibility can immediately make life better. When we stop blaming others for our problems and focus on what we can control, we gain the power to influence our circumstances and our future.

> "Life instantly improves when we don't blame other people and focus on what we can control." - James Clear (*Atomic Habits*)

This shift in mindset—away from finger-pointing and toward

self-agency—makes us more powerful and capable, not just in the eyes of others but, most importantly, within ourselves.

What Responsibility Looks Like

Responsibility is not just about doing what's expected; it's about actively choosing to engage with life. For many of us, it can be a way to unlock untapped potential. For teenage boys and men, in particular, the need for responsibility is especially profound. Without a sense of responsibility, there's often a default toward destructive behavior. But when we take on responsibility, men often find themselves leading, protecting, and providing in ways that bring value to the world.

"Opportunity lurks where responsibility has been abdicated." - Jordan B. Peterson (*Beyond Order*)

When others avoid responsibility, we have a chance to step up and make a real difference. This doesn't just apply to grand gestures; it can be as simple as noticing what needs to be done and asking, "What if I took this on?" Or "What else could I do?" In a workplace, for example, small tasks that others overlook or avoid become opportunities for us to stand out. By picking up the slack, we become someone who is needed—someone who is genuinely invaluable.

But it's important to start small. We need to take on challenges that are manageable but still push us to grow. If the challenge is too overwhelming, we risk failure; if it's too easy, we won't grow. Over time, small victories stack up, shaping us into people who can handle even greater responsibilities. These small wins are the building blocks of personal growth.

The Psychology of Responsibility

Responsibility isn't just about external tasks—it's about how we approach life itself. Viktor Frankl, a renowned psychologist and Holocaust survivor, believed that meaning comes from conscious engagement with life. He argued that our purpose is to maximize and perfect our states of consciousness by taking responsibility for our choices and actions. Meaning is not found passively; it is created through intentional living.

When we take responsibility, we align our actions with our values. We become active participants in our lives, rather than passive observers, and this leads to deeper fulfillment. Responsibility connects us to something bigger than ourselves and helps us build a life of meaning.

How to Start Taking Responsibility

So, how do we begin? First, we can start by recognizing areas where others are not stepping up. Often, the things left undone are risky, challenging, or simply undesirable—but they are also the tasks that bring the most growth. When we step into these gaps, we take on the challenges that others avoid, and in doing so, we build resilience and capability.

The key is to begin with small, manageable steps. Look for opportunities that push us slightly beyond our current comfort zone, but not so far that we feel overwhelmed. Each time we face these challenges, we learn more about ourselves and the world.

> "When we face a challenge, we grapple with the world and inform ourselves. This makes us more than we are. It makes us increasingly into who we could be." - Jordan B. Peterson (*Beyond Order*)

By confronting what scares us, we become stronger, more capable, and more confident. Each challenge, no matter how small, transforms us.

Responsibility also means holding ourselves accountable. When we avoid responsibility, we betray our own potential. We may start to feel disconnected from our work, relationships, or purpose. The sense of dissatisfaction is often a sign that we are neglecting something we could—and should—take responsibility for.

The Rewards of Responsibility

The rewards of responsibility are profound. When we pursue meaningful goals, we align our actions with something worth striving for. This alignment brings harmony and balance to our lives, creating a sense of purpose that goes beyond day-to-day tasks. Meaning is not something we wait for; it's something we create by taking responsibility for the parts of life that matter most to us.

A meaningful life starts with seeing responsibility not as a burden, but as an opportunity. Each time we seize that opportunity, we grow. We become more capable, more resilient, and more fulfilled. Over time, we align everything within us—our thoughts, actions, and values—toward something bigger than ourselves. This alignment creates a life filled with purpose and harmony.

When we embrace responsibility, we don't just improve the world around us; we transform ourselves into the best version of who we can be. By taking on the challenges that others avoid, we build strength, character, and, ultimately, a life filled with meaning and growth.

CREATING MEANING THROUGH SACRIFICE

PAIN, CARE, & IMITATION

"The purpose of life, as far as I can tell, is to find a mode of being that's so meaningful that the fact that life is suffering is no longer relevant." - Jordan Peterson (*Beyond Order*)

Sacrifice & Intentionality: A Necessary Pain

To achieve something real in life, we must be willing to sacrifice some of our potential. Without making that choice, we may remain lost in endless possibilities, never committing to one path. The refusal to sacrifice is like keeping all our options open yet never choosing one. In the end, this could leave us with nothing. Life, with all its challenges, can feel overwhelming. If we don't assign meaning to it through our actions, we risk being stuck in a place of aimless suffering.

When we sacrifice our potential for something tangible, we give up the possibility of everything for the reality of something. This decision not only moves us forward but also provides our lives with direction and meaning. Like a chess game, where we must sacrifice some pieces to win, we cannot keep everything—and that's okay. Sacrifice means letting go of something valuable now in exchange for something more valuable in the future. The risk is that we are often not guaranteed something more valuable in the future, and we may give something up now for nothing at all.

But sacrifice is not a passive act. We must be intentional with our choices. Without setting goals or disciplining ourselves to reach them, we become drifters—moving through life without purpose. And what's the consequence of drifting? All the suffering of life, but none of the meaning. That's why it's essential to aim at something and commit to the sacrifices necessary to achieve it, even if it means letting go of other possibilities.

Caring for Our Future Selves

When we think about self-care, it's not just about the version of us that exists today. We must also consider the person we'll become tomorrow, next week, next year, and even decades from now. Every decision we make today affects all of our future selves. In this sense, taking care of ourselves today is like nurturing an entire community of different versions of us in the future.

Neglecting ourselves in the present is not just a disservice to the current "us"; it's a betrayal of the people we will become. However, by taking responsibility for our lives today, we provide meaning and create a better life for all those future versions of ourselves. This kind of sacrifice is essential for long-term fulfillment.

The challenge lies in balancing what is best for us now with what will be best for us later. Is it more important to indulge in short-term comforts or to invest in our future well-being? The answer depends on our willingness to sacrifice immediate gratification for lasting rewards.

Awe and Imitation: Learning from What Inspires Us

When we feel awe, it's more than just a fleeting emotion—it's an invitation to learn, grow, and sacrifice for something greater. Awe shows us what's possible if we're willing to give up comfort and ease for the sake of something extraordinary. It pulls us toward a vision of what we could become if we're willing to make the right sacrifices.

Imitation plays a key role in this process. When we imitate what we find awe-inspiring, we're not merely copying—we're learning the patterns of our individualized success. By adopting the habits and practices of those who inspire us, we sacrifice old ways of being and step into a new reality. This transformation often involves giving up familiar comforts to pursue something greater.

SACRIFICE IS MORE than just a necessity—it's a form of growth. By making intentional choices, we discipline ourselves to move toward something meaningful, taking care not just of our present selves but of all the future versions of us. The awe we feel when we witness greatness can guide us, showing us what's possible when we let go of short-term comforts for long-term growth. In the end, sacrifice is not about loss—it's about creating the future we aspire to live.

THE FOUNDATION OF VIRTUE
WHY COURAGE MATTERS MOST

C ourage is the one thing that makes all other virtues possible. Without it, we can't consistently practice kindness, honesty, or love. It's the foundation upon which everything else rests.

But what is courage, really? And why is it so important?

Courage Means Facing Fear

The word courage comes from the same root as the French word *coeur*, meaning "heart." It's not about being fearless; it's about feeling fear and moving forward anyway.

Think of a superhero racing to save people from a collapsing bridge. Just seconds away from success, they are suddenly flooded with memories of failure and harsh words from the past. Doubts creep in, and instead of acting, they hesitate and give up. This is what happens when courage is missing—even heroes can falter without it.

Courage, however, is not the same as rashness. What might seem bold could be an unconscious attempt to prove hollow strength, a cover for deep-seated fear.

The Power of Courage in Our Lives

Courage is the foundation of everything we do. Without it, virtues like love and honesty lose their substance.

"Courage is not simply one of the virtues, but the form of every virtue at the testing point, which means at the point of highest reality." - C.S. Lewis (*The Screwtape Letters*)

In other words, when we are truly tested, courage is what allows us to hold on to our values.

"Courage is the most important of all the virtues, because without courage, we can't practice any other virtue consistently. We can practice any virtue erratically, but nothing consistently without courage." - Maya Angelou

Courage allows us to stay honest even when it's uncomfortable, to love even when it hurts, and to be kind even when we face criticism.

The Courage to Create

Rollo May, the renowned psychologist, explored the role of courage in creativity. He believed that creativity requires us to step into the unknown, to risk failure, and to express our true selves despite the fear of judgment.

May spoke about *"learned helplessness"*—a condition where we come to believe we have no control over our situation. He referred to a famous study by Martin Seligman in which two dogs were given electric shocks. One dog could stop the shocks, while the other couldn't. Later, when both dogs were given the chance to escape, only the dog that had control tried to flee. The other dog had learned to be helpless.

Feeling in control of our lives is important, but as May argued, control isn't enough. What truly matters is having the courage to face challenges and push through difficulties. If we fail to express our true ideas or embrace our potential, we betray ourselves and our community. When we lack courage, we withhold our contributions from the world.

Wisdom in Facing the Unknown

Courage is especially critical in times of change. We live in a world of constant flux—technology evolves, relationships shift, and our beliefs grow. It takes courage to navigate uncertainty and move forward when we don't know what lies ahead.

May also highlighted the paradox of courage: it's not about being free from doubt but about acting despite our doubts. True courage allows us to embrace uncertainty and act, knowing that the truth is always more complex than it first appears.

Social Courage

Courage isn't just about grand, heroic acts—it also shows up in our relationships and how we interact with others. May described "*social courage*" as the ability to open up, risk intimacy, and be vulnerable with others. This form of courage is about being authentic in our connections.

Social courage also involves "*perceptual courage*," which means recognizing and responding to the suffering of others. One of the most common forms of cowardice today is captured in the phrase, "I didn't want to get involved." True courage compels us to engage with others, even when it's difficult.

Otto Rank, an Austrian psychoanalyst, described two distinct fears that hinder social courage: "*life fear*" and "*death fear*." Life fear is the anxiety of living independently, the fear of being abandoned, and the desire to depend on others, sometimes so much that we lose ourselves in the process. Rank noted that this fear was more common among women, though it affects everyone.

Death fear, on the other hand, is the fear of being entirely engulfed by another person—of losing our independence and sense of self. Social courage lies in balancing these fears and embracing relationships while maintaining our identity.

Physical Courage

Physical courage is not just about strength or bravery in the face of danger. May often encountered men who, as sensitive boys, felt they were expected to dominate others, and when they didn't, they grew up feeling like cowards.

May argued for a new form of physical courage, one that doesn't rely on violence or dominance but rather on sensitivity and empathy. This kind of courage encourages us to listen with our bodies, to use our physical presence not to control but to express beauty and understanding. Nietzsche called this "learning to think with the body."

In a compassionate society, we should cultivate a physical courage that honors the inherent worth of every individual, regardless of their background or beliefs. This kind of courage doesn't glorify physical strength but rather celebrates sensitivity and connection.

The Paradox of Courage

People who believe their perspective is the only correct one can be dangerous. This kind of rigid certainty isn't just dogmatism; it's a form of fanaticism that shuts down the ability to learn and grow. This firm conviction is often a sign of unconscious doubt, leading the person to defend their stance even more aggressively to silence external opposition and internal uncertainties.

In contrast, it's much safer and healthier to have a leader who, like the rest of us, experiences doubts yet has the courage to move forward despite them. This kind of courage—acknowledging doubts while still making decisions—shows flexibility and openness to new truths.

Genuine commitment isn't about being free of doubt but staying committed even when doubts arise. Fully believing in something while also accepting that there might be more to learn is not a contradiction. Instead, it reflects a deep respect for the complexity of truth, recognizing that it always extends beyond what we can fully grasp at any given moment.

The Creative Act: A Struggle for Immortality

Creativity is a courageous battle against forces that push us toward conformity. According to May, creativity requires immense courage because it involves breaking rules, pushing boundaries, and daring to be different.

The myth of Prometheus, who stole fire from the gods to give to humanity, symbolizes creative courage. Prometheus was punished for his rebellion, but his defiance sparked the growth of civilization. Similarly, artists and creators challenge the status quo, bringing new ideas into the world despite the risks.

Courage as the Path Forward

Courage is not just a single act of bravery—it's a way of living that underlies everything we do. Whether we're creating art, building relationships, or facing our fears, courage drives us forward. It's the heart of every virtue, the foundation of a meaningful life, and the key to navigating the challenges of an ever-changing world.

Courage is not about the absence of fear, but about facing our fears and acting anyway. In those moments when doubt threatens to hold us back, it's courage that pushes us forward, allowing us to live authentically and contribute fully to the world.

MASTERING BEHAVIOR CONTROL
REINFORCEMENT AND PUNISHMENT

U nderstanding how we control behavior is fundamental to personal growth, relationships, and even success. By shaping our actions—whether to prevent bad habits or encourage positive ones—we gain the ability to influence our lives and those around us.

How We Control Behavior

> "Small and apparently insignificant details can have major impacts on people's behavior." - Richard H. Thaler and Cass R. Sunstein (*Nudge*)

When we want to control behavior, we generally have two goals:

1. *Prevent a behavior:* We don't want something to happen.
2. *Repeat a behavior:* We want something to happen again.

To achieve this, we rely on two main methods: *punishments* and *reinforcements*.

Positive and Negative Punishment: Stopping Behavior

We can accomplish the goal of stopping behavior through punishments. There are two kinds:

- *Positive Punishment:* This means adding something to stop a behavior. For example, touching a hot stove and getting burned is positive punishment. The added pain discourages us from touching the stove again.
- *Negative Punishment:* This involves taking something away to stop a behavior. For instance, when a child loses playtime for misbehaving, the loss of fun time is a negative punishment. The goal is to reduce bad behavior.

Positive and Negative Reinforcement: Encouraging Behavior

We can accomplish the goal of continuing behavior through reinforcements (also known as rewards). There are two kinds:

- *Positive Reinforcement:* We add something to encourage a behavior. If we perform well on a test and receive praise or a reward, that's positive reinforcement. The added good grade encourages us to study again later.
- *Negative Reinforcement:* We remove something to make a behavior happen again. For example, when we take painkillers for a headache and the pain goes away, removing the headache encourages us to take medicine in the future.

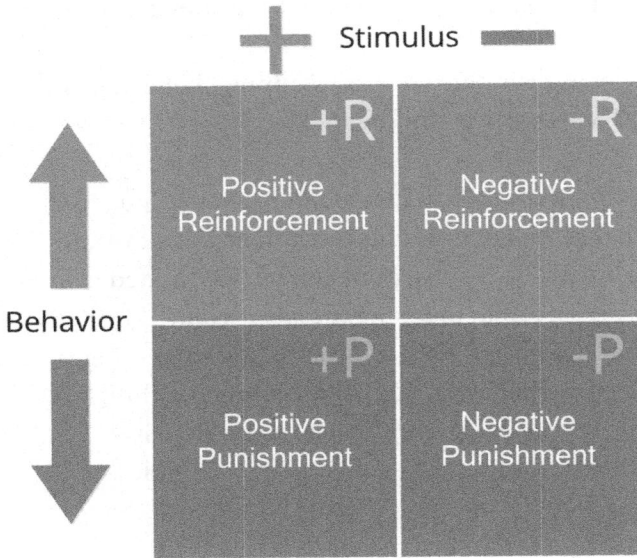

Image from simplepsychology.org

Short-Term vs. Long-Term Rewards

Our brains are wired to seek rewards, but not all rewards are equal. Some are short-term, like the pleasure of eating a donut, while others provide long-term benefits, like the health gains from eating spinach. Often, the challenge is prioritizing long-term rewards over immediate gratification. By becoming aware of this dynamic, we can start to make better choices.

Typically, short-term rewards yield less favorable long-term outcomes, while long-term rewards yield less favorable short-term outcomes. However, our brain frequently updates its reward system based on our current needs.

Mindful Consumption: Rewiring Our Brains

Sometimes, our brains hold on to old rewards, even when they no longer serve us. This is where *mindful consumption* comes in. Mindful consumption means paying close attention to what we're doing and how it feels. By focusing on the present moment, we can disrupt automatic behaviors and rewire our reward systems.

"Mindfulness means paying attention in a particular way: on purpose, in the present moment, and non-judgmentally." - Jon Kabat-Zinn (*Mindfulness for Beginners*)

For example, when we smoke a cigarette, we might take a moment to focus on the taste, smell, and how it makes us feel. We might realize that the habit isn't as rewarding as we once thought. This awareness allows our brain to update its understanding of what's truly rewarding, helping us make better decisions over time.

Rewards Can Shape Our Lives

By understanding how rewards work and applying principles of positive and negative reinforcement and punishment, we can shape our behavior and move closer to our goals. Whether we want to break a bad habit or build a positive one, becoming aware of what drives us can make a big difference.

The key is to start small—choose one behavior to focus on and practice mindfulness. As we do this, we'll find that we're not just controlling behavior; we're actively shaping the life we want to live.

RESTORING INTEGRITY
THE POWER OF KEEPING OUR WORD

"Be impeccable with your word." - Don Miguel Ruiz (*The Four Agreements*)

What is Integrity?

Integrity means being whole and complete. It's when our words and actions align perfectly, creating a sense of calm and confidence within us. When we keep our promises, our minds and bodies are in sync, allowing us to move through life with ease.

Integrity is like the foundation of a building. When it's strong, everything else stands firm. But when cracks appear, the whole structure is at risk. By honoring our commitments, we keep that foundation solid, and life becomes more balanced and fulfilling.

The Benefits of Living with Integrity

When we live with integrity, we feel good about ourselves. Our minds are clear, and it becomes easier to focus on what's ahead. Confidence builds, and our relationships become stronger because they're built on trust. Without the stress of broken promises, we experience a deep sense of peace.

Imagine we promise a friend to help them with a project. Following through not only strengthens our relationship with them but also reinforces the trust we have in ourselves. This creates a sense of accomplishment that boosts our long-term happiness and success.

The Consequences of Losing Integrity

But sometimes, things don't go as planned. We may fail to keep a promise or fulfill a commitment. When this happens, stress, anxiety, or a feeling of overwhelm can set in—signs that our integrity has been compromised.

For example, we might commit to finishing an important task at work but miss the deadline without any explanation. That guilt and tension weigh on us, and it may strain our relationships with colleagues. A loss of integrity can shake our confidence, making it harder to regain our footing.

How to Restore Integrity

"Kintsugi teaches that broken things can become more beautiful not despite the breakage but because of it." - Candice Kumai (*Kintsugi Wellness*)

The good news is that integrity can be restored. In fact, when we repair it, it often becomes even stronger, much like Kintsugi—the Japanese art of mending broken pottery with gold. Here's how we can restore integrity:

1. *Acknowledge the Broken Commitment:* If integrity is broken, that is usually a sign that a commitment wasn't fulfilled either. We start by admitting that a commitment

was broken. This acknowledgment is essential for both parties to understand and accept the situation.

2. *Share and Listen:* Both sides need to discuss how the broken commitment affected them. It's important to listen actively and without interruption. By sharing our perspectives, we foster empathy and begin the healing process. The person who broke the commitment can explain what led to it, not as an excuse but to offer context.

3. *Make a New Commitment:* After the conversation, we can agree on a new, more realistic commitment that honors both sides.

When we restore integrity in this way, we often feel immediate relief. The stress and negativity associated with broken promises fade, leaving us feeling whole again. If the process is handled sincerely and in good faith, the cracks in our integrity vanish. While the process is simple, these discussions are often difficult.

Practical Tips for Maintaining Integrity

- *Set Realistic Expectations:* We need to be careful not to overcommit. Making promises we know we can keep keeps our integrity whole with others, but most importantly with ourselves too.
- *Regular Check-Ins:* It's helpful to periodically review our commitments. Are we staying true to our word, or is something starting to slip?
- *Practice Active Listening:* When someone shares how a broken promise affected them, we should listen carefully and without interruption. Understanding their perspective is crucial for maintaining and restoring trust.

Integrity is the foundation of a balanced and fulfilling life. When our words and actions align, we feel confident, calm, and at peace. If our integrity is compromised, it can shake our very sense of self, leading to stress and uncertainty. Yet, the beauty of integrity is that it can always be restored, often stronger than before.

When we acknowledge broken commitments, share openly, and make new promises, we repair the cracks and rebuild trust in ourselves and our relationships. Setting realistic expectations, checking in regularly, and practicing active listening are key to maintaining integrity.

Are our words and actions in alignment? If not, what steps can we take to restore our integrity? By strengthening our foundation, we can move forward with peace and confidence, knowing that we are whole and complete.

THOUGHT & CRITICAL THINKING
HOW OUR THOUGHTS ARE SHAPED BY THE WORLD AROUND US

"A reliable way to make people believe in falsehoods is frequent repetition, because familiarity is not easily distinguished from truth." - Daniel Kahneman (*Thinking, Fast and Slow*)

Thinking as a Social Activity

I magine we're in a room full of people, each offering their thoughts, ideas, and insights. Even when we're alone, the voices of others echo in our minds, shaping our thinking. This is because thinking is not a solitary act—it's a social activity, constantly influenced by the people we meet, the books we read, and the conversations we have. Our thoughts are never truly isolated; they are the product of an ongoing dialogue with the world around us.

The Power of Questions

We have thousands of thoughts every day, but certain questions arise more often than others. These "dominant questions" guide our thinking, shaping how we see the world and respond to it.

For example, if someone constantly asks themselves, "How do I get people to like me?" their thoughts and actions will naturally focus on pleasing others. This may lead to a struggle with authenticity, as they continuously try to fit in. On the other hand, someone who regularly asks, "How do I make this moment magical?" will focus on creating joy and wonder in their life, elevating their experiences.

The questions we ask shape our perception of reality. To transform our thinking, we can start by becoming aware of the questions that dominate our inner dialogue. Once we identify them, we can consciously shift toward questions that inspire growth. Instead of asking, "How do I avoid failure?" we could ask, "What can I learn from this experience?" This subtle shift opens up new possibilities for growth and creativity, allowing us to move from a mindset of fear to one of curiosity and possibility.

Language as a Mirror and Mold for Thought

"Language is a window into human nature, exposing deep and universal features of our thoughts and feelings." - Steven Pinker (*The Stuff of Thought*)

Our thoughts are deeply shaped by language—not just as a tool for communication but as a reflection of our culture's values, assumptions, and perspectives. Language is a socially shared system that influences how we see the world. Because we absorb language from those around us, our thinking is inherently social, shaped by the collective ideas embedded within our words.

Consider metaphors. We rely on them to understand abstract concepts, yet they subtly direct our approach to life's challenges. Describing life as a "battle," "game," or "journey" frames our perspective: battles are fought, games are strategized, and journeys are explored. These metaphors shape our mindset without us even realizing it, highlighting the subtle ways that language impacts our mental landscape.

Language also mirrors societal norms. From an early age, we adopt patterns of speech that carry cultural assumptions, affecting how we interpret our own ideas and beliefs. Critical thinking begins here: not only questioning ideas but examining the language that conveys them. By choosing our words carefully and precisely, we gain control over our thinking, distinguishing what we truly believe from the influences we've passively absorbed.

When we put thoughts into words—whether written or spoken —we actively shape our understanding of them. Precision in speech sharpens our thinking, filtering out ambiguity and refining complex ideas. Language, then, is both a product of our social world and a tool for independent thought. The more precise we are in choosing our words, the clearer and more intentional our thinking becomes.

Thinking is Writing

> "Clear thinking becomes clear writing; one can't exist without the other." - William Zinsser (*On Writing Well*)

When we think, we are essentially writing in our minds. Just like writing, thinking helps us organize our ideas and make sense of the world. Writing forces us to put our thoughts into words, making them more straightforward and structured. This is why writing can be a powerful tool for improving our thinking.

Not only does writing help us organize our thoughts, but it also forces us to confront the gaps, contradictions, or uncertainties in our thinking. When we try to express an idea on paper, we often realize we haven't fully worked through it yet. Writing reveals the edges of our understanding, making it a powerful tool for refining and improving our thinking.

If we cannot write, we cannot think. The better we can write, the better we can think. By improving our writing skills, we directly improve the quality of our thoughts.

Learning from Others

It's crucial to surround ourselves with different types of thinkers. Spending time with people who think more deeply or creatively than we do is beneficial because they can challenge our ideas and help us grow. Connecting with those who share similar thinking patterns can provide support and validation for our ideas. Teaching those who are still developing their thinking skills also benefits us, as it forces us to clarify our thoughts and solidify what we know.

Consider how historical figures like Isaac Newton credited their breakthroughs to "standing on the shoulders of giants." Surrounding ourselves with diverse thinkers allows us to see further than we could on our own. Whether learning from mentors, peers, or even from those we teach, this exchange of ideas fuels both personal and intellectual growth. Additionally, surrounding ourselves with diverse thinkers gives us a better opportunity to think independently...as long as we do not mindlessly adopt the thoughts of others. When we have access to more perspective, we are able to form a more unique perspective of our own.

"The individual has always had to struggle to keep from being overwhelmed by the tribe. If you try it, you will be lonely often, and sometimes frightened. But no price is too high to pay for the privilege of owning yourself." - Friedrich Nietzsche

Overcoming Limiting Beliefs

Sometimes, our thoughts hold us back. These are called *limiting beliefs*. For example, if we believe we're not good at math, we might struggle with it even when we have the capacity to succeed. These beliefs can cause us to doubt ourselves, especially in high-pressure situations. I see limiting beliefs as the primary reason many public school students in the United States underperform compared to students in other countries in math and science.

Often, we aren't even aware of our limiting beliefs because they operate beneath the surface of our conscious thinking. One way to identify them is to notice recurring negative thoughts or feelings in specific situations. Journaling can help bring these patterns to light. Once identified, we can ask ourselves "Is there evidence for this belief?" If not, we may be falling into murky thinking. The next step is to actively challenge and replace them with beliefs that empower rather than limit us.

Critical Thinking and Assumptions

"We can be blind to the obvious, and we are also blind to our blindness." - Daniel Kahneman (*Thinking, Fast and Slow*)

We often hear that we should "think critically," but we're rarely given a clear definition of what that means. In my opinion, critical thinking involves being aware of the assumptions we make and questioning them. Deeper levels of critical thinking involve identifying and questioning the assumptions underlying other assumptions. For example, identifying why certain words are used to describe the assumptions can be a deeper level of critical thinking.

We often accept things as true without challenging them. But to think clearly, we need to identify these assumptions and decide if they are valid. For example, when we hear a piece of news that triggers a strong emotional reaction, it's easy to accept it as fact. But if we pause and ask ourselves, "What assumptions am I making? What evidence supports this? Is there an alternative explanation?" we open the door to clearer thinking and better decision-making.

Identifying our assumptions is key to avoiding mistakes and making more informed choices. By questioning what we take for granted, we can see the world more clearly and avoid the pitfalls of unexamined thinking.

THINKING IS RARELY JUST a solo activity. Every idea, assumption, and belief we hold is part of a larger conversation with the people we meet, the stories we hear, and the words we choose to carry forward. Whether it's the dominant questions shaping our lives, the language that molds our perceptions, or the critical examination of the beliefs we've inherited, each layer of our thinking draws from a shared human experience. By embracing precision in our words and openness in our minds, we reclaim a sense of ownership over our thoughts—allowing us to shape, question, and refine them until they truly reflect who we are.

DEEPER SELF-REFLECTION
MY PERSONAL METHODS OF REFLECTION

"Life can only be understood backwards; but it must be lived forwards." - Søren Kierkegaard (*Journals and Papers*)

My Personal Growth Strategy: Monthly Themes & Yearly Reviews

A few years ago, I was stuck in a rut. I kept repeating the same mistakes, struggling with the same challenges, and wondered why things weren't moving forward. It wasn't until I started dedicating time each month to reflect and set intentional themes for growth that I finally saw meaningful progress. Reflecting on my experiences and adjusting my path accordingly have been essential to achieving anything meaningful in my life. Without stopping to reflect, I'd still be running in circles.

Every month, I choose an area of my life to work on. I know I've chosen well when it feels uncomfortable—almost like resistance is trying to push me away. That discomfort is often a sign that it's exactly what I need to grow. When I chose the theme, I didn't do anything in particular to improve—I simply genuinely wanted to improve and knowing I had a theme kept it top of mind. For example, when I chose patience for my monthly theme, I went about my life and automatically noticed times when I was being patient and impatient. During the moments when I would act impatient, I noticed opportunities to be more patient. Simply keeping a theme changed my perceptions and I improved, most months.

"The more important a call or action is to our soul's evolution, the more Resistance we will feel toward pursuing it." - Steven Pressfield (*The War of Art*)

At the end of each year, I look back at these monthly themes and how they've shaped me. Revisiting my calendar, photos, and journal entries reminds me of the key experiences and lessons from the year. It's a time for me to connect the dots, see patterns in my growth, and set new intentions for the coming year.

This practice of reflection has taught me a lot about silencing my inner critic, understanding my strengths, and embracing my unique "genius." Here's how these ideas come together to create my holistic approach to personal growth:

Silencing the Inner Critic

A critical aspect of deeper self-refection is being able to quiet negative thoughts, embrace our strengths, and foster personal growth.

We all have an inner critic—the voice that says, "I'm not good enough," or "I'll never be able to do this." Dr. Jennice Vilhauer describes this voice as the part of us that judges, doubts, and belittles. It's more than a passing thought; it can hold us back from living fully. If left unchecked, it can lead to self-doubt, anxiety, and even depression.

One exercise that has helped me is to actually name this critic. Giving it a silly or quirky name makes it easier to distance myself from it. When it pipes up, I can acknowledge it, laugh a little, and let it go instead of letting it control me. For example, if my critic "Billy" says, "You're terrible at this," I can respond, "Thanks, Billy, but I'm going to keep trying." This simple shift lets me access different kinds of genius and opens my mind to new possibilities.

Understanding the Types of Genius

Many of us believe genius is something reserved for a select few. But the truth is, we each have unique areas of strength—a blend of genius that is distinctly ours. In ancient Greece, genius was not viewed as a personal trait or mere intellectual brilliance. Instead, it was seen as a guiding spirit or divine force, known as the *daemon*, which offered wisdom in the form of restraint. Socrates famously spoke of his *daemon* as an inner voice that only told him what *not* to do, acting more like a conscience than a source of ideas. This ancient idea reminds us that genius isn't solely about intelligence; it's about the qualities and abilities we each bring to the world.

In *Limitless*, Jim Kwik explains that understanding our unique blend of genius is key to silencing the inner critic and accessing a mind without limits. Here's a look at the different types of genius and how each one can thrive:

- *Dynamo Genius:* Creative thinkers who love developing new ideas. Think of figures like Steve Jobs or Picasso— people who saw the world differently and created something new.
- *Blaze Genius:* Masters of communication who excel in social settings. Oprah Winfrey is a classic example— someone who thrives by connecting and building relationships.
- *Tempo Genius:* Big-picture thinkers who keep everyone on track. They excel in fields requiring foresight and stability, like Warren Buffett in finance or conservationists focused on sustainability.
- *Steel Genius:* Detail-oriented thinkers who find patterns others miss. They're the analysts, the strategists—people

like Marie Curie, whose attention to detail led to breakthroughs in science.

Most of us are a blend of these genius types. When we understand where our strengths lie, we gain confidence, which helps quiet our inner critic. For instance, if we know we're Tempo Geniuses, we can embrace that skill rather than forcing ourselves into roles that don't fit. This self-awareness allows us to flourish in ways that align with our true genius. This has helped me set goals and focus on monthly themes that align with my nature.

Reflecting on Gratitude and Positive Emotions: Broaden & Build

When we're consumed by fear or self-doubt, our focus narrows, and our brains go into survival mode. This "fight or flight" reaction is sometimes helpful, like when we need to meet a deadline or face a specific challenge. But if we stay in this negative loop, it restricts our ability to see opportunities.

Dr. Barbara Fredrickson's *broaden and build* theory explains that positive emotions like joy and contentment broaden our minds, opening us up to new ideas and experiences. When I've applied this in my own life, I've found it helps me build resilience and approach life with a growth mindset. One way I cultivate positive emotions is through gratitude journaling. Reflecting on what's going well keeps my focus expansive and allows me to see possibilities I might have otherwise missed.

After a while, admittedly I would reflect on the same few things that I am grateful for and it would lose its effect. So when I do gratitude reflection, I try to not repeat any of the things I wrote down for the last three days. This keeps me searching for things to be grateful and keeps the practice meaningful.

Putting It All Together: Monthly Themes and Reflection

These tools—silencing the inner critic, understanding our genius, reframing limiting beliefs, and embracing positive emotions—are powerful on their own, but they're transformative when combined with regular reflection. Monthly themes give me focus, and yearly reviews let me see the big picture, track my progress, and set new intentions.

I encourage everyone to start their own monthly theme for growth. Choose an area that needs improvement, and remember, it's good if it feels uncomfortable. At the end of the month, we can reflect on the progress we made and set a new theme for the next month. Growth doesn't happen overnight, but with patience, reflection, and intentional action, we'll see meaningful progress over time.

TIMELESS LEADERSHIP

ESSENTIAL LESSONS FROM WINSTON CHURCHILL

Winston Churchill is widely recognized for his wisdom, courage, and resilience as a leader, especially during the turmoil of WWII. His life offers profound lessons that transcend time, speaking to anyone who aspires to lead with integrity and grit. Churchill embodied timeless principles that apply whether we're leading a team, a community, or simply leading ourselves.

Never Ever Stop

"If you're going through Hell, keep going." - Winston Churchill

Churchill endured countless hardships, from wartime battles to personal trials. He knew that life can sometimes feel relentless, but he also understood that the only way out is forward. His advice reminds us to persist, no matter how daunting the circumstances. When setbacks feel overwhelming, breaking down the challenge into smaller, achievable steps can help us stay on track. Make it a habit to set one goal each day that helps us move forward, even if it's just a small step.

Persistence not only gets us through tough times but also prepares us for whatever comes next. Determination can outweigh talent or resources. Successful leaders are those who keep trying, even when the odds seem insurmountable. It's useful to often think about a recent challenge we faced. How did we respond? Next time, how could we respond with relentless determination?

Intentionality Is for the Strong

"I like things to happen; if they don't happen, I like to make them happen." - Winston Churchill

Great leaders don't wait for the world to change—they take action to create the changes they envision. Churchill's words underscore the power of intentionality— setting a clear purpose and pursuing it with focus and determination. This mindset is vital, especially when faced with uncertainty. When we're intentional, we're not just responding to our circumstances; we're shaping them.

To develop this trait, we can visualize our goals regularly and identify the next steps to bring them closer. When I try to be intentional, I think of one goal I'd like to accomplish within the week. Then I ask myself "What steps can I take today to make it happen?" Leaders who approach life with intent build confidence, knowing they can make a difference no matter the odds.

Pick Our Battles

"You will never get to the end of the journey if you stop to shy a stone at every dog that barks." - Winston Churchill

Churchill also taught the value of selective focus. Not every challenge is worth our time and energy; wise leaders understand the importance of picking their battles. This lesson applies to both big goals and everyday interactions. Constantly getting caught up in small distractions or conflicts can keep us from making meaningful progress on what truly matters.

If we are getting bogged down by minor setbacks or irritations, we can take a step back to refocus. We can ask ourselves "What's most important in our journey?" Prioritize those answers, and let go of the rest. I also try to reflect on recent conflicts I've encountered. I ask myself "Was it worth my energy, or could it have been a distraction?"

Sometimes we can solve problems by simply deciding they are not.

Move Beyond Failure

"Success consists of going from failure to failure without loss of enthusiasm." - Winston Churchill

Churchill knew that failure was inevitable, but he refused to let it define him. Every failure can be a stepping stone if we learn from it. Great leaders embrace failure as part of the growth process, maintaining their enthusiasm even when things don't go as planned.

To adopt this mindset, view each setback as an opportunity for insight. After experiencing failure, we can take a moment to reflect on what went wrong and how we can improve. As we encounter future challenges, we can remind ourselves that every "no" is bringing us closer to a "yes." When I reflect on this, I think about a time I failed, how it felt, and how I could approach similar setbacks in the future with resilience and optimism.

We Are Never Done

"Success is not final, failure is not fatal; it is the courage to continue that counts." - Winston Churchill

Churchill understood that both success and failure are temporary. He didn't allow his victories to make him complacent or his defeats to discourage him for long. True leadership is an ongoing journey that requires us to continually face new challenges and push for growth.

It's easy to rest on past successes or dwell on failures, but Churchill's wisdom reminds us to keep moving forward. Each day is a new opportunity to learn, grow, and face the next challenge. I frequently ask myself, how can I be a better version of myself? Success is wonderful, but the courage to persevere is what's necessary for greatness.

Essential Leadership Traits

Now that we've explored Churchill's life lessons, let's take a closer look at twelve essential traits that define effective leaders. These qualities help leaders inspire, make tough decisions, and bring out the best in others.

- *Self-Awareness:* Understanding our strengths and weaknesses. Leaders who are self-aware make more strategic choices and know when to seek support. I try to practice self-reflection by identifying one area for improvement each month.
- *Respect:* Showing respect for others' perspectives. Building trust and avoiding unnecessary conflicts often come from demonstrating genuine respect.
- *Compassion:* Acting on what we learn from others' concerns. Compassionate leaders create a collaborative environment where people feel valued.
- *Vision:* Setting clear, compelling goals for the future. Having a vision gives both the leader and the team something inspiring to work toward.
- *Communication:* Effective communication bridges gaps.

Whether addressing a large group or one person, aim to speak with clarity and empathy.

- *Learning Agility:* Being open to learning and adapt to new situations quickly. In a world that's constantly changing, agility is a crucial leadership skill.
- *Collaboration:* Valuing teamwork and cooperation. Great leaders foster an inclusive environment where everyone feels empowered to contribute.
- *Influence:* Leaders inspire and persuade others thoughtfully and authentically to work toward common goals.
- *Integrity:* Be honest, ethical, and consistent in our actions. Trustworthy leaders build loyal teams who respect them.
- *Courage:* Boldness in action and words, especially during tough situations, is the mark of a leader unafraid to stand up for what's right.
- *Gratitude:* Acknowledging and appreciating others. Gratitude creates a motivated and positive atmosphere.
- *Resilience:* Bouncing back from setbacks. Resilient leaders turn challenges into opportunities, inspiring those around them to persevere.

LEADERSHIP ISN'T JUST about giving orders—it's about inspiring others, navigating setbacks, and continuing the journey, no matter what challenges arise. We can integrate Churchill's advice and these twelve traits into our own lives. I personally work on two traits a month, but we can always focus on just one. Leadership isn't something that we are born with, it is something that is developed and refined over time.

TOUGH LESSONS I LEARNED THE HARD WAY
UNPLEASANT TRUTHS

"Life's tough. It's tougher if we're stupid." - John Wayne

L ife has proven tough, and every year, I rediscover that I still have a lot to learn. There's humility in admitting our own ignorance, and with humility comes the opportunity for growth.

Life is filled with challenges, and no one is coming to save us—there's no backup, no cavalry. If we don't take responsibility and act, failure is inevitable. Here are a few lessons learned the hard way, shared in the hope that others might take something from these scars.

Our Pain is Not Unique

We're all unique, yes, but in a way that's shared by everyone. However, believing the universe has singled us out to endure the worst pain imaginable can lead us into self-pity and resentment. It's a form of narcissism to assume our suffering is somehow more profound or exceptional than anyone else. Gratitude helps reframe this thinking, grounding us in the reality that no matter how bad things seem, they could always be worse.

I highly recommend practicing gratitude daily and focusing on what we can control.

We Choose Unhappiness Over Uncertainty

We often cling to the familiar, even when it's unhealthy, because stepping into the unknown seems risky. We will often choose the devil we know, over the devil we don't. We prefer the comfort of misery to the fear of change. But staying in that comfort zone guarantees dissatisfaction.

Take a leap when things feel stagnant; the unknown can lead to deeper fulfillment than the familiar ever could. The line between known and unknown is where the adventure of our life is.

Pain is Inevitable, Suffering is Not

Pain is part of life, and it's not going away. Instead of avoiding it, we can learn to embrace it. Rather than having the pain lead to suffering, the pain can lead to growth. Pain has taught some of our most valuable lessons. Neurobiologically, learning happens when we face and process our discomfort.

> "People cling to hate because they know, once hate is gone, they'll have to face their pain." - James Baldwin (*The Fire Next Time*)

Letting go of resentment means embracing our wounds and seeing them as teachers rather than punishments. When I experience pain, I try to ask myself "what can I learn from this?"

When pain arises, try to sit with it. Journal about what it reveals and learn from it. Pain isn't something that needs to cause suffering, even though it is inevitable.

We Do Not Suffer From Events, But Our Judgments of Them

"We do not suffer from the events in our lives, but our judgments about them." - Epictetus (*Enchiridion*)

It's not what happens to us but how we interpret it that defines our experience.

At times, I've fallen into the trap of victimhood, believing circumstances were working against me. When I stopped judging events as unfair or unjust, life became easier to navigate. Our perceptions hold the power to shape our experiences.

Now I try to challenge my negative judgments, and consider reframing setbacks as neutral or even positive.

Commitment = Sacrifice

Commitment and sacrifice are two sides of the same coin. Pursuing a goal means giving things up—whether it's time, comfort, or sometimes relationships. The cost of what we want is often higher than expected.

Since learning this, I regularly reassess my priorities and am prepared to give up what's not essential to make room for long-term goals. If I am truly committed to something, I must be willing to give up something else.

We Fall to the Level of Our Training

It's easy to dream big, but we don't rise to meet our expectations; we fall to the level of our preparation. If we're not ready, things will fall apart. This means practicing and training constantly, even when it's uncomfortable.

I try to create small, consistent routines to build my foundation, so when challenges come, I'm prepared.

Not Everyone is On Our Team

Not everyone we meet will support our journey, and that's okay. Some people may actively root against us or even try to harm us. Recognizing this helps us set boundaries and keep our focus on those who genuinely support us.

I recommend surrounding ourselves with people who lift us up, and letting go of those who drag us down.

We Are Above Nothing

No job or task is too small for us. I once met a homeless man who believed he was too good to work at a fast-food restaurant. This kind of pride keeps us stuck. True humility isn't about feeling inferior; it's about recognizing we're not above doing what's necessary. Sometimes, life humbles us to open doors.

Whenever I face a task that feels "beneath" me, I try to remember that humility can be a strength.

Privilege is About What We Don't Have to Overcome

Privilege is less about what we have and more about the obstacles we don't face. While one person might have financial security, another might have the advantage of health or a supportive family. Recognizing both our advantages and disadvantages helps us grow with self-awareness.

Since learning this, I've learned to identify my unique privileges and leverage them with gratitude.

Our Adversity is Our Advantage

Our struggles are not roadblocks; they are stepping stones. Every setback brings insight and resilience that those who haven't faced similar obstacles may lack. This adversity becomes an edge, something we can use to our advantage.

I've been able to grow much more since accepting difficulty as a teacher, and allowing it to build my resilience.

Accept Setbacks and Move Forward

Failure is part of success. Setbacks happen, but they don't define us. Quickly forgiving ourselves, adjusting, and getting back up is key. Keeping a list of our achievements can help remind us of how far we've come, especially when self-doubt creeps in.

Now whenever I stumble, I take stock of my accomplishments to reinforce my sense of progress.

Be Aware of Our Weaknesses

None of us are perfect. We all have areas that need work. Being humble enough to acknowledge our weaknesses allows us to address them rather than let them fester. Whether it's learning new skills or asking for help, addressing these gaps strengthens us.

I try to frequently identify where I'm lacking and take practical steps to improve, one area at a time.

There's No Substitute for Hard Work

Hard work is the only true path to lasting success. We may have guidance or luck, but ultimately, it's up to us to put in the effort. Doing our best isn't always enough; sometimes, we need to push even harder.

I often hear people say "work smarter, not harder" but to be able to work smart, we have to first work hard. Only working hard will not get us to where we need to go, but working smart only becomes clear once we work hard.

Where We Aren't is Just as Important as Where We Are

Where we are is important, but so is where we aren't. Reflecting on the paths we didn't take offers valuable perspective. Sometimes, realizing the roads we left behind can clarify the direction we truly want to pursue.

I try to consider my choices from all angles to make better decisions moving forward and find perspective when I am unhappy with where I am.

We Will Die

Remembering our mortality can be the key to living intentionally. Time is limited, so let's use it wisely. When we understand that life is finite, we can focus on what truly matters and cut out the trivial distractions. Memento mori—remember, we will die. Our limited time is what makes everything special and miraculous. Seeing life this way helps me cultivate gratitude and prioritize what I believe to be truly important, especially in the face of death.

THESE LESSONS AREN'T magic solutions; they're tools. We may stumble and fail repeatedly, but by internalizing these principles, we become better equipped for whatever life throws our way.

LEARNING IN THE SOCIAL MEDIA AGE

TURNING SOCIAL FEEDS INTO GROWTH TOOLS

"If an endless amount of information is at our fingertips, but our ability to process it is compromised, then we're no better off than if we were in a state of ignorance." - Jim Kwik (*Limitless*)

The Struggles of the Digital Age

Technology surrounds us in today's world, transforming everything from how we connect to how we learn and entertain ourselves. It's amazing to have so much power at our fingertips, yet it's also challenging in ways we rarely consider. Imagine a day when we scroll through countless headlines, check notifications every few minutes, and ask our devices for every piece of information we need. We often feel productive, even connected, yet surprisingly drained. This sensation isn't just in our heads; our brains genuinely struggle to adapt to this digital age.

Brain and learning expert Jim Kwik calls this struggle the "four horsemen" of the digital age: digital deluge, digital distraction, digital dementia, and digital deduction. Each horseman challenges our brain's natural abilities to focus, remember, and think critically.

Digital Deluge: Too Much Information

We live in an age where, for the first time, ignorance is a choice. Every day, we encounter more information than people in the 1400s would have absorbed in a lifetime. But like our diets, not all information nourishes us. Some information is like the brain's equivalent of junk food: tasty but unsatisfying, filling our minds with trivia that doesn't help us grow. Just as overloading on sugar can make our bodies sluggish, consuming too much low-quality content can leave us mentally foggy and exhausted.

To combat this, we can treat our minds like we treat our bodies —by setting aside time to digest and rest. Try scheduling just 30 minutes of downtime each week where we put away screens and let our minds wander. This "brain detox" allows us to process what we've absorbed and enhances our memory. Small breaks aren't indulgences; they're necessary for clarity in an otherwise overwhelming digital storm.

Digital Distraction: Losing Focus

"Distraction is not about the inability to pay attention; it's about the struggle to control what we pay attention to." - Adam Gazzaley and Larry Rosen (*The Distracted Mind*)

How often do we check our phones when we are supposed to be working, relaxing, or engaging with others? Digital distraction is an ever-present temptation. In fact, studies show that people who keep their phones nearby—even when they're not in use—report feeling more distracted and enjoy their activities less. Multitasking, too, adds strain; every time we switch tasks, our brain burns more energy, leading to mental fatigue.

Social media can amplify this distraction. Studies reveal that young adults who use social media excessively—over 300 minutes a day—are nearly three times more likely to develop depression within six months. The constant scrolling, comparing, and dopamine-seeking on platforms like Facebook, Instagram, and Snapchat exhausts our minds. The design of these platforms, while addictively engaging, often pulls us away from the present moment and from ourselves.

To reduce distraction, let's create mindful routines. For instance, we could turn off notifications during specific times or try leaving our phones in another room while we eat. These small boundaries can help us regain focus and find greater enjoyment in our day-to-day lives. I personally have no notifications on my phone for this reason—the only notifications I allow are when my wife contacts me, my garage door opens, my doorbell rings, or my bank account falls below a certain threshold.

> "Digital minimalism definitely does not reject the innovations of the internet age, but instead rejects the way so many people currently engage with these tools." - Cal Newport (*Digital Minimalism*)

Digital Dementia: Forgetting How to Remember

Technology is our go-to source for everything, from navigation to daily reminders. While helpful, this reliance on devices weakens our memory. Neuroscientist Manfred Spitzer calls this phenomenon "digital dementia." When we turn to our devices for every answer, we bypass the mental workout our brains need to stay sharp.

> "Our brains are not wired to process multiple streams of information simultaneously, and doing so can actually diminish our cognitive capacity." - Adam Gazzaley and Larry Rosen (*The Distracted Mind*)

Each time we actively recall information without assistance, we strengthen our memory pathways. This "use it or lose it" principle reminds us that just like physical exercise builds our muscles, mental exercise builds cognitive strength. Instead of immediately looking things up, we can challenge ourselves to remember first. Whether it's recalling someone's name or remembering directions, relying on our minds helps us preserve this essential skill.

Digital Deduction: Overconfidence and Poor Thinking

"Our technology and devices, while powerful, can become a crutch, making our brains dependent on them, weakening our ability to think, remember, and learn on our own." - Jim Kwok (*Limitless*)

With instant access to answers online, we sometimes overestimate our knowledge. This reliance can lead to weak problem-solving skills and poor decision-making. When we depend too much on technology to "think" for us, we risk losing the critical thinking and deduction skills that have fueled human progress.

Deduction is more than just recalling facts; it's about interpreting, reasoning, and drawing connections based on what we know. Studies show that students who use laptops during class often retain less because they rely on the internet instead of engaging deeply with the material. By building our deduction skills, we sharpen our ability to think critically and make informed decisions.

Social Feeds to Growth Tools: Using Social Media to Our Advantage

While social media and technology can distract us, we can use it to our benefit—if we do it wisely. We can take control of our social media feeds by curating them. This means liking and following content that helps us learn and grow and disliking content that isn't useful. We can even create a new account and shape the algorithm to show us what we want to see.

For example, my YouTube feed contains content on investing,

technology, and market trends. This helps me stay on the cutting edge of innovation and learn valuable skills. If we don't curate our feeds, we'll see the same things over and over or content that appeals to our base animalistic desires instead of helping us grow. When we have curated feeds showing us a particular topic, we can supercharge our learning by having these algorithms teach us things we didn't know or didn't know. Of course, we want to cross-reference what we find online from multiple sources.

Additionally, the endless scrolling features can be used for good. While apps often use endless scrolling to keep us on their platforms longer, we can use this feature to keep reading and learning on platforms like Kindle. By making conscious choices, we can turn social media into a tool for personal growth.

A Digital Health Checklist for Modern Life

Technology is here to stay, but we hold the power to shape how it impacts us. Let's be mindful of the digital deluge, distraction, dementia, and deduction in our lives to protect our mental health. Here's a simple checklist we can follow to stay in control:

- *Take breaks:* Schedule at least 30 minutes of screen-free time each day to recharge and process information.
- *Manage distractions:* Turn off notifications during focused activities, meals, and conversations.
- *Challenge memory:* Try remembering names, directions, or small facts before reaching for our phones.
- *Strengthen critical thinking:* Spend time reflecting on ideas and solving problems without immediate digital help.
- *Curate our feeds:* Follow content that supports our growth and ignore content that doesn't.

When we use this checklist, we can turn technology from a

source of strain into a valuable partner in our growth. When we choose what to absorb, focus on real conversations, and engage our minds, we preserve our humanity in a world that constantly tugs at our attention.

PERFORMANCE REQUIREMENTS
AN INTRODUCTION TO NOURISHING THE MIND AND BODY

"Our mind is first and foremost a physical system. Oftentimes, what we experience as mental fatigue or emotional distress is simply a signal from our body that we're not getting enough of something we physically need: nutrients, exercise, or rest." - Josh Kaufman *(Personal MBA)*

Our Brains Deserve Premium Fuel

Our brain is a high-performance engine, thriving on high-quality nutrients. Dr. Eva Selhub likens it to an expensive car that runs best on premium fuel. When we nourish ourselves with foods rich in vitamins, minerals, and antioxidants, we protect our brains from oxidative stress—a damaging process caused by free radicals that can harm brain cells.

To operate at peak performance, our brain needs 45 essential nutrients. While our bodies produce some of these nutrients, others must come from our diet. So, what should we eat?

Top 10 Brain Foods

Here are ten foods that can help us stay sharp, energized, and focused (in no particular order):

- *Avocados:* Packed with healthy fats that protect brain cells and encourage good blood flow.
- *Blueberries:* Loaded with antioxidants, these berries help prevent brain damage and improve memory.
- *Broccoli:* High in vitamins and antioxidants, broccoli enhances brain power and protects against cognitive decline.
- *Dark Chocolate:* Rich in flavonoids, dark chocolate supports memory, attention, and focus.
- *Eggs:* A valuable source of choline, which helps memory and communication between brain cells.
- *Leafy Greens:* Spinach, kale, and other greens slow brain aging with essential protective nutrients.
- *Salmon, Sardines, and Caviar:* These fish are high in omega-3 fatty acids, which are vital for brain health and can reduce inflammation.
- *Turmeric:* Contains curcumin, a powerful compound that reduces brain inflammation and slows cognitive decline.
- *Walnuts:* Rich in omega-3s and antioxidants, walnuts improve memory and brain function.
- *Water:* Staying hydrated is crucial for focus, memory, and overall cognitive function.

I recommend incorporating at least one brain food into each meal and prioritizing hydration; even mild dehydration can impact concentration.

Brain-Boosting Recipes to Get Started

Here are some tasty ways to fuel our brains:

- *Morning Brain Tonic:* This drink combines ginger, turmeric, and green tea to reduce inflammation and give our brains a gentle boost.
- *Morning Magic Smoothie:* A blend of blueberries, spinach, and hemp seeds provides a quick nutrient-packed start to the day.
- *Brain Boost Salad:* Arugula, spinach, pomegranate seeds, walnuts, and avocado make for a brain-healthy salad rich in antioxidants and healthy fats.
- *Roasted Salmon & Broccoli:* A simple meal of salmon and broccoli supports brain health with omega-3s and vitamins.
- *Cocoa-Cinnamon-Ginger Hot Chocolate:* This cozy drink of almond milk, ginger, cocoa, and cinnamon reduces inflammation and enhances brain function.

Fueling Throughout the Day

To prevent energy crashes, it is wise to eat small, nutrient-dense snacks or meals every 2 to 3 hours. Almonds, fresh fruit, or a handful of walnuts can help keep our blood sugar stable and our brains focused.

Exercise: A Brain-Boosting Essential

Regular exercise isn't only for our bodies—it's crucial for our brains. Research from the University of British Columbia shows that aerobic exercise helps expand the hippocampus, a part of the brain responsible for memory and learning. When we exercise, blood and oxygen flow to our brain increases, making it function more effectively. Exercise helps us build new brain cells, manage stress, and potentially slow down age-related cognitive decline.

In *Brain Rules*, John Medina notes that even light physical activity boosts our energy, enhances thinking, and improves focus. A daily 10-minute walk can boost our energy and focus. Strength-based exercises like yoga or light weights can improve coordination.

Why Exercise Matters

- Exercise strengthens muscles and joints, allowing us to move with less effort.
- As we exercise, our cells become more efficient at absorbing nutrients and storing energy.
- Our nervous system improves muscle coordination, making our movements more precise and saving energy.
- Exercise stimulates the production of mood-enhancing chemicals like endorphins, improving our outlook and reducing stress.

Mental Wellness: Clean Thoughts, Clean Space

Our brains perform best in a clean, clear environment—both physically and mentally.

- *Avoid Automatic Negative Thoughts (ANTs):* Challenging these thoughts prevents them from limiting our potential. Remember, "If we fight for our limitations, we get to keep them."
- *Tidy Space, Clear Mind:* A clutter-free space reduces mental clutter. Research shows poor air quality is linked to conditions like strokes and dementia, so fresh air is also key.
- *Positive Connections:* Our brains are influenced by those around us. Social support from friends and family positively impacts decision-making and brain health.

Protecting Our Brains: Preventative Measures

Protecting our brains is an investment in our long-term health:

- *Avoid High-Risk Sports:* High-contact sports can harm the brain; wearing protective headgear is essential.
- *Keep Learning:* Our brains grow and adapt when we challenge them with new skills and activities.
- *Manage Stress:* Chronic stress can physically alter the brain, strengthening survival mechanisms while weakening problem-solving areas. Mindfulness, meditation, and other stress management techniques are crucial.

Sleep & Rest: The Brain's Reset Button

Sleep is like a restorative wash cycle for our brain. During sleep, our brain removes toxins that build up during the day, including amyloid-beta, a compound linked to Alzheimer's disease. Getting 7–8 hours of sleep per night is essential for memory, mood stability, and long-term brain health.

Additionally, our brains need downtime to stay productive. Short naps (10-20 minutes) or a full 90-minute nap can refresh us, improving our focus and memory.

Lifestyle Choices and Brain Health

Being mindful of our diet, exercise, and other habits can keep us mentally sharp:

- *Choose Whole Foods:* Opt for whole foods over processed ones and minimize refined sugars.
- *Consider Caffeine Intake:* Caffeine's half-life means it stays in our system for hours. Switching to tea can be a gentler option.
- *Vitamin D from Sunlight:* Sunlight is the best source of vitamin D. While it's important to avoid overexposure, spending a few minutes in the sun daily can help.

Experimenting with various diets or trying meal prep on a budget can give us insights into what makes us feel our best.

The Power of Purpose

"One, remember to look up at the stars and not down at your feet. Two, never give up work. Work gives you meaning and purpose and life is empty without it. Three, if you are lucky enough to find love, remember it is there and don't throw it away." - Stephen Hawking (*My Brief History*)

We can optimize all the diet, rest, and exercise we want without purpose - it will all fade away.

Having a sense of purpose can significantly impact our ability to perform and excel in whatever we do—understanding the "why" behind our actions fuels motivation, focus, and perseverance. Purpose guides us, giving meaning to our efforts and making even difficult tasks feel more worthwhile.

When we feel a strong sense of purpose, we're more likely to stay committed, even facing challenges. It helps us push through obstacles, stay disciplined, and remain dedicated to long-term goals. Purpose transforms tasks from mere obligations into meaningful pursuits, elevating our mental and physical performance.

Research has shown that having a clear sense of purpose can enhance cognitive function and decision-making abilities. When we know what we're working toward, our brain engages more fully, helping us to stay focused, solve problems, and stay productive for more extended periods of time. Purpose also helps reduce stress and anxiety, giving us a sense of control and direction. Instead of feeling lost or overwhelmed, we feel driven by something bigger than ourselves.

Additionally, having a purpose can improve resilience. When we face setbacks or failures, those with a clear sense of purpose are more likely to bounce back quickly because they're grounded in their bigger mission. Purpose can make challenges seem like temporary hurdles rather than insurmountable problems.

Purpose fuels our performance by giving us a reason to push harder, stay focused, and persevere when things get tough. It connects us to a bigger picture, making our work feel valuable, meaningful, and ultimately more rewarding.

A Balanced Approach to Health

Taking care of our brain and body is a holistic process that includes proper nutrition, regular exercise, restful sleep, and a clear sense of purpose. By fueling our minds with the nutrients they need, staying physically active, and maintaining a positive mindset, we can boost our cognitive well-being and overall happiness. Yet, without a sense of purpose, these efforts risk feeling empty. Purpose is the compass that guides us, helping us overcome obstacles and making each day more meaningful. When we align our physical health with a strong sense of purpose, we set ourselves up for a fulfilling and enriched life.

SUBSTANCE USE

A CRITICAL EXAMINATION OF DRUGS

"All things are poison, and nothing is without poison; the dosage alone makes it so a thing is not a poison." - Paracelsus

I magine we're at a social gathering, and someone offers us a drink or a hit from a vape. We might feel tempted, thinking it could help us unwind or fit in. But there's often a voice inside reminding us to think carefully about our choices. Substance use can offer enjoyment, relaxation, or even a boost in creativity, but if we're not mindful, it can lead us down a path we didn't intend. We can use substances responsibly once we understand both their benefits and risks, so we can make healthy, informed decisions.

Drugs: A Complex Category with Many Faces

When we think of "drugs," our minds might jump to harmful substances or illegal activities, but the reality is far broader. Drugs include everything from the caffeine in our coffee and life-saving prescriptions to substances responsible for the deaths of millions. Each has different effects and risks depending on how they interact with our bodies. Our approach to each kind of substance matters, and knowing the nuances can make all the difference.

The Many Types of Drugs

- *Everyday Drugs:* Some drugs are embedded in our routines, like caffeine in our morning coffee or tea. Caffeine is a stimulant, helping us feel more awake and alert. While a cup or two can give us that much-needed energy, too much caffeine can make us jittery, anxious, and disrupt our sleep.
- *Prescription Drugs:* Many of us use prescription drugs to manage health conditions. Antibiotics treat infections, and medications like ibuprofen reduce pain and inflammation. Under a doctor's guidance, these drugs are typically safe, but misuse—such as taking too much or using them without a prescription—can lead to addiction or harmful side effects.
- *Over-the-Counter (OTC) Drugs:* Common OTC drugs, like cold medicine or pain relievers, can be purchased without a prescription and are generally safe in recommended doses. However, misusing them, like taking extra painkillers, can harm our liver or kidneys.
- *Recreational and Illegal Drugs:* Some substances, like marijuana, cocaine, or heroin, are used recreationally but come with higher risks. These can change how our brain functions, often causing euphoria or relaxation. However, they carry a high risk of addiction and can damage our health, affecting our heart, mental well-being, and overall quality of life.

Understanding Risks and Rewards

"Every action has its pleasures and its price." —Socrates

The key to understanding drugs is recognizing that not all drugs are harmful, but all drugs have risks if they're misused. Even something as common as caffeine, which most of us think of as harmless, can cause problems if we consume too much, such as headaches, anxiety, or insomnia. On the other hand, prescription medications have clear benefits when used as directed, but they can be dangerous if we take them in ways other than intended.

Setting Personal Guidelines

One of the best ways we can stay safe around drugs and alcohol is by setting our own guidelines. When we know our boundaries, we're more likely to make thoughtful decisions. Here are a few guidelines to consider:

- *Know our limits:* Deciding in advance how much is comfortable for us helps us stick to it, even when others might be doing more.
- *Choose the right time and place:* We should only consider substances in safe, familiar environments where we feel in control.
- *Take breaks:* Giving ourselves permission to say no can be powerful. Just because something is available doesn't mean we have to partake.

Having these guidelines gives us a plan to follow, helping us stay in control and avoid making impulsive decisions. These limits are unique to each of us but are much easier to uphold when we decide ahead of time.

How Substances Can Change Our Experiences

Sometimes, we use substances because we think they'll enhance how we feel in specific situations. For example:

- *Relaxing with alcohol:* A drink or two might help us feel less nervous in social settings.
- *Boosting energy with caffeine:* Many of us rely on caffeine to stay awake or focused for a short time.
- *Enhancing creativity:* Some people believe that certain substances make creative activities like art or writing more engaging.

While these benefits can be appealing, they also come with risks if we're not careful about moderation.

Recognizing Consequences: What to Watch Out For

Even though substances might seem to make experiences better, they can lead to serious issues if overused:

- *Addiction and dependence:* Regular use of drugs or alcohol can make our bodies crave them, leading to dependency.
- *Health problems:* Overusing substances like alcohol or drugs can harm organs like the liver or brain.
- *Mood swings and mental health issues:* Substances that make us feel good at first can lead to anxiety or sadness, especially when overused.

The Role of Positive and Negative Feedback Loops

Our brain relies on neurotransmitters—chemicals that allow brain cells to communicate with each other—to control how we feel and behave. When we use drugs or alcohol, they interfere with the average production of these neurotransmitters, either boosting or suppressing their levels.

Positive Feedback Loops with Neurotransmitters

A *positive feedback loop* happens when our bodies increase the production of something. Regarding the brain, we have positive feedback loops with neurotransmitters in response to something pleasurable. For example, caffeine works by blocking adenosine receptors in the brain. Adenosine is a neurotransmitter that promotes relaxation and sleepiness, especially as it accumulates throughout the day. When we regularly consume caffeine, our brain adapts by increasing the number of adenosine receptors to counteract caffeine's blocking effect. This increased receptor sensitivity means that when we stop consuming caffeine, there are more adenosine receptors actively responding to natural adenosine levels.

As a result, during caffeine withdrawal, we may feel more tired, sluggish, and experience increased drowsiness. This is because, in the absence of caffeine, the brain responds to normal adenosine levels with an intensified effect due to the upregulation of adenosine receptors, which leads to more significant feelings of tiredness and fatigue.

Negative Feedback Loops with Neurotransmitters

A *negative feedback loop* works in the opposite way. This is when our bodies decrease the production of something. When we overuse a substance like drugs or alcohol, our brain may start sending signals to reduce or stop the production of certain neurotransmitters. For instance, alcohol increases the activity of GABA, a neurotransmitter that helps us feel calm and relaxed. With frequent alcohol use, however, the brain may begin to reduce its natural production of GABA to prevent overstimulation. This can result in feelings of anxiety or tension when not drinking, as the brain adjusts to lower GABA levels.

Staying Aware of These Loops

When we under stand how these positive and negative feedback loops work, we can become more aware of how substances like drugs and alcohol affect our brains. Positive feedback means that our bodies produce more of something, while negative feedback signals us to produce less. By listening to both types of signals, we can make healthier decisions and avoid getting caught in a cycle of addiction.

Tips for Staying Healthy and Safe

Here are a few ways we can maintain control and make mindful choices:

- *Listen to our bodies:* If we start feeling unwell or out of control, it's a signal to stop. Our bodies are good at telling us when something's off.
- *Talk to someone we trust:* If we're struggling or feel like we're losing control, reaching out to a friend or family member can offer support and perspective.
- *Find other ways to relax and have fun:* We don't always need substances to enjoy ourselves. Exploring hobbies, sports, or activities with friends can be just as rewarding without the risks.

Balancing Rewards and Risks

While substances can sometimes help us feel more relaxed or focused, these effects are temporary, whereas the potential consequences can last. If we choose to use substances, practicing moderation is essential. We can also find other ways to relax and engage without the same risks. Drugs and alcohol have a complex role in our lives. They can offer enjoyment and even some benefits, but they also carry significant risks. Even everyday substances, if overused, can become harmful.

When we understand different types of drugs and the feedback loops in our brains, we can make informed decisions. Setting personal guidelines for ourselves and staying aware of the potential pitfalls helps us enjoy life responsibly. In the end, making mindful, balanced choices lets us appreciate the moment while protecting our health and future well-being. It's about respecting our bodies, understanding the risks, and knowing that we are in control of what we put into our lives.

REPUTATION & INNER PEACE
A BALANCING ACT

"Reputation is the cornerstone of power. Through reputation alone you can intimidate and win; once it slips, however, you are vulnerable, and will be attacked on all sides." - Robert Greene (*The 48 Laws of Power*)

Our reputation is a powerful tool for navigating life. Whether we realize it or not, how others view us can influence our relationships, opportunities, and success. Yet, it's essential to remember that while reputation is valuable, it's not everything. Accountability plays a crucial role in maintaining a strong reputation while also keeping us grounded in our inner values.

Reputation can be a powerful tool if we can learn how to not become trapped by it and balance external validation with inner peace.

What Is Reputation?

Reputation is the image people form of us based on our actions, character, and associations. It's a kind of "social currency," often built on four key pillars:

- *Character* – Keeping our promises, acting with integrity, and aligning actions with words.
- *Experience* – Showing proof of accomplishments and handling challenges effectively.
- *Knowledge* – Knowing our field or role deeply and applying this understanding.
- *Association* – Surrounding ourselves with people who hold positive reputations, as trust and credibility can sometimes be "borrowed."

Imagine someone who has built a reputation in their field, not just because they're skilled, but because they consistently act with integrity. By upholding character, experience, knowledge, and association, they're trusted even when challenges arise. This trust opens doors that may otherwise would be hard to access.

We can begin molding our reputation by taking a moment to think about how we are perceived in each area of our lives. Do people see us as reliable? Knowledgeable?

Why Reputation Matters

A strong reputation can open doors and create opportunities. A good reputation encourages trust, which in turn leads to more positive connections and possibilities. However, if we aren't careful we can place too much weight on the opinions of others. Other people do not define our happiness.

"People generally think too much about the opinion which others form of them; although the slightest reflection will show that this opinion, whatever it may be, is not in itself essential to happiness."
- Arthur Schopenhauer (*The Wisdom of Life*)

Reputation can be essential but should not be the source of our self-worth or contentment.

However, it is worth considering that a bad reputation will close doors and create additional (and unnecessary) obstacles for us.

Psychologists today recognize that while reputation can enhance social standing, self-worth is best grounded in intrinsic factors like values and inner growth. Relying solely on others' views often leads to emotional instability. Building an "internal compass" for validation is key.

What Is Accountability?

Accountability is the practice of taking responsibility for our actions—both successes and mistakes. When we're accountable, we show others that we can be trusted to do what we say we'll do, and that we're willing to learn from our mistakes. This reliability builds credibility and strengthens our reputation over time.

For example, consider a colleague who consistently meets deadlines and admits when they make mistakes. Their willingness to take responsibility makes them a trustworthy teammate, regardless of occasional errors. This accountability is the foundation of their positive reputation.

The first step to develop our accountability is reflecting on recent moments when we were either accountable or avoided responsibility. Without accountability, we cannot build credibility.

Accountability as a Path to a Strong Reputation

Accountability not only fosters trust but is one of the surest ways to improve reputation. When we consistently act with responsibility, people view us as reliable and trustworthy. Accountability fortifies reputation in three ways:

- *Consistency* – Doing what we promise builds trust. When

we are reliable, our reputation grows stronger over time and solidifies our reputation.

- *Learning from Mistakes* – Everyone makes mistakes. Taking responsibility when things go wrong shows maturity and helps rebuild trust.
- *Earning Respect* – Being accountable earns respect. People appreciate when we own up to our actions and follow through on commitments.

Balancing Accountability and Self-Compassion

People who seek praise or fear criticism may struggle with accountability. When we limit our concern for external opinions and focus on developing our internal benchmarks, it becomes easier to develop accountability,

> "It is advisable... to set limits to this weakness, and duly to consider and rightly to estimate the relative value of advantages... Otherwise, a man is the slave of what other people are pleased to think."
> - Arthur Schopenhauer (*The Wisdom of Life*)

Accountability is not about pleasing others—it's about growth. We can use feedback as a tool for self-improvement without letting it control our happiness. Feedback is a learning opportunity rather than a judgment. By focusing on improvement, we strengthen both our reputation and our sense of self.

Balancing Reputation and Inner Peace

While reputation is valuable, overvaluing others' opinions can trap us. Obsessing over how others see us can make us slaves to their approval.

> "To lay great value upon what other people say is to pay them too much honor." - Arthur Schopenhauer (*The Wisdom of Life*)

In today's culture of social media and constant comparison, it's easy to become fixated on public image. But inner peace comes from grounding ourselves in reality and finding satisfaction within. Imagine someone who is respected in their community but deeply anxious about maintaining that image. Rather than enjoying their accomplishments, they're always seeking external validation. In contrast, someone who is internally grounded is at peace, content with their own growth regardless of others' opinions.

It is easier to find satisfaction within ourselves when we identify the personal values that matter most to us. Aligning our actions with these values, rather than external expectations, helps balance our reputation with inner peace.

Reputation as a Tool, Not a Trap

Reputation is an invaluable tool, but when we allow it to dominate our sense of self, it becomes a trap. People often spend their lives seeking others' approval through wealth, titles, or social status, leading to a distorted self-worth.

> "People reverse the natural order, regarding the opinions of others as real existence and their own consciousness as something shadowy." - Arthur Schopenhauer (*The Wisdom of Life*)

The true key to happiness lies in balance. Our reputation can help us succeed, but our peace of mind and self-worth should not depend solely on it.

> "Happiness... consists for the most part in peace of mind and contentment." - Arthur Schopenhauer (*The Wisdom of Life*)

Treat reputation as a tool for achieving goals, rather than the goal itself. I often ask myself, "what goals are worth my energy, independent of others' opinions?" When I ask myself this question,

I get clear on the things that I want to accomplish for myself rather than for others.

BUILDING A STRONG REPUTATION REQUIRES TIME, consistency, and accountability. By taking responsibility and learning from mistakes, we can naturally improve how others view us. Yet, as Schopenhauer cautions, we should not let others' opinions define our happiness. Instead, focusing on our inner growth first allows our reputation to reflect our true character—serving as a powerful, but not overpowering, guide in our lives.

By treating reputation as a tool and grounding ourselves in values, we can achieve both external success and inner peace. Striking this balance is easier said than done and needs to be reevaluated constantly.

NETWORKING

WINNING ISN'T THE GOAL—IT'S ABOUT HOW WE PLAY THE GAME

"The rules of the game are not only compulsory; they are also sacred and inviolable. They represent a transcendent order to which all players must submit." - Jean Piaget (*The Moral Judgment of the Child*)

Life as a Series of Games

Networking is not about who we know but about who knows us. We can enhance who knows us by understanding life as a game. However, life isn't about playing and winning just one game—it's about staying in the game over a lifetime. Networking follows this pattern: the goal isn't to impress someone once but to become the kind of person others want to keep inviting back. Real success, then, is about who we become, not just what we achieve in one isolated game.

"To be valuable in the broadest possible range of contexts, you must learn to be a flexible, competent, intelligent, courageous, honest citizen in a social hierarchy that could stretch as far as any horizon that you can conceive of." - Jordan Peterson (*Beyond Order*)

Life is a series of games and we're not just playing for ourselves; we're learning the group's values and understanding where we fit within them. We observe the rules that others follow, recognizing what matters in each "game." The more we play, the better we become at navigating complex interactions, leading us to succeed across different areas of life.

This understanding is key to networking. Success isn't just about one encounter or one connection; it's about building relationships that transcend a single moment. The more games we play, the better we get at reading people, understanding what they value, and finding ways to add value to their lives.

From Simple Games to Complex Interactions

As we grow older, the "games" of life become more complex. When we're kids, the games are simple, with straightforward rules and clear winners and losers. But as we move into adulthood, life's games—whether they involve relationships, career, or networking—demand more nuanced skills, like emotional intelligence and patience.

Psychologist Jean Piaget, who studied children's cognitive development, observed that playing games only works when there's a shared goal. This principle translates well into adult life: to achieve something meaningful together, people must agree on the rules and purposes of the "game." Collaboration, empathy, and flexibility become essential skills for winning in these more sophisticated games.

Peterson takes this further, pointing out that life is a series of interconnected games. Winning one round doesn't matter much if it means people don't want to play with us again. While strategies like lying or manipulation might seem effective in the short term, they erode trust and close doors over time. The real winners are those who approach life as a long game, where the ultimate goal is to keep getting invited back.

The Power of Choice in Playing the Game

Piaget also noticed that voluntary games—those played by choice, not force—are far more powerful. When we willingly join in, we engage more fully and play better. Peterson adds that the best players in life know how to cooperate, manage emotions, and compete fairly, building trust and respect from others. In networking, this means showing up authentically, playing by the rules, and being a good sport. People value those who play fairly, work toward collective goals, and contribute positively to the group.

Imagine a professional setting where someone volunteers to help with a challenging project. When participation is voluntary, their enthusiasm and effort show, and others take notice. Contrast this with someone reluctantly assigned to the same project—their impact is less likely to leave a positive impression. By choosing to engage meaningfully, we build relationships based on trust and shared values.

Humility as a Networking Strength

Networking rarely begins with immediate rewards or high-status connections. Often, we start at the bottom, which isn't glamorous but is invaluable. Being a beginner teaches us the importance of humility and gratitude, both of which can help us navigate the networking "game" more effectively.

Gratitude, in particular, helps us see others as resources rather than threats. There are always people who know more than we do; rather than feeling competitive or insecure, we can appreciate their expertise and learn from them. Humility enables us to approach situations with an open mind, allowing us to grow and understand the nuances of the game.

Psychiatrist Carl Jung highlighted the importance of embracing the "fool" archetype. The fool often starts at the bottom, willing to make mistakes and learn. It's this willingness to learn and grow that eventually transforms the fool into a hero. In networking, staying humble allows us to absorb wisdom from those around us, moving from a beginner to a respected player over time.

Benjamin Franklin: A Master of Building Connections

Benjamin Franklin serves as a classic example of someone who played the networking game masterfully. He wasn't just a scientist, writer, or politician; he was exceptionally skilled at building and sustaining connections.

Franklin famously used his ability to connect with people by asking for their help or advice. He believed that people like to feel useful and that he could build strong relationships by asking for small favors. Over time, these relationships grew, and Franklin became one of the most connected people of his time. He knew how to make people feel important, which kept him in the game across multiple areas of life.

Franklin also excelled at code-switching—a skill we now define as adapting one's language or behavior to fit different social situations. Whether he was talking to scientists, politicians, or everyday people, Franklin knew how to present himself in a way that made others want to engage with him. His adaptability kept him invited back to different "games" in society, demonstrating the value of versatility in networking.

Tim Ferriss: Networking as a Long Game

Author and investor Tim Ferriss advocates for a patient, long-term approach to networking. Ferriss emphasizes self-improvement, believing that when we focus on learning new skills and growing, the right connections naturally come to us. This perspective shifts networking from a desperate pursuit to a natural extension of our personal growth.

Ferriss suggests increasing our exposure to opportunities by positioning ourselves in high-density environments, whether physically or digitally. For example, moving to cities with active industries or participating in online communities relevant to our interests increases our chances of meeting people who share our values and goals. Ferriss also recommends volunteering at events, where a positive impression can lead to valuable connections with key players in the field.

> "No matter how isolated you are and how lonely you feel, if you do your work truly and conscientiously, unknown friends will come and seek you." – Carl Jung

THE GOAL of networking isn't to impress one person or win one game. The people with the most robust networks are those others want to keep inviting back, time after time. By focusing on growth, humility, and adaptability, we position ourselves as reliable and valued players in the game of life. It's about building relationships that endure, not just winning once.

So, we play the long game—not for quick wins but for lasting connections. We show up with curiosity and humility, engage willingly, and adapt to various settings. This approach naturally attracts the right network to us, ensuring that the games we play today continue to invite us back tomorrow.

ON LUCK

WE ARE NOT LOTTERY TICKETS

"Success is just a matter of luck. Ask any failure." - Earl Wilson

When we talk about success, it's common to think of luck. Many believe that success is a stroke of good fortune, something that either happens or doesn't. Luck isn't a strategy. Rather than waiting for life to go our way, we should focus on what we can control and create our own opportunities.

Self-Honesty: The Foundation of Growth

The first step to success is being honest with ourselves about where we are. Big goals can feel overwhelming, but self-awareness helps us break things down, staying realistic about our strengths and areas for growth. By focusing on specific steps, we can take action with confidence and avoid the trap of taking on too much at once. After all, luck alone doesn't solve problems—consistent, focused effort does.

"Success isn't about luck. Success is about intentionally aligning every aspect of your life with what you want." - Josh Kaufman (*The Personal MBA*)

Creating Conditions for Luck

"There's a difference between luck that happens by chance and the luck we create by taking action, being prepared, and putting ourselves in the right position." - Shane Parrish (*Clear Thinking*)

While pure, random luck isn't something we can control, we can influence our chances of success by preparing and positioning ourselves well. In his book, *Clear Thinking*, Shane Parrish breaks down luck into five types, four of which we can actively cultivate:

- *Blind Luck* – The kind of luck that happens by chance.
- *Action Luck* – Luck that arises when we take action and create momentum.
- *Preparation Luck* – When readiness meets opportunity, opening doors for us.
- *Persistence Luck* – The luck that shows up when we don't give up.
- *Reputation Luck* – When our character attracts opportunities others might call "luck."

Blind luck may be random, but we can influence the other types by taking action, preparing, persisting, and building a solid reputation. When we create favorable conditions, we put chance on our side.

"One of the best ways to improve your chances of success is by developing the character traits that increase your odds of favorable outcomes." - Shane Parrish (*Clear Thinking*)

Success Is Never Accidental

"Success is never accidental." - Jack Dorsey

When we look at people who've achieved great things, it's easy to think they just got lucky. But success is built on deliberate work, preparation, and a clear understanding of what's possible. Companies may launch in unique circumstances, but each one relies on a plan, effort, and a vision for the future.

If we treat the future as something we can shape, we'll work to make it better. But if we think life is purely random, it's easy to become passive and let things happen to us. Success comes from believing we can shape the future.

Turning Failure into Strength

"Shallow men believe in luck, believe in circumstances.... Strong men believe in cause and effect." - Ralph Waldo Emerson (*Self-Reliance*)

Failure isn't the opposite of success; it's an essential part of the journey. Learning from our failures builds experience and strengthens us, preparing us for future opportunities. Instead of hoping for a stroke of luck, we can focus on sharpening our skills so we're ready to seize chances when they arise. Consistent "failure" creates more success than aiming for perfection.

While persistence is about not giving up, resilience is about how we handle setbacks. Failure can be discouraging, but our ability to bounce back and keep going is essential to lasting success. Resilience is the "muscle" that powers persistence over the long term.

"Fall seven times, stand up eight." - Japanese Proverb

Those who rise after setbacks often find that resilience—the ability to stand back up—is the real difference-maker in their journey to success.

"You will come across obstacles in life—fair and unfair. And you will discover, time and time again, that what matters most is not what these obstacles are but how we see them, how we react to them, and whether we keep our composure." - Ryan Holiday (*The Obstacle Is the Way*)

Increasing Our Chances of Luck

So, how can we increase our chances of luck?

Stay Curious and Sensitive to Change

Stay curious, continuously learn, and pay attention to shifts others may miss. This way, when opportunities come, we can recognize them. A prepared mind sees openings that others overlook. I like to pay attention to people I believe are intelligent and notice how they spend their time during nights and weekends.

"If you want to see what's going to happen in the future, look at what's happening on the fringes of society now." - Naval Ravikant

For example, Steve Jobs demonstrated the power of staying curious and paying attention to emerging trends in design and technology. His obsession with exploring how technology could integrate seamlessly into people's lives led to innovations that revolutionized industries from computing to mobile phones.

Another example is Elon Musk. His curiosity about complex fields like space exploration and sustainable energy led him to establish groundbreaking companies like SpaceX and Tesla. By constantly seeking answers and paying attention to new developments, he transformed industries that once seemed unchangeable.

I would be remiss to not mention Marie Curie, she pioneered research into radioactivity, uncovering elements like radium and polonium. She was dedicated to understanding the unknown, despite significant risks. Her discoveries not only advanced scientific knowledge but also transformed medicine.

All of these people changed the world and found tremendous "luck" by recognizing opportunities that other people ignored.

Hustle Until We Stumble On It

Keep working, even when nothing seems to happen. The more we put ourselves out there and take action, the more chances we create for success. As we move forward, we encounter situations that lead to unexpected opportunities. We can make something happen, or we can let something happen to us. Moving toward our goal with action increases our chances of success far more than hoping ever could. Action produces information, so when we act we can better align our actions to suit out goals.

For example, the founder of Spanx, Sara Blakely, started with just $5,000 and no background in fashion or business. Her hustle—cold-calling manufacturers, promoting her product herself, and handling every aspect of the business—turned Spanx into a billion-dollar brand. She learned and created opportunities along the way, she didn't wait for "luck" to find her.

Let's took a look at Thomas Edison. He has an unyielding dedication to his work which led him to file over 1,000 patents. These resulted in transformative inventions like the phonograph and the practical light bulb. His luck sprang from his continuous experimentation, refusal to give up, and consistent hands-on effort.

Become the Best at What We Do

"Become the best in the world at what you do. Keep redefining what you do until this is true." - Naval Ravikant

When we refine our skills to a high level, opportunities begin to seek us out. Hard work is essential, but developing our abilities until we're among the best draws others to us and positions us for success that appears like "luck."

Take Warren Buffet, for example, he is known as one of the greatest investors of all time. His mastery of financial analysis and market trends sets him apart. From a young age, he immersed himself in studying businesses, honing his ability to evaluate companies and make informed investments. Buffett's expertise, coupled with his disciplined, long-term approach, has made him an unmissable figure in the financial world. Because of this, Buffet gets opportunities simply because he is Warren Buffet. During the 2008 financial crisis, Goldman Sachs approached Buffett for a $5 billion investment to stabilize the company. Buffett's expertise in financial markets and reputation for sound judgment made him the go-to person when companies needed not just funding but also the credibility that came from his backing. Additionally, Buffett's Berkshire Hathaway regularly receives investment proposals before they're available to the general market because people trust his insight.

We can also see this with Wolfgang Amadeus Mozart. His skill in composition and music theory, honed from childhood, made him one of history's most celebrated composers. His deep understanding of music, combined with endless practice and innovation, allowed him to compose complex and moving pieces that still resonate today. Mozart's reputation as a musical prodigy and his unparalleled skill in composition led to commissions from European royalty and nobility. For instance, Emperor Joseph II of Austria invited Mozart to become his court composer, giving him opportunities to create and perform for elite audiences across Europe. He also attracted the patrons who provided financial support, allowing him to compose freely and focus on his work. This support enabled Mozart to write masterpieces that continue to be celebrated centuries later

Character and Reputation Matter

"Your character and your reputation are things you can build, which will let you take advantage of opportunities other people may characterize as lucky, but you know it wasn't luck." - Naval Ravikant

Reputation and character play a huge role in creating "luck." When people trust us, opportunities come our way because we're seen as reliable and capable. Building a strong reputation puts us in a position to succeed even more. Reputation and character create luck, but we can create our reputation and character.

WHILE LUCK MAY SEEM RANDOM, we have more control over our future than we think. By being honest with ourselves, learning from failure, and staying persistent, we create conditions for success. When we prepare, take action, and continually refine our skills, what others call "luck" becomes the outcome of our hard work.

"Victory awaits him who has everything in order—luck, people call it." - Roald Amundsen

In truth, success doesn't happen by accident—it happens when we make room for it. We get lucky when we stop waiting for a lucky break and start building our own path forward. What others call luck is, more often than not, the result of deliberate choices and actions.

UNDERSTANDING LEVERAGE & JUDGEMENT

FOR SUCCESS & WEALTH BUILDING

In today's fast-changing world, wealth creation isn't just about hard work; it's about making informed decisions, leveraging technology, and owning something valuable. Naval Ravikant teaches us that good judgment is critical to lasting success. Judgment—the ability to make the right calls at the right time—guides us through the complexities of wealth-building.

Those who combine sound judgment with creativity and ownership will thrive in an age defined by technology and leverage. This requires a shift in thinking: from working harder to working smarter, from chasing short-term wins to pursuing long-term gains. By understanding this, we can build wealth, achieve freedom, and gain greater control over our lives.

Naval Ravikant, an entrepreneur, investor, and philosopher, has spent years studying and sharing his wisdom on these topics. Many trust his insights because he's built his wealth and helped guide some of the world's most successful companies, like Twitter and Uber. Naval's philosophy combines deep thinking with practical advice, making him an essential voice in the conversation on wealth-building and judgment.

Leverage: The Multiplier of Effort

To understand how to build wealth, we first need to grasp leverage. Leverage allows us to multiply our efforts and amplify the results of our decisions—both good and bad.

Leverage allows us to do more with less.

Leverage comes in many forms—money, technology, labor, media, or code—and magnifies our choices' effects. If we make a good decision, leverage can multiply the positive outcomes. However, the same goes for poor decisions; leverage will multiply negative outcomes as well.

Leverage can be divided into two types: permission and permissionless. Money and labor require permission from others to obtain the benefits of leverage. Media and code, on the other hand, are permissionless, meaning they do not need permission from others.

"Leverage magnifies those differences even more. Being at the extreme in your art is very important in the age of leverage." - Naval Ravikant

We live in a world of nearly limitless leverage, especially with the internet allowing one person to reach millions. Code, media, and capital give us leverage without physical boundaries. This abundance of leverage means that the quality of our judgment— the soundness of our decisions—matters more than ever. A good decision can yield enormous gains, while poor judgment can lead to equally significant losses.

To wield leverage effectively, we must understand its power. When combined with sound judgment, leverage becomes a tool that multiplies our potential, allowing us to create lasting and influential success.

"A leveraged worker can out-produce a non-leveraged worker by a factor of one thousand or ten thousand. With a leveraged worker, judgment is far more important than how much time they put in or how hard they work." - Naval Ravikant

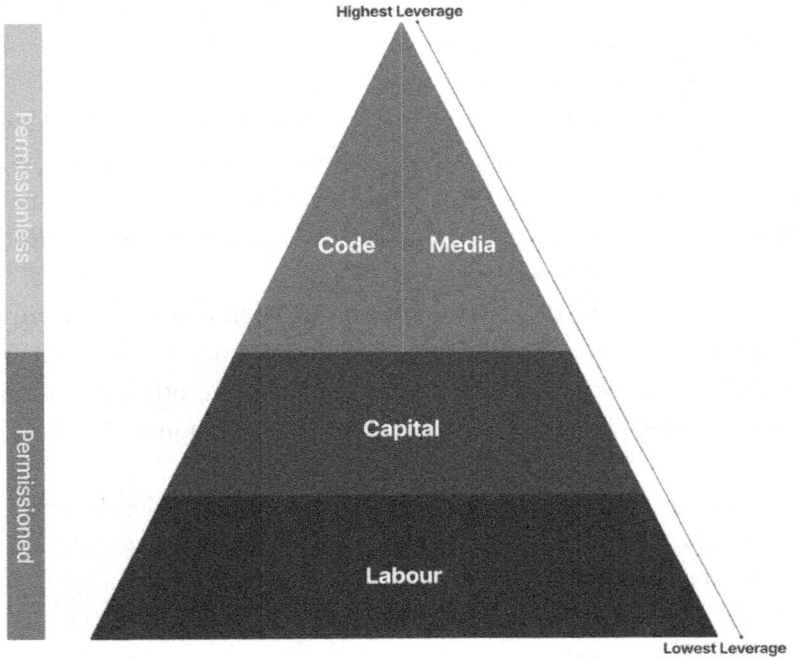

Image by Darien Tan / Medium

Building Judgment: The Core of Long-Term Success

In a modern age driven by artificial intelligence and rapid change, developing strong judgment is one of the most valuable skills we can cultivate. The ability to make intelligent, well-informed decisions will shape our lives more profoundly than hard work or luck.

Consider our choice of career or field. Selecting work that aligns with our values and skills isn't just about making money; it's about creating freedom. Judgment enables us to choose paths that expand our options rather than limiting them. Wise decisions give us more time and control over how we spend it.

"Choosing what kinds of jobs, careers, or fields you get into and what sort of deals you're willing to take from your employer will give you much more free time. Then, you don't have to worry as much about time management." - Naval Ravikant

In Naval's view, the future will be one where robots and computers handle much of the labor, while people are paid for their judgment. Building sharp judgment now prepares us to be among those who thrive in that future.

The Power of Small Differences in Judgment

Small differences in judgment can lead to huge differences in outcomes, especially when paired with leverage. Just as .01 seconds to an Olympic sprinter makes a champion, being slightly better at decision-making can create a massive advantage.

"Small differences in judgment and capability really get amplified." - Naval Ravikant

Consistency in good judgment is crucial. It builds trust and credibility, essential for succeeding in any marketplace or community. The goal isn't to make a few good decisions but to show a reliable pattern of sound judgment over time. Warren Buffet isn't considered one of the best financial analysts of all time because of one good trade, but because he has repeatedly demonstrated he can make good choices.

"Demonstrated judgment—credibility around the judgment—is so critical." - Naval Ravikant

In a world with infinite leverage, poor judgment leads to amplified poor outcomes. But with strong, consistent judgment, we turn leverage into an ally, multiplying positive outcomes.

Long-Term Thinking: Choosing the Right Direction

One key to improving our judgment is focusing on the long-term effects of our actions. Naval Ravikant defines wisdom as understanding the long-term consequences of our choices. When we apply wisdom to solve external problems, that's judgment.

> "My definition of wisdom is knowing the long-term consequences of your actions. Wisdom applied to external problems is judgment." - Naval Ravikant

In a leveraged world, picking the right direction matters more than speed. A well-chosen path, combined with steady effort, yields far greater rewards than rushing in the wrong direction.

> "The direction you're heading in matters more than how fast you move, especially with leverage." - Naval Ravikant

Hard work alone isn't enough; we must pair it with wise decisions to reach our full potential.

Clear Thinking and Independent Decisions

Good judgment comes from clear thinking. Richard Feynman famously said that if we can't explain a concept simply, we don't truly understand it. Naval emphasizes that clear thinkers who understand fundamentals are more valuable than those who simply memorize complex ideas.

> "If you can't explain it to a child, then you don't know it." - Richard Feynman

To develop clear judgment, we must seek understanding, not just knowledge. Independent thinking is equally important. In a world where many follow the crowd, those who reason for themselves will stand out.

> "A contrarian isn't one who always objects—that's a conformist of a different sort. A contrarian reasons independently from the ground up and resists pressure to conform." - Naval Ravikant

Embracing Reality: Facing the Uncomfortable

Sound judgment also means facing the truth, even when it's uncomfortable. Pain and hardship often reveal reality, forcing us to see things clearly and make better decisions.

> "The moment of suffering—when you're in pain—is a moment of truth. It is a moment where you're forced to embrace reality the way it actually is." - Naval Ravikant

To make wise decisions, we must look at facts rather than how we wish things were. Real change begins with seeing the world as it truly is, even if that means confronting difficult truths.

> "What we wish to be true clouds our perception of what is true. Suffering is the moment when we can no longer deny reality." - Naval Ravikant

In today's world, developing judgment has never been more essential. Whether choosing a career, leveraging technology, or navigating personal goals, judgment helps us make decisions that lead to long-term success. Embracing clear thinking, long-term perspective, and the reality of the world builds a track record of sound judgment that amplifies our efforts.

Building Wealth Through Value Creation and Ownership

Wealth isn't about competing with others for limited resources; it's about creating new value that benefits society. When we create something that society needs but doesn't yet have, we're on the path to success.

> "Wealth creation is an evolutionarily recent positive-sum game. Status is an old zero-sum game. Those attacking wealth creation are often just seeking status." - Naval Ravikant

The key to wealth creation is finding a product or service that aligns with our natural abilities. When we master this, we create real value.

> "Society will pay you for creating things it wants. But society doesn't yet know how to create those things." - Naval Ravikant

Owning something valuable is essential to becoming truly wealthy. Whether it's a product, intellectual property, or a business, ownership allows us to create value without tying ourselves to hourly work.

> "Without ownership, when you're sleeping, you're not earning." - Naval Ravikant

Ownership gives us the potential for unlimited growth, unlike debt, which offers limited gains. It allows wealth to accumulate even while we're doing other things—like spending time with loved ones or pursuing passions.

ULTIMATELY, creating wealth is about smart choices and using the right tools to expand our impact. Naval teaches us that good judgment—knowing when and how to act—is the secret to lasting success. By pairing judgment with leverage, like technology, money, or media, we multiply our results and create real value.

Wealth creation isn't about competing with others but creating something valuable and owning a part of it. This gives us control over our time and finances. With better decisions and effective tools, we can all build a life of freedom, purpose, and fulfillment.

NAVIGATING CAREERS
WHAT WE DO, NOT WHO WE ARE

Our Ever-Evolving Journey

Careers are not fixed destinations—they're dynamic, evolving journeys shaped by the choices we make along the way. Much like a ship navigating the open ocean, we have the power to steer, even if changing direction requires effort, especially as we go deeper into a specific path. The important thing is to remember: our career is what we do, not who we are. They are a series of actions, not an identity. Additionally, most people do not have careers. Most people have jobs. Careers are create when a set of experiences or jobs are linked together with a common theme. Regardless, our jobs or careers are not who we are, but simply actions we take.

As the world of work changes rapidly, the best way to prepare for an unpredictable future is to take control of our own learning. By continuously building our skills and expanding our knowledge, we ensure that we're not just keeping up but staying ahead, ready to face new challenges and seize new opportunities.

Growing Within Our Work

When choosing a workplace, it's crucial to find an environment where we can grow. Look for roles that challenge us but still allow room for improvement. The goal is to be in a place that stretches our abilities without overwhelming us—a balance that promotes both performance and well-being. Think of it as finding a mentor and protégé role in one space: someone to learn from and others we can help elevate.

Thriving in the Expert Economy

We live in an "expert economy" where our ability to think, solve problems, and innovate is more valuable than physical strength.

> "Your ability to think, solve problems, make the right decisions, create, innovate, and imagine is how we add value." - Jim Kwik (*Limitless*)

In this age, our most valuable asset is what's between our ears. The faster we can learn, the faster we can grow and adapt to this ever-shifting landscape. Think of reading and learning as installing new software in our brain, updating our internal "operating system" to meet the demands of the future.

Preparing for Future Opportunities

One of the biggest lessons I've learned in my career journey is that the future holds countless unseen possibilities. A few years ago, jobs like "podcast producer" or "data privacy officer" didn't exist, but now they're sought-after roles. This is why we should *focus on skills that intrigue us*; if we love learning something new, chances are that future job opportunities will reward our unique skill set.

By honing in on our passions, we stay open to evolving opportunities we might not yet imagine. As new roles emerge, our skills and interests prepare us to pivot seamlessly into spaces that didn't exist before. However, it is critical to keep in mind that solely focusing on on our passions may not necessarily give us opportunities. There are skills that we may not be passionate about that are necessary to combine with our passions. For example, someone who is a podcast producer may be passionate about connecting with people but may need to develop deep technical skill in audio engineering. Bonus points if they are passionate about both.

Switching Modes for Renewed Growth

At one point, while working on my resume, I felt stuck and burned out. I had been experimenting and trying new things but realized I needed a shift. Instead of testing new skills, I began refining and presenting what I already had. Sometimes, burnout isn't a sign of doing too much—it's a signal that we need a change in perspective. Switching from *experimenting to improving* can be just the refresh we need to unlock new growth. For example, I spent a lot of time and effort learning new skills and exploring fields that we seemingly unrelated— music, medicine, education, & business. After a while, I decided to improve my skills with education to grow in a different way. This led me down a path of becoming a teacher and author.

The Power of Relationships

Building strong, authentic relationships is key to any career. Showing kindness, honoring commitments, and maintaining integrity can be 70% of success. Early in our careers, relationships are fresh and untested. It's essential to care for these connections by addressing and repairing issues early. For example, if a relationship at work is strained, address it by mentioning what went wrong, offering a solution, and committing to making things right. This level of interpersonal care can surprise people and strengthen our professional network.

The Two Phases of a Career: Learning and Earning

Career journeys often have two main stages:

1. *Learning Stage:* Early in our careers, say yes to opportunities that expand our experience. This phase is about exploration, whether through side projects or diverse roles. Think of it as gathering "tools" in our toolkit until we find what fits best.
2. *Earning Stage:* Once we know what aligns with our skills and goals, it's time to specialize. Focus on the skills that bring the most success, honing them to maximize our earning potential and become an expert in our chosen field.

Career Paths After High School

After high school, various paths open up:

- *College:* A traditional route that can lead to advanced education.
- *Military:* Offers structure, discipline, and career benefits.
- *Jobs:* Enter the workforce to gain experience and income right away.
- *Trade/Technical Schools:* Provide hands-on skills for specific careers.
- *Combination:* A mix of work and education can be beneficial, particularly in the learning phase of a career, as it provides a well-rounded experience without splitting focus.

I did a combination of all of these choices, with the exception of the military, when we left high school and found that they are all valuable in their own way.

Reverse-Engineering Career Goals

One powerful way to map out a career is by reverse-engineering our goals. Start by visualizing our ultimate career position—whether that's a specialized role, leadership position, or entrepreneurial path. Then, work backward to understand the steps needed to get there, such as specific training, experience, or connections.

This process provides clarity and direction, helping us build a solid plan to reach our goals. For example, if we aim to be a medical doctor, identify the required certifications, degrees, and experience, and begin setting small goals toward each milestone.

The Value of Letters of Recommendation or References

Letters of recommendation (LOR) or references are essential when applying for jobs or schools. They help prove what we say on our applications, like our skills and experience. Anyone can claim something, but a good recommendation shows it's true.

We can do a few things to help us stand out.

- *Content:* A strong LOR should highlight both skills and character, matching the specific job or program requirements. The letter should match the job or profession. Letters from people in higher positions carry more weight.
- *Uniqueness:* Everyone has a letter of recommendation, but ours needs to stand out. It should show what makes us unique. We need to think about our special qualities and make sure the letter talks about those. The letter should show why we're the perfect fit, not just tell.
- *Right Recommender:* It's best if the letter comes from a professional we've worked with, not a family member. This makes it more credible. We should build strong

relationships with people who could be our recommenders, like teachers, bosses, or mentors.

- *Ease for the Recommender:* Sometimes, it's been a while since we worked with the recommender. We should make it easy for them by giving them plenty of time to write the letter. It helps to provide them with all the necessary information, like details about the job or school we're applying to.

In competitive fields, having a great letter of recommendation can make us stand out. It's an extra effort, but it's worth it to make sure our letters help our application, not hurt it.

By putting care into our letters of recommendation and choosing the right people to write them, we can increase our chances of success in competitive spaces.

In the advent of AI, I suspect many letters of recommendation will not be as influential in decision-making, but these tips can also work for references. Letters and references are designed to prove what is already on our applications or resumes. Unfortunately, many people lie on their applications or resumes, but a letter or reference could bolster the experiences.

Navigating a Raise and Salary Negotiations

Negotiating a raise or salary can be intimidating, but preparation and strategy can help. Here are key steps:

1. *Document Achievements:* Keep track of accomplishments to showcase our impact.
2. *Set Salary Goals:* Don't just hope for a raise—we need to regularly discuss our progress with our boss.
3. *Frame the Raise as a Mutual Benefit:* Present reasons why our raise benefits the company. Highlighting both potential benefits and challenges if it doesn't happen makes a persuasive case. When making requests from

others, it is best to appeal to their self-interest, not our own.

Chris Voss's negotiation tips can also apply here:

- *Ask "what" or "how" questions, not "why":* These invite discussion rather than defensiveness. Asking "why" questions will subconsciously put people on defense.
- *Let the other person speak first:* It's helpful to let the other person share their expectations before we make our case. This gives us more information to work with and helps guide the conversation.
- *Use emotional anchoring:* We can use humor or soften our requests to make them more appealing. For example, at a hotel, we might say, "I'm going to make your day tough —I'm asking for an upgrade," then follow it up with, "Just kidding, I'm hoping for an upgrade." This makes the request feel less demanding.
- *Summarize what they say:* Before we respond, it's smart to mirror what the other person says. This lowers their guard and shows we're listening.

By focusing on building a win-win relationship, we set the foundation for a positive outcome. When negotiating big decisions, it's important to make the other person feel heard. Even in tough situations, like hostage negotiations, Chris Voss says people want to feel understood. By showing empathy, we can sometimes help people meet us halfway without conflict.

Standing Out in Interviews

Preparing for interviews is a game-changer. Here's a quick rundown of how to make an impression:

- *Know the company:* Research and connect your skills to the company's needs. We shouldn't have a generic answer. Instead, we should mention 2-3 specific things we like about the company. This shows we're serious about working there.
- *Craft a compelling pitch:* Share why we're a great fit, using 2-3 examples to support our case. We can research the values of the company and refer to stories that demonstrate how we exemplified those experiences.
- *Practice key responses:* Anticipate common interview questions and practice answers. Most common interview questions are usually asking something different under the surface. I recommend looking up Sahil Bloom's 20 *Common Interview Questions, What They Really Mean, & How To Answer Them*, then coming up with answers to each of those questions.

When it's our turn to ask questions, don't settle for generic ones. Show that we're invested by asking something unique, like, "If you hired me and six months from now I was the best employee you ever had, what are some of the things I did?"

Practical Tips for Career Success

Our career journey isn't only about finding a job—it's about creating a fulfilling path that grows with us. Here are a few final tips:

- *Build a tailored resume:* Customize it for each role, focusing on achievements and relevant keywords. Action words and numbers help the most here.
- *Network intentionally:* Attend events and build connections in companies we admire.
- *Stay current:* Regularly update skills and remove outdated information.

. . .

NAVIGATING our careers is about more than just finding a job—it's about continuously learning, building strong relationships, and strategically positioning ourselves for success. Careers are what we do, not who we are, and they can change and grow as we do. By focusing on developing skills, making connections, and keeping our goals in sight, we can be ready for whatever the future holds.

The workplace is constantly evolving, and so should we. Whether learning new skills, preparing for a raise, or navigating an interview, the key to success is being adaptable, patient, and persistent. We take control of our professional paths by understanding how to reverse-engineer our careers, stand out with tailored resumes and strong interview strategies, and negotiate confidently.

Success isn't just about getting ahead—it's about doing meaningful work that aligns with our values and goals. These strategies allow us to thrive in an ever-changing world and create a fulfilling, rewarding career journey.

WINNING THE GAME OF LIFE
MASTERING ATTENTION & SPEECH

Winning the Series of Games

"Where you spend your attention is where you spend your life." - James Clear

Ever since I was a kid, I've been obsessed with discovering what makes people win. I used to think what made someone good at one thing was different than what made them good at another, and while there is some truth to that, I've noticed that there are a few things that make people good at everything. It's almost like a Pareto distribution of skills necessary for winning.

There are a handful of skills and traits that we can learn that can help us get to the top of all the pyramids.

While analyzing the "winners" of our society, I've noticed that they all possess certain traits to get to the top of their fields.

What makes a successful professor is different from what makes a successful athlete is different from what makes a successful musician, or businessman, or mother, or soldier, or fashion designer...so on and so forth.

Each one of these people has developed themselves in the areas they need to reach the top of their game.

But, life is more than just one game, it's a series of games.

The skills and traits needed to win a series of games are different than the ones needed to win one game.

What it takes to win one particular game, but in other ways, it's also the same. That led to me looking for patterns, not only in successful people of my time but in the heroes of the myths of all cultures.

What does it take to win the series of games?

For generations, even predating written history, people have been trying to figure out this question and share their findings with the next generation. They shared these ideas through stories of heroes who would display the traits and ways of being necessary for "winning."

For example, Hercules is a kind, strong, brave, and persistent young man, and because of that, the story ends well for him. When little boys are told the story of Hercules, they want to emulate his heroic qualities and be one themselves. Adults are happy to tell them this story because they know (subconsciously) that these lessons will help the children win the game of games, and life. The same can be found in religious stories, ancient myths, and popular culture. The Avengers is another great example of this. Spider-Man is my personal favorite.

So I started thinking, what if I analyzed what was common among these hero myths?

Will I find the skills needed for success everywhere?

I don't know exactly what will make someone successful everywhere, but I have compiled some similarities between the heroes in every story I've seen.

I do not have an exhaustive list of these traits and skills, but they are the ones I've found to be most important:

- Attention
- Speech

The Osiris Myth & Attention

This story has a similar arc to Disney's famous *The Lion King*, one of my favorite movies ever. I'll make various connections to *The Lion King* and its relevance to the modern world throughout the story. I'll be interjecting with some *analysis in italics* throughout the story.

This story is one of the oldest, but most elaborate and influential, myths of the Egyptian Gods. This is the Osiris Myth.

IT BEGINS with the god Osiris, the King of Egypt, ruling a fair and prosperous kingdom. Osiris is extremely wise and well-liked by his subjects. He's harsh with his judgments but fair with his punishments.

Osiris is analogous to Mufasa in The Lion King. They are both a representation of The Wise King archetype.

Osiris was married to Isis, the Goddess of health, marriage, and fertility. They had a good marriage and Isis was lovingly devoted to Osiris. Osiris also had a brother named Set, the God of deserts, disorder, and violence.

Isis seems to be the ancient Egyptian representation of the anima. Set is analogous to Scar from The Lion King. Like Scar and Mufasa, Set's relationship to Osiris represents "the hostile brothers" archetype.

Set was jealous of Osiris and his power. He wanted to be the King of Egypt. Osiris knew his brother had these feelings but chose not to acknowledge them. Instead, he was willfully blind to his brother's hostility. Set used his brother's voluntary ignorance against him and killed Osiris. Set chopped Osiris into little pieces and spread his body parts across Egypt.

These different pieces represented the different districts in ancient Egypt and were believed to be the origins of their old borders.

Mufasa was killed by Scar because Mufasa did not want to see the evil in his brother. He chose to be willfully ignorant. Just like in The Lion King, Set was able to kill Osiris because Osiris didn't want to see the evil in Set.

This is one of the biggest lessons I took from this story: Willful ignorance is strong enough to take down a good, powerful, and wise leader. Or maybe the ancient Egyptians were trying to say that only willful ignorance is strong enough to take down a wise, powerful, and good leader. Either way, willful ignorance is destructive and the forces working against us will use our ignorance to catch us off guard. Choosing to not see the evil will kill us, maybe when others may need us the most.

When a king dies, it's big news and Isis shortly finds out. She's furious and goes around to each district gathering Osiris's parts. Eventually, she finds his phallus and impregnates herself. While pregnant, she leaves for the underworld to raise her baby, the hero, Horus the Younger, away from the disorder and violence of Set's reign.

Horus the Younger is commonly depicted as a falcon-headed man because he represents attention. The agent of attention is born from the wise king and the anima. I think it's also worth mentioning that Horus was raised in the underworld. To the modern Westerner, the underworld has connotations of Hell or other terrible places, but in ancient Egyptian mythology, the underworld was another dimension where the gods could watch the humans from afar.

Horus, the agent of attention, is raised in a world separate from the one he will inherit. Similar to how children are raised in environments separate from "the real world."

This is where the Osiris myth diverges from The Lion King a bit. In The

Lion King, Simba (Horus analogous) "grows up" with Timon and Pumba singing Hakuna Matata, whereas Horus was raised in the underworld by Isis. Those are different, but in some ways they are similar. Our heroes are learning in a haven away from the real burden of responsibility.

As Horus gets older, he learns the truth about his father. That Set usurped him and rules Egypt into the ground. Horus decides to return to Egypt, confront Set, and avenge his father.

This is like when Simba decides to leave Timone and Pumba to go take his rightful place as king. This is the quintessential coming of age story (at least for boys), a boy leaves his friends so he can go and answer the calling to be greater. Usually catalyzed by a woman, in Simba's case, it's Nala.

When Horus returns, Set tries to win Horus the same way he did with Osiris. But Horus has something his father didn't: the gift of true attention. With his attention, Horus could see Set for what he was, an agent of betrayal and malevolence. When Horus confronts Set, they have a great battle. Set tears out one of Horus's eyes, but Horus ultimately defeats him. Since gods cannot truly be killed, Horus banishes Set from the Kingdom.

This is one of my favorite parts of the story because it has so many of the lessons that make this story worthwhile.

- *Attention is the one thing that will give us a fighting chance against the forces of malevolence.*
- *When we are confronting the forces of malevolence and disorder, we will get hurt in a serious way.*
- *We'll never truly destroy the forces working against us, we can only fight them off and make them leave temporarily.*

Horus picks up his eye and returns to the underworld, where Isis had kept all the pieces of Osiris. Horus gives Osiris his eye, restores attention to the old corpus of wisdom, and together they rule Egypt into prosperity and peace.

The ancient Egyptians believed that the pharaoh represented the union between Osiris and Horus. A good ruler needs the wisdom of the past and attention to the present to lead the people into a prosperous future. Horus knew that by giving attention informed by the wisdom of his dead father, he would do what is best for Egypt.

When we combine the attention of the youth with the wisdom of the old, we access profound meaning that runs deep within the soul of every human being. There are so many myths that depict that exact journey.

It is not solely attention nor wisdom that will lead us to freedom and prosperity, but the union of both in a way that allows us to recognize and overcome the forces working against us.

ATTENTION IS what brings us to the top of every hierarchy and overcomes the forces of evil. This idea has been expressed through archetypal images and myths throughout history and cross-culturally.

We can see this with the image on the back of the American dollar bill. Attention is the thing that is at the top of the pyramid, but it's also more than that too. Attention transcends the rest of the pyramid, as if the ones who are paying attention are no longer part of the rest of the pyramid.

Attention is the thing that will take us to the top of every hierarchy and overcome the forces of evil.

But why does attention sit on top of the hierarchy?

I believe that with the power of attention we can:

• plan for the unknown
• create the future
• avoid danger

• predict the future.

I believe this is a huge part of the reason why so many internet influencers, the Kardashians, and the like, make so much money. When we harness people's attention, we have the ultimate power. Our attention is the most powerful thing any of us has to offer. This is partly why companies are willing to pay millions of dollars for advertisements and people will dedicate their lives to being famous. Attention is the real currency, everything else is an illusion.

Paying attention to where we pay attention is critical for living a powerful and fulfilled life.

When we pay attention to our minds, we can improve our mental health. When we pay attention to our bodies, we can improve our physical health. When we pay attention to anything, we can improve it. What gets measured gets managed, and what gets managed gets improved. Attention is the first step to all of that.

I recommend looking into mindfulness exercises and practices. I use meditation as a way I to train myself in paying attention to my mind and myself. There's so much research that grounds the value of paying attention to ourselves.

Pay attention to where you pay attention. It's the most valuable thing we have to offer.

The Invisible World of Speech

"A problem well put is half-solved." - John Dewey

Similar to attention, speech is highly overlooked.

In *Sapiens: A Brief History of Humankind*, renowned Israeli historian, Yuval Noah Harari, provides a beautiful timeline of history. It starts with matter and energy appearing marking the dawn of physics and takes us to the present and into a potential future. In this timeline, different human species appear and either evolve or die out. We know how this story ends. We, the homo sapiens, end up dominating the planet.

But what makes homo sapiens the dominant human species? Harari argues that is it our unique ability to communicate through complex language. Homo sapiens were the only human species that were capable of communicating on a massive scale. That gives us a huge advantage over the other species. That combined with our unprecedented cognitive abilities makes us the most powerful creatures on earth.

Everything we do on this planet is created by us and our ability to communicate through complex language. Yuval talks about this idea of living in two worlds simultaneously; the real tangible world and the "imaginary" world of conversation. I like to think of this "imaginary" world as *the world of conversation*, speech, or logos rather than "imaginary." Referring to this world as imaginary carries implications that it's not real. If anything, the world of conversation is *more* real than the tangible world.

From my experience and observations, unless overridden by conscious free will, the human being primarily lives in the world of conversation. We experience our lives as a narrative, a conversation, but we also create things external to us in that conversational world.

For example, businesses in society are not physical entities, but simply a conversation we are having with one another.

In *Sapiens*, Harari brings up Google to illustrate this point. If we were to destroy the Google headquarters, would Google disappear?

No, it wouldn't because we could rebuild it.

If we replaced all the people who worked for Google with a whole new batch of people, would Google disappear?

No, not really. It might be a different company, but it could still be Google as we know it.

This little thought experiment is fun because it highlights the fallacies in thinking that we live in a purely physical and tangible world. Google exists in the world of conversation and because of that, we could destroy the things that represent Google in the real world, and Google could still exist.

I argue that the conversations we are a part of matter much more than where we are in the physical world. I've seen happy people in terrible places and miserable people in beautiful places. What determines their happiness or misery is the conversation they're in.

People live in conversations.

Businesses are conversations. Relationships are conversations. Jobs are conversations.

Sometimes we add tangible symbols to keep the conversation boundaries clear in the physical world. We see this in things like wedding rings or uniforms. Nothing changes *physically* when someone gets married, but we all understand that there's still a huge transformation that takes place. When someone changes from fiancé to wife or husband, there's a transformation in the conversation & the way we act changes along with that conversation. We symbolize that change in the physical world with wedding rings, marriage certificates, and other things.

When my wife and I first started dating, nothing changed *physically*, but we started changing how we behaved because things have changed in the world of conversation. The same thing happened when we got married.

The same thing happened when I became an EMT. Nothing changed physically, except maybe a few neural pathways. I was physically the same person, but the conversation I participated in was different. The same thing happened when I became a teacher.

We create the world with our language. Change the conversation, change the world.

I know this idea seems extreme, but it seems like the Mesopotamians understood this as well.

Tiamat vs. Marduk

This story depicts how the Mesopotamians believed the world came to be and the origins of the first men. It's one of the oldest stories known to man and it is filled to the brim with powerful and timeless lessons. I'll be interjecting with some *analysis in italics* throughout the story.

IT BEGINS WITH TIAMAT, the goddess of saltwater, and Apsu, the god of freshwater coming together in the Tigris and Euphrates rivers to create the world of Mesopotamia.

Tiamat is more than just the goddess of saltwater, she is also the mother of everything and the goddess of Chaos. Together, Tiamat and Apsu populated Mesopotamia with young gods.

Tiamat is the archetypical representation of the anima. She is the chaos from which life springs and Apsu is the penetrative decisive force necessary to keep them alive. In some ways, Apsu is the archetypical old wise king, the positive masculine, and the animus.

There are also representations of Tiamat and Apsu drawn as serpents wrapped around each other and look eerily similar to DNA. How the Mesopotamians knew that is way beyond me.

As time goes on, the young gods become troublesome and begin to act recklessly. One night, the young gods disturb Apsu while he's sleeping. In frustration, Apsu tells Tiamat they should destroy the younger gods because they aren't acting properly. Tiamat disagrees with Apsu and urges him to protect the young gods, but it is too late. Ea, (a god of knowledge, mischief, and sweet water) discovers Apsu's plan to destroy the young gods and sends him into an eternal sleep, death.

Naturally, the younger generations start acting in ways that the

judgmental father (animus archetype) does not approve of. Apsu doesn't
believe his creations bring order to the chaos, judges them accordingly,
and wants to destroy them. Not surprising considering that the animus
archetype either protects or destroys. Of course, like any good mother,
Tiamat strives to protect her children (a hallmark anima trait) but in the
end, the young gods end up destroying Apsu, the order of the old.

Younger generations are constantly looking to understand the world
around them and older generations are constantly working to give them
answers. The issue arises when the younger generation doesn't see the
value in the old ways. Perhaps the old ways of doing things are outdated
and need change. Perhaps the new ways of doing things aren't the best
and the young people who practice these methods are doomed to repeat
mistakes. Either way, there is a mismatch between the young and old and
it almost always results in the young destroying the old ways.
So what happens when we destroy what our predecessors have given us?

Chaos reigns.

Tiamat hears of Apsu's death and is furious. She creates an
army of monsters to destroy the young gods in retribution for the
death of Apsu. She places Qingu, one of the few gods she trusts, as
head of the army and gives him the Tablet of Destinies to wear as a
breastplate. The Tablet of Destinies was the story of the world and
what was written on the tablet is what happened. Because of this,
the tablet gave Qingu immense power.

Tiamat's rage echoes themes of flood myths. In most cultures, you can
find a myth of a great flood wiping out the world. In this story, Tiamat
doesn't necessarily drown the world but she is the goddess of chaos and
saltwater and her will is to destroy the world because it has become too
corrupt.

The young gods are terrified of Tiamat's wrath and know they
cannot defeat her despite their powers, so they elect a champion,

Marduk, to fight. Marduk had eyes all around his head and could speak magic words. He was the only god brave and strong enough to take on this battle. He made a deal with the younger gods and told them that if he defeated Tiamat, they must make him king of the gods and give him the Tablet of Destinies.

Marduk, the hero of the gods, the only opportunity to overcome chaos, harnesses the power of attention and speech. I think this idea is so powerful. The only way we can have a fighting chance to triumph over chaos is through our attention and speech.

The younger gods want to give him the Tablet of Destinies if he can defeat chaos. The hero that uses their powers of attention and speech to overcome chaos, will determine what happens in the world. The hero's will can surpass the will of the gods. The hero will no longer be under the influence of the gods and can create the world in his image.

So Marduk went to war. He armed himself with a net and a sword. The battle was long and difficult. The more Marduk would attack Tiamat the stronger she became. She grew more monstrous with every swing of his sword. Tiamat becomes a dragon and destroys everything around her, but Marduk doesn't quit. Eventually, he catches Tiamat in his net and chops her into pieces.

From her body, Marduk creates the sky and the earth. From her blood, he creates the first man tasked to serve the gods who had a responsibility to maintain order and keep chaos at bay.

Marduk, the hero, confronts chaos with his net and his sword. This is particularly interesting because this is similar to how we psychologically grasp the unknown. When we are confronted with something that we don't know, we grab a general understanding (the net) and learn the details in pieces (the sword).

I like to use this idea to study better. We can create a general knowledge frame to understand something new, then learn the details second. This makes learning complicated concepts much more manageable.

When Marduk went to war with Tiamat she grew stronger with every attempt to contain her and eventually began destroying everything around her. When we confront chaos, it will get ugly and things will be destroyed, but persistence will be the only way to victory. Finding the balance between tolerable destruction and irreparable damage is difficult, but we can find solace by expecting things to get ugly.

Notice how humans are created from Tiamat (life; the anima) and the thing that harnesses attention and speech. I think this shows that the Mesopotamians noticed that a part of us, human beings, had powers like Marduk but was placed in bodies created from Tiamat.

I've also heard versions where the people were created from the blood of Qingu. I think that's an interesting take on the story and also carries wisdom, but I'm not going to dive too deep into that here.

Not only were we created from the same thing that created everything else, but we were also tasked to serve the gods and mediate between chaos and order. This gave the Mesopotamians an understanding of why we felt controlled by things beyond us at times. Like jealousy or lust. The Mesopotamian gods represent what modern people would call emotional states. Carl Jung said when we stopped believing in the gods, we put them inside us.

It is also our job to be like Marduk and maintain chaos and order. If we do, we get to be like Marduk. Access to the Tablet of Destinies and be king of the gods. This is an idea I think the Mesopotamians captured well: the hero who maintains a proper balance between chaos and order will determine what happens in the world and will not unwillingly fall to the influence of their emotions or primal instincts.

SIMILAR TO MARDUK, human beings speak magic words. We use our speech to craft the world around us and it's truly magical how it happens. What we say has a very real impact on the world as we know it. From the story, we know that the hero who harnesses speech and attention and willingly confronts chaos gets to determine what happens. This is a powerful lesson, but that leaves us with an important question:

What does it mean to harness speech?

I don't have a clear answer, but I think it's something like understanding that there is immense power in what we say, but to take it further and use that power to confront potential and bring about our will.

Harnessing speech requires us to focus our attention on our language.

How we phrase things is how we understand them.

Harnessing speech involves practicing multiple iterations of phrasing ideas while refining the meaning more accurately each time.

Harnessing speech involves practicing specificity.

From my experience, whenever I've experienced frustration or irritation, it comes from a lack of specificity or too much generality. For example, when I was first working on my YouTube channel I was frequently frustrated because there were so many little decisions to make. I had no idea where to start.

But then I started writing down the issues one by one. What's the font for my brand? What is my logo? What are the structures of the beats? What are my upload days? What genre of music am I making?

Slowly, the task became less and less frustrating.

I had to focus and articulate the chaos into something small and actionable.

Once I started doing that, there was another layer of specificity. What font size should I use? What are my brand colors? What are the titles of the videos I'm uploading? What time am I uploading?

I was reminded of Marduk throughout the process — using my speech to slowly cut the chaos into smaller and smaller pieces.

We overcome chaos by using our language to break up the overwhelming monster into manageable pieces.

So this poses the question: if the Mesopotampians meant this, then why didn't they just say it?

This is not a perfect answer, but I think it's because language development is a long and difficult process. The Mesopotamians saw this lesson. They knew it to be true. But they could not say it outright because we, as a human race, did not have enough iterations to spell out that message. Today, we can because we've had thousands of years to be able to retell the story, refining the message with every rep.

This also mirrors the battle between Marduk and Tiamat. The battle was long, but after a while, Marduk was able to capture the Tiamat (chaos, the unknown) and chop it up. The Mesopotampians captured this idea, so to speak, but we have been able to chop it up and understand it on a deeper and clearer level.

Over time, messages from the great myths become clearer and clearer, provided that the ones confronting the unknown are harnessing their powers of attention and speech responsibly and constructively.

I've seen this to be true in writing too. The age-old phrase that I'm learning to accept captures it perfectly — *writing is rewriting.* I used to think that writers just wrote down whatever they wanted to write the first time through, but I'm starting to see that there are significant differences between the first and second iterations...and the 10th....and the 20th.

I try to embrace this principle and use it to write my ideas. I usually write something that barely makes any sense at first, then I try to make it clearer with each rewrite.

This chapter started as "Mesopotamian God Story – the being that confronts chaos is the thing that chooses the destiny – articulation – logos – speech." As you can see, I've fleshed it out a bit more.

Another place I've seen this idea is in Napoleon Hill's fantastic

book, *Outwitting the Devil*. In his book, he talks about the importance of definitive purpose and how it's what separates the drifters
from the non-drifters: those who act on purpose from those who
act on accident.

The act of defining purpose is a form of harnessing speech.
Defining purpose requires us to use language to carve out
exactly what we want from the unknown. Creating or defining
purpose is a great way to get people to consciously grab hold and
actively participate in the world of conversation, especially if they
don't have the vocabulary to do so.

It's worth mentioning that our brains have systems for dealing
with environments that we don't understand. These systems in our
brains are primarily associated with negative emotions. We experience negative emotions when we find ourselves in places that we
don't know how to navigate (chaotic environments). When we're in
predictable environments, we experience positive emotions. Like
the humans created in the story, we manage the balance between
chaos and order. We get access to positive emotion from
confronting the chaos and turning it into order through harnessing
speech and focused articulation.

This is something that I try to actively practice, especially in
highly stressful or overwhelming times. Believe it or not, one great
way to practice this is to create checklists. Whenever I feel like a
challenge is too much to overcome, I emulate Marduk and chop the
great dragon into little actionable tasks. This simplifies the situation, instead of trying to control for all the variables, my task
becomes one easy thing — cross things off the list.

I recommend checking out *The Checklist Manifesto* by Atul
Gawande. It's a beautifully written book on the hidden (and
extremely underrated) powers of checklists. It's cool to see how
using checklists can completely eradicate mistakes and move
projects along faster. He also goes over what makes checklists effective and what makes them more trouble than their worth. Using
checklists to practice harnessing speech is so powerful. More accu-

rate articulation comes from multiple reps, your first checklists aren't going to be very good.

When it comes to being an effective student, determining what we need to get accomplished or what we need to learn is a fantastic way to practice harnessing speech. What we say creates who we are. We see this in jobs and our relationships with people. I try to make this known to my students — the only reason they see me as a teacher is that we agree that in the world of conversation, I am a teacher. There is nothing that's physically different between me and them (except a few neural pathways). I find that this helps them feel like they could learn the material too, despite their failures in the past. It also humanizes me and makes me more relatable. When I'm teaching, things run smoother if my student sees me as similar to them rather than some "science guy" who knows the answer all the time.

Our language plays such a huge role in the world we participate in. I try not to write about what people ought to do, but we should treat our powers of speech with respect and use them to build a better place for everyone.

"Life punishes the vague wish and rewards the specific ask." - Tim Ferriss

Learning to make ourselves articulate in writing, thinking, and speaking makes us powerful and gives us a defense against the tragedy of life. We can create strategies, communicate them with others, and act them out in the world. The most articulate person always rises above the rest.

LEARNING HAPPINESS & CHOOSING OURSELVES

A SKILL, NOT A DESTINATION

Learning Happiness

Happiness isn't something we stumble upon, nor is it a destination we reach. Instead, it's a skill we cultivate through intentional choices and practices. It isn't "one-size-fits-all"; what brings one person happiness may not work for someone else. Over the years, I've learned happiness requires intentionality, reflection, and consistent habit-building.

Happiness as Our Default State

Naval Ravikant suggests that happiness is our natural state. When we feel like nothing is missing, the mind stops wandering to the past or future, regrets dissolve, and planning takes a backseat. Testing this idea over the last few months, I've found a deeper sense of peace by focusing less on what I lack and more on what I have.

> "Happiness is the state when nothing is missing. When nothing is missing, your mind shuts down and stops running into the past

or future to regret something or plan something." - Naval
Ravikant

This insight shifted my perspective: Happiness isn't about
adding anything but about letting go of the notion that something
is missing. This idea reminds me of Schopenhauer's insight, "What
a man sees in the world is what he has in his heart," or as Anaïs Nin
puts it, "We don't see things as they are; we see them as we are."

Discovering the Insignificance of Self

A pivotal part of this journey was realizing the small, fleeting
nature of the self. Understanding my own insignificance didn't
diminish my happiness; instead, it freed me. At first, it was uncomfortable to think that my life might be just a "blink of a firefly in the
night," as Naval puts it. But once I accepted this, I felt liberated to
make the most of every moment.

"Our lives are a blink of a firefly in the night... Every second you
have on this planet is precious, and it's your responsibility to make
sure you're happy and interpreting everything in the best possible
way." - Naval Ravikant

When we let go of trying to change the world and focus on
what we can control—ourselves—the need for constant validation
or striving fades. We are left with the choice to live in alignment
with our values.

Happiness as a Choice

Happiness is not something we find but something we choose. Like
love or peace, happiness is a commitment to see things positively. I
realized the biggest obstacle to my happiness was my own mind—
the voice that magnified anxieties, doubts, and fears. The problem
wasn't the voice itself, but accepting it as truth.

Now, when a difficult thought surfaces, I ask myself, "Would I rather be at peace or dwell on this?" If I'm honest, the answer is almost always peace. By making this choice, I understand that a "happy" person isn't always in a state of joy. Rather, they choose not to let other things disturb their peace.

"Desire is a contract you make with yourself to be unhappy until you get what you want." - Naval Ravikant

Many of us think happiness is about getting what we want, but I've found that happiness is about wanting less. When I experience a strong desire, I ask, "Will I truly be unhappy if this doesn't happen?" More often than not, I realize it's unnecessary for my peace.

The Role of "Should"

The word "should" is often an enemy to happiness. I try to minimize my "shoulds" because they often reflect societal expectations I haven't consciously chosen. "Shoulds" can drain energy and steal peace, distracting me from what genuinely matters. I focus instead on moral "shoulds" that align with my values, leaving other "shoulds" behind.

"Life is a single-player game. You're born alone. You're going to die alone. All of your interpretations are alone. All your memories are alone." - Naval Ravikant

True happiness doesn't require validation or external rewards. It's an internal journey, one we take alone. Yet, we often focus on multiplayer games—like status or social acceptance—mistaking them for happiness.

Building Habits for Happiness

Happiness is a skill developed through intentional habits. Our environment, the people we spend time with, and our daily routines all influence this skill. Surrounding myself with positive influences, limiting social media, and being mindful of my physical and mental environment have helped build a foundation for happiness.

Here are a few habits that have supported my journey:

- *Meditation:* Practicing choiceless awareness—observing thoughts without judgment—has helped quiet my mind. I notice how many thoughts are driven by fear or desire, and as I sit still, my mind begins to settle, allowing me to see life's simple beauties. Meditation has shown me that the mind can serve us rather than control us.
- *Sunlight:* Spending time outdoors has stabilized my mood and boosted my energy.
- *Limiting caffeine:* I'm a coffee lover, but when I notice dips in happiness, switching to tea or going without caffeine resets my mood.
- *Limiting screen time:* Screens often drain happiness; I find that activities away from screens nourish peace.
- *Exercise:* A peaceful mind is easier to find in a peaceful body.
- *Honesty:* Being truthful with myself and others keeps me aligned with my values and reduces internal conflict.
- *Enjoying natural things:* I prioritize experiences like food and nature over possessions.
- *Declaring myself a happy person:* This reinforces accountability for my mindset and choices.
- *Avoiding news:* News often triggers anxiety, so I focus on uplifting topics instead.

- *Choosing positive-sum games:* Games like entrepreneurship or personal growth are positive-sum—everyone benefits. This helps me avoid zero-sum competitions in areas like social status or politics.

Happiness Questions

A few simple questions keep me grounded:

- "What's the positive interpretation of this?" when I catch myself judging someone.
- "Will I be truly unhappy if this doesn't happen?" when I feel a strong desire.

These questions remind me to choose peace over negativity and help me center myself in the present.

Finding Happiness in Acceptance

In every situation, we have three choices: change it, accept it, or leave it. Most suffering, I've found, lies not in the situation itself but in avoidance. When we accept what is, we can shift from suffering to peace, focusing instead on perseverance.

Choosing one priority at a time also helps reduce distraction and overwhelm. This approach has allowed me to bring more intentional focus to my goals, cultivating happiness without a constant chase.

Choosing Ourselves

The hardest part of life isn't doing what we want—it's knowing what we want. Often, we try to live as others do, but true happiness requires that we live for ourselves. There's no competition when we're true to ourselves.

"No one in the world is going to beat you at being you." - Naval
Ravikant

When we stop trying to follow the paths of others, we get the
chance to listen to ourselves. This self-guidance is a path of courage
and authenticity, where each person has unique experiences, skills,
and desires that no one else can replicate.

Changing Ourselves

Our environment shapes our minds, but we can use our minds to
influence our environment too. I've learned to focus on internal
change rather than external. Real transformation often means
being patient with results while being impatient with taking action.
Change doesn't happen overnight, but the journey itself is a reward.

Living Our Values

Living according to our values creates a strong foundation for
happiness. Honesty is one of my core values; I find that aligning
with it brings a sense of peace. Knowing that we only have peer
relationships—no one is above or below us—brings freedom from
social pressures and expectations.

"To find a worthy mate, be worthy of a worthy mate." - Charlie Munger

Clear values help us stay true to ourselves, especially when
others expect us to live differently. When we live according to our
own values, we find other people who are worthy of our time.

Lessons on Happiness

Through the years, I've gathered insights that remind me of the
path to happiness when I lose my way:

- Stay present—trying to live our whole life at once creates misery and disturbs peace.
- Desire creates suffering; letting go frees us — many problems are solved by deciding they aren't.
- Anger is like drinking poison and expecting someone else to suffer.
- Learning is invaluable; it's a skill that can be traded for anything.
- Most effort is wasted, and that's okay.
- If it can't be done forever, don't do it even for a day.
- Honesty and positivity are always possible.
- All greatness comes from suffering.
- Watch every thought; not all are worth believing.
- Love is something to give, not something we wait to receive.

CHOOSING happiness is about choosing ourselves. It means living on our terms, aligned with our values, rather than what society or others expect. This single-player game has no real competition; it's a journey to cultivate peace, let go of distractions, and focus on the present—where life truly happens.

In letting go of external expectations, we gain the freedom to live authentically. And in that freedom, happiness thrives.

BOOK REFERENCES & RECOMMENDATIONS
FOR INTEGRATIVE GROWTH

"It's not about the book, it's about the book the book leads you to."
- Austin Kleon

Book References & Recommendations

<u>Why Reading Matters: How Reading Can Change Lives</u>

- **"Games People Play"** by Eric Berne
- **"Limitless"** by Jim Kwik
- **"The Naval Almanack"** by Eric Jorgenson (featuring ideas by Naval Ravikant)

<u>The Call to Adventure: A Path We All Can Take</u>

- **"The Hero with a Thousand Faces"** by Joseph Campbell
- **"Beyond Order"** by Jordan Peterson
- **"The Bible"** (Various Authors)

- "The Matrix" (film directed by Lana and Lilly Wachowski)
- "The Karate Kid" (film directed by John G. Avildsen)
- "The Wizard of Oz" by L. Frank Baum
- "Being and Nothingness" by Jean-Paul Sartre

Rewriting Our Story: How Changing Our Narrative Leads to Growth & Fulfillment

- "Fight Club" by Chuck Palahniuk
- "The Brothers Karamazov" by Fyodor Dostoevsky
- "Recovery" by Russell Brand
- "The 4-Hour Workweek" by Tim Ferriss
- "I Will Teach You to Be Rich" by Ramit Sethi
- "Getting Things Done" by David Allen

The Art of Patience: The Secret Weapon for Achieving Goals, Success, & Happiness

- "The Practicing Mind" by Thomas M. Sterner
- "Atomic Habits" by James Clear
- "The Power of Now" by Eckhart Tolle
- "Man's Search for Meaning" by Viktor Frankl
- "The Obstacle Is the Way" by Ryan Holiday
- "The Subtle Art of Not Giving a F*ck" by Mark Manson
- "Patience" by Allan Lokos
- "Human, All Too Human" by Friedrich Nietzsche

Responsibility: Creating Our Own Opportunities

- "Limitless" by Jim Kwik
- "Atomic Habits" by James Clear
- "Man's Search for Meaning" by Viktor Frankl
- "Beyond Order" by Jordan B. Peterson
- "12 Rules for Life" by Jordan B. Peterson

- **"Extreme Ownership"** by Jocko Willink and Leif Babin

Creating Meaning Through Sacrifice: Pain, Care & Imitation

- **"The War of Art"** by Steven Pressfield
- **"Beyond Order"** by Jordan B. Peterson
- **"Man's Search for Meaning"** by Viktor Frankl
- **"Essentialism"** by Greg McKeown
- **"The Slight Edge"** by Jeff Olson
- **"The 7 Habits of Highly Effective People"** by Stephen R. Covey

The Foundation of Virtue: Why Courage Matters Most

- **"The Courage to Create"** by Rollo May
- **"The Screwtape Letters"** by C.S. Lewis
- **"The War of Art"** by Steven Pressfield
- **"Beyond Good and Evil"** by Friedrich Nietzsche
- **"12 Rules for Life"** by Jordan B. Peterson
- **"The Hero with a Thousand Faces"** by Joseph Campbell
- **"Man's Search for Meaning"** by Viktor Frankl
- **"The Myth of Sisyphus"** by Albert Camus
- **"I Know Why the Caged Bird Sings"** by Maya Angelou
- **"The Denial of Death"** by Ernest Becker

Mastering Behavior Control: Reinforcement and Punishment

- **"Thinking, Fast and Slow"** by Daniel Kahneman
- **"The Power of Habit"** by Charles Duhigg
- **"Atomic Habits"** by James Clear
- **"Nudge"** by Richard H. Thaler and Cass R. Sunstein
- **"Mindfulness for Beginners"** by Jon Kabat-Zinn
- **"Influence"** by Robert B. Cialdini
- **"Drive"** by Daniel H. Pink

- "The Brain That Changes Itself" by Norman Doidge

Restoring Integrity: The Power of Keeping Our Word

- "The Four Agreements" by Don Miguel Ruiz
- "Integrity: The Courage to Meet the Demands of Reality" by Henry Cloud
- "Daring Greatly" by Brené Brown
- "The Power of Integrity" by John MacArthur
- "Kintsugi Wellness" by Candice Kumai
- "The Seven Habits of Highly Effective People" by Stephen R. Covey

Thought & Critical Thinking: How Our Thoughts Are Shaped by The World Around Us

- "Thinking, Fast and Slow" by Daniel Kahneman
- "The Power of Now" by Eckhart Tolle
- "The Art of Thinking Clearly" by Rolf Dobelli
- "Limitless" by Jim Kwik
- "Mindset" by Carol S. Dweck
- "The Four Agreements" by Don Miguel Ruiz
- "On Writing Well" by William Zinsser
- "How to Think Like a Roman Emperor" by Donald Robertson
- "Beyond Good and Evil" - Friedrich Nietzsche
- "Thus Spoke Zarathustra" - Friedrich Nietzsche
- "The Stuff Of Thought - Steven Pinker

Deeper Self-Reflection: My Personal Methods of Reflection

- "Journals and Papers" by Søren Kierkegaard
- "Limitless" by Jim Kwik
- "Mindset" by Carol S. Dweck
- "The War of Art" by Steven Pressfield

- **"Think Forward to Thrive"** by Jennice Vilhauer
- **"The Power of Now"** by Eckhart Tolle
- **"Big Magic"** by Elizabeth Gilbert
- **"Flourish"** by Martin Seligman
- **"Positivity"** by Barbara Fredrickson

Timeless Leadership: Essential Lessons from Winston Churchill

- **"Churchill"** by Andrew Roberts
- **"Never Give In! The Best of Winston Churchill's Speeches"** by Winston Churchill
- **"The Last Lion"** by William Manchester and Paul Reid
- **"Team of Rivals"** by Doris Kearns Goodwin
- **"Leadership in War"** by Andrew Roberts
- **"Extreme Ownership"** by Jocko Willink and Leif Babin
- **"Leaders Eat Last"** by Simon Sinek

Tough Lessons I Learned The Hard Way: Unpleasant Truths

- **"Meditations"** by Marcus Aurelius
- **"The Fire Next Time"** by James Baldwin
- **"Enchiridion"** by Epictetus
- **"The Obstacle Is the Way"** by Ryan Holiday
- **"Man's Search for Meaning"** by Viktor Frankl
- **"Letters from a Stoic"** by Seneca
- **"The War of Art"** by Steven Pressfield
- **"Can't Hurt Me"** by David Goggins
- **"Atomic Habits"** by James Clear
- **"Extreme Ownership"** by Jocko Willink and Leif Babin
- **"The Gifts of Imperfection"** by Brené Brown

Learning in the Social Media Age: Turning Social Feeds into Growth Tools

- **"Limitless"** by Jim Kwik

- **"Deep Work"** by Cal Newport
- **"The Shallows"** by Nicholas Carr
- **"The Power of Habit"** by Charles Duhigg
- **"Digital Minimalism"** by Cal Newport
- **"The Distracted Mind"** by Adam Gazzaley and Larry D. Rosen
- **"Brain Rules"** by John Medina
- **"How to Break Up with Your Phone"** by Catherine Price

Performance Requirements: An Introduction to Nourishing The Mind and Body

- **"Personal MBA"** by Josh Kaufman
- **"Your Brain on Nature"** by Eva Selhub
- **"Brain Rules"** by John Medina
- **"Keep Sharp"** by Sanjay Gupta
- **"The UltraMind Solution"** by Mark Hyman
- **"Why We Sleep"** by Matthew Walker
- **"Spark"** by John J. Ratey
- **"How Not to Die"** by Michael Greger
- **"My Brief History"** by Stephen Hawking
- **"The Purpose Driven Life"** by Rick Warren

Substance Use: A Critical Examination of Drugs

- **"The Personal MBA"** by Josh Kaufman
- **"In the Realm of Hungry Ghosts"** by Gabor Maté
- **"The Biology of Desire"** by Marc Lewis
- **"Dopamine Nation"** by Anna Lembke
- **"How to Change Your Mind"** by Michael Pollan
- **"The Power of Habit"** by Charles Duhigg
- **"This Naked Mind"** by Annie Grace
- **"Clean"** by David Sheff

Reputation & Inner Peace: A Balancing Act

- **"The Wisdom of Life"** by Arthur Schopenhauer
- **"The 48 Laws of Power"** by Robert Greene
- **"Dare to Lead"** by Brené Brown
- **"Extreme Ownership"** by Jocko Willink and Leif Babin
- **"The Reputation Game"** by David Waller and Rupert Younger
- **"Ego is the Enemy"** by Ryan Holiday
- **"Leaders Eat Last"** by Simon Sinek

Networking: Winning Isn't the Goal—It's About How We Play the Game

- **"Beyond Order"** by Jordan B. Peterson
- **"The 48 Laws of Power"** by Robert Greene
- **"The Moral Judgment of the Child"** by Jean Piaget
- **"Play, Dreams and Imitation in Childhood"** by Jean Piaget
- **"Man and His Symbols"** by Carl Jung
- **"Poor Richard's Almanack"** by Benjamin Franklin
- **"The Four-Hour Workweek"** by Tim Ferriss
- **"The Social Animal"** by David Brooks
- **"How to Win Friends and Influence People"** by Dale Carnegie

On Luck: We Are Not Lottery Tickets

- **"Zero to One"** by Peter Thiel
- **"Clear Thinking"** by Shane Parrish
- **"The Almanack of Naval Ravikant"** by Eric Jorgenson
- **"The Personal MBA"** by Josh Kaufman
- **"The Obstacle Is the Way"** by Ryan Holiday
- **"Outliers"** by Malcolm Gladwell
- **"Atomic Habits"** by James Clear

- **"Grit"** by Angela Duckworth

Understanding Leverage & Judgement: For Success & Wealth Building

- **"The Almanack of Naval Ravikant"** by Eric Jorgenson
- **"Zero to One"** by Peter Thiel
- **"The Lean Startup"** by Eric Ries
- **"Principles"** by Ray Dalio
- **"The Innovator's Dilemma"** by Clayton Christensen
- **"Antifragile"** by Nassim Nicholas Taleb
- **"Thinking, Fast and Slow"** by Daniel Kahneman

Navigating Careers: What We Do, Not Who We Are

- **"Limitless"** by Jim Kwik
- **"Beyond Order"** by Jordan Peterson
- **"Never Split the Difference"** by Chris Voss
- **"The Four-Hour Workweek"** by Tim Ferriss
- **"The Personal MBA"** by Josh Kaufman
- **"Zero to One"** by Peter Thiel
- **"20 Common Interview Questions, What They Really Mean, & How To Answer Them."** by Sahil Bloom (blog)

Winning the Game of Life: Mastering Attention & Speech

- **"Atomic Habits"** by James Clear
- **"Sapiens"** by Yuval Noah Harari
- **"Outwitting the Devil"** by Napoleon Hill
- **"The Checklist Manifesto"** by Atul Gawande
- **"Tools of Titans"** by Tim Ferriss
- **"Beyond Order"** by Jordan B. Peterson

Learning Happiness & Choosing Ourselves: A Skill, Not A Destination

- **"The Almanack of Naval Ravikant"** by Eric Jorgenson
- **"Limitless"** by Jim Kwik
- **"The Wisdom of Life"** by Arthur Schopenhauer
- **"The Iliad"** by Homer
- **"Self-Reliance"** by Ralph Waldo Emerson
- **"Confucius: The Analects"** by Confucius
- **"Poor Charlie's Almanack"** by Charlie Munger

WHAT THIS BOOK MEANS TO ME

Finishing this book feels like a major victory—another reminder to myself that I can accomplish things I once thought were "impossible." There was a time when words intimidated me. In 6th grade, I struggled with reading, writing, and spelling tests. I'd run to math and science because they made me feel smart, while words left me feeling lost.

But I didn't write this book to feel competent. I didn't write it for praise or attention either. I wrote it because I wanted to see who I became in the process. The greatest lesson I learned wasn't just about how to write—it was about how the work we do shapes us. In fact, I've come to believe that our work works on us more than we work on it. Writing this book has not only made me a better communicator, but it has also sharpened my thinking in ways I never could have imagined.

The process taught me so much: how to be consistent, how to think deeply, how to focus, how to be patient, and how to be courageous. I had to confront my doubts and stay true to myself, even when it wasn't easy.

This book feels uniquely mine—like something only I could write. It's filled with the messages I want my students and my children to understand, lessons that I could only learn when I stopped running from who I am and embraced what truly interested me. For me, this book isn't just a finished project. It's proof that I can do hard things, even things that scare me.

"...each man is called upon to say his piece, lest the world suffer in the absence of that singular and unique truth. That every man who fails to offer his best and who hides his light and his talent leaves a hole in the world that the offering of his best could have f-illed— a failure that is on him. That every person bears the responsibility to keep the ship of state afloat, to repent even in the depths of hell, and to journey to the very place where destiny is trying to make itself manifest." - Jordan B. Peterson (*We Who Wrestle with God*)

ABOUT THE AUTHOR

Christopher Mukiibi is a Southern California native with a wide range of talents and interests. He grew up in a middle-class family with a younger sister and a strong connection to his extended family. His parents immigrated to the U.S. in the 1970s and '80s from Uganda and the Philippines, bringing with them a rich cultural heritage that continues to shape his life.

Christopher has many interests—he's deeply drawn to music, science, psychology, philosophy, and education. He's a lifelong learner and a natural teacher. Since 2014, he's taught and mentored hundreds of students, helping them reach their academic and career goals. With a Bachelor's degree in Chemical Engineering and a Master's in Education, he spent his college years actively supporting his peers and students in their studies.

During college, he co-founded a tutoring company with former teachers in his hometown. At the same time, he worked as an R&D chemist and took on small consulting roles in chemical engineering. For a time, he considered becoming a doctor, becoming an EMT and rigorously preparing for med school. But this journey eventually led him to his true passion: education.

Writing has become an important part of Christopher's life. Through his work, he shares insights on education, productivity, and well-being. He aims to promote the value of excellence while exploring topics like learning, wealth, health, happiness, and creativity.

Christopher teaches high school chemistry and AVID, and he also advises the school's Young Investors Society and Black Student Union. His goal is to empower students with the skills they need to lead fulfilling lives.

Beyond education, Christopher and his wife co-run an eco-friendly skincare brand, Sioné. This business combines his love for chemistry, business, and sustainability, addressing the need for affordable high quality skincare and reducing plastic waste. Their products use earth-derived and responsibly sourced ingredients.

Music is another deep passion for Christopher. He sees it as a profound expression of human creativity. As a music producer, he gravitates toward rock, hip-hop, R&B, and EDM as well as plays six different musical instruments.

Today, he lives in Southern California with his wife and two daughters, living a life filled with constructive struggle, purpose, and creativity.

X x.com/chris_mukiibi
instagram.com/mrmukiibi

Made in the USA
Las Vegas, NV
13 January 2025

16086012R10400